Controlling-Profitability Analysis (CO-PA) with SAP®

 PRESS

SAP PRESS is a joint initiative of SAP and Galileo Press. The know-how offered by SAP specialists combined with the expertise of the publishing house Galileo Press offers the reader expert books in the field. SAP PRESS features first-hand information and expert advice, and provides useful skills for professional decision-making.

SAP PRESS offers a variety of books on technical and business related topics for the SAP user. For further information, please visit our website: *www.sap-press.com*.

Gary Nolan
Efficient BW Implementation and Project Management
2007, app. 300 pp.
ISBN 978-1-59229-105-2

Ryan Leask and Mathias Pöhling
SAP xApp Analytics
2006, 408 pp.
ISBN 978-1-59229-102-1

Matthias Melich and Marc O. Schäfer
SAP Solution Manager
2007, app. 492 pp.
ISBN 978-1-59229-091-8

Ulrich Schmidt and Gerd Hartmann
Product Lifecycle Management with SAP
2006, 613 pp.
ISBN 978-1-59229-036-9

Marco Sisfontes-Monge

Controlling-Profitability Analysis (CO-PA) with SAP®

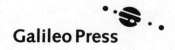

Galileo Press

Bonn • Boston

ISBN 978-1-59229-137-3

1st edition 2008

Acquisitions Editor Jawahara Saidullah
Developmental Editor Jutta VanStean
Copy Editor Mike Beady
Cover Design Silke Braun
Layout Design Vera Brauner
Production Vera Brauner
Typesetting Typographie & Computer, Krefeld
Printed and bound in Germany

Contents

4 Configuring Costing-Based CO-PA 75

5 Master Data in CO-PA 129

6 Introduction to CO-PA Planning 183

Acknowledgments

"We are living in a new world — the world of a global capitalist economy that is vastly more flexible, resilient, open, self-correcting, and fast-changing than it was even a quarter century earlier. It's a world that presents us with enormous new possibilities but also enormous new challenges."
Alan Greenspan (Former US Federal Reserve Chairman), The Age of Turbulence

I would like to thank all of those individuals that in one way or another influenced this publication. First, I would like to thank my parents, Francisco and Oralia Sisfontes, for their unconditional support in the good and bad times in my life. I would also like to thank John and Carol Reese for being great friends and my family away from home.

I would like to express my special thanks to my editors, Jawahara Saidullah and Jutta VanStean, and to all of the people involved from Galileo Press, and SAP AG for their guidance and patience while working on this publication. Also, I would like to thank Lesbia Lemus from the Risk Management Division at Citigroup; Martin Schloegelhofer, Head of Business Development/Banking Division, Hypo-Alpe-Adria Leasing Holding AG's Austria office; Szu Fen HSing, MS, SAP Consultant, from Abeam Consulting in Taipei, Taiwan; Professor Dr. Naoki Kambe from Kanda University of International Studies in Tokyo, Japan; Hugo Ayala from a Big 4 Accounting Consulting Firm in Minneapolis, MN; Dr. Elena Davidiak from Hofstra University, NY; and Adriana Sisfontes, MS, from Dole Corporation in Monterey, CA.

Finally, thank you to all of you who have trusted in me to guide you in this learning process. I have tried my best to not disappoint you, and hopefully this book will be helpful as you continue your SAP development.

Dr. Marco Sisfontes
New York

Preface

Right now I am having a latte near Wall St., and it is simply difficult to believe that so much money is won and lost everyday inside the New York Stock Exchange (NYSE). Yes, money is flowing all over the place and you do not see it, which is the best part. Being an investor, entrepreneur, and consultant myself, I have seen many times how simple decisions that could have been avoided, significantly affected a company's profits.

The question: what makes a company profitable? Sounds more like a philosophical and ethical issue with no correct or incorrect answers rather than a business question. This fact puzzles business experts who try to make corporations as lucrative and profitable as possible without negatively affecting shareholders, employees, vendors, suppliers, the environment, and clients.

As professionals in the SAP arena, we know for a fact that the cost of a project going wrong is significant, without mentioning the impact on the reputation of the people involved. It is not a secret that knowledge is power, and SAP is a clear example of that as it defines whether a project succeeds or fails. Therefore, I hope that the contents of this book will help initiate your learning process with CO-PA and its related systems.

I encourage you to use the information inside this book to help you achieve the best results for your projects, your clients, and your company. I have tried my best to provide the most complete and accurate information for you, but, as always, not everything can be covered or alternative procedures can be followed. It is an honor for me to have the support of SAP AG, Galileo Press, my editors, and all of you with this new publication, and I hope I can provide a little more help on this topic.

Thank you,

Dr. Marco Sisfontes
New York

Welcome to the world of Profitability Analysis with SAP. This chapter describes the basic objectives and contents of this book, by individual chapter.

1 Introduction and Overview

We'll start this book with a story. A long time ago, a young engineer was looking for a job right out of school. After studying hard and getting good grades, he had a job offer in hand from a worldwide technology company, to work in the process improvement division (Six Sigma). His future, highly lucrative, job was simple — use the latest mathematical and software tools to improve assembly, materials costs, and anything else required to make the best product that money can buy.

The high-tech company was one of the best and biggest technology companies in the world. The human resources manager who interviewed the young engineer assured rapid growth within the company, a close working relationship with the production manager, and that he was the final candidate after many interview rounds. Everything sounded like a dream, and the best part was that a close friend of his was working at the same company and could help him with his training.

Before making a decision, the young engineer also requested a tour of the company to have a look at the systems and processes. He saw the different production lines, packaging, and robotic and manual assemblies scheduled to work 24 hours a day, 7 days a week. One department team had saved over 1.4 million USD improving material usage and flow, making it the most profitable and productive center for the entire corporation, worldwide. Highly impressed with what he saw, and knowing that the name of the company by itself was a boost to his career, the young engineer considered taking the position right away. What more could a young gun want than to join a well-known and profitable company?

However, before accepting the job, the young engineer did one more thing. He went online and checked the company's performance on the New York Stock Exchange (NYSE), and what he found was disturbing. The overall corporation inventory turnover was excessively low in comparison with that of the industry, the operating profit was in the red in the last two quarters in comparison to competitors, the yearly demand forecasts were cut in half one week before, and the stock price had gone down more than 30 % in less than two months prior to his investigation.

To make things worse, the demand for the company's main product was being negatively affected by an Asian invention disclosed two weeks before, and that completely changed the way new technology was provided to the consumer. After reading several news reports about this, the young engineer realized that this invention was threatening almost 40 % of the company's product line because it affected the main components of the company's final product. This analysis took a little while, but it was enough to make the young engineer think twice about taking the job, and to call the following Monday and kindly decline the offer. He instead decided to join a consulting firm using software that he had never heard of before.

The next month, the young engineer received a call from his friend who had worked at the company, to let him know that he, along with nearly 70 % of the workforce of the facility, had been laid off (including the HR manager who had interviewed him). Only one person was left in the department where he was supposed to work, the production manager. The high-tech equipment was sold as scrap to junk yards, or shipped overseas for adaptation to new technology for use in another country. Also, four more facilities and research centers around the globe were closed.

After this reality check, the young engineer completely understood that there is more to making a company profitable than massive production, the best technology, and the best qualified individuals. At this point, nobody was interested in the best facility in the world, with the best financial indicators just one month ago, and with the best and most qualified labor force of a technology that was now obsolete. What the young engineer also realized was that profitability, growth, and financial performance were highly inter-related.

Many years have passed since this close encounter with a potentially bitter experience, but from that day forward, and before appearing in front of any client, the engineer always makes sure to completely understand a company's situation, its financials, ethics, shareholder and clients' opinions, and the latest financial news, to have a clear picture of the situations he will face. In addition, these analyses can play an important role in deciding whether to ultimately take on a project, regardless of what a company's reputation is, and how wonderful of a place it seems to be.

Hopefully, this short story has drawn your attention to some considerations behind profitability analysis, and the vision toward the development and implementation of a profitability system. Profitability Analysis requires not only financial transactions that measure a company's success, such as revenues or sales, but also strategic decisions that make the products or services of a company attractive in the marketplace to satisfy the changing demands of customers and keep up with the competition.

1.1   The Purpose of this Book

Welcome to Profitability Analysis with CO-PA, or, in technical terms, with SAP ERP Central Component (ECC) 6.0 and R/3. Before we begin, let me say that it is quite challenging to develop a book for a module that has been on the market for quite a while with very successful results, but with very little good or up-to-date documentation. Therefore, this book has been primarily designed to provide a reference guide for intermediate and advanced users of SAP software that already have basic knowledge of the concepts of CO-PA. Also, because CO-PA can be considered an integrator within the SAP Controlling (CO) component, a certain minimum level of expertise in other SAP components and modules is required to fully understand CO-PA's potential.

However, with a little extra work, beginners will also find the information in this book useful to mastering the basic elements required for a successful CO-PA implementation, or to just explore the capabilities of the system. In this book, not every element of the module will be explained. Rather, we will explore the most important functionalities.

The purpose of this book is to explain CO-PA configuration and techniques with a technical and theoretical, but also hands-on, approach. CO-PA is a widely used module in the industry that can simplify the data extraction processes and fulfill reporting requirements. It supports the implementation of a revenue, cost, and expense analysis toward the calculation of measures such as net revenue, contribution margins, cost of goods sold, costs of goods manufactured, and operating profit.

> **Note**
>
> The activities performed or explained in this book use the standard SAP IMG Activity help environment. Therefore, if you get lost, want more information, or simply do not believe everything that you are reading, you can quickly complement your learning process using IMG Activity Help information. Additional places to look for help include *http://help.sap.com*, and *http://sdn.sap.com*.

1.2 How this Book is Organized

As we mentioned, this book has been structured following the IMG Activity CO-PA menus. However, depending on the level of implementation of CO-PA within the SAP system in your organization, you might not need to use all of the CO-PA submenus. Also, because costing-based CO-PA is the more complex implementation model, it has been given priority in the discussion and revision of the associated elements, however, most of the functionalities used with this model can be applied with account-based CO-PA as well. For this reason, we can say that if you implement costing-based CO-PA you are getting account-based CO-PA for free. Here's a quick overview of what you'll do and learn reading this book:

- Gain a basic understanding of CO-PA concepts in Chapter 2. This should be useful, especially for beginners that require additional clarification of concepts behind Profitability Analysis with SAP.

- Work with business content and get an overview of the functionalities and configuration components of CO-PA in Chapter 3.

- Explore the configuration settings to define the basic CO-PA components in Chapters 4 and 5.

- Configure a planning application using the CO-PA Planning Framework in Chapters 6 and 7.

- Get an overview of how to transfer actual data from other SAP components such as Financials (FI), Sales and Distribution (SD), Materials Management (MM), and others in Chapter 8.

- Create reports within the CO-PA environment using the CO-PA Information System menu in Chapters 9 and 10.

- Review briefly the general configuration modifications required to change from a CO-PA costing-based analysis to an account-based analysis in Chapter 11.

▶ Review some useful tips and tricks in Chapter 12 to improve your reporting and system performance.

▶ Review what you have learned in this book in Chapter 13.

Each chapter of the book has been written independently, meaning that you should be able to work with it without the need to move back and forth between chapters. However, there are references between chapters to complement your learning, in case an important concept requires additional clarification that depends on concepts discussed in other chapters. In order to speed up the learning process, SAP-delivered business content (CO-PA templates) is used and populated with actual and plan data to get you started with CO-PA tools in no time.

Note that it is not the intention of the author to provide a complete overview of all of the capabilities and configuration steps required to use CO-PA. This module is quite sophisticated, and some of the functions that CO-PA performs are very difficult to replicate with alternative modules such as SAP Business Warehouse (BW), SAP NetWeaver Business Intelligence (BI), SAP NetWeaver BI Integrated Planning (IP), Business Planning and Simulation (BPS), and others. Only the most significant components are reviewed in this book; however, readers are given pointers to additional documentation, components, transaction codes, and procedures that can support the functionalities reviewed. So, without further delays, welcome to the CO-PA environment!

1.3 Summary

The CO-PA module of your SAP system's CO component is a powerful application with extensive functionality. Although you might not require every single component that we will review, by reading this book you will get a broad overview of almost all of the menus available in CO-PA. This will allow you to quickly identify what functionalities you can use, and which ones you won't need, which you should make sure to do.

Looking ahead, in Chapter 2 we will briefly review some general and basic components to consider before initiating your work in CO-PA, as well as the financial and accounting terms to expect during your implementation because it is important to clearly understand the difference, for example, between variable and fixed costs, and the types of documents available inside the SAP system to accomplish the consolidation.

Chapter 2 will also briefly provide an overview of another key element related to Profitability Analysis in the enterprise: Economic Value Added (EVA). This indicator is often used as the final financial number that many Corporate Financial Officers (CFOs) require that your CO-PA reports deliver.

Before initiating our review of CO-PA, it is important to consider basic concepts behind the application. Profitability analysis itself is a multidimensional process that allows analysis of different pieces of information based on relevance and importance to the generation of value for the corporation, which in turn is based on concepts such as revenues, profit margins, fixed and variable costs, and EVA.

2 Basics of Profitability Analysis

Key decision makers in any industry have the responsibility to make a business profitable, or at least to make decisions that do not make the company lose money or that reduce the risk of doing so. However, the only way for a manager or decision maker to do so successfully is by having access to a combination of facts and numbers coming from financial data. In this chapter, we will review and describe basic principles to determine whether a company is making decisions that will help it to be profitable. These are basic principles to consider for your CO-PA applications that will directly affect your implementation.

> **Note**
>
> This chapter provides a brief overview of important elements to consider when working with CO-PA. However, if you lack formal training in the areas of financial and cost accounting, economics, and general business analysis, we recommend that you also consult books on these topics to complement your learning.

2.1 Fundamental Principles

You can perform profitability analysis in three ways:

► **Historic comparison**
Evaluation of different time periods to identify the best alternative. For example, you might compare two consecutive time periods, such as month to month, or period to period, such as year to year.

> ▶ **Selecting between different alternatives**
> For example, you might choose between two machines, or projects, or include only projects that meet a minimum level of profitability using criteria such as net present value or internal rate of return (IRR).

> ▶ **Differential cost analysis**
> Evaluation of how much money can be obtained from current operations in comparison with an alternative. For example, the analysis with higher net present value or IRR, depending on your decision criteria, might be selected based on its incremental cost or value.

We define profit as the difference between revenues and total costs (that is, revenue − cost = profit). In an SAP system, each of these components is split into multiple accounts and document types, depending on the transaction generated. Furthermore, each of these components requires the creation of cost elements and general ledger accounts (GLs) that control documents inside the system that carry data and information to calculate the relationship between revenues and costs such as:

▶ Billing documents

▶ Purchase orders

▶ Sales orders

▶ Accounts payable

▶ Accounts receivable

▶ Invoices

▶ Allocations

▶ Project order settlements

▶ Internal orders

▶ Credit memos

▶ Production orders

▶ Inventory movements

▶ Overhead

▶ Investments

▶ Rebates

The documents listed are just a few examples and do not take into consideration any additional company-specified documents required to control debit and credit movements inside the financial system. In addition, some of these documents occur within the SAP Financials (FI) application, and others occur inside the SAP Controlling (CO) application used for external and internal parties respectively.

Using this information, the SAP system can calculate revenues such as sales — sales discounts, sales rebates, returns, and allowances. Total costs can be classified in multiple ways, depending on a company's operations. Generally, they include expenses such as utilities, office supplies, insurance, shipping, and anything not directly related to a company's operations but that helps support the processes. Costs are more associated with the transactions directly related to maintaining a company's operations, such as labor and materials.

Generally, CO-PA is useful to calculate all of the elements involved in the profit and loss statement (P&L) that quantifies the flows of revenues and costs in the company. However, to generate the balance sheet, additional connections might be required, either using integrators within CO-PA to access information coming from other modules, or using SAP Business Warehouse (BW) or SAP NetWeaver Business Intelligence (BI) to complete the generation of the P&L. In the income statement, or P&L, there is an operating section that describes only revenues and expenses, and a non-operating section that describes other revenues and other expenses and losses.

> **Note**
>
> If you are a CPA or a highly accounting-oriented person, the information presented here is likely to be very basic, and is only meant to provide the link between SAP and traditional accounting.

Profitability analysis can be a sophisticated or a simple process within the SAP system, and for this reason is considered to be multidimensional. This topic is discussed in the next section.

2.2 Profitability Analysis as Multidimensional Analysis

Multidimensional analysis is one of the most frequently used terms when working with business intelligence technologies, such as SAP BW and SAP NetWeaver BI. However, this term is also applicable to analytical-oriented and transactional applications delivered with CO-PA without leaving the basic Online Transaction Processing (OLTP) system. This means that the information is not provided in real time and that there might be some delay in the information reported because some structures require uploading data outside the transactional system and updating the data targets.

CO-PA allows a similar multidimensional analysis without leaving the transactional system. Thus, you can analyze profit contribution for a complete company code, by individual customer or market segment (profitability segment). Using Figure 2.1, you can review how the concept of multidimensional analysis of profitability is defined. At the bottom of Figure 2.1, you see a cube of data or data sets that we are interested in reviewing using specific characteristics, such as **Region**, **Division**, and **Customer group**.

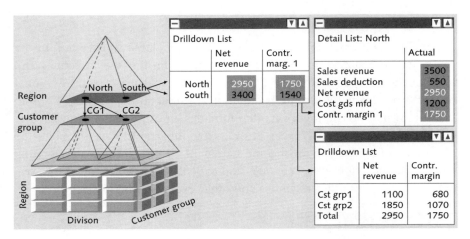

Figure 2.1 Multidimensional Analysis of Profitability

Also, notice that there are small cubes that define small segments that we can use to summarize our data at different hierarchical levels. For example, there is a drilldown displaying **Net revenue** and **Contr. margin** (contribution margin) for two customer groups (**Cst grp1 and Cst grp2**) and also information for the **North** region with its actual data in a separate environment, shown in **Detail List: North**. The small cubes can be used to share information at different levels based on the characteristics available, making it possible to be more selective how the information can be displayed and modified in the system, depending on the role of the user.

However, CO-PA is a process rather than a data display at different levels. This profitability analysis process is reviewed in the next section, and should be used as a reference when working with your traditional ASAP methodology.

2.3   The Profitability Analysis Process

The process of profitability analysis is considered intrinsically linked with the concept of Economic Value Added (EVA). EVA-based management links the creation of shareholder wealth over time with a common standard index that measures the differences and growth of the company overall as a single entity. The EVA index is very popular among Corporate Financial Officers (CFOs), Corporate Executive Officers (CEOs), and, of course, many people in Human Resources (HR) departments. The use of this index, especially in publicly-traded companies, provides a general overview of the company's health in its efforts to create value for the shareholders using the minimum rate of return (K) that shareholders and lenders could get by investing their money elsewhere with a similar level of risk.

It is possible to define EVA as:

EVA = Net Operating Profit After Taxes (NOPAT) – Capital x Cost of Capital (K)

For our purposes, let us consider profitability analysis as a process that highly depends on how accurate and simplified the information is to calculate the EVA value. With the concept in mind that every single component in an organization is dependent on this EVA index, let us review Figure 2.2.

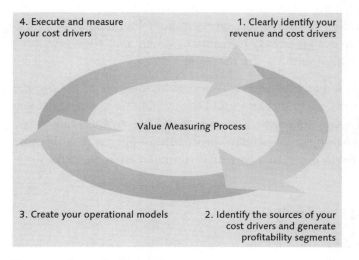

Figure 2.2 The Profitability Analysis Process

As shown in Figure 2.2, the goal is to generate the EVA by implementing a **Value Measuring Process** using cost and value drivers. To do so, perform the following steps:

1. **Clearly identify your revenue and cost drivers.**
   Use current reports, management reviews, dashboards, and analytical applications to fully understand your core measurement system.

2. **Identify the sources of your cost drivers and generate profitability segments.**
   Once you know what to measure, spend your time determining how data will flow into your profitability system. Will you have SAP data? Third-party systems? SQL systems from 20 years ago? Make sure you understand your data flow before you even begin with your profitability analysis.

3. **Create your operational models.**
   Once you are ready to start building your different CO-PA structures and components, create a model description that includes your data flows, sources, and required outputs, keeping in mind how your users will access your data. Also, consider system performance along the way.

4. **Execute and measure your cost drivers.**
   You can also call them value drivers depending on how you handle your value measuring process. Cost drivers are considered those financial measures identified to describe the performance of your key business areas, such as net revenue, sales per square foot, and revenues per product line. Once you initiate the CO-PA measuring process with reports and planning applications, make sure that your core cost drivers are clearly identified and allocated to the correct levels in your hierarchical organization. You need to design an easy-to-maintain system that allows multiple users to work with it without any problem.

As we mentioned, and as you can see from reading these steps, the profitability analysis process can be a complement to the ASAP methodology, if you desire a more practical approach. However, if you are an EVA consultant, you'll likely prefer using your standard procedures. Either way is fine; the process we outlined in this section is a suggestion, not a requirement.

2.4   Break-Even Analysis

The goal of any manager or company is to at least "break even," which means that the total fixed and variable costs are equal to the total revenues. In other words, the company has the minimum amount of money required to pay all of its liabilities for a particular time period. To know where the break-even point is or how to calculate it, we need to review revenues, fixed and variable costs, and the concept of a break-even analysis in a little more detail.

2.4.1 Revenues, Fixed and Variable Costs

A break-even analysis requires either using a chart or mathematical calculations to estimate the point of equilibrium where costs equal revenues. That point of equilibrium is the minimum level of provided production, sales, or services required for a time period in order to guarantee that you are maintaining value or creating value. It is clear that if you are below that point you are literally "destroying value." Let us review a few terms related to break-even analysis:

▶ **Revenues**: Describe a relationship, such as *product x price*, that generates the revenue of the company.

▶ **Fixed costs**: Costs such as direct labor, so if you produce 100 parts or 200 parts you always pay the same. However, in the long term fixed costs become variable costs.

▶ **Variable costs**: Costs such as materials, that change depending on the level of production, that is, you do not pay the same if you produce 100 or 200 parts for reasons of volume. However, in the long term variable costs become fixed.

▶ **Relationship**: The relationship of the three previously outlined components is thought to be linear, which is not always true but simplifies the calculations.

▶ **Formula**: Standard formula used to calculate the break-even point is as follows:

$Y = a + bX$

Where:

▸ Y = revenues or total sales

▸ a = fixed costs, constant

▸ b = average cost per unit produced

▸ X = total production units

For example, a company called ABC has total fixed costs of 4 USD per month and average material cost is 2 USD/unit. The company's previous analysis shows that they must have a minimum of 200 USD per month to cover costs. However, the company wants to know what the minimum number of parts required to break-even is. Let's find out:

$Y = 4 + 2 * X$

This means:

```
200 USD = 4 + 2 * X
```

This in turn means:

```
(200 - 4) = 2 X
```

Therefore, the company needs to produce X=98 units in order to achieve 200 USD per month to break even. If they produce more, they will generate a profit.

2.4.2 Sunken Costs

Decision making can only be affected by elements that will affect the future, meaning that any economic resources already committed must be excluded from any new scenario comparison or managerial analysis.

These types of economic effects are called *sunken costs*. For example, if you already invested 1,000 USD as a down payment to build a new facility, and you already committed to a mortgage of 100 USD per month for 30 years, then this money is committed; you have already spent it, so there is no reason to include these costs as part of any new project comparisons.

Therefore, sunken costs are final commitments that are part of the daily life of operations, and there are no increments unless you chose a flexible interest rate, which might require additional analysis. Costs can be classified in different ways, so next, let's look at different types of cost classifications.

2.5 Cost Classifications

When working with accounting to measure profitability, you have to identify the cost drivers that truly represent the behavior of your activities, profit centers, cost centers, processes, or systems. For that, it is quite useful to understand the different cost classifications under which your profitability models can be created. We'll review them in detail in the following sections.

2.5.1 Costs Based on their Function

Costs based on their function are strongly associated with the departments or areas of the organization where they occur, and can be classified as follows:

▶ **Production costs**: These can be further classified as the following:

  ▸ **Direct materials**: Costs that are directly related to the product, such as sugar in candy.

  ▸ **Direct labor**: Costs such as the salary of workers on an assembly line.

  ▸ **Indirect labor**: Costs not directly related to product or services delivered, such as inspections and supervision.

▶ **Distribution or sales costs**: Incurred to move the products from the company's facilities and delivered to the customer. Examples are advertising, shipping costs, and commissions.

▶ **Administrative costs**: For example administrative salaries, phone, and general expenses.

2.5.2 Costs Based on Activity

Costs based on activity, and that are directly related to the final product or service of a company, can be divided as follows:

▶ **Direct costs**: Identified with an activity, department, or product. For example, the salary of the marketing manager's secretary is a direct cost for the marketing department.

▶ **Indirect costs**: Cannot be identified and associated with a particular activity. For example, the salary of the secretary from marketing is a direct cost for the marketing department, but an indirect cost for the product.

2.5.3 Costs Depending on When They Are Charged Against Revenues

Costs that depend on when they are charged against revenues describe the moment when costs are considered reported, depending on their purpose. These costs can be classified as follows:

▶ **Costs of the period**: Identified based on the time interval and not with the products or services. Example: monthly rent for a building, because it is always incurred, regardless of when products or services are provided to customers.

▶ **Costs of the product**: Costs of goods sold (COGS), regardless how goods were sold, via credit or full payment.

2.5.4 Costs Depending on the Authority

Costs that require approval or a certain level of managerial control can be classified as follows:

▶ **Controllable**: One person has the authority to incur the cost. For example, the sales director has the authority to accept (or decline) the expenses of sales representatives.

▶ **Noncontrollable**: These are costs incurred without control, for example, machine depreciation.

2.5.5 Costs based on Their Importance to Decision Making

When evaluating different options, managers and analysts must focus their attention on costs that are important. For example, when evaluating a multi-million dollar contract, travel expenses might not have a significant impact. Therefore, these type of costs fall into one of the following classifications:

▶ **Relevant costs**: Also known as differential costs. These costs change depending on decisions made, and remove any sunken costs (sunken costs were explained a bit earlier in this chapter) associated with the decision.

▶ **Irrelevant costs**: Not directly related to the activity in question, or too small to make a difference. Therefore, management can decide to remove these costs from the final decision while concentrating only on the relevant costs.

One final point: because working with financial transactions is a delicate task, unless you are an expert on the topic in your region of the world, you should always partner with the accounting and financial departments of your client, company, or organization when working with CO-PA.

2.6 Summary

This chapter provided you with a quick overview of concepts, terminology, and elements that are part of profitability analysis, and that you will likely encounter when interacting with other members of your team or organization during your implementation. However, it is not enough to simply understand these terms; it is highly recommended to complement your SAP knowledge with financial and cost accounting information to understand why the different cost elements, general ledger accounts, cost centers, profit centers, internal orders, and other transactions within your transactional system have been set up the way that they have.

Chapter 3 provides a more hands-on overview of the general concepts associated with CO-PA using SAP-delivered templates or business content within the SAP ERP ECC 6.0 or R/3 environment. We will review the general components and structures that create an operating concern, and explore basic reporting capabilities available in CO-PA.

Working with SAP-delivered templates is the best way to get you started with your implementation and with basic CO-PA Concepts. In this chapter, we will review the basic functionalities that describe the CO-PA environment.

3   Introducing CO-PA with SAP

Welcome to the SAP Controlling (CO) module for Profitability Analysis or, in technical terms, CO-PA. As its technical name shows, CO-PA is part of the Controlling module of SAP, and thus it is related to the internal transactions of a company. In this chapter, we will review the basic functionalities of CO-PA, including the basic components that define the module and the CO-PA model required to define the approach. We will also look at how to activate and work with predefined business content delivered within the R/3 or SAP ERP ECC 6.0 environment, and how to set up the system to read the information for each structure created (operating concern).

As part of our discussion, we will provide an overview of the general functionalities of each of the Profitability Analysis menus and functionalities such as master data, planning, flows of actual values, tools, reports and forms, and generation of testing data for our examples. Now, let us have a quick look at the capabilities of CO-PA before initiating our detailed discussion in the following chapters.

3.1   General Overview of CO-PA

The Controlling Profitability Analysis (CO-PA) component is a subcomponent of the SAP Controlling (CO) module that integrates information coming from different platforms such as Sales and Distribution (SD), Materials Management (MM), Financials (FI), CO, Production (PP), and others. Think of CO-PA as a window to look inside the SAP database using selective extraction and reporting capabilities to either provide saved and thus static, or real-time and thus dynamic, information.

Regardless of the module on which you have expertise, you likely know that the SAP platform is designed around the financial elements of a company. Thus, it does not matter if you work with web technologies, ABAP, MM, SD, or any other module of SAP; the information available in any system is limited by the rules defined in the FI module. Thus, the FI module becomes the core of the organization in terms of reporting, value and money flow, as well as administration and development. Should you have doubts about this, ask your implementation team which is the first component to implement in your organization, and the answer would be...yes, Financials!

Because high-level enterprise resource planning (ERP) technologies focus first on controlling how the money flows in the enterprise and later on how that information is going to be reported or shared, CO-PA interacts with both of these worlds. That is, CO-PA allows access to the Online Transaction Processing (OLTP) structures, or the core of SAP database tables, and it also allows the creation of structures that are later used by Online Analytical Processing (OLAP) applications to generate multidimensional, analytical, and reporting components based on OLTP data such as that delivered in SAP NetWeaver Business Intelligence (BI) 7.0. Let's look at OLTP and OLAP in a bit more detail.

3.1.1 OLTP

OLTP structures are the industry standard for applications that require multiple data entry and retrieval transaction processes, such as creation of purchase orders, invoices, and others. These OLTP databases are also the standard way of storing transactional data generated from those multiple processes, allowing the system to respond faster to database and user requests. However, OLTP databases, like the core database of SAP, have limitations in reporting capabilities because their main purpose is to *generate and store day-to-day data as fast as possible* and general reporting is not their main strength.

3.1.2 OLAP

To resolve these reporting issues, OLAP structures are used separate from OLTP structures, and their main purpose is to *provide a better view of how data is organized and identify patterns based on segmentation or limitations in data display*. Some examples of OLAP applications are analytical and reporting operations such as dimensional analysis, slicing and dicing, drill-down, and data mining.

An example of OLAP is SAP NetWeaver BI 7.0 or any other data warehousing application that can extract information from the core of the SAP tables and enhance the reporting capabilities of the data initially stored in OLTP format. Performing advanced reporting processes in the OLTP environment, however, consumes computer resources to a degree that significantly reduces system performance. On the other hand, storing and generating transactional data in OLAP applications causes the same problem. That's why the two structures operate separately; OLTP to store and generate data, and OLAP to read, report, and analyze data.

3.1.3   Linking OLTP and OLAP

CO-PA is the recommended standard practice to make the link between both worlds (OLTP and OLAP). Using CO-PA, OLTP data can be shared and used in SAP NetWeaver BI. Furthermore, data that exists in SAP NetWeaver BI 7.0 can be stored inside the core tables of SAP and you can use CO-PA as the way to find data inside the SAP database. The beauty of CO-PA lies in the capability of performing somewhat sophisticated planning and reporting processes similar to those available in SAP NetWeaver BI 7.0, but working with OLTP data, which means that your reports can display information available in SAP in real time.

> **Note**
>
> Information displayed in SAP NetWeaver BI 7.0 is not real time; rather it reflects information with a delay caused by the update and transformation processes.

For this reason, CO-PA allows some level of OLAP reporting while working within an OLTP environment. This is quite useful when the reporting and planning requirements do not demand a high level of sophistication, and the data does not need to be transferred to an external platform. However, the drawback of CO-PA is that if the information is not correctly limited when performing the extraction or a search, system performance might be negatively affected. If so, the data will need to be moved to SAP NetWeaver BI 7.0 using special objects to fully deliver more complex requirements.

3.1.4   SAP ERP ECC 6.0 — Specific Recommendations

As you've seen, SAP's CO-PA submodule is the window and the door to two worlds: OLTP and OLAP. As such, CO-PA makes it possible to work with transactional data coming directly from SAP tables and in real time while performing reporting, planning, and analytical operations similar to those of SAP NetWeaver BI 7.0 or other modules, such as SAP Business Warehouse–Business Planning and Simulation (SAP BW-BPS) or Strategic Enterprise Management–Business Planning and Simulation (SEM-BPS), which basically provide the same functionalities. For this reason, you should use CO-PA as the first choice for SAP ERP Central Component (ECC) 6.0 data analysis and reporting requirements. If your requirements are more complex, then use the more powerful tools available in SAP NetWeaver BI 7.0 using CO-PA as the interface to collect and control the data extraction (from SAP ERP ECC 6.0 to SAP NetWeaver BI 7.0) and retraction (from SAP NetWeaver BI 7.0 to SAP ERP ECC 6.0).

Let's now take a detailed look at the CO-PA profitability model and the two types of transactions that can be used: account-based and costing-based.

3.2   The SAP Profitability Model

From a profitability point of view, SAP ERP ECC 6.0 is a collection of tables and fields that store data, and CO-PA is the interface to access saved (frozen) or real-time data. The main element in CO-PA is called *operating concern*, which can be understood as an *InfoCube* for those familiar with the SAP data warehouse applications, or simply as a small group of selected data objects that will be extracted from specific SAP Tables and that are part of what are called *profitability segments*. Profitability segments can be considered the link between Profitability Analysis and Profit Center Accounting, establishing the connection with the complete SAP ERP ECC 6.0 system into a common analysis, reporting, and display environment.

The SAP system uses two data models: *account-based* and *costing-based*. These two data storage or reporting models are the references for any data-sharing applications in the SAP environment, and also limit the type and level of detail of the data reported. These two models control how the information is posted inside the financial modules in SAP, and also how CO-PA accesses and reports the information.

We can simplify all of these relationships and interactions into a summarized model, as shown in Figure 3.1. This model describes the information flow between the different SAP modules and CO-PA. Notice that the SAP R/3 or SAP ERP ECC 6.0 environment is the most important source of data displayed in CO-PA, from modules such as FI, CO, SD, PP, MM, and Project Management (PS).

Also, notice that the information transferred into CO-PA can be costing-based, account-based, or both formats reported at the same time. The kind of information that flows from the different SAP modules depends on how the transactions are defined in the OLTP system, and thus can be slightly different depending on your reporting and planning requirements, and the account-based or costing-based models that describe how the data is stored or generated.

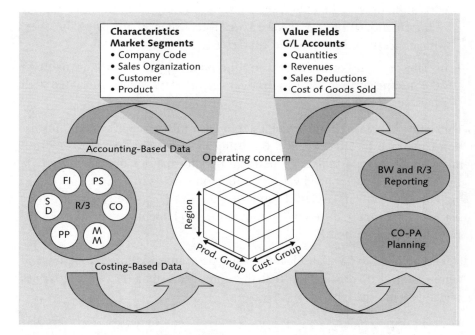

Figure 3.1 SAP Profitability Analysis Model

As you are probably aware, objects inside an SAP system are either called *characteristics* or *value fields*. Characteristics describe the data stored in the system, such as customer ID, billing date, or product ID. These characteristics can be used to limit the data extraction with the definition of profitability segments or market segments. Value fields store data as currency, quantity, or amounts, such as sales, cost of goods sold, and others. For example, if we have the following information in a purchase order: customer ID:

AA3223, purchase order number: 11224, and sale=1,000 USD; then the customer ID and order number are the characteristics, and the sale is the value field.

Once the operating concern is created inside the R/3 or SAP ERP ECC 6.0 platform, the values of the selected tables are transferred, increasing the level of detail by the creation of profitability segments that also limit the information to display outside the operating concern. The SAP system is now ready to initiate two processes, as shown in Figure 3.1:

1. Start reporting the data using the traditional SAP ERP ECC 6.0 reporting environment with the CO-PA reporting capabilities, or initiate the transfer of information from SAP tables to SAP NetWeaver BI 7.0 using the operating concern and the selected characteristics and value fields.

2. Initiate planning of the data using the planning framework available in CO-PA to perform modifications over specific data values associated with a particular object.

This lets you create charts, graphics, and customized reports with information contained in SAP ERP ECC 6.0 using the available reporting environment, or generate a budget or perform transformations over the raw data and store it in a customized value field that only exists in a particular operating concern. With this view in mind of the CO-PA process, you are now ready to explore the different components and elements involved in Profitability Analysis with SAP.

Next, you need to have an idea of what type of information to look for and where to find it, considering that there are more than 17,000 SAP tables available to do the job.

> **Note**
>
> There are several online resources where you can obtain the names of the SAP tables, including **www.sapgenie.com**. For our purposes, we will limit the discussion to only the tables and fields we are interested in studying.

Table 3.1 provides a general overview of several specific modules, documents, and information contained in some of the main SAP ERP ECC 6.0 modules and their SAP tables. For example, production order, which is part of the PP module, stores production variances that can be assessed in real time and that can be either shared with different users or that can be user specific.

Module	SAP Objects	Data
SD	Billing documents	Quantities, revenues, sales deductions, cost of sales
CO-PC	Cost estimates	Variable and fixed costs of goods manufactured
FI	GL account posting	Rebates and freights
CO-OM	Cost center Order Process	Sales and administrative costs Marketing costs Variances
PS	Work breakdown structure (WBS) elements Network activity	R&D costs
PP	Production order	Production variances
MM	Material ledger	Quantity flows
CO-PA tables	Additional costs (user-defined)	Accrued discounts and rebates

Table 3.1 Some CO-PA Data Sources

Looking at Figure 3.1 and Table 3.1 together, you should have a better understanding of the functionality of CO-PA and its interface with different modules. Further, CO-PA not only interacts with other modules but allows you to create additional information, such as user-defined characteristics and value fields that can store customized data.

CO-PA is also important within the CO module as a tool for internal reporting and interaction with other CO components, such as Profit Center Accounting (CO-PCA), Product Cost Controlling (CO-PC), Overhead Cost Controlling (CO-OM), Cost Center Accounting (CO-CCA), Cost Element Accounting (CO-CEL), and others. As shown in Figure 3.2, the goal of SAP financial systems as a whole is to provide the platform to use each major business unit as an income generator instead of a cost carrier with CO-PCA.

If each business unit in a corporation were a profit center rather than a cost center, that would be the dream of any CEO and shareholder. However, a limited number of profit centers and a large number of cost centers is actually the norm. Cost centers absorb the resources generated from profit centers because their function is limited to support the strategic process to continue generating income or simply being operational. Also, the role of a profit center can be considered to be more high level in the company's structure, such as that of a division or business unit that carries a considerable number of resources and generates income from a market segment or an important geographical location, such as Germany, USA, or New York.

In Figure 3.2, only the most important components are described, however, these modules contain submodules, so in reality the flow of information is considerably more complex.

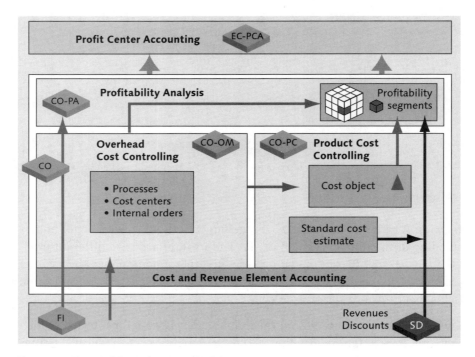

Figure 3.2 Financial Data Flow in an SAP System

You should now have a clear picture of the importance of CO-PA within the R/3 or SAP ERP ECC 6.0 platform, especially to consolidate data for external use, such as in SAP BW, SAP BW-BPS, and SEM.

> **Note**
>
> CO-PA not only allows exporting data, but also controls the communication structures that import data into SAP ERP ECC 6.0, which is called *retraction*. This is not a very common procedure, but it is useful if you require information that flows from SAP ERP ECC 6.0 into SAP NetWeaver BI 7.0, and vice versa. An example of using data retraction is if you complete your planning outside SAP ERP ECC 6.0 using SAP-BW-BPS and then transfer the final budget into the plan data inside SAP ERP ECC 6.0.

In the next section, we will explore in more detail how to access and start working with CO-PA and its components, and we will provide you with a general idea of the elements that form part of this module. More detail on each of these elements will be provided in subsequent chapters.

3.3 Components of CO-PA

To work with CO-PA in SAP ERP ECC 6.0, one can choose to work with the traditional path **Accounting • Controlling • Profitability Analysis,** as shown in Figure 3.3, or another environment called the IMG Activity. We will use the IMG Activity because it provides additional help capabilities and a more user-friendly environment to navigate and access the different CO-PA objects and menus, as shown in Figure 3.4.

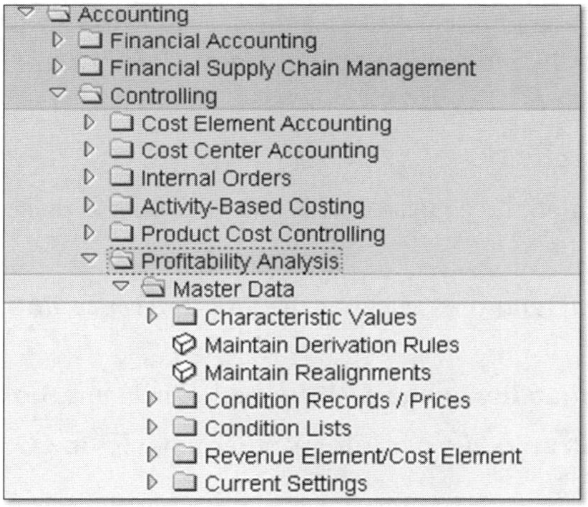

Figure 3.3 Contents of SAP Profitability Analysis Standard Menus

> **Tip**
>
> The menus that display on your screen may be different from those presented in Figure 3.3 and Figure 3.4, depending on your level of authorization and the processes you are allowed to perform. If you have problems accessing the screens presented in this book contact your system administrator for clarification.

41

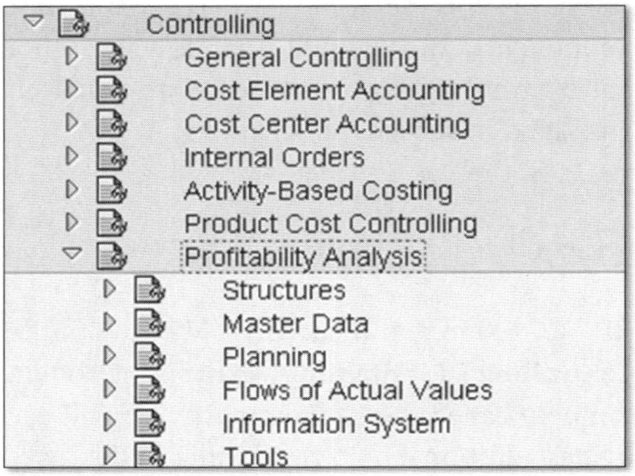

Figure 3.4 Display of the IMG Activity Menu

Once you are comfortable working with the application, you can complete your learning by exploring the traditional SAP menus, because the IMG Activity provides access only to the most commonly used functionalities.

3.3.1 Accessing the IMG Activity

To access the IMG Activity, enter the Transaction SPRO and follow these steps:

1. Press Enter on your keyboard, and then click on the **SAP Reference IMG** button.

2. Navigate to **Controlling • Profitability Analysis**, shown earlier in Figure 3.4.

3. Notice that CO-PA has a similar module structure as other modules in CO, such as CO-CCA.

3.3.2 Profitability Analysis Menu Items

The structure of this book follows the main menu items displayed in the IMG Activity for Profitability Analysis and can be described as follows:

▶ **Structures**
Lets you define the objects and relationships required to perform CO-PA. Without configuring the structures, you cannot work with any CO-PA functionalities.

▶ **Master Data**

Master data provides the fundamental data and content of the previously created structures using characteristics and value fields.

▶ **Planning**

Planning allows you to perform sales, profit, and revenue planning using selected profitability segments.

▶ **Flows of Actual Values**

You can extract data from the OLTP transactional fields and link it to value fields in CO-PA. This submenu allows you to transfer information coming from modules such as FI, SD, or MM.

▶ **Information System**

Lets you perform drilldown reporting to improve data analysis using individual elements that can be linked to reports.

▶ **Tools**

Tools allow you to access functions applicable to all of CO-PA, including authorizations, summarization levels, Schedule Manager, and others.

We will now look at the components included in the CO-PA module, and analyze SAP-delivered templates to further your understanding of CO-PA.

> **Note**
>
> If you get lost along the way, you can also use the available help information that is part of the IMG Activity to support your learning process.

Structures

As its name implies, *structures* are the basic components of any CO-PA project that control the implementation. As shown in Figure 3.5, the **Structures** menu displays different options that control the organization of the following CO-PA information:

▶ Characteristics, which describe the data.

▶ Value fields, which store quantity or amount values.

▶ Operating concerns, which store characteristics and value fields.

▶ Profitability segments, which limit the characteristic data displayed inside the operating concern and the data to be transferred as account- or costing-based into the operating concern.

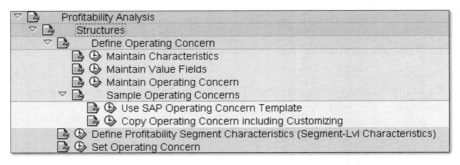

Figure 3.5 Components of the Structures Menu

To access individual elements inside the CO-PA module, click on the clock with the checkmark icon next to the appropriate object. For example, by clicking on this icon for **Maintain Characteristics** (shown in Figure 3.5), you access the screen shown in Figure 3.6, where you can create, change, or display the characteristics available in CO-PA for reporting as part of an operating concern.

Char.	Description	Short text	DTyp	Lgth.	Origin Table	Origin field d
BONUS	Vol. rebate grp	Rebate grp	CHAR	2	MVKE	BONUS
BRSCH	Industry	Industry	CHAR	4	KNA1	BRSCH
BZIRK	Sales district	District	CHAR	6	KNVV	BZIRK
COPA_KOSTL	Cost center	Cost ctr	CHAR	10		
COPA_PRZNR	Business Proc.	BusProcess	CHAR	12		
CRMCSTY	CRM Cost Elmnt	CRM CstElm	CHAR	10		
CRMELEM	Marketing Element	Mrkt.Elem.	NUMC	8		
CRMFIGR	CRM Key Figure	CRM KF	CHAR	16		
EFORM	Form of manufacture	Manuf.form	CHAR	5		
GEBIE	Area	Area	CHAR	4		
KDGRP	Customer group	Cust.group	CHAR	2	KNVV	KDGRP
KMATYP	Aircraft type	Plane type	NUMC	2		
KMBRND	Brand	Brand	NUMC	2		
KMCATG	Business field	Bus. field	NUMC	2		
KMDEST	Destination	Destin.	CHAR	5		
KMFLTN	Flight number	Flight no.	CHAR	8		
KMFLTY	Flight type	FlightType	CHAR	4		
KMHI01	CustomerHier01	CustHier01	CHAR	10	PAPARTNER	HIE01
KMHI02	CustomerHier02	CustHier02	CHAR	10	PAPARTNER	HIE02
KMHI03	CustomerHier03	CustHier03	CHAR	10	PAPARTNER	HIE03
KMIATA	IATA season	IATA seas.	CHAR	5		
KMKDGR	Customer group	Cust.group	CHAR	2	KNVV	KDGRP
KMLAND	Country	Country	CHAR	3	KNA1	LAND1
KMLEGS	Route segment	RouteSegmt	CHAR	7		
KMMAKL	Material Group	Matl Group	CHAR	9	MARA	MATKL
KMNIEL	Nielsen ID	Nielsen ID	CHAR	2	KNA1	NIELS
KMOPDY	Day of operation	OperatnDay	CHAR	2		
KMORIG	Departure Location	Depart Loc.	CHAR	5		

Figure 3.6 Maintain Characteristics Overview

The screen displayed in Figure 3.6 shows characteristics that either extract information contained in the default SAP tables or characteristics that were created by a user for data load. An important part of the **Structures** menu is that it allows you to navigate to and identify the complete set of information available in CO-PA to create operating concerns and profitability segments. Also, accessing the screen in Figure 3.6 allows you to access the value field screen. In both cases, the information shown includes a **Description**, **Short text**, **DType** (data type), **Lgth.** (length), **Origin Table**, and **Origin Field** to make sure that you are getting the correct data.

Data structures defined in the **Structures** menu of the IMG Activity establish what type of data you can access later on in the **Master Data** menu. However, they also tell you what information you will be reporting, planning, or monitoring in CO-PA because you already defined an operating concern and its contents.

The challenge begins in what additional information is necessary to comply with profitability requirements that are not available in the SAP tables, because we need to add user-defined values, hierarchies, and automatic rules that control the calculation of additional data based on valuation rules and predefined conditions.

To resolve these issues, you must configure additional rules in the **Master Data** menu, which we'll look at next. Basically, in the **Structures** menu you identify "what" you are interested to find or work with, and in the **Master Data** menu, you configure additional rules about "how" to work with that data.

3.3.3   Master Data

The **Master Data** menu, as shown in Figure 3.7, lets you configure the basic settings that determine the structure and contents of Profitability Analysis in your system.

Using this menu, you access the configuration of the characteristic values, derivation, and valuation to either manually or automatically create values or hierarchies based on predefined criteria to be used in profitability segments.

The elements presented in Figure 3.7 are reviewed in more detail in Chapter 5, where you will learn how to configure derivation rules and valuation strategies based on predefined criteria. Notice that there is more than just one

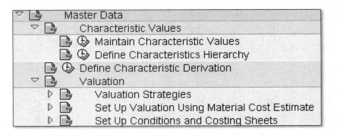

Figure 3.7 The Master Data Menu

way to work with valuation, and the way it is configured increases the level of sophistication of your data process.

At this point, we should mention that you do not have to configure each of the options available in the **Master Data** menu, so always focus on your requirements to identify which components you need to work with besides the definition of your structures. In this book, we will show you what can be done so you can decide what to apply to your particular project. Note also that sometimes CO-PA is unable to handle the types of transactions required by a massive implementation and interfaces with SAP NetWeaver BI 7.0 or other external systems to the core of the SAP system are required. As such, the items in the **Master Data** menu can be considered optional for configuration. You must, however, configure the items in the **Structures** menu to be able to work with CO-PA.

In many cases, SAP provides several tools that deliver similar results. For example, the CO-PA planning framework that we'll look at in the next section is similar to other SAP planning applications, such as SAP NetWeaver BI IP, SEM-BPS, and SAP BW-BPS. While the CO-PA planning framework is also not mandatory, you are encouraged to explore its potential as a planning application as much as possible before deciding to increase your application requirements by using one of the other tools mentioned.

3.3.4 Planning

Planning in CO-PA is done with the CO-PA planning framework. As mentioned, this framework is similar to other SAP applications, for example the SAP BW-BPS application, but they run in different environments. CO-PA allows you to modify and display information from real-time or frozen data inside the R/3 or SAP ERP ECC 6.0 system. In comparison, SAP BW-BPS requires the creation of SAP BW InfoCubes, which are outside the SAP R/3 or SAP ERP ECC 6.0 platform, before any type of reporting and planning is allowed. Furthermore, the use of data in OLAP format is not real time but limited to the creation of data extraction applications.

The capabilities of the CO-PA planning framework are not as powerful as those of SAP NetWeaver BI Integrated Planning or SAP BW-BPS. However, the CO-PA planning framework provides useful functionalities to perform the most common calculations and avoid development or creation of extraction objects that move data outside the SAP ERP ECC 6.0 tables. For this reason, the CO-PA planning framework can provide a great level of sophistication for data planning or manipulation without leaving the SAP ERP ECC 6.0 environment.

The CO-PA planning framework provides different types of planning functions that allow users to revaluate, copy, forecast, and distribute large amounts of data that can later be distributed using the manual planning functions. Another useful feature of the CO-PA planning framework is the transfer of plan data from other applications such as Sales and Operations Planning (SOP), Cost Center Planning (CO-CCA), or the Logistic Information System (LIS). For those familiar with SAP BW-BPS, this topic is quite easy, but if you are not familiar do not be worried; we will review these elements extensively in Chapter 7.

Figure 3.8 shows the **Planning** menu and its submenus. For now, just be aware of its existence. In a later chapter, we will create a customized application and use the different functions available in this menu to modify the data extracted from the SAP tables, user-defined characteristics, or value fields. Also, an important element of the CO-PA planning framework is its interaction with information created in the Master Data menus, such as valuation strategies, and rules and conditions that can significantly increase the power and complexity of a planning application.

If you need to interact with different components, such as SD or MM, you must configure different interfaces so CO-PA can extract and display the information coming from those applications. The menu **Flows of Actual Values** provides the capability to do so, and these types of requirements allow CO-PA to combine and access data easily and efficiently without the need for major ABAP developments or customizations. Everything comes SAP-delivered or "inside the box" and such interfaces are already configured and ready to use.

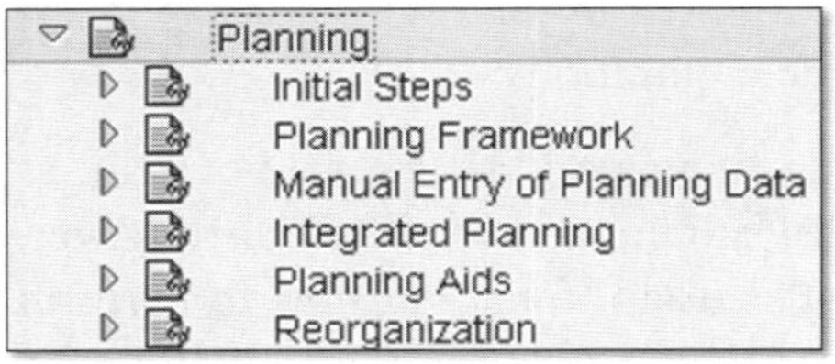

Figure 3.8 The Planning Menu

3.3.5 Flows of Actual Values

Profitability Analysis with SAP is about combining the sources of revenue and costs into a common communication, reporting, and planning environment. Therefore, we should be able to quantify whether the company is making or losing money at any particular moment because CO-PA allows you to create interfaces to interact with different SAP accounting, financial, and operational modules and subcomponents.

To that end, when working with the menu **Flows of Actual Values,** we will explore the basic settings required to access and consolidate data coming from SD, FI, CO, and other SAP modules. For example, to quantify the estimated sales value of an organization for a particular time period, you might require transferring information from incoming sales orders to CO-PA and assigning those to value fields or quantity fields.

Figure 3.9 provides a quick overview of the main menu components of **Flows of Actual Values**, and shows the options to transfer information coming from different modules, which include, among others:

- **Transfer of Incoming Sales Orders**
- **Transfer of Billing Documents**
- **Direct Posting from FI/MM**
- **Settlement of Production Variances**
- **Transfer of Overhead**

The **Information System** menu of CO-PA, which we'll look at next, provides great flexibility in the generation of customized reports, forms, and variables (similar to what you can do in SAP NetWeaver BI 7.0). Reporting is one of the most important parts of the SAP system, and the flexibility delivered with CO-PA can satisfy quite complex requirements, thereby reducing the complexity of implementations, especially those that require extensive reports and scenarios.

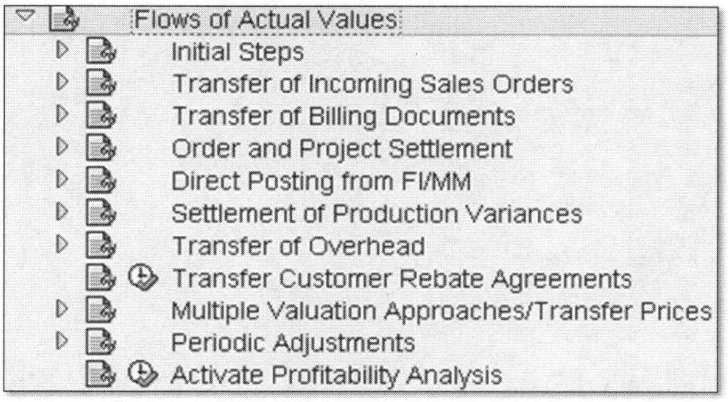

Figure 3.9 The Flows of Actual Values Menu

> **Note**
>
> If you are an advanced user who knows that sometimes these type of extractors are not enough for the type of requirements or functionalities demanded by your projects, you can also perform a generic data extraction into SAP NetWeaver BI or SAP BW. Note that the concept of generic data extraction is not reviewed in this book because its concepts go beyond the scope of our discussion. If necessary, you can consult additional SAP-BW documentation for guidance on this subject, such as *http://help.sap.com* or *http://sdn.sap.com*.

3.3.6 Information System

The **Information System** menu can be considered the most important menu besides the **Structures** menu in defining the overall CO-PA environment. In comparison with BEx or similar reporting applications in SAP NetWeaver BI, the **Information System** menu lets you perform flexible data reporting and analysis using different types of graphics. It also enables the execution of variables behind the scenes within the ABAP environment to automatically update and control the data update to improve reporting performance without coding! As shown in Figure 3.10, in the **Information System** menu you can perform the following:

▶ Create individual components of reports

▶ Create reports

▶ Store report data

▶ Define a report tree

▶ Define authorization objects for the information system

▶ Reorganize your information system

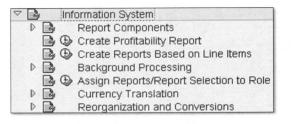

Figure 3.10 The Information System Menu

Once an operating concern has been created, activated, and loaded with data, the **Information System** menu allows you to use system-specific reports or create your own. You can also create sophisticated reports that allow drilldown and filtering using reports or forms. Note that even though CO-PA allows access to see real-time data, this does not mean that you will see the latest data all of the time. If you have a report open, you need to refresh it periodically, or, using variables defined as variants, execute it in the background with an ABAP program and schedule its behavior. All of these options will be reviewed later on in Chapter 9.

Finally, the **Tools** menu delivers additional functionalities, such as summarization levels, SAP enhancements, and access to the authorization management system. These are not required for an implementation, but provide system performance improvements.

3.3.7 Tools

Tools in this case are additional functionalities that are not key elements of CO-PA but they are nice to have. They relate to performance, security, analysis, simulation, and general revision of the objects created in CO-PA. Also, using the **Tools** menu, you can perform transports, imports, and deletion of transactional data, and post billing documents and sales orders to Profitability Analysis retroactively if you went productive with SD before you implemented CO-PA.

Another important feature available in this menu is **Authorization Management**, which allows setting up authorization levels for CO-PA objects in planning and for basic and baseline items reports. In addition, as with any other SAP application, the definition of roles and profiles is also included in this component.

Figure 3.11 provides a general overview of the contents of this menu, but we will review this information in detail in the "Tips and Tricks with CO-PA" chapter, Chapter 12. These are important elements that need specific attention, especially when you are ready for implementation. Do not review these elements on your own until we reach that chapter, because using them is, for the most, part limited to system administrators or high-level power users.

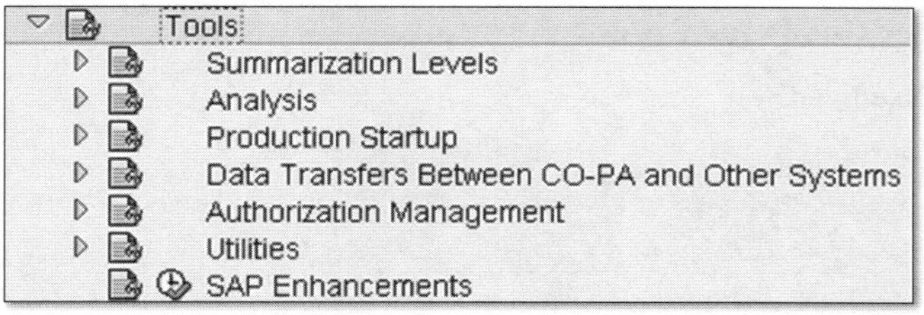

Figure 3.11 The Tools Menu

As is the case with most of the SAP modules, predefined content is delivered in SAP ERP ECC or R/3 for CO-PA; namely SAP operating concern templates, which provide you with preconfigured environments you can use as a reference during your implementation. In the next section, we will explore these templates in detail.

3.4 Working with SAP Operating Concern Templates

SAP-delivered business content exists for CO-PA in the form of different templates that can be activated and populated with data to assist your implementation. These templates have predefined operating concerns, which are complete structures that you must generate, activate, and populate with testing data to use them as part of a reference for your implementation. These templates are standard SAP objects that are protected and cannot be modified, so you always have a clean version ready to use as a reference.

> **Note**
>
> You might ask yourself: Why should I use these templates? The answer is simple: they were created to be used as examples for simple and complex implementations providing reports, planning layouts, and other objects that can be used to end up with a successful CO-PA implementation. The only way to learn SAP software, or any other application, is by having a good idea first of what is expected and what kind of general functionalities are available, so you can "play" and learn along the way, without risking or modifying real data or objects.

There are four SAP-delivered templates in the system, as also shown in Figure 3.12:

- ▶ **Model Bank E_B1**
- ▶ **Airline Route Profitability S_AL**
- ▶ **Template Consumer Goods Ind S_CP**
- ▶ **Quickstart Template S_GO**

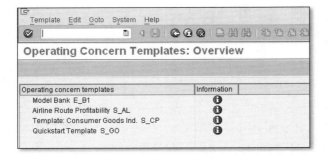

Figure 3.12 SAP-Delivered Operating Concern Templates

To access any of these operating concern templates, follow this path in the IMG Activity: **Controlling • Profitability Analysis • Structures • Define Operating Concern • Sample Operating Concern • Use SAP Operating Concern Template**.

Notice in Figure 3.12 that the cells in the **Information** column contain an icon with an "i" inside a circle. If you click on this icon, you will access additional help documentation that describes the elements and procedures for each of the objects included in the respective operating concern template. For our purposes, we will use the operating concern named **Quickstart S_GO** because it is the most basic application of all of the available operating concern templates and thus the easiest to understand.

3.4.1 The Quickstart S_GO Operating Concern Template

This section will describe how to activate and access the different predefined objects included inside the Quickstart S_GO (S_GO is its technical name) operating concern template only, which is similar to the other SAP-delivered operating concern templates. Before we can start working on the information configured in this object, however, we need to generate the objects as well as the data inside this operating concern:

1. Double-click on the operating concern named **Quickstart Template S_GO** and you will receive a message notifying you that the client system (development, production, or testing) will be updated with the test data and the required tables.

2. Click on the checkmark icon. The system will now automatically generate all of the structures and objects required for the Quickstart S_GO template, however, the objects will not contain data. You are creating only the data structures or "buckets" were the data will later be stored or extracted.

Activating and Generating Sample Data

Now, to generate and activate the sample data available with the Quickstart Template S_GO template, follow this procedure:

1. Double-click on **Quickstart Template S_GO** again, and you see the information displayed in Figure 3.13, which describes the template and its three submenus: **Customizing**, **Application examples**, and **Tools**.

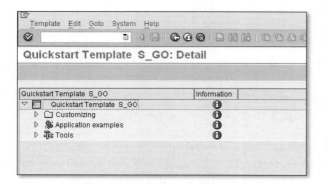

Figure 3.13 Working with the Quickstart Template S_GO Template

2. Next, to generate data for the operating concern Quickstart S_GO, follow this path: **Application Examples • Prepare application examples • Create example data**.

3. Double-click on **Create example data**, shown in Figure 3.14.

4. In the **Generate Example Data** screen shown in Figure 3.15, select the radio button **Create planning data**, and enter a fiscal year for which the data is going to be generated, in our case "2009."

5. Click on the green checkmark icon.

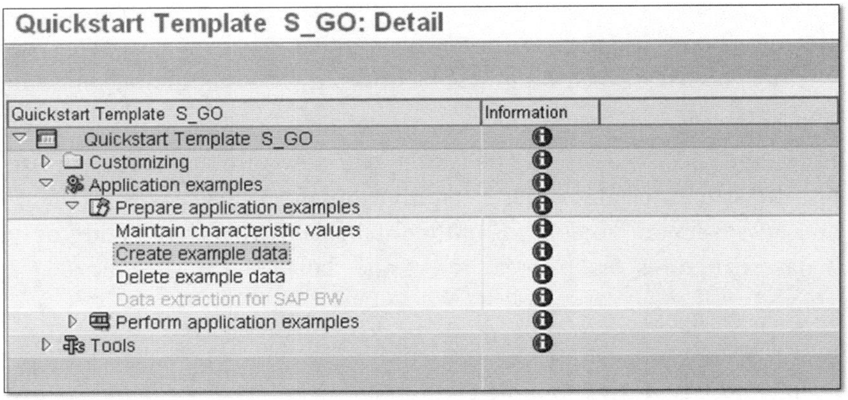

Figure 3.14 Creating Data in Your S_GO Template

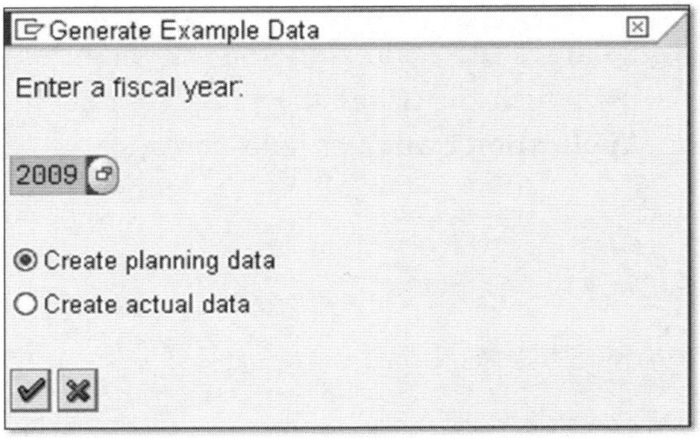

Figure 3.15 Generating Example Data in the Quickstart S_GO Template

6. The message **Example data has been created** appears on the screen, notifying you that the data was successfully generated. If you want to create actual data, go back and select the **Create actual data** radio button, and then click on the checkmark icon again.

3.4.2 Customizing

Now you are ready to navigate and review the predefined elements inside the CO-PA module using the Quickstart Template S_GO. First, we will look at each of the functions in the **Customizing** object.

Display Characteristics/Value Fields

The first function in the **Customizing** object is **Display Characteristics/Value Fields**:

1. Open the **Customizing** menu and select **Display Characteristics/Value Fields** to highlight this menu item, as shown in Figure 3.16.

Quickstart Template S_GO	Information
▽ ▦ Quickstart Template S_GO	ⓘ
▽ 🗁 Customizing	ⓘ
Display Characteristics / Value Fields	ⓘ
Display/Define Characteristic Derivation	ⓘ
Preparation in Planning	ⓘ
Display / Define Planning Layouts	ⓘ
Flows of Actual Values	ⓘ
Display / Define Key Figure Scheme	ⓘ
Display / Define Forms	ⓘ
Display/Define Profitability Reports	ⓘ
Connection to SAP BW	ⓘ
▽ 🐾 Application examples	ⓘ
▷ 📖 Prepare application examples	ⓘ
▷ 📇 Perform application examples	ⓘ
▷ 🛠 Tools	ⓘ

Figure 3.16 Display Characteristics/Value Fields

2. Click on **Display Characteristics/Value Fields** again to access the IMG Activity menu that will let us review the structure and configuration of the operating concern, shown in Figure 3.17.

▽ 📑 Profitability Analysis
▽ 📑 Structures
▽ 📑 Define Operating Concern
📑 ⊕ Maintain Characteristics
📑 ⊕ Maintain Value Fields
📑 ⊕ Maintain Operating Concern
▷ 📑 Sample Operating Concerns
📑 ⊕ Define Profitability Segment Characteristics (Segment-Lvl Characteristics)
📑 ⊕ Set Operating Concern

Figure 3.17 Accessing Characteristics/Value Field Information

> **Note**
>
> To access the IMG Activity associated with any item in the menu structure shown in Figure 3.16, you can either select the item to highlight it and then click on it to access the IMG Activity, or you can double-click on the item.

3. Find the item **Maintain Operating Concern** and then click on the clock with the checkmark icon to execute the function, shown in Figure 3.17.

4. The screen shown in Figure 3.18 appears, where you can modify the structure of any operating concern. Click on the change/modify icon, (the pencil with glasses), and the message **Caution! You are changing/deleting cross-client settings** appears. The SAP system is letting you know that you are accessing objects used in different components.

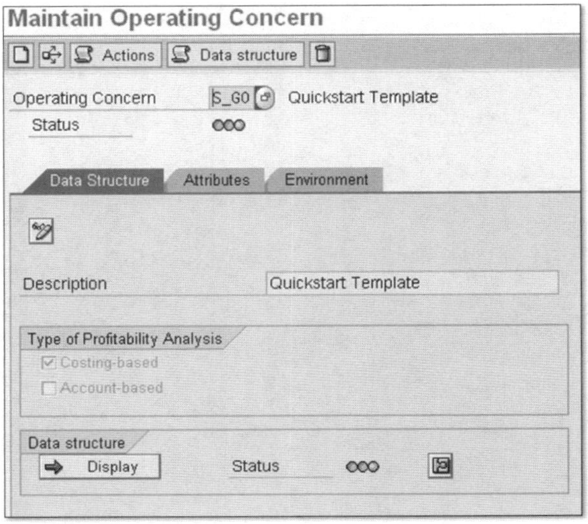

Figure 3.18 Reviewing the Contents of an Operating Concern

5. Click on the green checkmark icon.

> **Tip**
>
> When you need to run the activation process, you can click on the change/modify icon, use the combination Ctrl+F3, or click on the cigar icon in the icon bar. Because the Quickstart template is default SAP business content, however, you are not actually allowed to modify any part of its configuration; you can only display its contents. However, in an operating concern created from scratch, you can modify any part of the structure and you will need to activate these changes.

6. You can now review the information contained on the **Chars** (Characteristics) and **Value Fields** tabs of the operating concern, as shown in Figure 3.19 and Figure 3.20. Notice the technical names that identify the characteristics and the origin SAP tables.

Characteristic	Description	Cat.	Length	Check table	Origin table	Doma
BRSCH	Industry	CHAR	4	T016	KNA1	BRSCI
BZIRK	Sales district	CHAR	6	T171	KNVV	BZIRI
KDGRP	Customer group	CHAR	2	T151	KNVV	KDGRI
KMVKBU	Sales Office	CHAR	4	TVBUR	KNVV	VKBUI
KMVTNR	Sales employee	NUMC	8		PAPARTNER	PERNI
MATKL	Material Group	CHAR	9	T023	MARA	MATKI
VKGRP	Sales Group	CHAR	3	TVKGR	KNVV	VKGRI
KMWNHG	Main material group	NUMC	2	T2246		RKESI

Figure 3.19 Characteristics of the Operating Concern Quickstart

Value field	Description	Cat.
KWBRUM	Gross sales	Amount
KWBONI	Bonuses	Amount
KWKDRB	Customer Discount	Amount
KWMGRB	Quantity discount	Amount
KWMARB	Material discount	Amount
KWSKTO	Cash discount	Amount
KWVKPV	Sales commission	Amount
KWVSEK	SalesSpecDirectCosts	Amount
KWKLFK	Anticipd ship. costs	Amount
KWMAGK	Mat. overhead costs	Amount
KWMAEK	Direct mat. costs	Amount
KWFKFX	Fixed prod. costs	Amount

Figure 3.20 Value Fields of the Operating Concern Quickstart

7. Once you have finished reviewing this information, click on the back icon to return to the original screen of the Quickstart template.

8. After completing your changes, also review the **Status** indicator shown earlier in Figure 3.18, which must be set to green. Otherwise, there might be errors in the latest modifications that you need to review.

9. Select the **Attributes** tab as shown in Figure 3.21 and notice that the operating concern requires an **Operating concern currency** for costing-based CO-PA and a **Fiscal year variant**. Generally, **K4** (calendar year with 4 special posting periods) is the most common for SAP reporting.

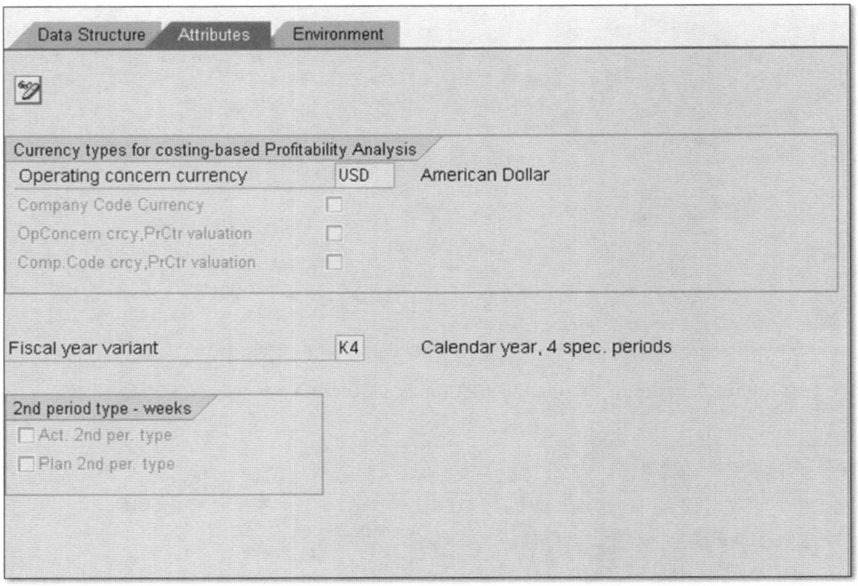

Figure 3.21 Reviewing the Attributes Tabs

10. The **Environment** tab (shown later in the chapter in Figure 3.33) provides a general review of the status of the operating concern cross-client (programs, screens, and any other objects). Also, this tab provides information if the operating concern has been configured properly. The other status indicator is the client-specific part that identifies whether any objects, such as number range objects, attributes, or control table entries are working properly.

Display/Define Characteristic Derivation

We'll now take a quick look at characteristic derivation:

1. Return to the Quickstart main menu, and double-click on **Display/Define Characteristic Derivation**, shown in Figure 3.22. We will look at derivation in detail in Chapter 5, however; we can say that derivation lets you find values for certain characteristics automatically, based on the known values of other characteristics, where these characteristics are logically dependent on one another.

2. Select **Profitability Analysis**, click on the checkmark icon, and then access the IMG Activity menu called **Define Characteristic Derivation**, as also shown in Figure 3.22.

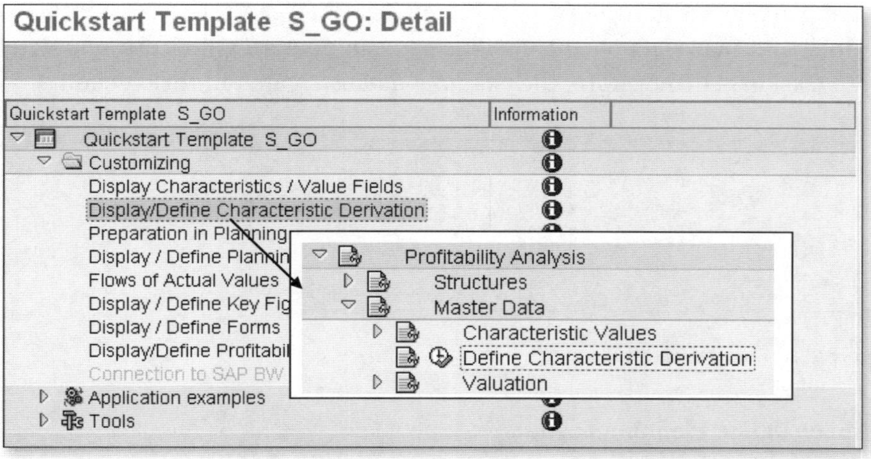

Figure 3.22 Accessing Characteristic Derivation

Notice that, as shown in Figure 3.23, the main component that controls the **Define Characteristic Derivation** menu item is the **Derivation rule**, which can be considered to be the inference engine that controls the relationships between different characteristics and generates the new data values in the predefined characteristic that exists inside an operation concern.

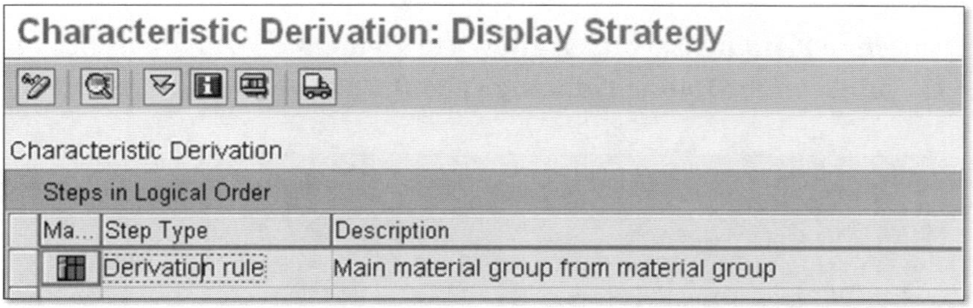

Figure 3.23 Characteristic Derivation

Preparation in Planning

Next, we'll look at preparation in planning:

1. Return to the main menu of the Quickstart template, and follow this path: **Customizing • Preparation in Planning**.

2. Select **Profitability Analysis** and click on the checkmark. This lets you access the CO-PA **Planning** menu as shown in Figure 3.24. In this menu, you can display the settings made in planning for the operating concern

59

template Quickstart: version maintenance is organized across applications and plan version 0 is assigned to the operating concern template Quickstart. Furthermore, the example data is created in this version.

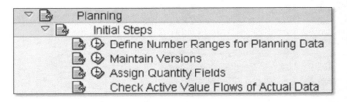

Figure 3.24 Preparation for Planning

Display/Define Planning Layouts

As mentioned earlier, the CO-PA planning framework is an important component in the success of a CO-PA implementation, especially when you start transferring information from other modules. We will explore the CO-PA planning framework features in detail in Chapter 6; for now, we will simply review the information presented for the Quickstart template using the **Display/Define Planning Layouts** option:

1. Click on the back icon to access the main screen of the Quickstart template.

2. Double-click on **Display/Define Planning Layout**.

3. Select **Define Planning Layout**, as shown in Figure 3.25, and then click on the execute icon for **Define Planning Layout**.

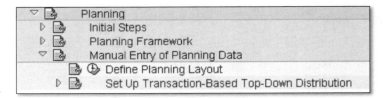

Figure 3.25 Defining Planning Layouts

4. Select **Create planning layout**, **Change planning layout**, or **Display planning layout**, depending on whether you want to create a new planning layout, modify an existing layout object, or display an existing layout object.

The Quickstart template contains several predefined planning layouts, as shown in Figure 3.26. For those familiar with SAP BW-BPS, the concept of *layout* should be more than clear. A *planning layout* is a spreadsheet-like environment that allows you to perform planning operations that can interact with SAP software and Microsoft Excel at the same time. Planning layouts interact directly with the information stored in your operating concern and are created using the SAP ERP ECC 6.0 application called Report Painter, which we will also review in Chapter 9.

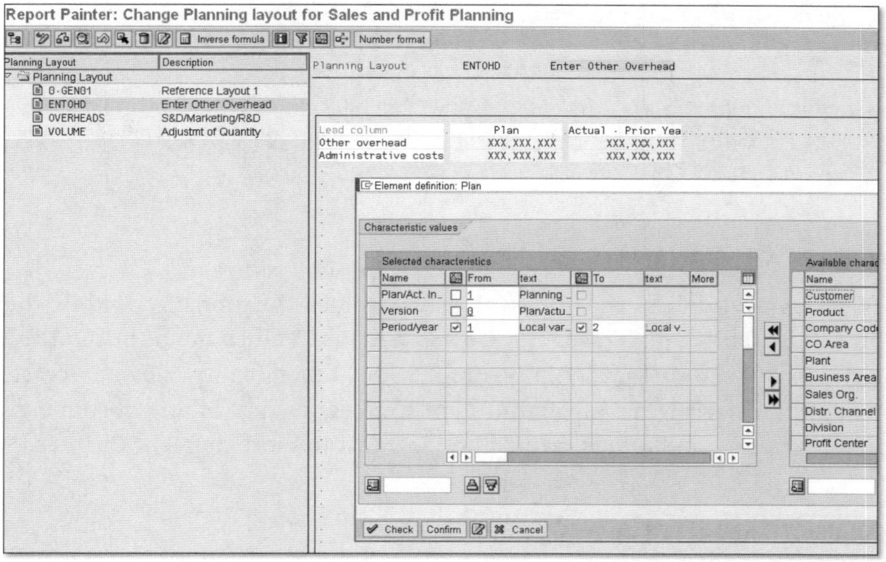

Figure 3.26 Quickstart Template: Predefined Planning Layouts

The functionality of each of the planning layouts shown in Figure 3.26 is as follows:

▶ In planning layout **0-GEN01**, the basic layout includes a number of predefined variables that collect and present information based on amount, unit, and distribution key. Use this for a quick reference for a basic layout that you can adapt to other needs, depending on the characteristics of your data.

▶ In planning layout **ENTOHD**, other overhead costs and administration costs are planned at the highest level under record type D. The numbers from the previous year are displayed for comparison purposes.

▶ Planning layout **OVERHEADS** is used for entering R&D, marketing, and sales overhead. Planning occurs at the distribution channel and main material group under record type D.

61

▶ In planning layout **VOLUME**, you can make adjustments to quantities at the customer group, material group, and distribution channel level under record type F.

> **Note**
>
> An operating concern works quite similar to an SAP BW InfoCube in the sense that it interacts with layouts to extract and modify the information they contain. An operating concern is also the link required to establish data extraction architectures between SAP R/3 or SAP ERP ECC 6.0 and SAP NetWeaver BI, as discussed in Chapter 9. Hopefully, the model presented earlier in Figure 3.1 is clearer now; otherwise, wait until we review each of the components in more detail in later chapters.

Flows of Actual Values

As its name implies, the flows of actual values functionality within the Quickstart template accesses the **Flows of Actual Values** menu in the IMG Activity. As seen previously in Figure 3.9, this functionality allows interacting and transferring data from different sources, such as billing documents, direct postings, and others. We will review this in more detail in Chapter 8.

Display/Define Key Figure Scheme

This component is quite important to simplify the calculation of values in CO-PA. This menu of the Quickstart template can be compared to a *calculated key figure* (CKF) or *restricted key figure* (RKF) in SAP BW-BEx because it establishes predefined structures and relationships and stores individual values. For example, we can create a key figure scheme (an object with formulas attached) called Net Sales and place it in a column as part of a report, but in reality it is an object that includes the formula sales-total costs, and its value is what we use in any report. This shows you that CO-PA is a quick and agile reporting tool and its interaction with Microsoft Excel makes it very desirable for end users.

To work with key figure schemes:

1. Return to the Quickstart main menu and double-click on **Display/Define Key Figure Scheme** in the **Customizing** menu.

2. In the IMG Activity, execute the function **Define Key Figure Schemes** to access the screen shown in Figure 3.27.

Here, the key figure scheme **Total var. COGM** is shown, and the formula used to calculate its result is presented as:

+ 'Direct MaterialCosts' + 'Var. Production costs'

Direct MaterialCosts and **Var. Production costs** are also key figure schemes with a lower sequence value that extract the information using a specific element based on a **Value Field**, **Formula**, and **Function**.

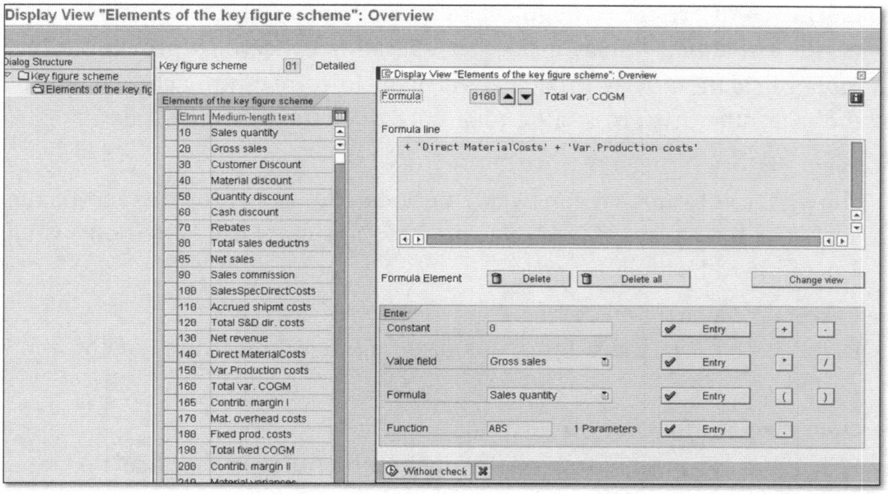

Figure 3.27 Example of a Key Figure Scheme

> **Note**
>
> We will discuss this topic in more detail in Chapter 10 on CO-PA reporting. For now, you just need to understand that you can create your own objects inside CO-PA that allow you to work similarly to how you would work with SAP BW with calculated key figures or with preconfigured formulas, and that they are called key figure schemes.

Display/Define Forms

The **Display/Define Forms** function in the main menu of the Quickstart template allows you to access information of profitability reports that can be based on objects called *forms*. Forms work as templates that define the key figure or value fields to display in rows and columns within a report. You can use forms as a template for complex reports in as many reports as required or to maintain a standard format used by departments or business units with similar information. In addition, the Quickstart template includes seven pre-defined forms, as shown in Figure 3.28 and described here:

▶ **Sales/Sales Volume (SGOF01)**
Calculates the total value of net sales using the information coming from sales quantity, gross sales, customer discount, material and quantity discount, cash discount, rebates, and total sale deductions.

▶ **Target Achievement (SGOF02)**
Calculates the relative weight or percentage of achievement of the plan versus actual data values inside the operating concern. It provides a formula calculation between actual versus plan to measure achievement of the sales quantity, gross sales, total sales reductions, and net sales.

▶ **Price History (SGOF03)**
Shows the information for twelve periods and a total for the end of the year. The total year value is calculated as the sum of the 12 periods using a predefined formula.

▶ **Customer Sales (SGOF04)**
Displays the total sales for all of the customers, regardless of the time period.

▶ **Operating Profit Analysis (SGOF05)**
Provides a clear view on how the operating profit can be calculated, and additional features that can be configured as part of a report. For example, you can extract the actual and plan values, and perform comparisons with previous years and make a calculation in the percentages of change for each value type. Also, there are different levels to how the Net Revenue and the Contribution Margins are calculated, depending on the desired deductions at each step. However, the values are defined only for pre-defined value fields without any further definitions.

▶ **Incoming Orders (SGOF06)**
Extracts information from other SAP modules, and how this information can be used and displayed by different users. Most of the value fields have not been preconfigured, and only the calculation of contribution margin per unit (CM II/Unit) and contribution margin per net sales (CM II/Net Sales) have actual formulas assigned to their objects.

▶ **Analysis CM II (SGOF07)**

Presents a more detailed overview of the calculation of the contribution margin and a comparison with previous years.

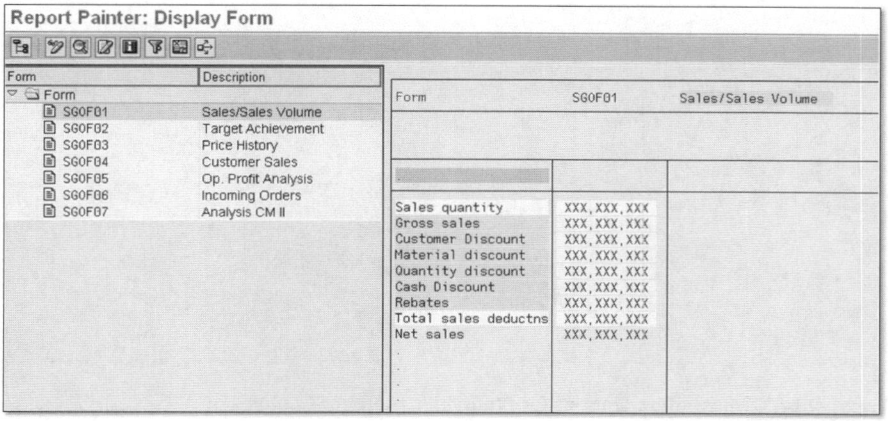

Figure 3.28 Display/Define Forms with the Report Painter

You can use these SAP-delivered forms as a template for your own forms, customize them to suit your requirements, or as a reference to create new forms.

Display/Define Profitability Reports

Profitability reports are the ultimate goal of CO-PA because they give managers and users direct access to the information they need that is stored in SAP R/3 or SAP ERP ECC 6.0. In comparison with forms, profitability reports, shown in Figure 3.29, are individual objects that you can customize and modify but that you cannot use as templates to control other reports' behavior. The Quickstart template delivers seven reports using the forms displayed in Figure 3.29 as templates:

▶ **SGOB01**

Allows you to analyze the short-term sales and volume figures. In particular, you can explore in detail the structure of the discounts granted. Because this information reaches Profitability Analysis from billing documents, you can run an analysis at the customer or product level.

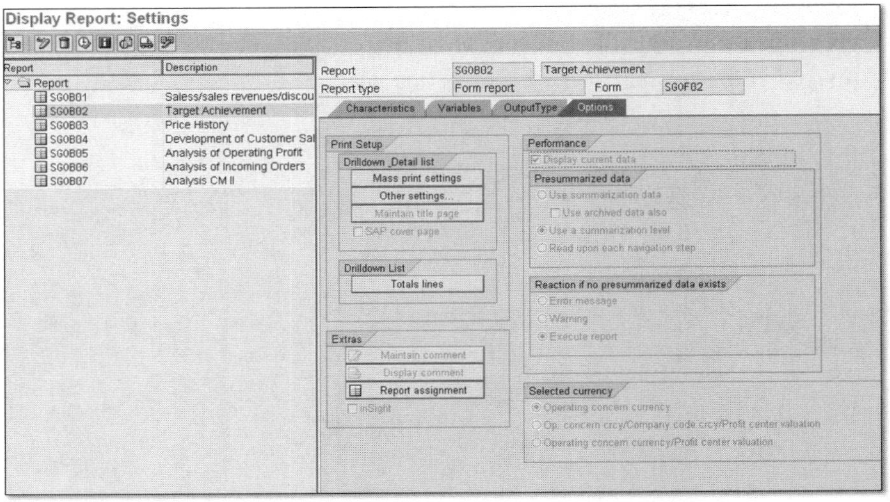

Figure 3.29 Configuration Options for Profitability Report SGOB02

▶ **SGOB02**

Shows the extent to which planned targets have been attained. Because planning often occurs at a higher level than the customer or product level, you cannot drill down from these characteristics.

▶ **SGOB03**

Shows the gross and net price history during a given year. Depending on the selection you make, you can display this information for planning or actual data. You can drill down via all of the characteristics in the product hierarchy.

▶ **SGOB04**

Lets you analyze sales volumes in the customer hierarchy. For this, you can either specify a specific period or display an overview of all periods. You can tailor the graphic to meet your requirements.

▶ **SGOB05**

Allows you to compare the actual data — within a given period interval — with the planning data and the data for the previous year (up to the operating profit or loss) for the entire contribution margin scheme. You can drill down from the characteristics if overhead costs occur at that level. The only costs to be represented at the level of the entire company are administration costs.

▶ **SGOB06**

Provides you with a comparison of the incoming sales in a given period interval and the 12 previous periods (that is, the previous year). The information includes everything up to contribution margin II. You can use this report to display early warning information.

▶ **SGOB07**

Allows you to analyze short-term company success (that is, CM II), without taking periodic overhead into account. Moreover, the report also displays two key figures on the profit-sales ratio.

To access profitability reports in the Quickstart template, follow this procedure:

1. Return to the main menu of the Quickstart template.

2. Double-click on **Display/Define Profitability** in the **Customizing** menu.

3. Select **Profitability Analysis** and click on the checkmark icon.

4. Click on the execute icon for the IMG Activity object named **Create Profitability Report**.

5. Choose an activity, either **Create**, **Change**, or **Display**. For our purposes, we'll choose **Display** to navigate and review the configurations without changing any important information.

6. Double-click on any object to review its configuration. For example, Figure 3.29 displays the report **Target Achievement (SGOB02)** and the **Characteristics**, **Variables**, **Output Type**, and **Options** tabs that control its behavior. For now, access this information and become familiar with it, we will review it in more detail in Chapter 8.

7. You can execute any profitability report anytime using the same procedure we just used to view the target achievement report.

The final results of executing a profitability report are presented in Figure 3.30 using **1/2009** as the starting period. Notice the different components, such as characteristics used for **Navigation,** value fields for **Sales Quantity**, **Gross sales**, and others; as well as charts and totals for a particular characteristic for a given time period are shown. The customization options available in the Report Painter allow CO-PA to be a flexible application to design new and improved ways to analyze different sources of data.

CO-PA reporting also requires performance tuning if the amount of data extracted increases with time, so you need to be aware of new techniques or simplifications to avoid performance issues when running your reports.

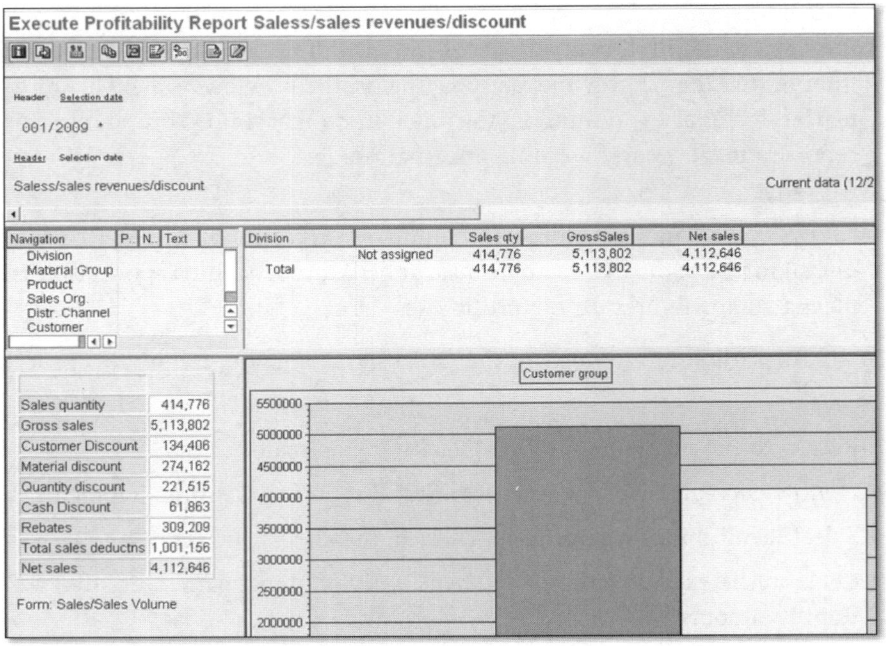

Figure 3.30 Example of Profitability Report SGOB01

3.4.3 Application Examples: Prepare Application Examples

We'll now look at the functions in the **Application examples · Prepare application examples** menu of the Quickstart template, shown earlier in Figure 3.16.

Maintaining Characteristic Values

A market segment is made up of a combination of characteristic values, and the **Maintain Characteristic Values** function allows maintaining these values for selected characteristics that can be deleted, changed, or added. Characteristic values are used to generate sample data when activating your Quickstart template. To access this functionality follow these steps:

1. Follow this path in the Quickstart Template main menu: **Application examples · Prepare application examples** and double-click on **Maintain Characteristic Values**.

2. The screen shown in Figure 3.31 appears and displays the available characteristic values for the operating concern **S_GO Quickstart Template**.

3. Click on the **Customer group** characteristic and see the values as shown on the right side of Figure 3.31. You can modify, delete, copy, and change the values displayed in your system to match your needs.

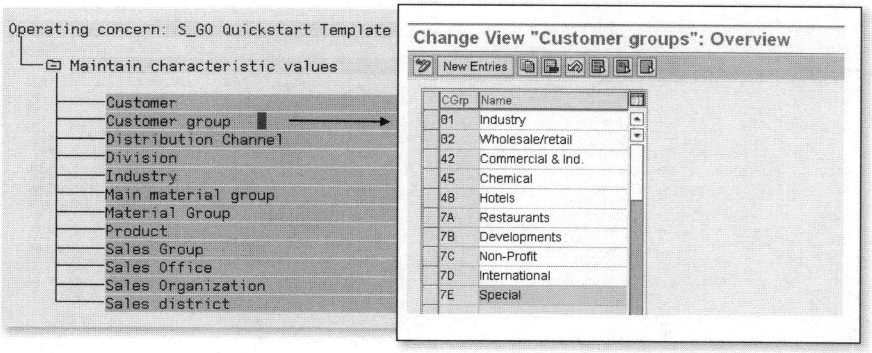

Figure 3.31 Maintaining Characteristic Values

Create/Delete Example Data

We have already covered creating example data earlier in this chapter so we won't look at the **Create example data** option here. The option **Delete example data** lets you completely remove the sample data from your system.

3.4.4 Application Examples: Perform Application Examples

We'll now look at the options in the **Application examples · Perform application examples** menu of the Quickstart Template.

Execute Profitability Report

You can access the **Execute Profitability Report** function by following this path: **Perform Application example · Execute Profitability Report**. We won't go into further detail here because we have already executed a report and also have a good idea on how to display reports on the screen, based on Figure 3.30. Further detail will be provided in Chapters 9 and 10.

Execute Planning Method

The **Execute planning method** function lets you directly access planning layouts (the objects that allow users to make modifications to data inside the core SAP tables or user-defined values) using the path: **Application examples · Perform application examples · Execute planning method**. As mentioned before, we will explain these concepts in more detail in Chapter 6, so for now simply navigate and become familiar with the planning framework environment shown in Figure 3.32.

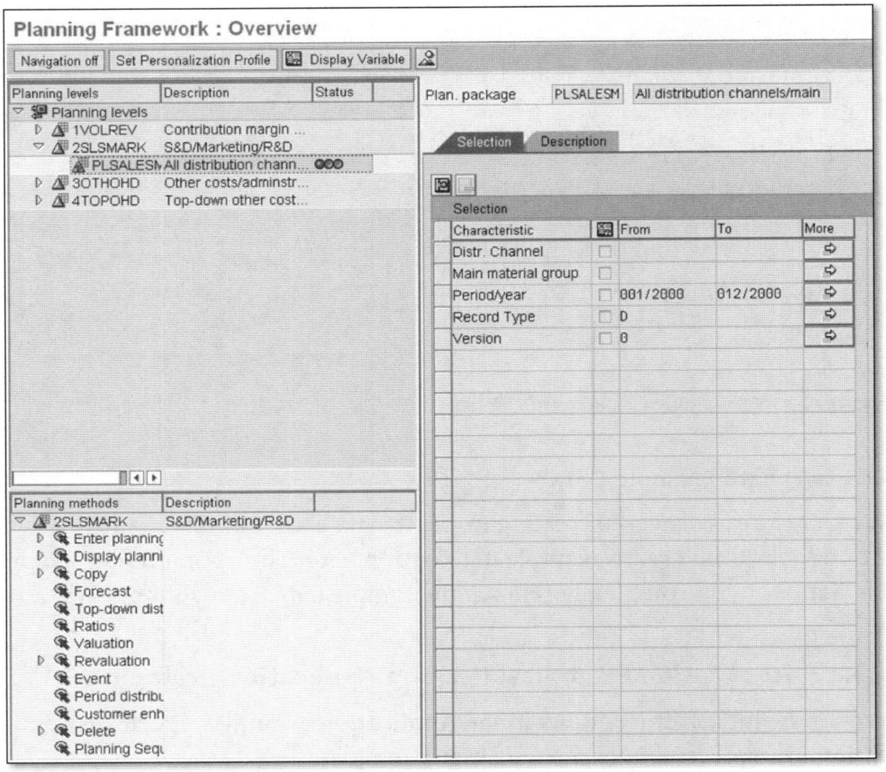

Figure 3.32 The CO-PA Planning Framework

3.4.5 Tools

The last menu of the Quickstart operating concern template is **Tools**. CO-PA provides an extensive number of tools to improve analysis, performance, and other elements. However, the **Tools** menu for Quickstart is limited to the following tools:

► **Copy Operating Concern Template**
This function lets you copy the selected operating concern template, including the changes you have made to it. You can then make further changes to this copied operating concern and use the relevant customizing settings to integrate it into the other application components. Give the operating concern a name that does not fall within the SAP name range (S_xx).

▶ **Reset Operating Concern Template**
This functions lets you reset the operating concern template to its original SAP-delivered state. This process erases any changes you have made to the template and any example data generated. Note that the characteristic values you have maintained are not deleted.

Once all of these components are working, and you have finished creating and configuring your CO-PA applications, you must activate each operating concern and set it as current so you can extract your data and generate reports according to your specifications. This process is discussed in the following section.

3.5 Manually Activating an Operating Concern and Setting it as Current

For changes made to an operating concern to affect all of the objects included in the operating concern, the operating concern must be activated. You can do this by either answering **Yes** to the message you receive after adding characteristics and value fields to the operating concern when working with the function **Maintain Operating Concern** in the **Structures** menu (shown earlier in Figure 3.5), or by manually activating the operating concern at a later point in time. To manually activate an operating concern, follow this procedure:

1. Follow this path in the IMG Activity: **Profitability Analysis • Structures • Maintain Operating Concern** and click on the execute icon.

2. Select the **Environment** tab, shown in Figure 3.33.

3. To activate either of the two available components, **Cross-client part** (external to CO-PA) or **Client-specific part** (internal to CO-PA), click on the cigar-like icons in the respective sections. These two components are critical for the data structures and information extracted and shared within the CO-PA application. Your objects are now ready to be accessed by any reports or planning applications.

> **Note**
>
> You should always make sure that the **Status** icons on the **Environment** tab, as well as those on the **Data Structure** tab, are green, to be certain that there are no problems or errors left in the system. The SAP system will prompt you if any errors were identified in the data structures of the operating concern that you are trying to activate.

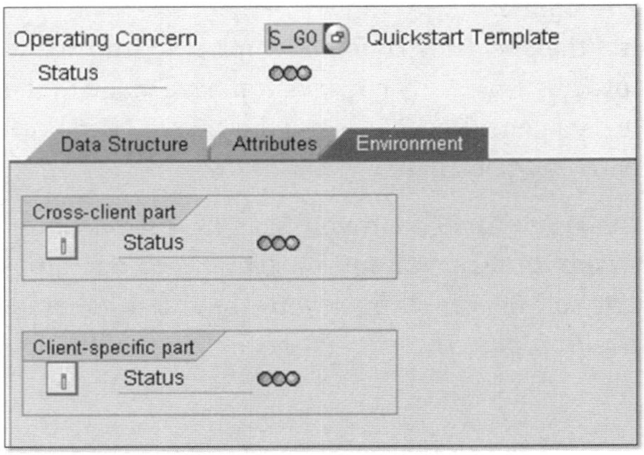

Figure 3.33 Activating Your Operating Concern

When you are certain that your operating concern has only the group of characteristics and value fields you want, is correctly configured (status green), has been activated (to reflect the latest data structure), and you are clear what you want to do with it, you are ready to make it the current operating concern, using the **Set Operating Concern** function in the IMG Activity **Structures** menu.

Only the operating concern that is current will be affected by any modification, change, report extraction, and update of objects. Further, any objects such as planning layouts, forms, and reports that are attached to an operating concern are only available if the correct operating concern has been set up as current. Making sure that the appropriate operating concern is set up as current is extremely important; you don't want to make changes to, or use data from, an incorrect operating concern.

Example

For example, if you have two operating concerns, Europe and USA, and you set Europe as current, the USA information will not be affected by any changes you make in data, reports, layouts, and other information (as long as the two operating concerns' information does not overlap in the data structures). Also, the information contained in the USA operating concern will not be available when working with the Europe operating concern, and vice versa, unless you select the **Set Operating Concern** function again, and change this relationship.

To set the Quickstart operating concern current:

1. Follow the IMG Activity menu path **Profitability Analysis · Structures · Set Operating Concern**, as shown in Figure 3.34, and click on the execute icon.

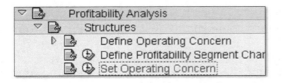

Figure 3.34 The Set Operating Concern Function

2. Review the information presented in the screen shown in Figure 3.35. There is a **Status** icon that lets you know how if the operating concern is ready to be used. Further, the **Type of Profit. Analysis** that this object will perform is identified (either **costing-based** or **account-based)**, which also affects the way that information is posted and displayed into CO-PA.

3. Click on the checkmark icon to set the operating concern current.

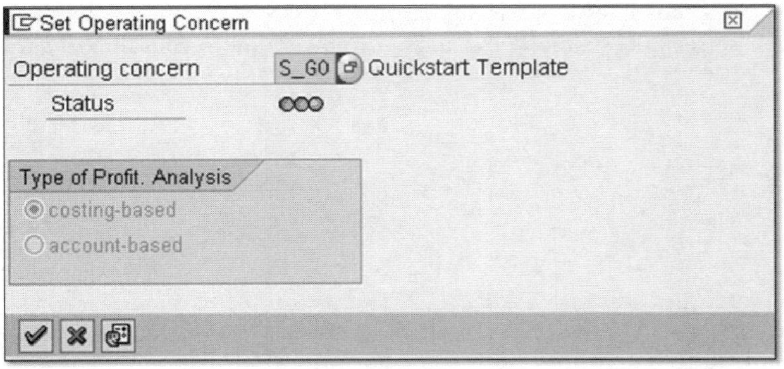

Figure 3.35 Making an Operating Concern Current

> **Note**
>
> We recommend that you do not perform any additional transactions until you understand the ideas and general concepts presented in the next two chapters. Also, remember that you have several SAP-delivered templates that follow the same format of the Quickstart template that you can activate, and whose structures and configurations you can review to complement your learning.

3.6   Summary

In this chapter we explored the basic functionalities of CO-PA from a general point of view. We showed you what type of information CO-PA can handle in R/3 or SAP ERP ECC 6.0, how you can access this information in a template, and, in general, helped you become familiar with the CO-PA environment.

In Chapter 4, we will analyze in more detail the concept of an operating concern, and of CO-PA and its role as main integrator within an SAP system of OLTP and OLAP data. We'll also analyze in more detail the differences between costing-based and account-based CO-PA.

> **Note**
>
> Should you still be confused about the topics or terms discussed in this chapter, or how to navigate inside the SAP IMG Activity, don't worry; we will continue our discussion in more detail in the chapters that follow and you will get the hang of things. Also, remember that this book is written for intermediate and advanced users, but beginners of CO-PA can catch up quickly with the help of other team members and using the material in this book. Further, the SAP community continuously evolves, so seek the help of a consultant or power user in your firm to get you started.

Costing-based CO-PA is considered the most intensive and common application of Profitability Analysis. However, when you configure costing-based CO-PA, you are also creating an account-based environment at no additional charge.

4   Configuring Costing-Based CO-PA

The most popular type of Profitability Analysis is costing-based CO-PA because it is easy to configure and provides a reasonable level of detail without having to worry about account or cost elements in the system, and it gives meaningful information to decision makers. In this chapter, we will explore in detail the creation and configuration of a CO-PA costing-based operating concern and the major options required to set it up. In addition, we will activate all of the account-based CO-PA options along the way so you can review them when we explore account-based CO-PA in more detail in Chapter 11.

4.1   General CO-PA Overview

In general, CO-PA is a module that allows the analysis and combination of different types of documents, such as:

- Invoices from the SD module
- Direct journal entries from FI
- Cost center assessments from CO
- Settlement of production orders from Production Planning (PP)
- Quantity flows from Material Management (MM)
- Work Breakdown Structure (WBS) elements from Project System (PS), among others

All of this documentation carries information related to customers, billing information, dates, products, variances, cost allocations, and hierarchies, and allows the creation of up to 30 additional user-defined characteristics and up to 120 additional value fields (key figures) to complement the different analyses. Moreover, the creation of CO-PA documents for each line item, sales order, cost assessment, and production order allows creating profitability segments or market segments that identify the data with specific characteristics.

> **Note**
>
> Profitability segments allow CO-PA to perform transactions between controlling objects, such as cost centers or production orders, and the profitability segments. However, once the values have been allocated inside CO-PA, the revenue and cost elements require special processing procedures to be allocated outside this environment.

As you can see in Figure 4.1, the role of CO-PA is to consolidate and access information coming from different areas of the SAP ERP ECC 6.0 system, based on the documents previously discussed. The **Value Flow** shown in Figure 4.1 describes the availability of key financial data coming from either Financial (**FI**) or Controlling (**CO**) modules, which are the two key elements for any posting inside an SAP system. At the end you can see what management wants to visualize in terms of how each transaction affects financials, while thinking ahead to the balance sheet and the income statement reports.

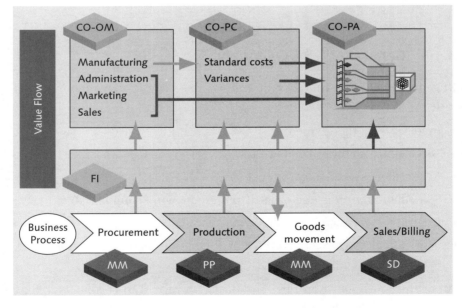

Figure 4.1 The CO-PA Value Flow and Business Process Model

> **Note**
>
> Remember, an operating concern can be defined as the SAP ERP ECC 6.0 version of an SAP BW InfoCube in that its main function is not storing data but rather creating a window into the SAP tables that store the transactional data.

4.2 Costing-based CO-PA versus Account-based CO-PA

Part of the decisions required to work with CO-PA is how to configure and control how your data flows, which is done using one of two models: costing-based or account-based. Each allows posting information at different stages of the sales cycle, and also the type of information displayed differs slightly. In simple terms, the two basic CO-PA approaches are:

▶ **Costing-based**: Uses value fields and does not use General Ledger (GL) accounts to perform any type of reconciliation with FI or cost-element accounting. Advantages of costing-based CO-PA include:

  ▶ Contribution margin can be calculated, automatically accessing the standard cost estimates of the product valuation approaches.

  ▶ Variance categories can be mapped to value fields.

  ▶ Flexible reporting capabilities are available for analysis of several characteristics.

  ▶ Standard cost estimate is used to show a split by cost component of the bills information extracted from the product costing module.

▶ **Account-based**: Is directly related to GL account posting and for this reason makes it more exact and requires summarization levels to facilitate data consolidation. The advantage of account-based Profitability Analysis is that it is permanently reconciled with financial accounting. However, the fact that it uses accounts to get values makes it less powerful. No contribution margin planning can be done because it cannot access the standard cost estimate in account-based CO-PA and no variance analysis is readily available.

The main difference, however, between the two CO-PA methods is how and when postings are performed inside the system. Table 4.1 provides a description of these specific differences and how their transactions are posted into the financial and controlling systems, dealing with three major issues:

▶ Passing an invoice to accounting updates the revenue, discount, freight, and cost of sales value fields.

▶ Settling production order variance updates the variance fields that are related to the cost of goods sold (COGS) cost components.

▶ Assessing cost centers updates the cost center variance fields.

Account-based	Costing-based
Invoice information and financial postings are performed at the same time when calculating the cost of sales.	Cost of sales captured at the time of invoice but the financial posting is done at the time of delivery. Meaning there is a time lag between these two transactions.
The cost of sales is no longer exactly matched with the revenue that is posted at the time of invoicing.	The cost component detail for variances is available for production order settlement and production cost collector hierarchy.
The details of the COGS components are not available.	Cost elements and GL accounts are not available.
The cost of sales is not captured when invoicing a customer because it was already done when doing the financial entry.	Reconciliation using value fields and high-level characteristics (such as region, business area, and others).
Revenue is posted into CO-PA during billing.	The postings are recorded in a CO-PA document.
Production variances (order settlement and cost collector hierarchy) are not available, but variance is captured via one cost element.	Costing-based CO-PA uses a cost-of-sales approach, where the standard cost of sales is not recognized until a product is sold.
It is more detailed than costing-based because it discloses the different GL accounts and cost elements.	
The postings are recorded in a standard controlling document.	

Table 4.1 Comparison between Account-based and Costing-based CO-PA

Note

If both costing-based and account-based CO-PA are activated, when the settlement to CO-PA takes place, a posting is made to both types of CO-PA. The account-based CO-PA posting is recorded in a standard controlling document and the costing-based CO-PA posting is recorded in a CO-PA document.

If R/3 or SAP ERP ECC 6.0 do not give you the type of information that you want, you can use SAP NetWeaver Business Intelligence (BI)/SAP Business

Warehouse (BW). If you want to customize something beyond that, using ABAP or another programming language, remember the following:

► Customization affects system performance and it is directly affected by future system upgrades.

► Modifications to the standard system functionalities centralizes power in the hands of a few people who might not be around all of the time.

► The lack of documentation generally available during and after a major system customization provides more room for the people who built the system, to, under negative circumstances, possibly halt the system.

► Customizations mostly add costs rather than value; consultants love to bill you for a new system and the periodic maintenance, but the SAP system has enough tools to avoid major customizations. Limit yourself to what the system provides and you will find that you are able to access the information that you need without major customizations.

► Limit the use of ABAP for:

  ► Major "your boat is sinking" type of scenarios in SAP and other GUI components

  ► Simple queries using an ABAP query with table joins or direct access

  ► Interacting in the SAP NetWeaver BI 7.0 environment on the Web.

  Do not use ABAP for:

  ► Major customizations that modify default SAP objects

  ► Creating applications that can be easily delivered with alternative methods, such as FOX code and Formula Editor (available in SAP NetWeaver BI 7.0 and CO-PA Report Painter).

► Try to maximize the usage of available standard SAP extractors. SAP BW generic data extraction can be very handy when exporting information outside SAP ERP ECC 6.0 if the capabilities of CO-PA Report Painter or CO-PA Planning are not enough.

With all these practices and tips in mind, we are now ready to start our discussion of extracting information from R/3 or SAP ERP ECC 6.0 using costing-based CO-PA.

4.3   Creating Characteristics and Value Fields

The following is a general rule in SAP Controlling:

"Company codes are assigned to controlling areas, and controlling areas are assigned to operating concerns."

A *controlling area* is the highest level of aggregation that covers the activities of Cost Center Accounting, Product Costing, Profitability Analysis and Profit Center Accounting. An *operating concern* is the highest node in Profitability Analysis that limits the activities and elements that can be accessed and modified inside SAP ERP ECC 6.0 or R/3 and is limited by characteristics and value fields. Figure 4.2 provides an overview of the major components that are part of the **Structures** menu of the IMG Activity (Transaction **SPRO**) as part of the **Profitability Analysis** menu.

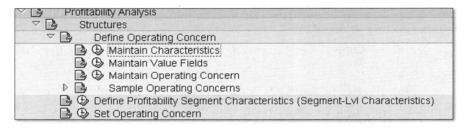

Figure 4.2 The CO-PA Structures Menu

The individual configurable items include the following:

▶ **Maintain Characteristics**: create, modify, or change all available characteristics. Some of the CO-PA characteristics required for reconciliation usually include company code, business area, and cost element. When working with reports, additional characteristics, such as high-level material groups, may also be used or defined as user-defined elements that are part of a derivation rule based on current SAP information to derive new values.

▶ **Maintain Value Fields**: create, modify, or change all available value fields. You can choose to either store or extract data as amount or quantity. For example, the value Sales can be stored with a unit of measure as US dollars or euros as a quantity, but Inventory can simply be stored as "100," regardless of unit value as an amount or vice versa.

▶ **Maintain Operating Concern**: create, modify, or change operating concerns. This is where you establish the link between characteristics and value fields to create your operating concern and control the information displayed in reports or planned in CO-PA.

▶ **Define Profitability Segment Characteristics**: these elements are additional "partitions" or pieces of your operating concern and are defined via characteristics. You select which characteristics are available for the information system and later on in planning. The remaining characteristics are considered line items and will not be used to generate any type of classification inside the operating concern.

▶ **Set Operating Concern**: determines which operating concern is current in the system, and is affected by any operations, reports, extractions, derivations, and so on. The current operating concern carries the information defined inside the system, such as reports and planning layouts. For example, if operating concern A has report X attached, and operating concern B has report XX attached, only X or XX is available to perform the operations over the respective operating concern and the respective data. For this reason, it is important to know in which operating concern you are working, and that operating concern is current in the system until you exit the system or run this option again to change into another current operating concern.

Now we will review in more detail, and learn how to create, the structures that define the basic behavior of the information inside CO-PA and that control the access and display of information, namely characteristics and value fields.

Characteristics

To access the characteristics definition:

1. Follow this IMG path (or use Transaction SPRO): **Controlling • Profitability Analysis • Structures • Define Operating Concern • Maintain Characteristics.**

2. Double-click on the clock with the checkmark icon next to **Maintain Characteristics.**

3. You will see the **Edit Characteristics: Start** screen, displayed in Figure 4.3. You can now click on **Create/Change, Display,** or **Change,** depending on what you want to do.

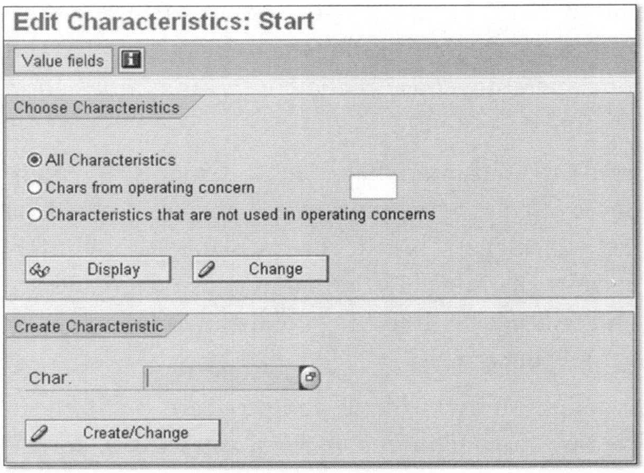

Figure 4.3 The Edit Characteristics: Start Screen

4. Click on **Create/Change**. The message **Caution you are processing cross-client data structures** appears.

5. Click the checkmark icon to accept the message.

6. Review the screen **Change Characteristics: Overview** that appears, as shown in Figure 4.4. It displays all of the characteristics available in the system you can allocate to an operating concern. User-defined characteristics are displayed in white and can be modified. SAP standard characteristics extracted from specific SAP tables are grayed out and can't be modified. For example, **BONUS** is an SAP default characteristic coming from the origin table **MVKE,** and **EFORM** is a user-defined characteristic.

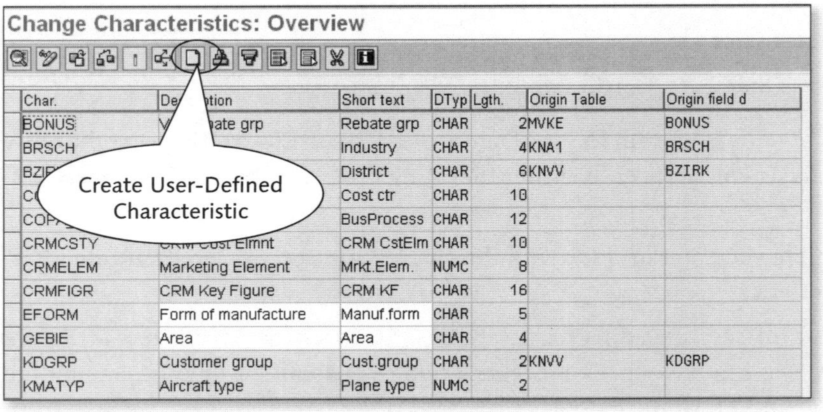

Figure 4.4 Available Characteristics in CO-PA

As discussed in the previous step, SAP default characteristics are clearly identified with their original SAP tables that store the transactional information and data fields. However, you can also create your own characteristics that you will either populate with data or use for different calculations or planning applications later on in the process. To create a user-defined characteristic:

1. Click on the create icon located at the top of the screen shown in Figure 4.4.

2. Select **User defined**, as shown in Figure 4.5.

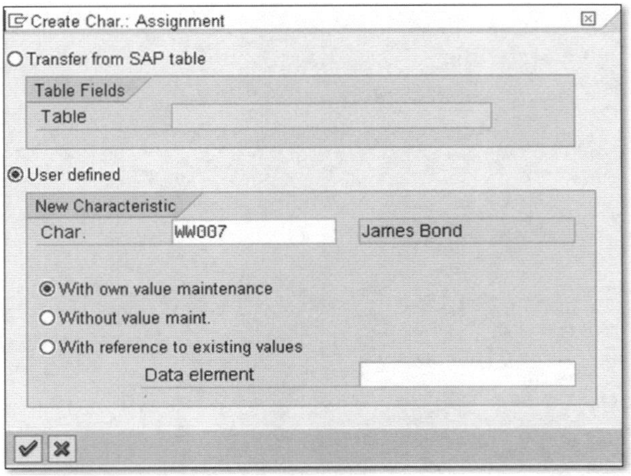

Figure 4.5 Creating a User-Defined Characteristic

3. In the **New Characteristic** section you need to configure two input boxes. The first box contains the field name or unique identifier of the characteristic and must begin with "WW," followed by a standard SAP nomenclature to make the system identify these types of characteristics. The second box contains a description. For example, in Figure 4.5, **WW007** is a user-defined characteristic. Its name is identifier **007** and the description is **James Bond**.

4. After configuring the identifier and description, click on the checkmark icon and the screen shown in Figure 4.6 appears. The system now requires the definition of **Data type/length**. Specify "CHAR" to indicate that 007 is alphanumeric and specify "10" for the character length.

5. Click on the save icon to save your changes.

6. Click on the checkmark icon to create the characteristic from scratch, and click on **Yes**, despite the warnings.

7. Click on **Automatic**, and then click on the save icon. At the end of this process your screen must look like Figure 4.6. (The system copies the descrip-

tion information from the initial screen shown in Figure 4.5 into the **Description** and **Heading** boxes in the **Texts** section.)

8. To complete the process, click on the activation icon, which looks a bit like a cigar, located at the top of the screen, as shown in Figure 4.6.

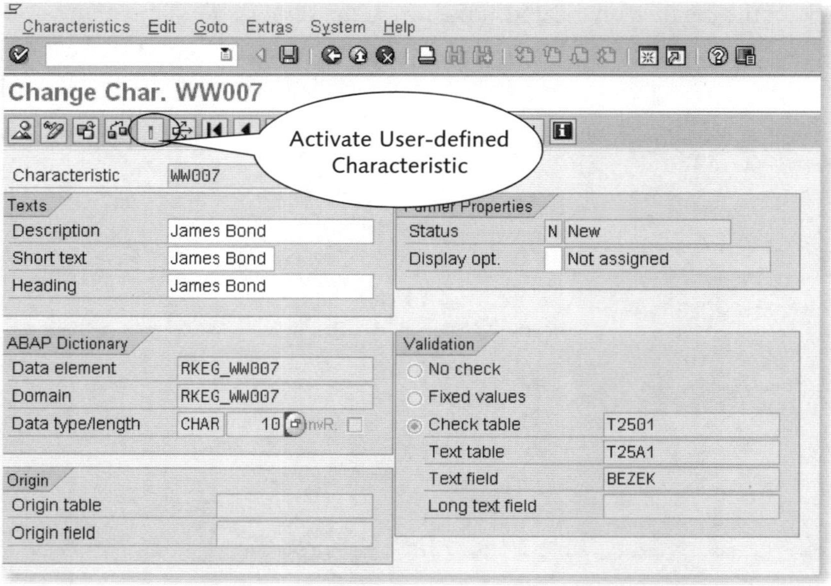

Figure 4.6 Creating a User-defined Characteristic in CO-PA

This user-defined characteristic is now available for use by different operating concerns.

> **Note**
>
> When creating a user-defined characteristic, a data class can be defined to describe the data format at the user interface. If a table field, structure field, or a data element is used in an ABAP program, the data class is converted to a format used by the ABAP processor. For this reason, when a table is created inside the SAP system, the data class of a table field is converted into a data format of the database system used.

Value Fields

In simple terms, value fields do not store descriptions of data but their results. You can access the information contained in value fields in one of two ways:

▶ Click on the button **Value Fields**, shown earlier in Figure 4.3.

▶ Follow the IMG path **Profitability Analysis** • **Structures** • **Define Operating Concern** • **Maintain Value Fields**.

As a result, the **Edit Value Fields: Start** screen appears, as shown in Figure 4.7.

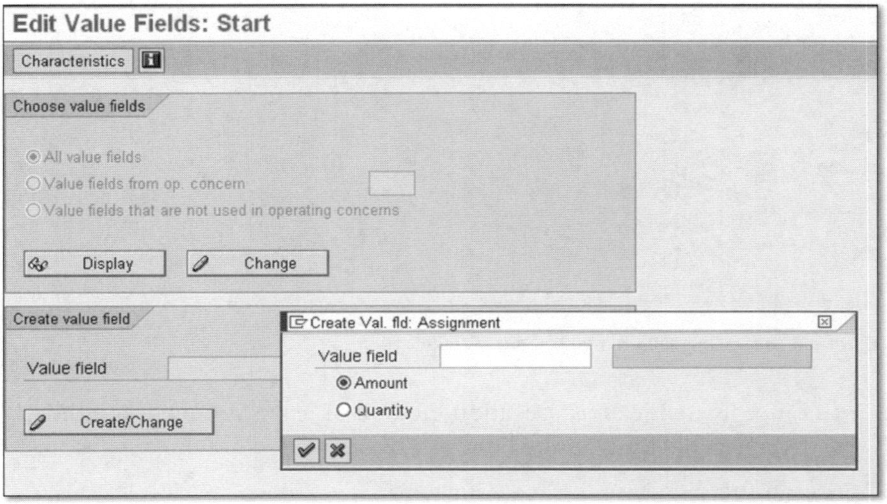

Figure 4.7 Accessing the Edit Value Fields: Start Screen

To create a new value field follow this procedure:

1. Click on **Create/Change.**

2. Click on the checkmark icon in the dialog box with the message **Caution you are processing cross-client data structures**, and an input box called **Create Val. fld: Assignment** appears, as shown in Figure 4.7.

3. Select either **Amount** or **Quantity**, depending on your requirements. We selected **Amount** for our example.

4. You now need to configure the technical name and a description in the two **Value Field** input boxes, as shown in Figure 4.7. The first input box describes the technical name that must start with "VV", followed by xxxx ("VVxxxx"). VV are the initial required letters for the system to identify this field as a value field and xxxx is the name of the value field, which must be between 4 and 5 characters long. The second input box is where you enter a description. For our example we entered "VVTES" in the first box, and "test1" in the second box.

5. Click on the checkmark icon to access the change value field screen (**Change Val. fld VVTES**) as shown in Figure 4.8.

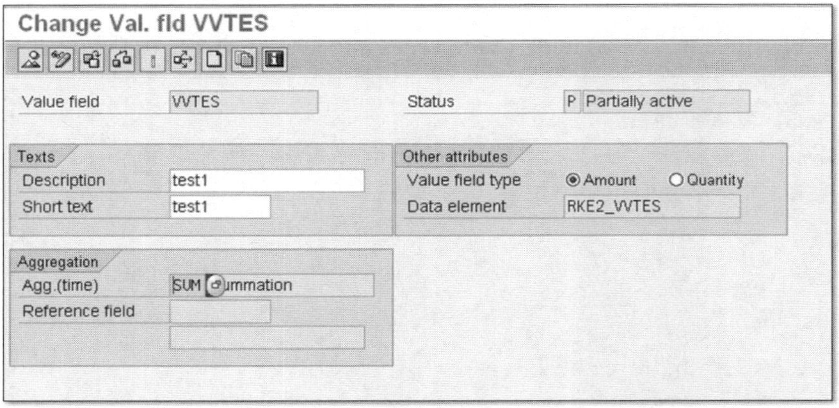

Figure 4.8 Accessing the Change Val. fld VVTES Screen

6. You can now define an aggregation method or leave Summation (**SUM**) as the default depending on the behavior of the value field during posting.

7. Click on the save icon to save your work.

Note

A time-based aggregation rule determines how a key figure is calculated when the reference field is a characteristic with a time dimension with three options:

▶ Aggregate or Average (AVG) value operation

▶ Summation (SUM) operation

▶ Last value (LAS)

The aggregation rule selected depends on the type of value field defined and its real-life behavior. For example, Revenue is a SUM value field because you want that to be added all of the time. Employees during a time period can be a SUM or an AVG depending on whether our calculations require total employees or average number of employees. Inventory price can be considered a LAS value field because you may only be interested in having the latest value of the price. We recommend that you review the SAP documentation to fully understand this functionality.

Tip

The aggregation rules "Last value" and "Average" are only useful for representing statistical and noncumulative values in value fields. Also, the reference period is always the period of a fiscal year. If your data is planned in weeks, the value fields cannot use the aggregation rules AVG or LAS.

---

8. Create additional value fields by clicking on the change/modify icon.

9. Click on **New Entries**.

10. Type the technical name in the **Value Field** column, then provide a **Description** and **Short text**. For our example, use the information for the value fields **VV01**, **VV012**, and **VV12**, as shown in Figure 4.9.

11. Specify for each value field whether it is an **Amount** or a **Qty**. (Amount value fields generally carry information, such as currency, and quantity fields carry data with units of measure, such as kilograms or number of produced units.) Once created, the value fields, as shown in Figure 4.9, are ready for use by any operating concern.

Change Value Fields: Overview

Value field	Description	Short text	Amount	Qty
SEKFF	Fixed SDCP	Fixed SDCP	●	○
SEKFP	Vbl. SDCP	Vbl. SDCP	●	○
STDPR	Standard price	Std.price	●	○
UMSLZ	Licensing Fees	Lic. fees	●	○
VRPRS	Stock Value	Stock val.	●	○
VSVP	DispatchPackag.	Disp.Pack.	●	○
VTRGK	Sales Overhead	Sales ovhd	●	○
VV01	Sales Unit	Sales Unit	○	●
VV012	Sales Unit	Sales Unit	○	●
VV12	Sales Unit	Sales Unit	○	●
VVTES	test1	test1	●	○
VWGK	Admin. Overhead	Admin Ovhd	●	○
WEINS	Goods usage	Gds usage	●	○

Figure 4.9 Accessing the Change Value Fields: Overview Screen

Like with characteristics, grayed out and white boxes are used to differentiate default SAP value fields from user-defined value fields. Notice that for the default SAP value fields, the radio buttons in the **Amount** and **Qty** (Quantity) columns are also grayed out, meaning you can't change them.

In the next section we will explore how to create an operating concern, using value fields and characteristics together to build a common structure that lets you extract or receive information.

Note

An exception exists to the rule that the fields of SAP-defined value fields display in gray: As shown in Figure 4.9, the value field **VRPRS** is an SAP-defined value field; however, it is possible to change its description and short text. Therefore, the **Description** and **Short text** fields for this value field display in white.

4.4   Maintaining an Operating Concern

Operating concerns in CO are the objects required by an SAP system to connect or interact with other structures inside R/3 or SAP ERP ECC 6.0, or external systems, such as SAP NetWeaver BI-IP, SAP SEM-BPS, or SAP BW-BPS.

4.4.1   Accessing and Creating Operating Concerns

To access existing and create new operating concerns, follow this procedure:

1. Follow the IMG path **Controlling · Profitability Analysis · Structures · Define Operating Concern · Maintain Operating Concern**.

2. Click on the execute icon to display the screen shown in Figure 4.10.

3. Here you can select any operating concern available in your system. For our example, we selected the **S_GO** operating concern template. Notice that once you select an operating concern you can check the **Status** of its configuration to give you an idea if the data structures were correctly defined.

4. Review the different options available, especially those on the **Data Structure** and **Environment** tabs. Also, notice that the operating concern requires defining a type of Profitability Analysis: **Costing-based, Account-based,** or both.

5. If necessary, select the **Data Structure** tab shown in Figure 4.10, and click on the change/modify icon (a pencil with glasses), and the message **Caution! You are changing/deleting cross-client settings** will appear.

6. Click on the checkmark icon to acknowledge the message.

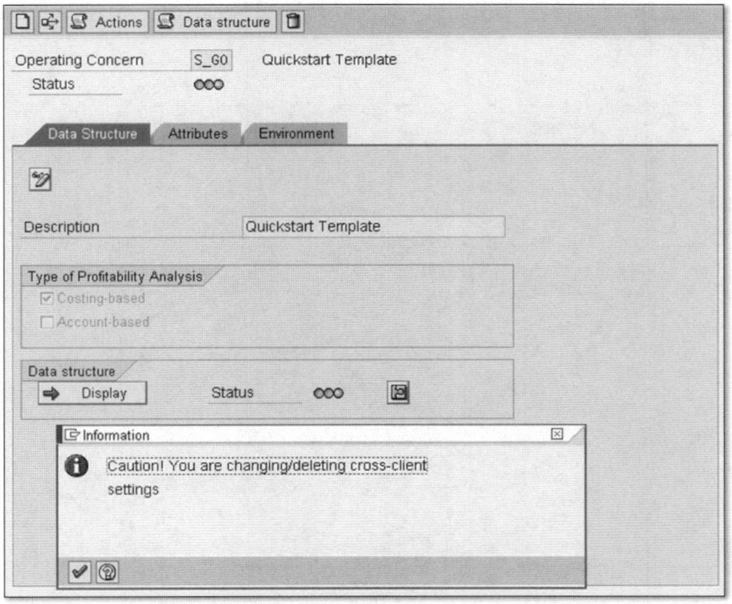

Figure 4.10 Maintain Operating Concern

7. Notice that the button located at the lower bottom of the screen in the **Data Structure** tab has changed from **Display** in Figure 4.10 to **Activate** in Figure 4.11.

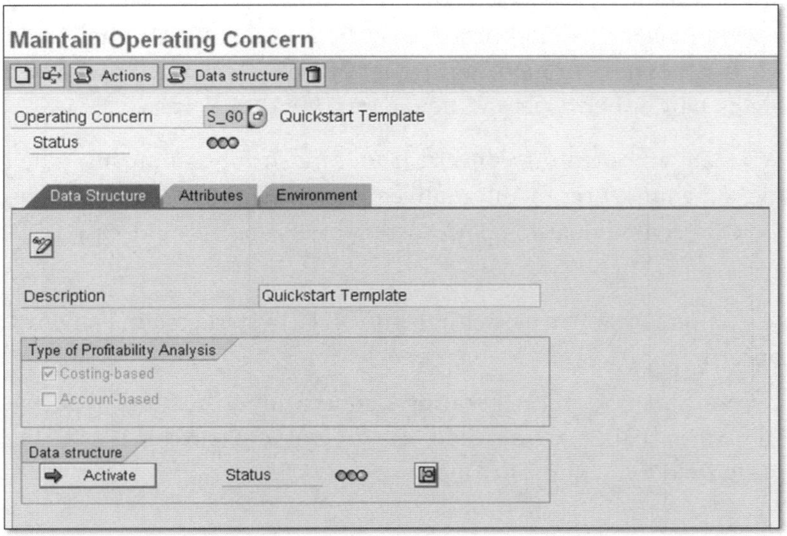

Figure 4.11 Operating Concern in the Change Mode

8. Click on **Activate** to access the configuration of the operating concern displayed in Figure 4.12.

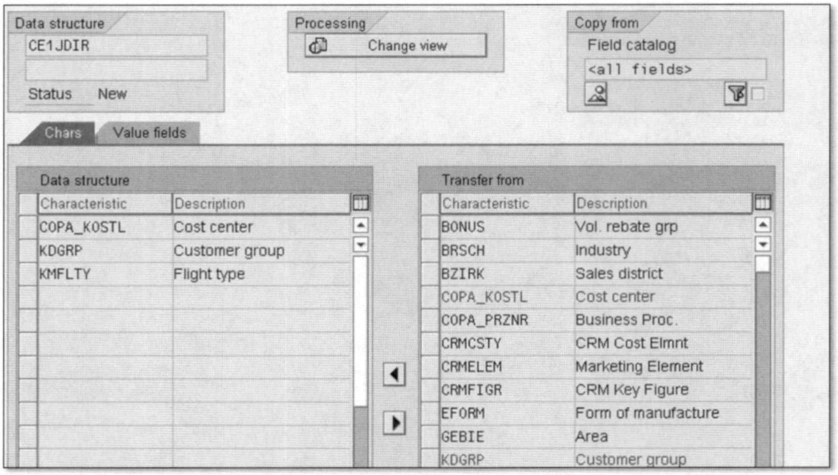

Figure 4.12 Data Structure for an Operating Concern

9. Notice that an operating concern structure contains the **Chars** (characteristics) and **Value Fields** tabs, as shown in Figure 4.12. You can see here how an operating concern is a collection of predefined objects that you want to have access to from the SAP tables or to store user-defined values. With predefined CO-PA–activated templates, such as **S_GO**, you are not allowed to make any modifications to the business content delivered with R/3. It is possible to modify the contents of the characteristics and **Value Fields** tabs only on a brand new operating concern.

Let us now create an operating concern from scratch for a company called Jon Dirr Inc, a manufacturer of automotive parts, that is interested in implementing the CO-PA module using both costing-based and account-based CO-PA:

1. Return to the screen shown earlier in Figure 4.11 to start creating an operating concern.

2. Position your cursor in the **Operating Concern** input box and type the technical name "JDIR" in the field, as shown in Figure 4.13. In the **Description** field, type "Jon Dirr Inc."

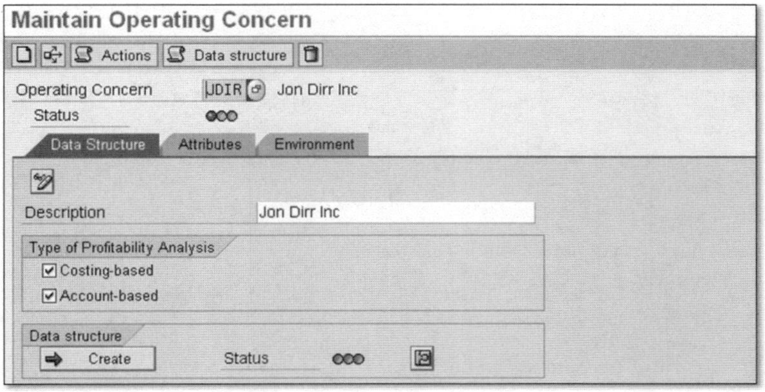

Figure 4.13 Creating a New Operating Concern

3. Select both **Costing-based** and **Account-based** in the section **Type of Profitability Analysis**, to allow you to switch between them later on in the process. We're doing so for our example because Jon Dirr Inc does not know exactly how it generates revenue and exactly how it is profitable, because the results and analysis are based on the final corporate P&L statements each quarter and while each plant around the world has its own SAP system, they have not yet been integrated.

4. Click on the standard SAP create icon (the white page icon). A screen similar to the one shown earlier in Figure 4.12 displays.

5. To include a characteristic or value field in the operating concern, select either the **Chars** or **Value fields** tab, then select a line in the **Transfer from** area and click on the left-arrow to move it to the **Data structure** area.

6. To remove a value field or characteristics from the operating concern, reverse the procedure by selecting a line in the **Data structure** area and clicking on the right-arrow to move it to the **Transfer from** area.

7. When you're done, save and activate your structure using the save and activate icons. Once completed, a green checkmark must appear at the bottom of your screen to notify you that the update was completed successfully.

At this stage several tables are created inside the system carrying the name of the operating concern (xxx reflects the name of the operating concern). For example, if CE1xxx is created from the SG operating concern, the new table name will carry the information CE1SG. The CO-PA tables generated when you save and activate the operating concern are quite important when performing reporting or extraction operations. Table 4.2 shows the most important tables for costing-based CO-PA and Table 4.3 shows the most important tables for account-based CO-PA.

Table name	Description
CE1xxxx	Actual data, costing-based CO-PA
CE2xxxx	Plan data, costing-based CO-PA
CE3xxxx	Segment level, CO-PA.
CE4xxxx	Characteristics table, and also similar to dimension table in SAP NetWeaver BI.
CE1xxxx_ACCT	Account assignment information, new for release R/3 4.5.
K81xxxx	Summarization levels, costing-based CO-PA
TKEBL	Currency of operating concern, costing-based CO-PA
COIX_DATAReport Data	Only converted in costing-based CO-PA.
TKEBZ	Exceptions for reports

Table 4.2 Important Tables for Costing-based CO-PA

Table name	Description
COEJ	Actual/plan line items (by year)
COEP	Actual/plan line items.
COSS	Totals records.
COSP	Totals records, account-based CO-PA

Table 4.3 Important Tables for Account-based CO-PA

4.4.2 Creating User-defined Value Fields and Characteristics Within an Operating Concern

It is also possible to create user-defined value fields and characteristics within an operating concern. To do this:

1. Access **Profitability Analysis • Structures • Define Operating Concern • Maintain Operating Concern**.

2. Select the **Chars** or **Value Fields** tab, depending on what type of component you want to create.

3. Select the create icon (showing a white page), as shown in Figure 4.14, step 1.

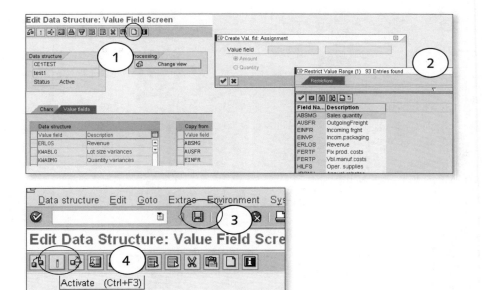

Figure 4.14 Creating User-Defined Value Fields and Characteristics from within an Operating Concern

4. Type the default VV or WW initial name, depending on whether it is a value field or a characteristic, and type a description as shown in Figure 4.14, step 2.

5. Click on the save icon as shown in Figure 4.14, step 3.

6. Finally activate your new value field or characteristic by clicking on the activate icon shown in Figure 4.14, step 4.

7. Now the system asks you to generate the operating concern, which means completing the update of the information contained in the operating concern and creating the CO-PA tables. Once you are ready, click on **Yes,** as shown in Figure 4.15, and if everything is correct the **Status** light will be green. Otherwise, go back to your structure and review your characteristics or value fields that caused the problem and correct it.

8. If you clicked **No** in the screen shown in Figure 4.15, then, as shown in Figure 4.16, you can go to the operating concern's **Environment** tab and activate this process manually using the appropriate **Activate** buttons. A green light next to the **Status** for the **Cross-client part** and **Client-specific part** is displayed if the process was performed successfully.

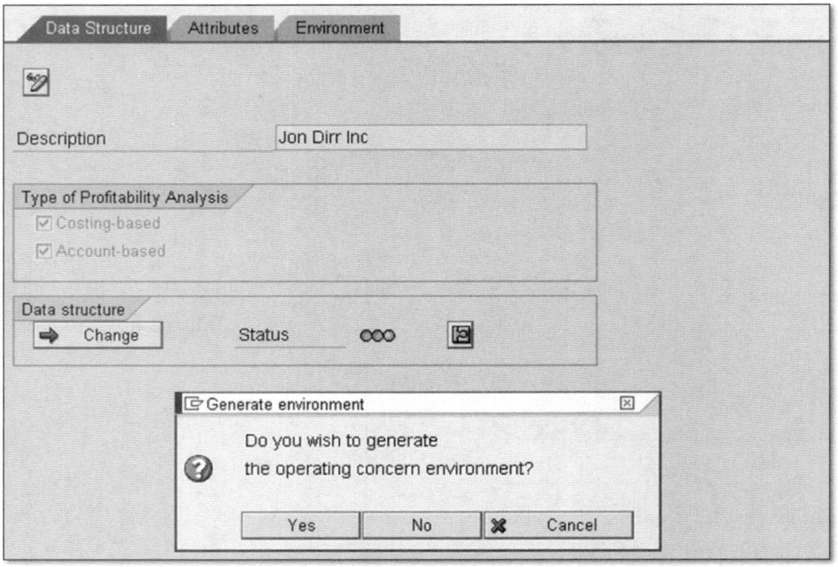

Figure 4.15 Generating the Operating Concern Environment

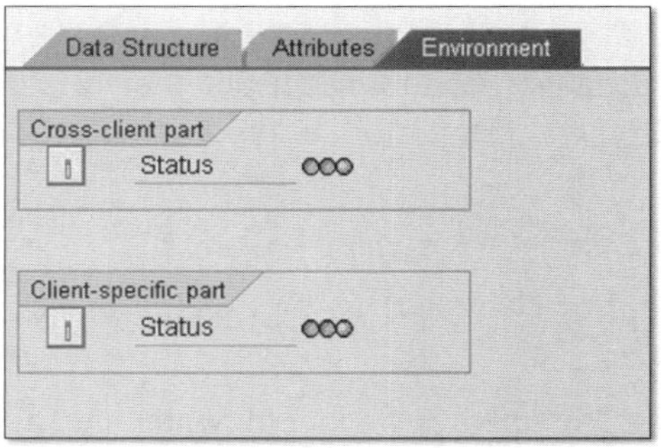

Figure 4.16 The Environment Tab of an Operating Concern

4.4.3 Specifying the Operating Concern Currency

Another important factor is the currency of your operating concern. To configure it:

1. Select the **Attributes** tab (shown in detail in Figure 4.20, located later in the chapter in Section 4.6).

2. Select the **Operating concern currency**; for our example we used **USD** as the default currency.

3. Specify **K4** as the **Fiscal year variant** to have a calendar year with four periods of reporting and four special periods.

We now have an operating concern almost ready for use. However, segments are another important part of the configuration, and using them significantly improves performance, limits the contents of the information inside operating concerns, and depends on the type(s) of accounting selected.

Therefore, in the next section we will explore how to work with profitability segments, and also how to include exceptions as part of the configuration. In general, the next section is to realize the possibility to perform a multidimensional analysis of R/3 or SAP ERP ECC 6.0 data to quickly access the required information.

4.5 Defining Profitability Segments and CO-PA Exceptions

In this section, you will learn how to specify whether a characteristic in CO-PA is assigned to profitability segments that are later available for use with the Information System and Planning menus of CO-PA. Remember that those characteristics that are not involved in the creation of profitability segments remain as line items in CO-PA.

4.5.1 Profitability Segments Overview

Using profitability segments improves the performance of your profitability analysis considerably by excluding characteristics that will otherwise slow down your system. SAP recommends the exclusion of characteristics that occur frequently and that have a different value with each posting (such as "part number" or "bar code"), and are thus not relevant for analysis. Furthermore, you can perform profitability analysis at the customer group level or at the product group level by ceasing to use certain customers or products in that analysis. Most of the time there are simply too many of them and retrieving all of that information at once as a profitability segment would require a considerable amount of resources.

> **Caution**
>
> Before you execute the first transfer of productive data to CO-PA, you should configure the appropriate setting, specifying which characteristics should be involved in creating profitability segments. The only type of change that you can make subsequently is the deactivation of more characteristics for the determination of a profitability segment. If you later include a characteristic in the determination process, your CO-PA data will be incomplete for all affected characteristics.

4.5.2 Exceptions Overview

Instead of excluding characteristics generally, you have the option of excluding a characteristic under certain conditions and thus define exceptions for how characteristics are used. Because of this option, make-to-order manufacturers with a spare parts business, for example, can exclude the spare parts business from their analyses, or wholesale manufacturers with a large number of customers can restrict their analysis at the customer level to key customers. The purpose of this function is to reduce the amount of created profitability segments by updating in detail only those values that are relevant for a particular analysis.

4.5.3 Automatically Excluded Characteristics

Elements such as "sales order," "order number," "WBS element," and "cost object" should not be used as characteristics in the formation of profitability segments for the previously discussed reasons (they occur frequently and their values are always different). Thus, when you create a new operating concern, the relevant table is automatically set so that the following characteristics are not used to form the profitability segments:

▶ **Sales order (KAUFN)**

▶ **Sales order item (KDPOS)**

▶ **Order (RKAUFNR)**

▶ **WBS element (PSPNR)**

▶ **Cost object (KSTRG)**

All other characteristics — including "customer" and "product" — are used and therefore are available for profitability reports, planning, and account assignments to profitability segments, for example. No exceptions are defined by default. If you need to make a change to these settings, change the entries accordingly. You should check the index to the object table, especially if you exclude the characteristics "customer" or "product." By defining an index that is most optimally reconciled to how the segment-level characteristics are used, you can improve performance considerably.

4.5.4 Defining Profitability Segment Characteristics

To define profitability segment characteristics, follow this procedure:

1. Follow the IMG path **Controlling · Profitability Analysis · Structures · Define Operating Concern · Define Profitability Segment Characteristics (Segment-Lvl Characteristics)**.

2. Click on the execute icon next to **Define Profitability Segment Characteristics (Segment-Lvl Characteristics)**, shown in Figure 4.17.

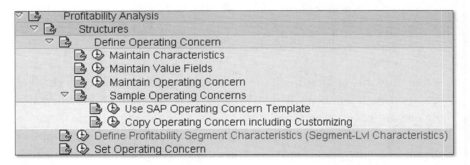

Figure 4.17 Accessing Profitability Segments Window

3. Now the screen displayed in Figure 4.18 shows the characteristics in the **Operating concern, S_GO** in this case, that can be used to configure your profitability segments. You can choose **Costing-Based** only, or **Costing-Based+Account-Based**, or you can exclude the characteristic as a profitability segment and leave it as a CO-PA line item by selecting **Not Used**.

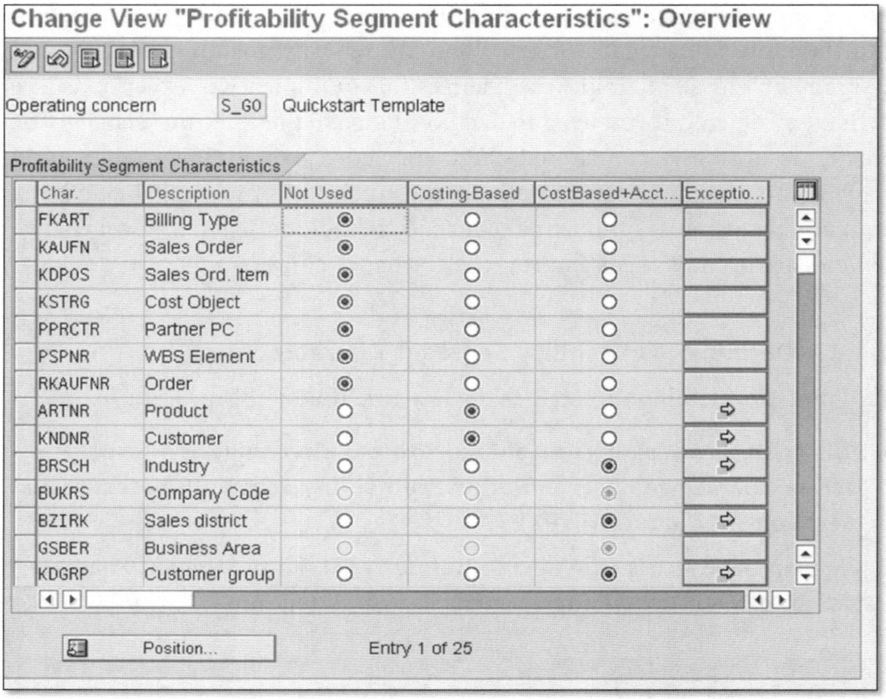

Figure 4.18 Profitability Segment Characteristics

4. To modify any contents of the operating concern, click on the change/
   modify icon (the pencil with glasses), and select the radio button depending on your requirements and future usage of the characteristics. Remember, if you are working in an SAP template, such as the **S_GO template**
   shown in Figure 4.18, the SAP system does not allow you to make modifications. However, that is not a problem when using an operating concern created from scratch.

Next, let's look at CO-PA exceptions in more detail.

4.5.5 Creating Exceptions

You specify an *exception* for a characteristic you generally do not wish to
include in creating profitability segments by defining the conditions when
the characteristic should be included among the segment-level characteristics. You do this by specifying the characteristic values. Let us say we are
interested in assigning exceptions to a characteristic called **Product**:

1. Click on the yellow arrow for the characteristic **Product**, located in the **Exceptions** column on the right side of the characteristic, as shown earlier in Figure 4.18. The screen shown in Figure 4.19 appears.

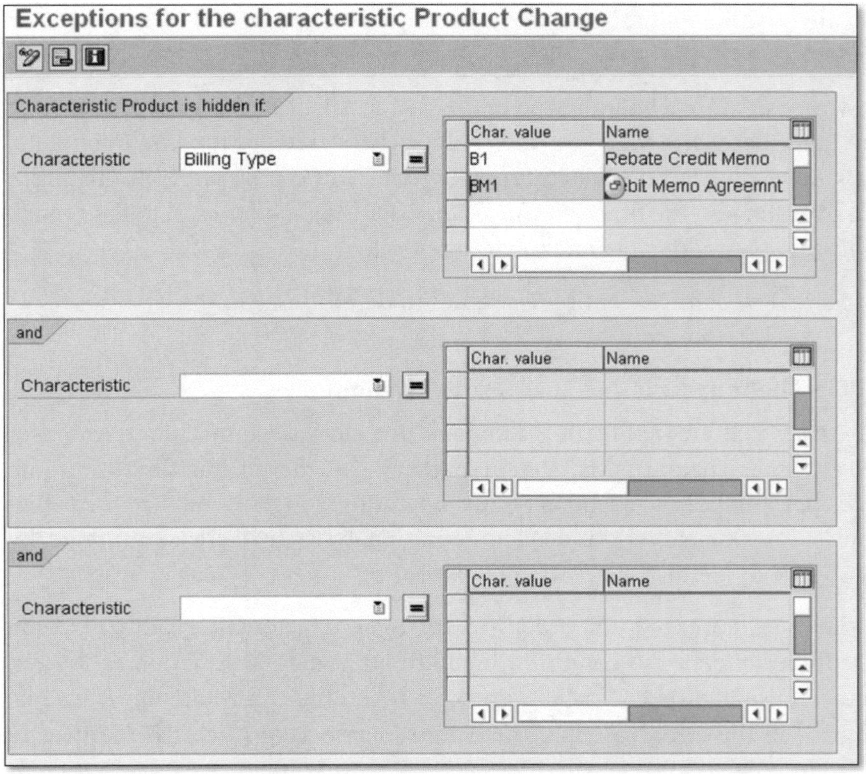

Figure 4.19 Creating Exceptions for a Characteristic

2. There are two areas you work with. The one on the left creates a Boolean logic described as **Characteristic Product is hidden if:**. The one on the right establishes the characteristic values used to limit the data display of the characteristic (**Product** in this case).

3. Notice that up to three characteristics and their values can be used to hide information that meets certain criteria. For example, as shown in Figure 4.19, for the characteristic **Product** the data values are hidden if the characteristic **Billing Type** is either **B1 (Rebate Credit Memo)** or **BM1 (Debit Memo Agreement)**.

Characteristics that are hidden due to an exception are still updated in the line item SAP table (CE1xxxx). Furthermore, they remain visible when you display the line items with the current structure. If a line item contains such a characteristic, the system always accesses the line item list to display the line items. This is also the case if you call up the line item display from a profitability report with the current structure. There, the affected characteristic has the value "initial" because the report accesses the segment level (CE4xxxx).

However, the initial value stored in the characteristic is also used to select the line item. Because a value for the characteristic exists in the line item table, the system cannot find the correct line item. You can circumvent this problem by calling up the function **Goto • Line Item** at a higher level in the report. That way, the hidden characteristic is not selected.

Let us review some exception examples in detail.

Hiding All Products in the Spare Parts Division

Let us say that an engineering company produces large machinery to order but also sells custom parts. Detailed analyses at the product level are only necessary for heavy machinery. The operating concern contains two divisions, heavy machinery and engineering analysis, that are determined by appropriately defined derivation steps.

In this case, an exception is defined for the characteristic Product. On the exceptions screen, the condition for hiding the data is specified as follows (you can use Figure 4.19 as a reference): When the characteristic "Division" (defined in the left area) takes the value "Engineering Analysis" (defined in the right area).

Hiding "Other Customers" by Defining the New Characteristic Key Customer Indicator

A repetitive manufacturer (those that manufacture or assemble large quantities of similar products, such as automotive components) does not want to analyze all of their data at the customer level. Instead, only a selection of key customers should be looked at in detail. However, there is no characteristic in the operating concern that makes any such distinction. Not only is it not possible to define an exception along the lines of "Hide characteristic customer when customer = A and customer = B and ...," but this would not be practical either. Hence, a new characteristic — with which a distinction can be made between key customers and other customers — needs to be created. It is possible, for example, to define an additional characteristic "key customer indicator" and then, by means of characteristic derivation, to set it to X for key customers and leave it empty for all other customers. For data that has already been posted, you have to run a realignment during which these other customers are set to the initial value.

The following exception can then be defined: The characteristic "customer" is hidden when the key customer indicator = initial (for the initial characteristic value, enter "#" (= non assigned) in the entry field). Once this exception has been applied, no further analysis can be run on the other customers at the customer level because the exception cannot be canceled.

4.5.6 Exception Recommendations

Consider the following recommendations when working with exceptions:

▸ You should only define an exception for characteristics representing a detailed level of analysis and that therefore take a large number of characteristic values. The larger portion of these characteristic values should be excluded as a result of the exception.

▸ Complicated conditions should not be defined in an exception because analysis with such a condition counteracts any improvements in performance. It makes better sense to use as your condition one or two characteristics, each having no more than two or three characteristic values. For best results, aim to keep the definition of your exception as basic as possible. To achieve this, it is sometimes necessary to create an additional characteristic.

▸ Exceptions should not be changed once applied in a productive system. In particular, such exceptions should not be deactivated because this prevents the data from being analyzed correctly. In certain cases, it is possible to maintain extra exceptions. However, you must run a realignment for the affected characteristic beforehand. To do this, select in the selection condition the characteristics and characteristic values specified in the exception. In the conversion rule, enter # for the characteristic for which the exception was defined.

▸ Characteristics that have an exception maintained for them cannot be changed by realignments!

▸ To define an exception, you can use almost all characteristics that create profitability segments (technically all of the characteristics from table CE4xxxx, where xxxx = operating concern). This does not apply in the case of unit of measure or the characteristic for which the exception has been defined.

▶ If you define an exception with dependent characteristics, then all of the characteristics in those dependencies should be included in that exception.

▶ Note that the definition of the exception applies for all flows of actual data, as well as for the summarized update of data during the transfer of billing documents. The setting does not apply in planning; there, the detail level for data entry is specified in the planning level. The detail level for planning should not be greater than that for the flow of actual data in order that useful comparisons between actual and planning data are possible.

Tip

When an exception is applied, the number of profitability segments generated is reduced, thereby improving performance in reporting and in the system in general. However, to ensure that system performance is actually enhanced, you should use this function sparingly and only use it in specific cases. Once applied in a productive system, an exception should no longer be changed, because changes to it would cause inconsistencies in your data, especially if you remove an exception and thereby include the corresponding characteristic in the creation of profitability segments.

Our efforts would not be complete without the configuration of the operating concern attributes that are closely related to the definitions of the data extracted from FI and CO. For this reason, it is highly recommended to review how your company's controlling areas and transaction attributes are related to the attributes used by your operating concern. These elements are discussed in the next section.

4.6   Operating Concern Attributes Tab

The **Attributes** tab of an operating concern, as shown in Figure 4.20, contains several options that are important to understand if your implementation increases the complexity of the behavior of your data.

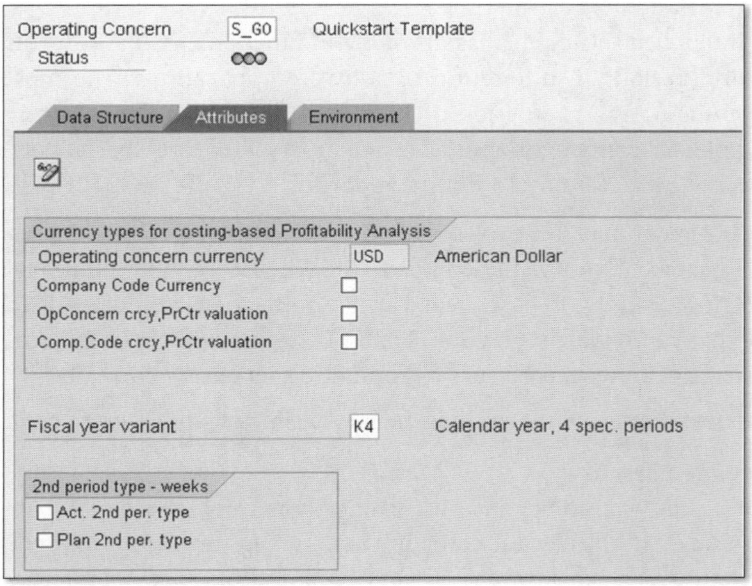

Figure 4.20 The Attributes Tab of an Operating Concern

Two main elements of the **Attributes** tab are **Operating concern currency** and **Fiscal year variant**, both of which we briefly looked at earlier in the chapter in Section 4.3, and will look at now in more detail:

▶ **Operating concern currency**
This setting determines how the operating concern is going to be valuated; it specifies the currency in which values in CO-PA are going to be displayed and planned. In costing-based Profitability Analysis, actual data is always updated in the operating concern currency. You can change the operating concern currency as long as no data has been posted in the operating concern. Once data has been posted, however, a change in the operating concern currency would cause the existing data to be interpreted as if it were posted in the new currency (for example: USD 1,000.00 in old currency might be reported as 1,000.00 Euros in new currency).

Be aware that actual data can be updated simultaneously in all of the combinations of currency type and valuation, increasing the data volume. In contrast, plan data is updated only with the currency specified in a particular plan version.

▶ **Fiscal year variant**
This is an important setting that is part of the FI functionality that controls the reporting periods in different SAP software applications. The most common configuration is a period of 12 months for which the company produces financial statements and takes inventory, with four special periods per year allowed for any additional reporting.

A fiscal year may or may not correspond to the calendar year, but depending on the characteristics of the company, it will also require additional special posting periods. A fiscal year can be both internal and legal, so make sure that you review with your FI and CO team members on the current FI practices so you can be sure to configure this setting correctly.

Now let us review the rest of the options on the **Attributes** tab in more detail:

▶ **Company Code Currency**
In addition to the operating concern currency, you can also store all data in the currency of the relevant company code using the **Company Code Currency** setting. This makes sense if your organization operates internationally and deals with exchange rates that change daily. It allows you to avoid differences due to different exchange rates and lets you reconcile CO-PA data directly with FI.

You can activate the company code currency at any time but this will not affect data that has already been posted. If you deactivate the company code currency, you can no longer use plan versions and reports that use the company code currency.

▶ **Profit center valuation**
In addition to storing data in these two currencies (company code and operating concern currencies) using the legal (= company code) valuation view, you can also store data in both of these currencies valuated from the viewpoint of individual profit centers. This yields the following possible combinations of currency type and valuation view (also called valuation approaches) as shown in Table 4.4.

Currency type	Valuation view
Operating concern currency	Legal valuation
Company code currency	Legal valuation
Operating concern currency	Profit center valuation
Company code currency	Profit center valuation

Table 4.4 Currency Type and Valuation View Combinations

With this information, you can set up actual data valuation from the profit center viewpoint using the IMG Activity path **Profitability Analysis • Flows of Actual Values • Multiple Valuation Approaches • Transfer Prices**. Whereas actual data is updated simultaneously in all of the selected combinations of currency type and valuation, plan data is always updated in one currency only — the currency specified for that particular plan version.

▶ **Second period type — weeks**
If you set any of the two indicators available in this area, namely **Act. 2nd per. type** or **Plan 2nd per type**, the system stores the actual or plan data in weeks when using costing-based Profitability Analysis. This increases the data volume in CO-PA and could lead to slow response times in the information system.

However, when using these indicators with account-based CO-PA there is no effect because there is no alternative period type available.

None of the above configuration steps and functionalities will take effect until you assign the controlling area to an operating concern. This procedure is discussed in the following section.

4.7 Assigning a Controlling Area to an Operating Concern

As mentioned earlier, you must make sure that there is a clear relationship between controlling areas and operating concerns if you want to build a framework to create business transactions and an integrated financial architecture that allows carrying out cross-company code cost accounting. In other words, you need to make sure that data is transferred from other financial modules correctly.

To do so, you assign to an operating concern the controlling areas you want to analyze together in Profitability Analysis because the goal is to connect to the rest of the architectures, described previously in Figure 3.2 in Chapter 3, to CO-PA. In order to start this assignment there are several steps and requirements. Let us look at them in detail.

4.7.1 Reviewing Controlling Area Components and Verifying the Existence of Operating Concerns

First, let us make sure you are familiar with what a controlling area and its components look like, and also verify that an operating concern has been created:

> **Note**
>
> Before you get started, a controlling area must exist and be correctly configured already. SAP provides several preconfigured controlling areas for your review, and you can use them to integrate with your CO-PA templates.

1. Access controlling areas by following the IMG path **Controlling • General Controlling • Organization • Maintain Controlling Area**.

2. Select the appropriate controlling area, for example, the **0001 SAP** controlling area, as shown in Figure 4.21.

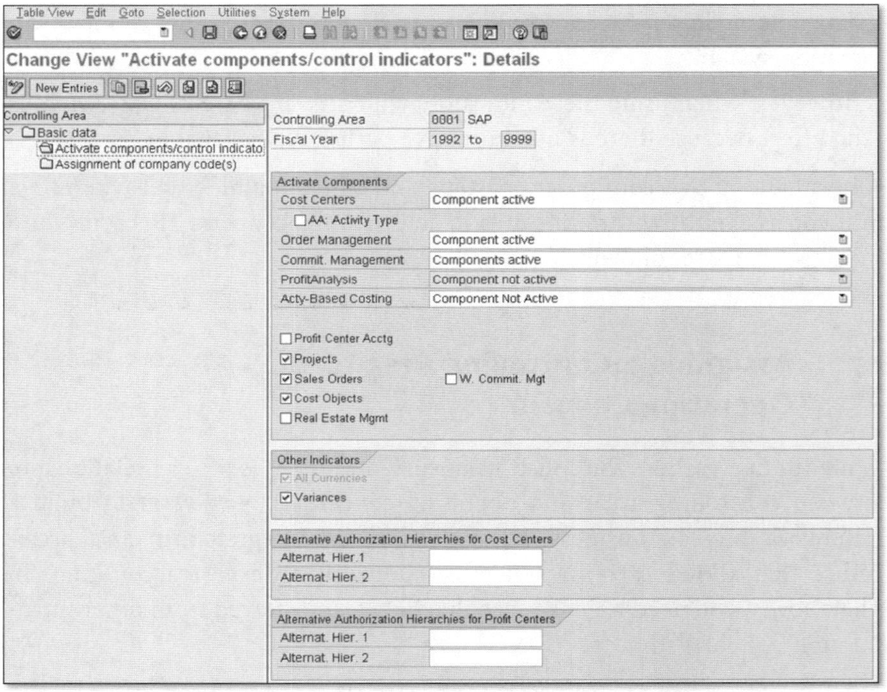

Figure 4.21 Reviewing Active Components of a Controlling Area

In this screen, you can determine which components of a controlling area are active. For example, Figure 4.21 shows that only Profitability Analysis and activity-based costing are not active in the controlling area **0001 SAP**, and we want to have CO-PA activated. For now, however, we are just exploring these options; you will learn how to activate CO-PA later in this chapter in Section 4.8 — it requires additional configuration to do so (notice that the option **ProfitAnalysis** is currently grayed out). Primarily, knowing that CO-PA hasn't been activated leaves you certain that no postings or any transactions have been affected in the controlling area with any information from CO-PA.

3. Next, use the IMG path **Controlling • Profitability Analysis • Structures • Define Operating Concern • Maintain Operating Concern** to access the screen shown in Figure 4.22 to verify that an operating concern with the elements you need exists, and thus can be assigned to a **Controlling Area**. If there is none, create one as previously explained in Section 4.5.

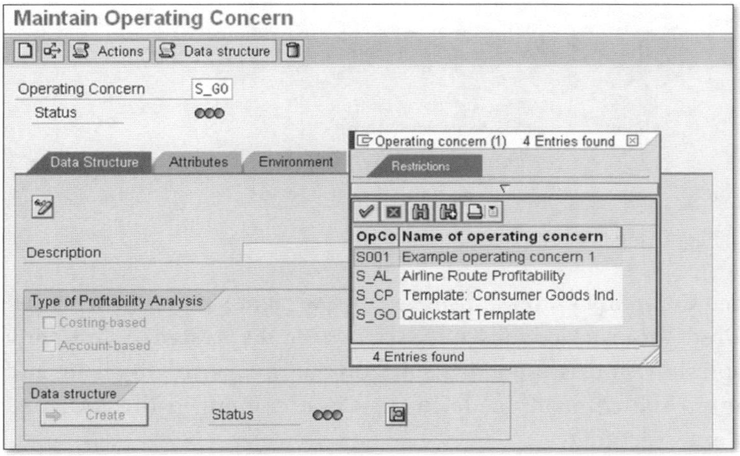

Figure 4.22 Creating or Maintaining an Operating Concern

Be aware that a company code will be affected by different transactions in different business areas, and you must make sure that it has been correctly configured to avoid posting problems later on in the process. Next, we'll look at assigning a company code to a controlling area.

> **Note**
>
> You will need additional background information in FI regarding the configuration and analysis of company codes. Review this information with your implementation team or project manager, as this topic is beyond the scope of this book.

4.7.2   Assigning a Company Code to a Controlling Area

To assign a company code to a controlling area:

1. Follow the IMG path **Enterprise Structure • Assignment • Controlling • Assign Company code to controlling area**.

2. Figure 4.23 shows the available controlling areas to which we can assign company codes so that the transactions in that area are limited to those

company codes. For our purposes **0001 SAP** is our controlling area, so select the appropriate line on the right side of the screen, and then double-click on **Assignment of company codes** on the left side of the screen.

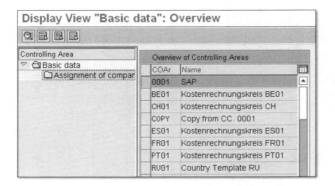

Figure 4.23 Assigning Company Codes to Controlling Areas

3. The **Assigned Company Codes** are shown on the right side of Figure 4.24. If the required company code is not assigned or the **Assigned Company Codes** section shows no assignments, click on the change/modify icon, and manually input the company code in the **CoCd** column in the **Assigned Company Codes** section.

In our example in Figure 4.24, we are assigning company code **0001 SAP** to controlling area **0001 SAP**. The fact that they have the same name and code is a coincidence. Therefore, review these assignments with your project manager and FI or CO implementation team before proceeding any further. Once this relationship has been created, all transactions associated with the company code will be limited to the controlling area definitions.

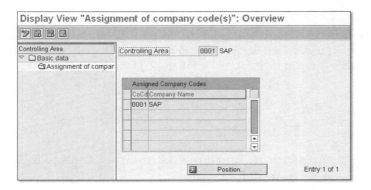

Figure 4.24 Linking Company Codes with Controlling Areas

Company codes, controlling areas, and operating concerns must have identical fiscal year variants, as shown in Figure 4.25, to avoid error messages or serious data inconsistencies during cost center assessments, settlements, or other types of postings. Review this issue with your FI or CO implementation team to make sure that all settings are correctly configured according to the company's ongoing implementation.

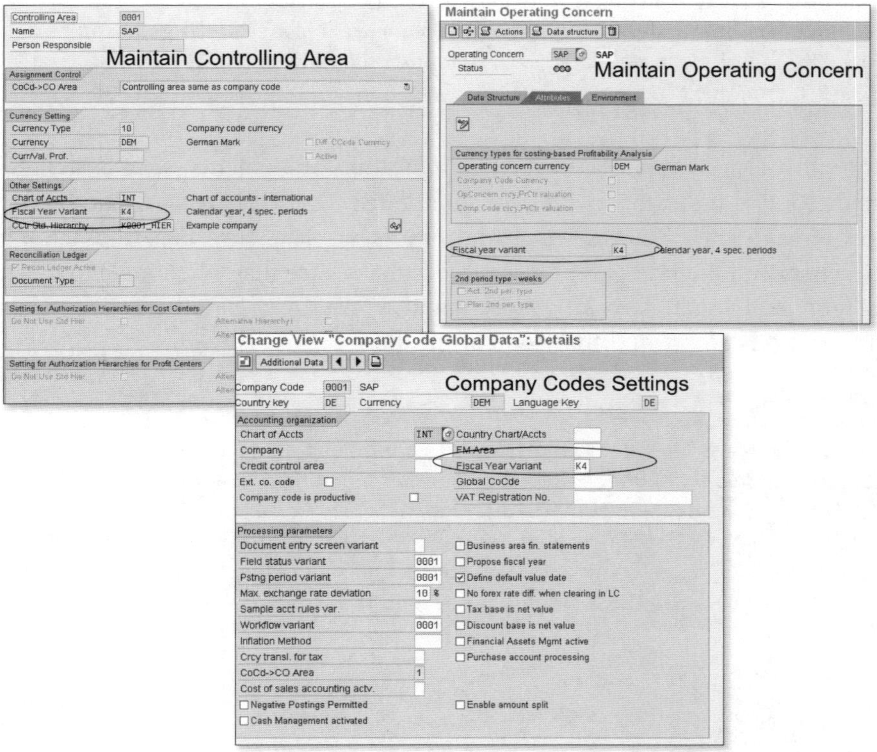

Figure 4.25 Reviewing the Configuration of Controlling Areas, Company Codes, and Operating Concerns

The relationships shown in Figure 4.25 between operating concerns, company codes, and controlling areas allow cross-application data transfers using the path **Enterprise Structure • Assignment • Controlling • Assign controlling area to operating concern**, shown in Figure 4.26.

This screen lets you complete the link by assigning an operating concern to a controlling area, using a simple table.

> **Note**
>
> The screen shown in Figure 4.26 is also where you specify the assignments between company codes and controlling areas, as we did a moment ago.

> **Tip**
>
> It is important to make sure that Profitability Analysis is activated in your controlling area to make the connection in both directions, meaning postings from FI and other CO modules can be accessed using the controlling area as the gate, and postings from CO-PA can be shared with other modules. We'll look at how to activate CO-PA in the next section.

You must also maintain a correct configuration of elements, such as assignment control indicator, chart of accounts, fiscal year variants, GL accounts, cost elements, currency settings and others to make sure that transactions flow between FI and CO. For this reason, make sure that when making these assignments you are working closely with your FI/CO team because further clarifications go beyond the scope of this book.

> **Note**
>
> Because some of the components, such as controlling area, company codes, cost centers, and so on, require knowledge of other modules of FI and CO, we will not go into much detail about them. Instead, we will limit our discussion to how to establish the relationships to link Profitability Analysis with the other controlling structures. The actual configuration, analysis, and requirements to correctly allow transactions between these systems go beyond the scope of the book.

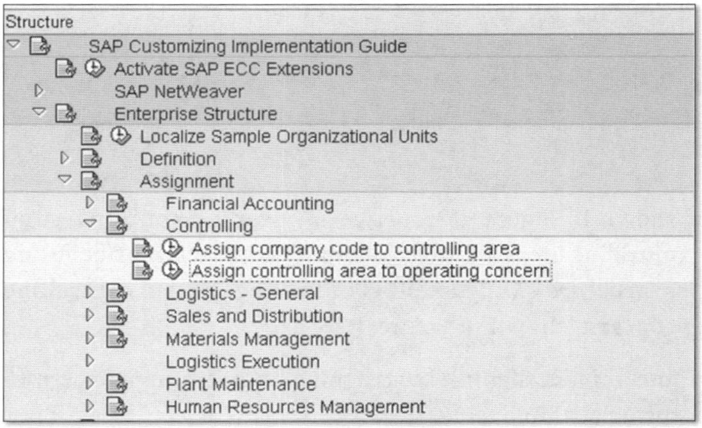

Figure 4.26 Linking Company Codes, Controlling Areas, and Operating Concerns

> **Tip**
>
> Before going any further with CO-PA, you should have a clear representation of the financial structures that control your different transactions inside your financial accounting and controlling areas. Therefore, you should link CO-PA to controlling areas to review the impact in your operations with your implementation team, and match the settings of your objects on both sides so the different postings behave the way they are supposed to.

Next, you'll learn how to activate the CO-PA module inside the R/3 or SAP ERP ECC 6.0 platform.

4.8   Activating CO-PA in R/3 or SAP ERP ECC 6.0

It is not enough to create an operating concern and a link between company codes and controlling areas. You also must perform a specific activation procedure to make sure that all of the individual components are ready to accept and share information between CO-PA and other components in FI/CO. First, however, let us review the status of Profitability Analysis in your controlling area; Profitability Analysis may already be activated, in which case you would not need to do anything else.

4.8.1   Checking the Current Profitability Analysis Activation Status

To check the current status of the Profitability Analysis activation, perform the following procedure:

1. Use Transaction OKKP to go to **Maintain Controlling Area Settings** and review the information as shown in Figure 4.27.

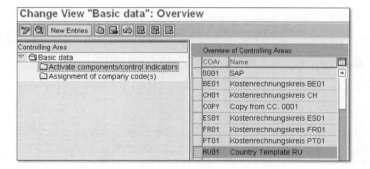

Figure 4.27 Reviewing the Activation Components for Controlling Area RU01

2. Select the Controlling Area **RU01 Country Template RU**, and click **Activate components/control indicators** on the left-hand side.

3. The status of the **Controlling Area RU01 Country Template RU** displays, as shown in Figure 4.28. You can see that the Profitability Analysis (**Profit-Analysis**) and activity-based costing (**Acty-Based Costing**) modules are not activated. Also, Profitability Analysis shows as **Component not active,** and is grayed out, so you cannot use the appropriate option from the dropdown menu to activate it like you can with the other modules. Instead, you need to perform additional configuration steps.

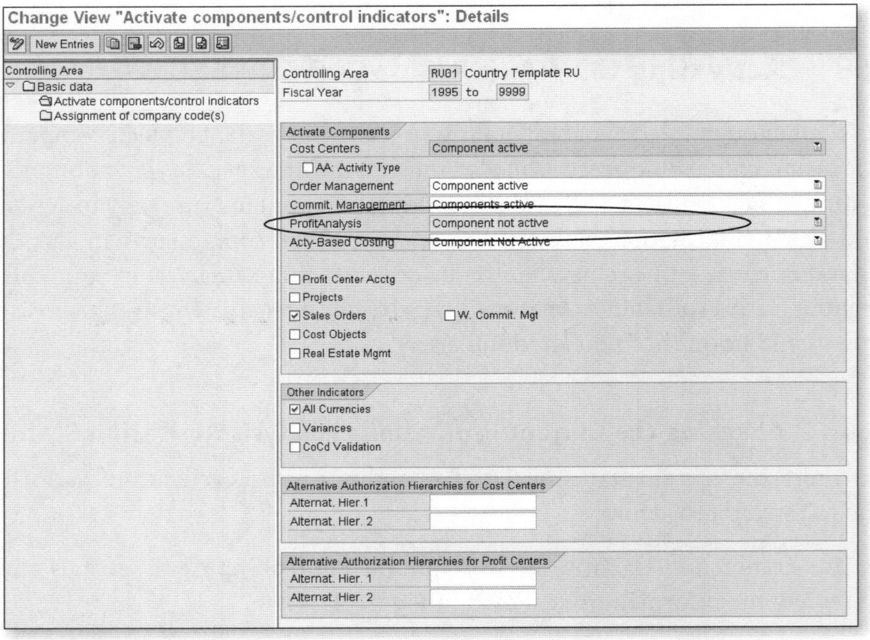

Figure 4.28 Reviewing Activation Status of CO-PA for RU01

4.8.2 Performing the Activation

Once you have finished all of the previous steps, you are ready to activate CO-PA by using the following procedure:

1. Follow the IMG Activity path **Controlling • Profitability Analysis • Flows of Actual Values • Activate Profitability Analysis**, as shown in Figure 4.29.

2. Execute the function **Activate Profitability Analysis** by clicking on the clock with the checkmark icon located next to the function.

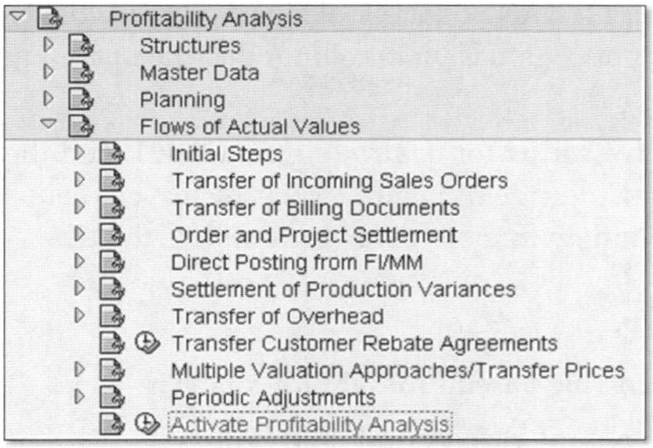

Figure 4.29 Activating Profitability Analysis

Tip

If someone else is using the active operating concern when you attempt to activate Profitability Analysis, the SAP system displays a message that the data is locked by a specific user ID, who is probably working in one of the configuration menus we discussed in this chapter. Contact that user to have him exit the objects he is modifying, or wait until his work is finished to perform the activation.

---

3. Next, the screen shown in Figure 4.30 appears, showing the table **CO-PA: Activate Flag for Profitability Analysis**.

Caution

It is important to know that the CO-PA: Activate Flag for Profitability Analysis table is the same table used when performing the function Activate Transfer of Incoming Sales Orders, as explained later in Chapter 8. Thus, keep in mind that any changes to this table affect both CO-PA activation and the activation of transfer of incoming sales orders.

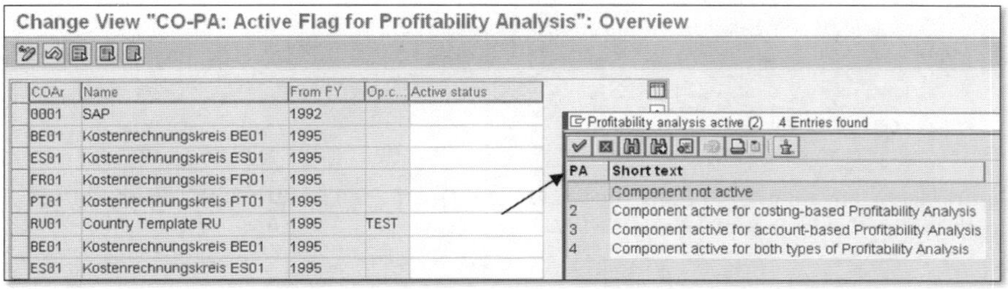

Figure 4.30 CO-PA: Active Flag for Profitability Analysis

4. Verify that the controlling area (**COAr**) you are looking for is available. In our case, this is **RU01**. Also, notice in the **Op c.** column that the operating concern **TEST** has been assigned.

5. Click on the blank field **Active status** for controlling area **RU01**, and the window shown on the right-hand side of Figure 4.30 is displayed. Let us review the options in this window in more detail to complete the CO-PA activation:

   ▶ **Blank: Component not active**

   ▶ **2: Component active for costing-based Profitability Analysis**

   ▶ **3: Component active for account-based Profitability Analysis**

   ▶ **4: Component active for both types of Profitability Analysis**

   Because there are several options from which to select, the SAP system does not allow you to activate CO-PA using the dropdown list shown earlier; selection of the correct option is a procedure that requires analysis and review to make sure that your components will do what you want them to do. For example, you do not want the system to perform account-based CO-PA when you need to use costing-based CO-PA, or vice versa.

6. Option **4** (activating CO-PA for any type of analysis, costing- or account-based) will make things easiest for you, so let us select it. The Active Status field will now look like that shown in Figure 4.31.

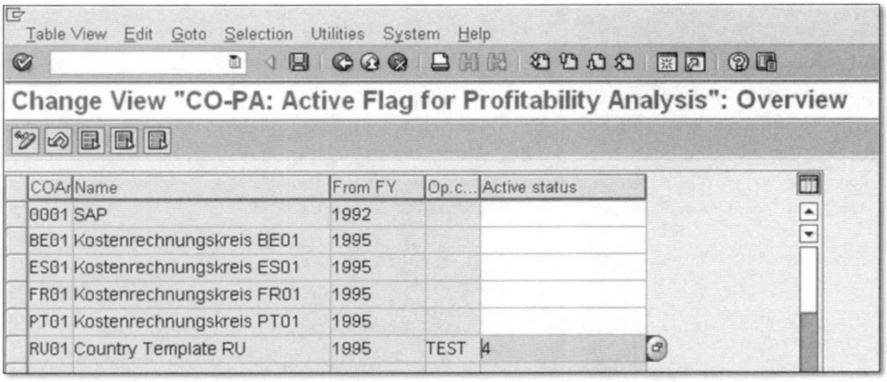

Figure 4.31 Activating Controlling Area RU01 and Operating Concern TEST to Use Both Costing-based and Account-based CO-PA

7. Click on the save icon to save your changes. CO-PA has now been activated for all types of Profitability Analysis.

4.8.3 Verifying the Activation

At this point, we also need to confirm the activation, following this procedure:

1. Run Transaction OKKP again.

2. Review the activation options of the **RU01 Controlling Area**, as shown in Figure 4.32. The grayed-out menu option has changed from the previous **Component Not Active** to **Component active for both types of Profitability Analysis**.

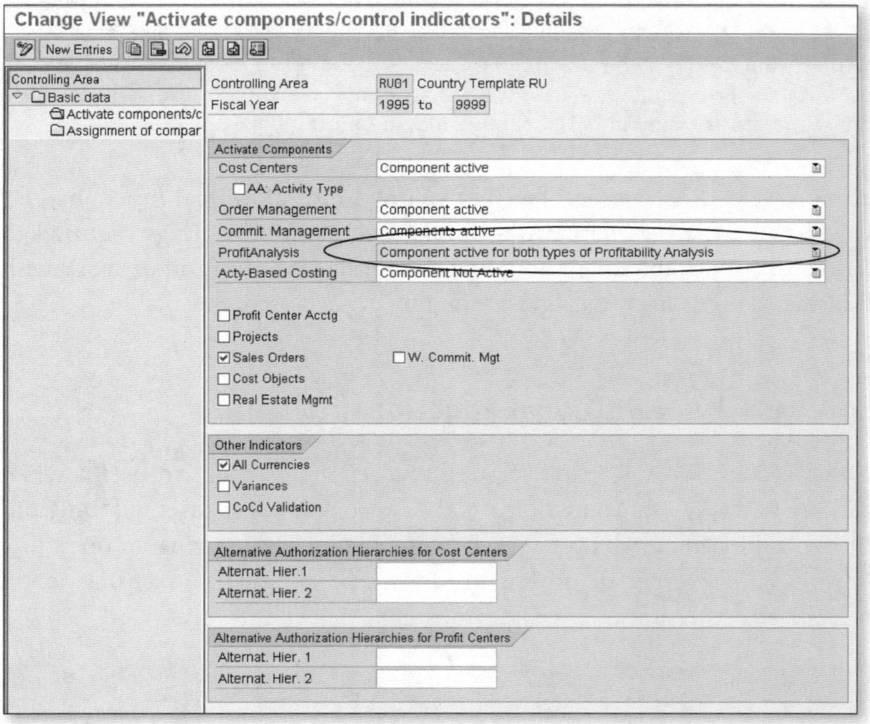

Figure 4.32 CO-PA is Active and Ready to Use Inside RU01

Once the Profitability Analysis module is activated, you can start transferring the actual postings into the predefined profitability segments. We will outline these elements briefly here; they are reviewed in more detail later on in Chapter 8:

▶ Automatic transfers of billing document data from SD

▶ Direct postings from FI

► Settlement of orders and projects

► Period-based allocations, such as the transfer of overhead

► Invoice receipt postings from MM

Also, you can now make plan data postings, such as the following:

► Period-based allocations, such as the transfer of planned overhead

► Settlement of planning data from orders and projects

> **Caution**
>
> We need to mention again, because it is very important, that when you carry out the activities Activate Profitability Analysis and Activate Transfer of Incoming Sales Orders, (the latter will be described in detail in Chapter 8), you are accessing the same table. Consequently, if you delete an entry on one of these screens, you affect the functionality in both components, so be careful!

In the next section, we will briefly explore a few additional functionalities available in CO-PA as part of the initial configuration settings required to start the CO-PA implementation. You do not have to perform or work with all of them, but it is important to remember that they are available.

4.9 CO-PA: Additional Functionalities

In this section we will explore additional elements that are useful when working with CO-PA. You will learn about the more user-oriented function-alities on the Structures menu, such as importing and copying an operating concern, copying specific objects inside an operating concern, using action and data structure buttons, and performing CO-PA transports.

> **Note**
>
> If you feel you are confident using these elements, feel free to continue with other parts of this book. Keep this section in mind, however, if you are interested in exploring the additional functionalities available in CO-PA if they are required later on in your implementation.

To access the copy functionality in CO-PA, follow this IMG Activity path:

Controlling • Profitability Analysis • Structures • Copy Operating Concern Including Customizing.

The screen shown in Figure 4.33 appears. There are three different tabs:

▶ **Import operating concern**

▶ **Copy operating concern**

▶ **Copy specific objects**

In addition, there is the **Copy** button at the top of the screen. Let us now look at the first tab, the **Import operating concern** tab in more detail.

Caution

Copy operations do not make copies of the transaction data stored in any of the operating concerns. That is, they perform changes to the objects of the operating concern, but not the data. Therefore, these operations are not meant for archiving or storage of data. For these functions, use the proper SAP tools; your SAP basis or security teams in your company should be able to assist you with this.

4.9.1 Import Operating Concern

The **Import operating concern** tab, shown in Figure 4.33, lets you select one of the sample SAP operating concern templates in source client **000** and copy it to a target client. The SAP template must not exist in the target client, and the source and target clients must have different values.

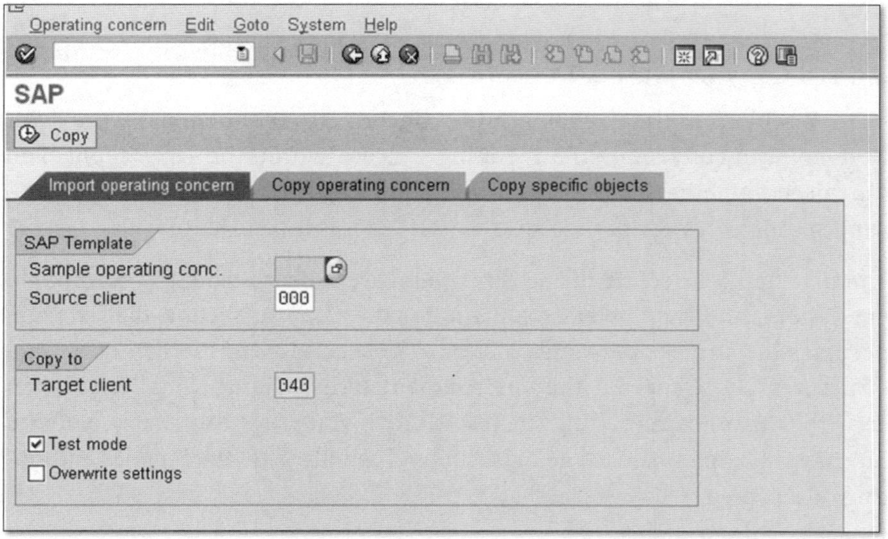

Figure 4.33 The Import Operating Concern Tab

In addition, the **Test mode** checkbox lets you copy the customizing settings in the test mode (with no changes being made to the database). A log tells you which tables and settings are copied when you select this feature and click on the **Copy** button.

Furthermore, the **Overwrite settings** checkbox determines how the system handles table entries that are not directly dependent on the operating concern but are still part of the customizing settings for the operating concern. If this field is not selected (default), these settings are not copied to the target client. Consequently, no existing settings in the target client are overwritten. If this field is selected, the existing settings in the target client are overwritten. This can lead to changes in the settings for other operating concerns that are in use.

Tip
Only select the **Overwrite settings** checkbox if the target client (= current client) has not yet been customized for any operating concerns, or if you want the source and target clients customized identically. Unlike the function import objects, this function copies all of the settings for the operating concern, not just individual objects. The logic for copying settings is different from the logic for transporting in that settings that simply reference the operating concern instead of being dependent on it (such as PA transfer structures) are copied as well. To avoid inadvertently overwriting settings in the target client, you should only use this function when the target client does not contain any customizing settings yet, or when you want customizing in the source and target clients to be identical.

4.9.2 Copy Operating Concern

Next, we'll look at the **Copy operating concern** tab, as shown in Figure 4.34. Here you can copy an entire operating concern within the same client. You can specify whether you want to copy the data structures only, the customizing settings only, or both. These are copied in separate steps.

The first step is selecting the **Source operating concern** from the current client system, and then creating a name for the **Copy to** section that later on becomes the **Target operating concern**. The second step is to copy the **Data structures** and **Generate the environment (cross-client)**. Finally, you can copy the **Customizing** settings in **Test Mode** if you select this checkbox (with no changes being made to the database). A log tells you which tables and settings are copied.

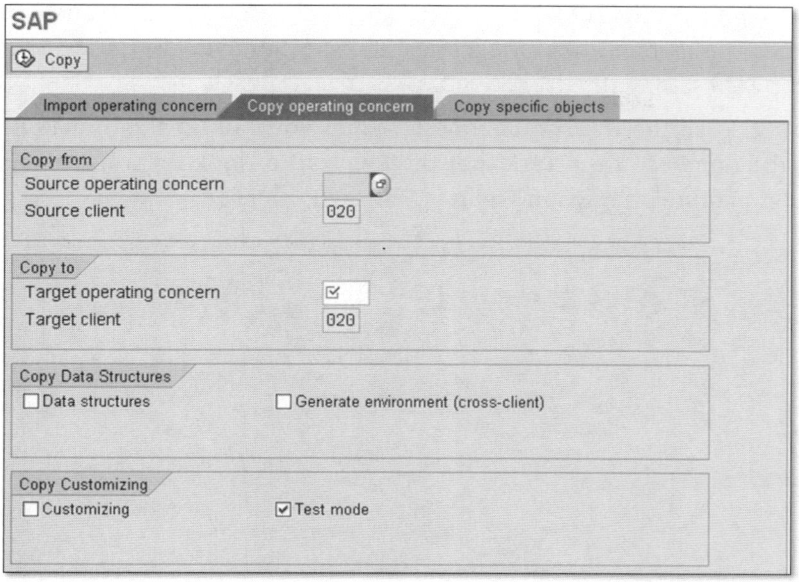

Figure 4.34 Copy Operating Concern Tab

> **Tip**
>
> The test mode cannot be used to copy data structures of the operating concern because those can be copied when you execute the function, provided that test mode has been activated for customizing.

Once you have generated the environment (cross-client) and the customizing in test mode, you can copy the customizing settings. You can also repeat this step as often as required and every time the system overwrites any existing settings. The data structures in the target operating concern must be active, and they must at least contain the same characteristics and value fields as the source operating concern. Next, let's look at the **Copy specific objects** tab.

4.9.3 Copy Specific Objects

The **Copy specific objects** tab allows copying specific customizing settings between clients or between operating concerns within one client. This means, that you can only copy the objects inside an operating concern to another one as long as it is within the same SAP system (production, QA, or test). For this, simply follow these steps:

1. Collect all of the relevant tables in a transport request using the **Transport Objects** Transaction **SE10** or the manual transport function in the transaction for each setting (the truck icon).

2. Do not release the transport request. When you call up this function, enter the number of the **Task** (not the **Request**) or look for it using the search capabilities shown in Figure 4.35.

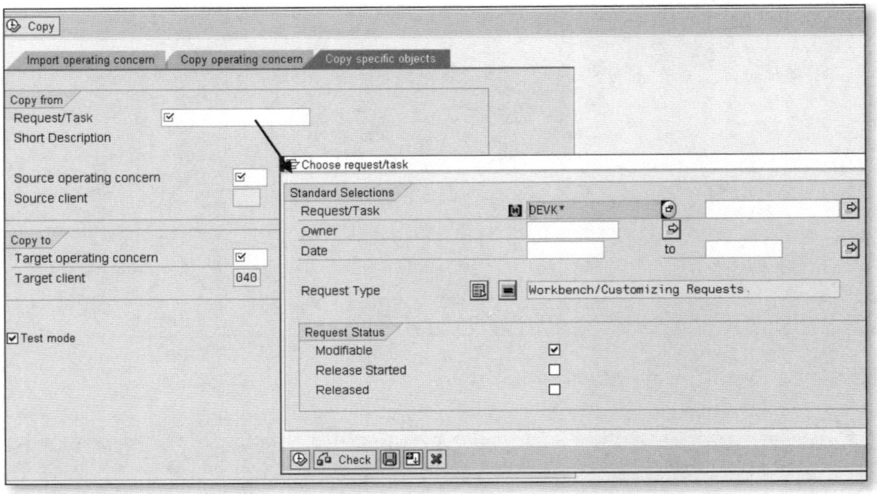

Figure 4.35 Choose Request/Task on the Copy Specific Objects Tab

3. The **Source client** is determined based on the client for which the transport request is defined. If you are copying between clients, you cannot change the operating concern. If you are copying between operating concerns, they must be in the same client.

4. Once you find the desired objects, select the **Request/Task** number that contains the objects that you want to copy and then select the **Source operating concern** as shown in Figure 4.36.

5. In the **Copy to** section, create a name for the **Target operating concern**. This needs to be a four-character description, as shown in Figure 4.36.

6. Click on the **Copy** button located on the top of the screen to perform the copy.

> **Caution**
>
> The system cannot automatically check whether all of the table entries in the transport request belong to the specified source operating concern. You need to pay special attention to this when you use this function.

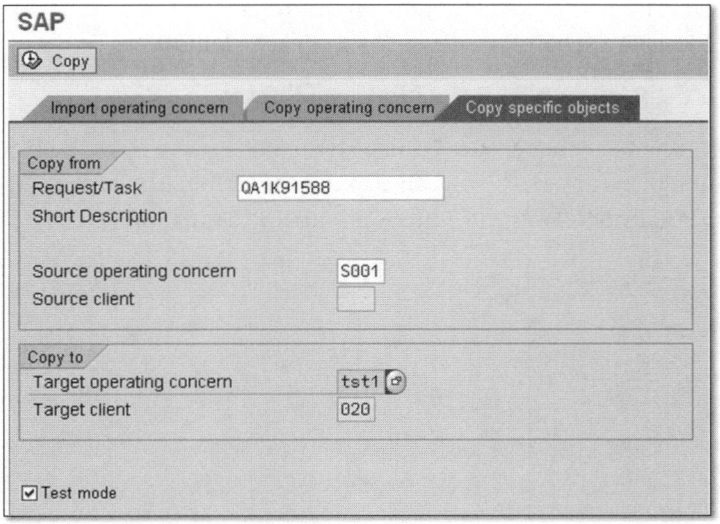

Figure 4.36 The Copy Specific Objects Tab

Eventually you will need to move your information from a testing environment into a production system. For this, it is important to review how to perform transports in CO-PA as we will do in the next section.

4.10   Performing CO-PA Transports

You move or transport objects (but not data) that exist inside an operating concern to another system for final testing or implementation using a *transport request*. With this function, the system collects all of the dependent objects in the source system and places them in the transport request. After importing the objects to the target system, it automatically activates the necessary objects in the *ABAP dictionary* (the data structures of the operating concern). For that, both the source and target systems must be of the same release and update level.

Best Practice is to use the following client sequence:

1. From development to testing (QA)

2. From testing to production

This sequence, or object flow, describes a secure way to avoid losing information on any server because it is unique, and reassures the implementation team that objects exist more than once in a client system. Also, because the original always exists in the development environment and can be transported again, objects are secure in case of corruption or failure.

The process of a CO-PA transport is described as follows:

1. Click on the execute icon next to **Transport** in the **Production Startup** menu, as shown in Figure 4.37. You can also use the IMG path **Controlling • Profitability Analysis • Tools • Production Startup • Transport**.

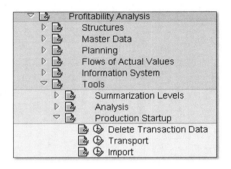

Figure 4.37 Accessing the Transport Functionality

2. The SAP Ecexutive Information System (EIS) transport tool starts and the screen shown in Figure 4.38 appears. You can now collect the objects that are linked to your CO-PA settings (table entries, data elements, domains, tables, and so on) in a transport request.

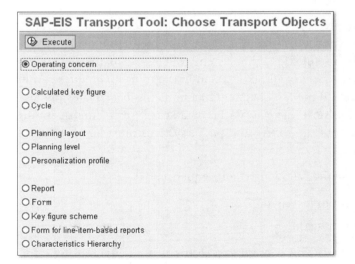

Figure 4.38 The SAP-EIS Transport Tool

3. For our example, we want to transport operating concerns, so select the radio button next to **Operating concern** and click **Execute**.

4. Next, the SAP system requires finding the customizing request that stores the information that you are looking to transport. Remember, we have created structures that interact with other objects. If those objects are already in a customizing or workbench request (if you are not familiar with these request types, we will explain what they are in more detail a little later in this section), we need to find them in the system. Click on the icon to the right of the **Customizing Request** box, as shown in Figure 4.39, to see the different options available, or you can create your own customizing request.

Figure 4.39 Accessing the Customizing Requests

5. You can work with the Transport Organizer (Transaction SE10) by clicking on the **Transport Organizer** button shown in Figure 4.39, and allowing any user to review any transport objects available in the system. Using the Transport Organizer you can create a transport request which lets you transport objects to a target system. Note that detailed information about the Transport Organizer is beyond the scope of this book.

> **Tip**
>
> Using the transport functionality creates a transport request based on the current settings of the operating concern; thus, no new CO-PA objects should be added and no setting changed while the transaction is running. Also, a transport request can be created and data transferred at different points in time. However, if you change any settings between the time when you create the transport request and when you carry out the transport, the system recognizes some of the changes but does not add any new objects to the transport request. This can lead to inconsistencies in the target system following the transport. For this reason, SAP recommends that you make no further settings in CO-PA between the time you create the request and when you export the settings.

When you create a transport request, the system is not able to check which of the objects to transport already exist in the target system. However, if objects already exist in the target system they are overwritten. To avoid this, you should set up one source system with the defined objects and then transfer the settings defined in this source system to other target system(s). Do not create any new CO-PA objects, such as operating concerns, characteristics, or value fields in the target systems if you are going to have transports between a source (development) and different target systems.

There are different types of CO-PA transports:

► Automatic transport or manual transport

► Transporting client-specific and cross-client settings

► Transporting translated settings (settings in different languages)

Next, we will analyze these to get a better understanding of the CO-PA transport process, and the types of transports available in the R/3 or SAP ERP ECC 6.0 systems.

4.10.1 Automatic Transport or Manual Transport

Even though CO-PA automatically collects the objects and stores them in a transport request, not all of the desired settings may be correctly collected and some objects might still be missing. To address this, you can use automatic transport to set up the overall structure of the required objects in the new system when performing the first move of individual objects to a new system.

If changes have happened to previously transported objects or not all of the objects are found in the new system, you can generate a manual transport, selecting individual components to include in a specific transport request. This is quite useful for large applications. Manual transports are also called *delta transports* because you only move the elements that have changed to the new system and not the complete set of objects.

You should use the Transport Organizer to manage your transported objects. However, coordinate with your SAP basis team, project manager, and security administrators about the company's procedure to perform and release transports to other systems before you generate one or verify that you are allowed to perform this process based on your individual role in the implementation.

4.10.2 Client-specific and Cross-client Settings

In CO-PA, customizing consists of cross-client settings (such as tables and data elements) and client-specific settings (such as customizing value flows). Two request categories are usually used in the SAP system, which are also available in the Transport Organizer:

► **Customizing requests**: Record the changes to the customizing settings. When you release the requests, the current status of the recorded settings is exported, and can then be imported into the consolidation system and, if necessary, into subsequent delivery systems. When you create customizing requests, the transport target is automatically assigned the standard transport layer by the SAP system.

► **Workbench requests:** These types of requests record the changes made to ABAP workbench objects, and can be either local or transportable workbench requests. The package of the object and the transport route settings in the transport management system is what determines if the changes are recorded in a local or transportable workbench request.

The customizing settings in CO-PA are split by default into these two request categories, depending on whether they are cross-client or client-specific settings. You can deactivate this splitting by using the **Goto • Settings** path in the SAP-EIS transport tool, as shown in Figure 4.40, and deselecting the option **Split into Workbench and Customizing Requests**.

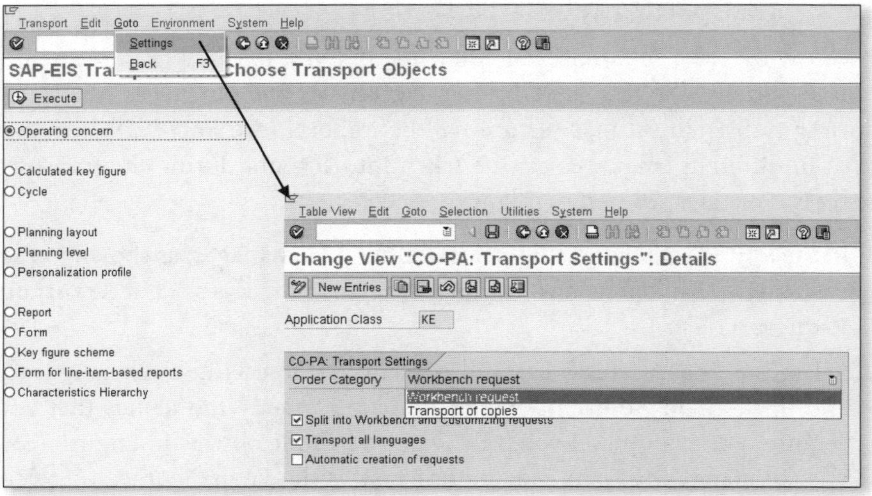

Figure 4.40 Accessing CO-PA Transport Settings

You use the customizing settings to specifically configure the transport options for CO-PA, and how the transported information will behave. There are two options on the **Order Category** dropdown list, as shown in Figure 4.40: **Workbench request** (default) and **Transport of copies**. You can also select the request type for cross-client objects in the CO-PA **Transport Settings • Order Category** section for cross-client objects.

The **Workbench request** (also called consolidation requests) option is set as the default request type. If the system has not been configured for transporting objects, it is possible to transfer the objects using the **Transports of copies** option. During a transport of copies, however, it is not possible to run checks on the transport system, and for this reason, this setting should only be used in exceptional cases.

If you select the option **Automatic creation of requests**, the system automatically creates the required transport requests depending on the category of the objects that will be transported: either client-specific or cross-client. Finally, if the sequence in which the transport occurs is important and if the split function is activated, make sure that the workbench request is released first (by following the proper transport release procedures) and then the customizing request because the first one moves the objects and the second one updates any changes generated over these objects that exist in your transport system.

4.10.3 Transporting Translated Settings

If you work for a multinational company and you have a big implementation, especially one that uses different currencies and languages, the transporting translated settings feature will be important to know. Objects that exist in different languages can be taken into account during the transport process. For this, proceed as follows:

1. In the SAP-EIS transport tool, select **Edit • Add Languages**, as shown in Figure 4.41. This opens the **Adding Foreign Languages to a Transport Request** screen.

2. Select the **Request/task** that will contain the objects in other languages and in the field **Additional languages** enter exactly the names that you require. For example, if you only want to include objects in English (EN) and German (DE) as part of a **Request/task** as shown in Figure 4.42, select the input box, right-click, and select the **Multiple selection** option as shown.

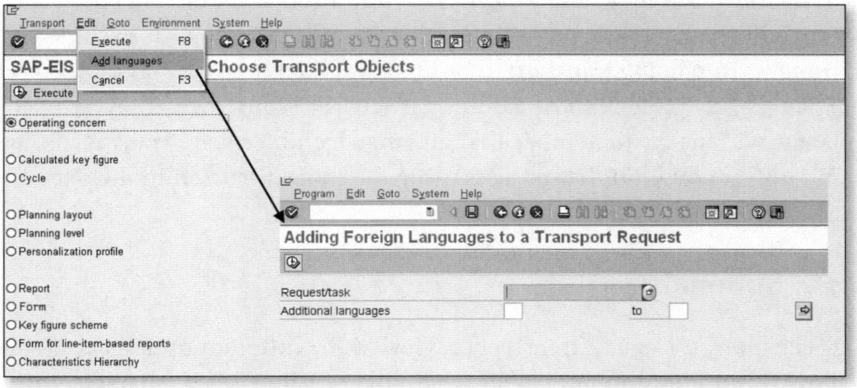

Figure 4.41 Adding Foreign Languages to a Transport Request

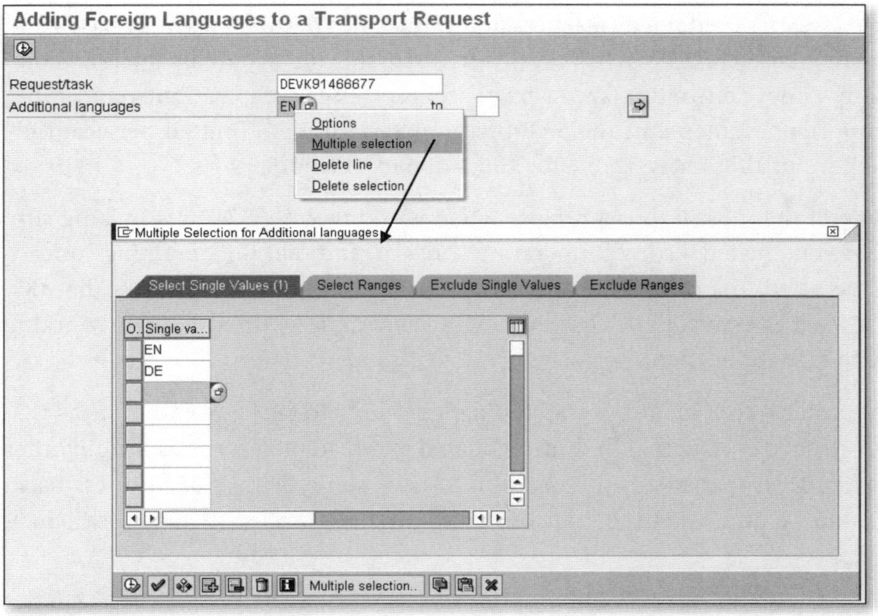

Figure 4.42 Multiple Selections for Additional Languages

3. Now the screen **Multiple Selection for Additional languages** appears, as also shown in Figure 4.42, which has several tabs. For our example, we only want English (EN) and German (DE) objects attached, so you should work on the **Select Single Values (1)** tab.

4. Once satisfied with your selections, click on the green checkmark icon located in the lower menu bar to accept them.

The remaining tabs let you select different options to limit the selection, such as transaction ranges, exclude single values from a selection, or exclude certain ranges from being transported or linked to the request or task, based on their language. Explore these additional tabs on your own; they are self-explanatory. Finally, remember that all language objects are transported by default unless you limit that process using the tools discussed in this section.

4.11   Summary

In this chapter, we have extensively reviewed the different options available to allow the system to understand what type of value fields, characteristics, and accounting type you want to use as part of your costing-based CO-PA configuration.

We also explored the differences and similarities between account-based and costing-based CO-PA. However, our discussion on elements such as company code, controlling areas, profit centers, fiscal year variants, and other important elements of the SAP financial system were limited because they require further analysis outside the scope of this book.

One of the most important parts when working with CO-PA is making sure that you created a correct operating concern, and that the operating concern is assigned to a controlling area. Furthermore, it is very important that CO-PA itself is activated so that the SAP system "knows" that you are working with this application.

We will explore in more detail in Chapter 5 how to take advantage of the CO-PA structures now that they are activated and ready to accept data from other systems. Note that it will be helpful to have some finance or business background to understand the functions and methods discussed in the next chapter.

Master data provides organizational rules that control the behavior of the data values stored in different characteristics inside the operating concern. In addition, master data allows you to perform characteristic valuation and derivation using predefined rules to generate new values based on stored data.

5 Master Data in CO-PA

In Profitability Analysis, master data provides the basis to build content within the structures you have already created with characteristics and value fields. That is, master data in CO-PA is the organizational rule for the structures created and stored inside an operating concern that limit the values, postings, and extraction procedures.

Master data defines the general components used in your CO-PA applications and will control how your data is reported, displayed, and analyzed. It is important to understand that master data is not actual data but rather metadata that regulates and controls the CO-PA structures discussed in Chapters 3 and 4. This is similar to the concept of InfoObjects that define the structure of InfoCubes in SAP Business Warehouse (BW) or SAP NetWeaver Business Intelligence (BI). In this chapter, we'll closely look at master data, how it relates to CO-PA, and how to configure it.

5.1 Components of Master Data Menus in CO-PA

Figure 5.1 provides a complete overview of the components inside the **Master Data** menu of CO-PA (Transaction SPRO); we'll now take a closer look at the most important of these components:

> **Tip**
>
> It is not always necessary to configure or add any of the **Master Data** menu components, especially if your only goal in CO-PA is to use it as a basic data layer to access OLTP data and move it to SAP NetWeaver BI/ SAP BW for reporting and additional manipulation.

- **Maintain Characteristic Values**: Lets you define specific sets of values for a particular characteristic included in an operating concern and also affecting profitability segments.

- **Define Characteristics Hierarchy**: Lets you define hierarchies that control the behavior and display of the characteristic values stored in a particular characteristic.

- **Define Characteristic Derivation**: Lets you generate values based on predefined rules and relationships to generate additional characteristic values inferred from the previously stored data. For example, if material type A and supplier B are data values available in the system, then we can find the characteristic C because it is only provided by supplier B and it is made of material A.

- **Valuation**: Valuation has several sub-items that are of importance and are as follows (note that some items in the following list are summaries of multiple subitems):

  - **Valuation Strategies**: Lets you configure automatic procedures based on specific rules and relationships following a sequence of events. For example, automatic calculation of commissions and discounts for specific material types.

  - **Keys for accessing material cost estimates, characteristics, and products**: Lets you configure automatic procedures to search or locate information using predefined criteria to access specific information based on data attributes. For example, for the calculation of the cost of goods manufactured you can subdivide your company's material value into fixed and variable cost components and their classification is identified by their costing key to differentiate between the two when calculating your profit margin.

  - **Assignment of value fields**: Lets you specify the value fields (key figures) to consider as part of the component structure to analyze with CO-PA. For example, you could specify the gross sales value field from operating concern A to be a variable amount and its actual data to be extracted using a real-time procedure (point of valuation).

CO-PA uses a combination of characteristic values to automatically create the affected market segment or profitability segment we discussed in Chapter 4 (and that can be considered SAP ERP ECC 6.0 InfoCubes but are completely transactional in nature from an SAP BW/SAP NetWeaver BI perspective).

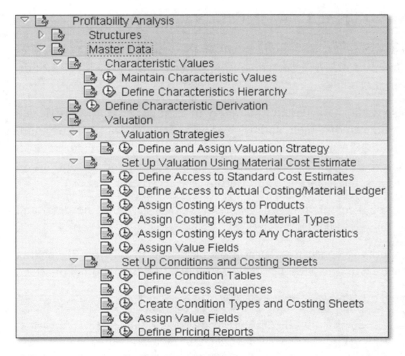

Figure 5.1 Reviewing the Master Data IMG Menu

These specifications for the characteristic values form the basis for the automatic determination of the profitability segment. Now you can specify the valid characteristic values for the new characteristics you have defined using the master data stored in your characteristics by limiting and controlling the types of transactions allowed inside the system.

Of the topics reviewed in this section, valuation and derivation are the most complex and sophisticated topics in master data CO-PA, because if not configured correctly, they can negatively affect system performance when working on a massive scale. However, they can also allow the user to generate sophisticated scenarios for calculating multiple pricing or costing procedures for multiple numbers of materials, products, parts, and others, and replicating such processes using SAP NetWeaver BI or SAP BW, SAP NetWeaver BI Integrated Planning (IP), and Business Planning and Simulation (BPS) might not be worth the effort. Let us now take a closer look at the topic of maintaining characteristic values.

5.2 Maintaining Characteristic Values

In this section, you'll learn how to maintain the values of the characteristics that you already defined in your operating concern within the SAP ERP ECC 6.0 environment.

You can also use a characteristics hierarchy to arrange the characteristic values in a tree-like environment and use it as part of a report or planning application in the CO-PA information system. As shown earlier in Figure 5.1, in the **Characteristic Values** menu you'll see the corresponding options of **Maintain Characteristic Values** and **Define Characteristics Hierarchy.**

Now, let's begin maintaining characteristic values (carrying the data) and texts (describing the data):

1. Set an operating concern as current (as described in Chapter 3), making sure you are working with the object you actually want to modify or affect.

> **Note**
>
> Remember from our discussion in Chapter 3 that to modify the contents of any elements in CO-PA that are included as part of an operating concern, the operating concern must be set up as current, using the IMG path **Profitability Analysis • Structures • Define Operating Concern • Set Operating Concern,** otherwise nothing will appear or your changes will be stored in the wrong operating concern.

2. Click on the **Maintain Characteristic Values** option shown earlier in Figure 5.1.

3. Now the operating concern set up as current, in this case **S_GO Quickstart Template**, and its available characteristics, display. This is shown in the box on the left of Figure 5.2.

4. Double-click on the **Customer group** characteristic and the screen **Change View "Customer groups": Overview** appears, as shown on the right side of Figure 5.2. Notice that there are two columns: **CGrp** for the technical name and **Name** for the description.

5. Click on the change/modify icon (pencil with glasses).

6. Click on the **New Entries** button and provide the necessary information to create your master data values attached to the **Customer group** characteristic.

7. Save your work by clicking on the save icon, and now all cross-client and client objects will be compiled and activated with this change.

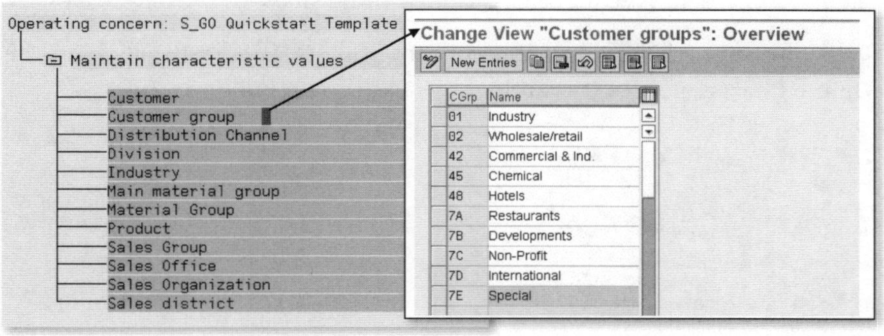

Figure 5.2 Maintaining the Characteristic Values

At this point, only the values set up in the master data characteristic are allowed for selection or generation inside CO-PA. In addition, you can organize characteristics using hierarchies to improve performance, planning, or reporting, depending on the complexity of the project, or if the project requires several levels of organization. Let us look at this next.

5.2.1 Define Characteristics Hierarchy

Hierarchies are one of the most important components in an SAP system, regardless of the environment. They are structures for characteristics that help to simplify and analyze data using the Information System menu that will be discussed in Chapters 6, 7, 9 and 10, for planning and reporting. For example, it is possible to set up a hierarchy structure for products or customers and categorize it by region.

Different characteristics that use the same master data table are grouped in the same characteristics hierarchy. It is not difficult to define external hierarchies for characteristics that do not have a check table or text table. In addition, only the characteristic values for one characteristic are grouped hierarchically for each hierarchy. And, each characteristic value can occur only once in the hierarchy. Thus each value is unique within the entire hierarchy. You can define alternative hierarchies for the same characteristic to simulate different ways of grouping the characteristic values. These alternative hierarchies are stored as hierarchy variants. You can define up to 999 different variants for each characteristic.

To define a characteristic hierarchy, follow these steps:

1. With the appropriate operating concern still set as current, click on the **Define Characteristics Hierarchy** object as shown in Figure 5.3.

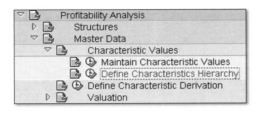

Figure 5.3 Define Characteristics Hierarchy

2. The screen displayed in Figure 5.4 appears, showing the **Char.** (characteristic) **Table** on the left. On the right side is the section **Choose Hierarchy**, where you can create a characteristic hierarchy associated with a specific characteristic.

3. As shown in Figure 5.4, select the characteristic **Zone** in the **Char. Table**, and enter "TST" in the **Variant** box to start creating a characteristic hierarchy associated with a variant called TST.

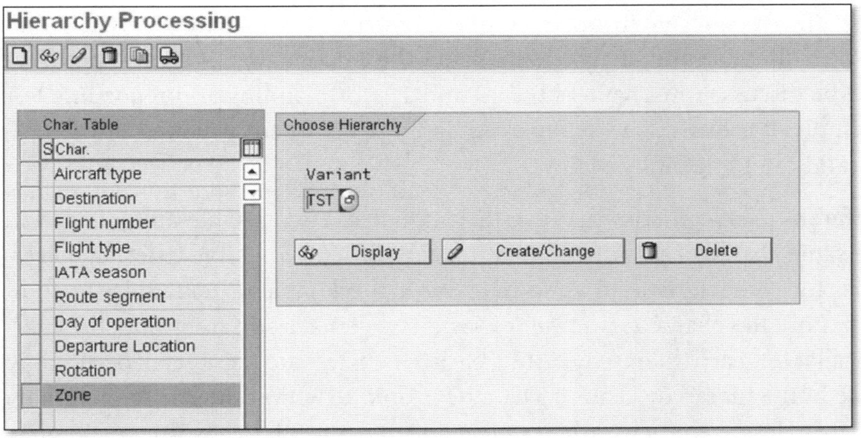

Figure 5.4 Creating a Hierarchy in CO-PA

4. Click on the **Create/Change** button shown in Figure 5.4 to create the variant variable that will store the characteristic hierarchy information. Notice that you can also **Display** and **Delete** a selected variant.

5. The screen displayed in Figure 5.5 appears. To complete the configuration of your hierarchy variant TST, type "This is a characteristic hierarchy" or any other description that you might require into the **Short description** box, and click on the **Hierarchy** button.

> **Tip**
>
> Notice in Figure 5.5, in the **Attributes** section, the checkbox called **Visible system-wide**. This controls whether the hierarchy variant will be active for all applications where master data hierarchies can be maintained. If not selected, the hierarchy variant is only available in the Enterprise Controlling Executive Information System (EC-EIS).

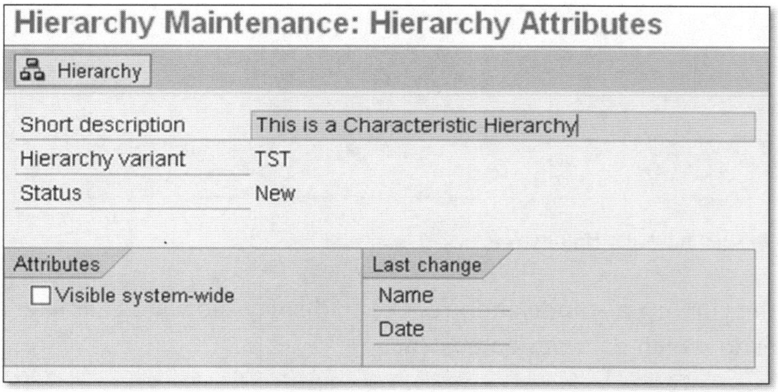

Figure 5.5 Configuring Your TST Hierarchy Variant

6. After completing the previous steps, your screen should now look similar to the **Hierarchy Processing: Maintain Hierarchy** screen shown in Figure 5.6. Here, the different standard nodes and levels that you can define are displayed as a hierarchical tree. There are several buttons at the top of the screen, such as **Same Level** (create object at the same level), **Lower Level** (create object at lower level), delete icon, cut icon, **Same Level** (paste operation at same level), **Lower Level** (paste operation at lower level), and **Empty Node**. All of these buttons and icons can be used to enhance or remove elements of the hierarchy.

You can now fill in the blanks of the different nodes and create your own hierarchy, or use the buttons to add, remove, or modify the current standard hierarchy configuration.

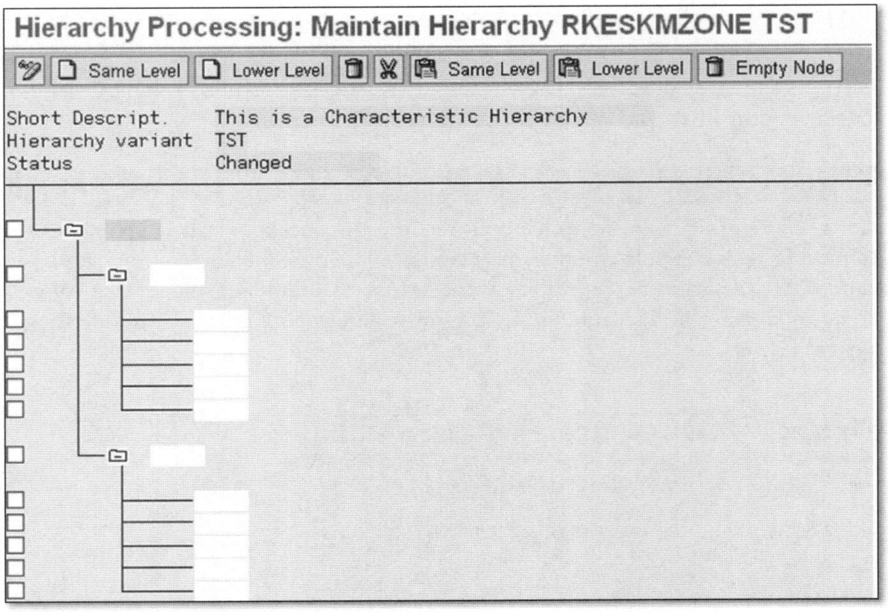

Figure 5.6 Empty Characteristic Hierarchy

7. Position the cursor on a node and press F4 to display the valid characteristic values to which data can be posted.

> **Tip**
>
> Each characteristic value can only be present once in the hierarchy variant. If a characteristic value is already present in the hierarchy, it no longer appears in the list of possible entries.

8. Choose the desired value or any existing node that cannot receive postings.

> **Tip**
>
> If you enter data for a nonchargeable node, this data is transferred to a table. To access this table, choose **Goto • Maintain nonchargeable nodes**.

9. Take a look at Figure 5.7, which shows a completed hierarchy for the **Zone** characteristic. The first node, called **ORIGIN NODE,** is considered the root node or dummy node, to which every other component is attached.

10. Save your work. Your hierarchy is now ready for use by the components of the Information System menu and the CO-PA planning framework.

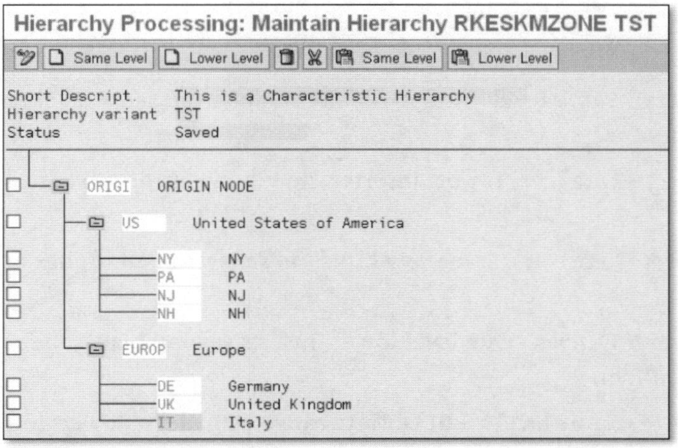

Figure 5.7 TST Characteristic Hierarchy for the Zone Characteristic

11. To open and close the hierarchy tree, click on the nodes at each of the higher levels to expand or collapse the structure below. Nodes that can be expanded have a plus (+) sign next to their name, and nodes that can be collapsed have a minus (-) sign next to their name.

> **Tip**
>
> Now you can use the hierarchy TST in the Information System menu to improve the system performance and access the information in levels of data and not all at once. You can consider each level node a level of aggregation that limits the search to that level, if selected in reporting or planning.

Additional functionalities are available when creating hierarchy variants. For example, explore the **Edit** option, as shown in Figure 5.8.

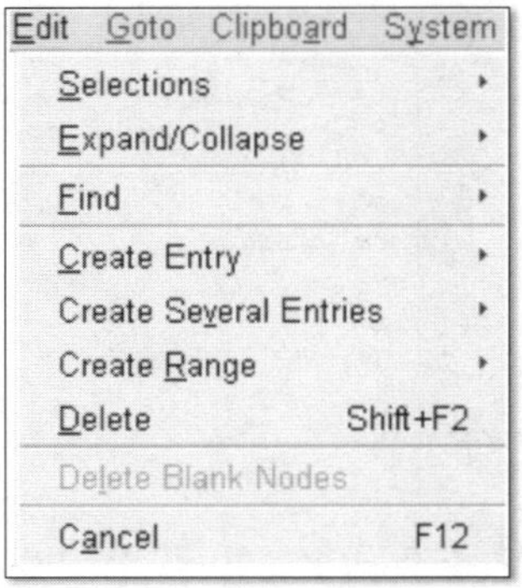

Figure 5.8 Reviewing the Edit Menu

There are several ways to create new nodes in the hierarchy as described below:

▶ **Edit • Create Entry • Same level**: inserts a blank node at the same level as the selected node.

▶ **Edit • Create Entry • One level lower**: inserts a new node at the next level down.

▶ **Edit • Create Several Entries • Same level**: inserts several blank nodes at the same level.

▶ **Edit • Create Several Entries • One level lower**: inserts several blank nodes at the next level down.

▶ **Edit • Create Range • Same level • Edit • Create range • One level lower**: lets you enter a range, such as "characteristic value X through characteristic value Z."

It is possible to change, display, copy, transport, delete, and modify the master data of the characteristic values at any time to update or adjust your hierarchy variant. You can also copy a hierarchy variant and change it to generate a brand new one. For example, follow the steps shown in Figure 5.9 to copy a hierarchy variant.

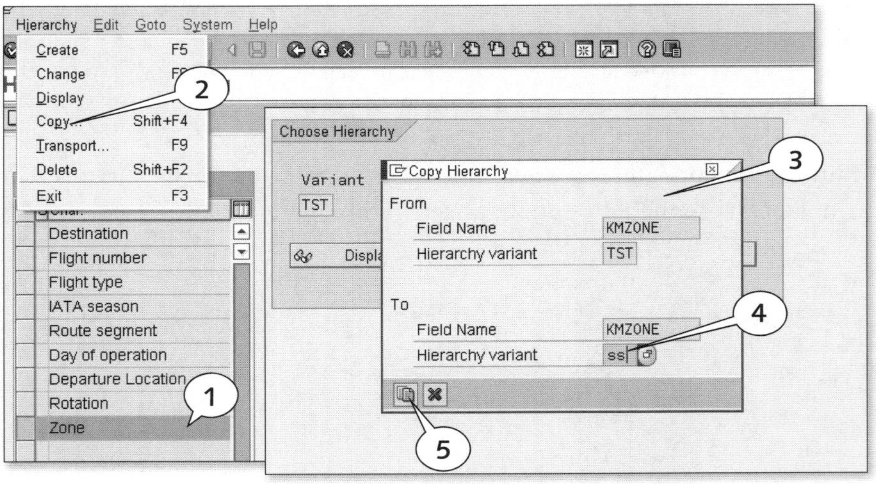

Figure 5.9 Copying a Hierarchy Variant for the Zone Characteristic

There are additional functionalities available in the screen presented in Figure 5.9 that are beyond the scope of this book. Feel free to explore and play with them to learn more about them. Remember, hierarchies become quite handy, especially when the number of products, materials, customers, regions, and their relationships becomes so large that it confuses data analysis and affects system performance due to the data volume.

In the following section, we will review in more detail the concept of derivation and the different types of rules that can be utilized to generate new characteristic values based on the relationships described, with data originally stored in the database.

> **Note**
>
> We will not be able to cover the concepts of derivation and valuation in great detail in this book because of their sophistication. This book will help you understand the basic functionalities and see how they can be integrated into more complex environments to automatically control and calculate the generation of new information and store it as part of your operating concern.

5.2.2 Derivation, Derivation Tables, and Rules Overview

Characteristic derivation is the process of inferring or estimating relationships for CO-PA values to a specific profitability-relevant business transaction. Think of characteristic derivation as a process that is based on specific sets of *rules* created using controlled and logically organized sequences of tasks in a *derivation table*. This entire process is called the *derivation strategy*.

A caution right up front: Be careful when generating new values while working with derivation and valuation because their effect might seriously affect your final data, especially when the calculations run in the background. Depending on complexity, potential problems might be very difficult to resolve. Therefore, you should pay special attention to the alternative usage of valuation and derivation as shown in the Planning Framework and reviewed in Chapter 7.

With derivation, not all of the desired outputs are generated at once, because one task can generate outputs required to execute or generate the following set of activities to come up with the desired result. Let us review a traditional philosophical example, if characteristics material type = "wood," tool type = "ladder," and object = "tree" our characteristic derivation rules might look like this:

▶ **Rule 1**: Ladder is made of wood: the computer will understand it if tool type = "ladder" and material type = "wood."

▶ **Rule 2**: Tree is made of wood: the computer will be able to say that we have a tree if object = "tree" and material type = "wood."

When these rules are met, our new characteristic value "tree is a ladder" can be populated. In other words, we would say "yes" to the statement "tree is a ladder" only when object = "tree" and tool type = "ladder" are true and if both have material type = "wood." These relationships can be generated combining both rules in a derivation table to generate a third and true statement based on the information available.

As shown in Figure 5.10, derivation requires a sequence of events that is logically organized to use the current input data, shown on the left side of the figure, and transform and generate additional data to store in CO-PA and create an enhanced output, shown on the right side of the figure. As also shown in Figure 5.10, we are using three characteristics and their values (**Customer, Product, and Sales rep.**) to generate data for six different characteristics populated based on the relationships of the characteristic values of the initial three characteristics.

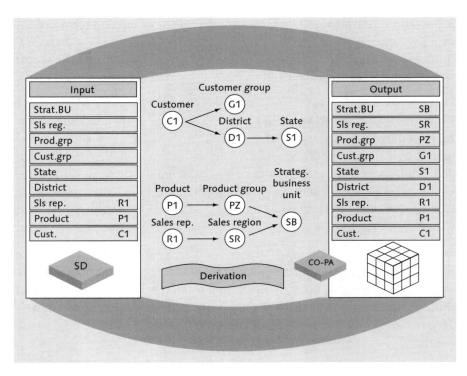

Figure 5.10 The Derivation Concept

The same idea behind these rules is what controls the generation of values using derivation. We can generate a third characteristic that we do not currently have, based on the characteristic values of our current data values stored in a characteristic. For example, if product A and region B are in the same transaction line, we can generate values for a characteristic called "industry sector" and generate a characteristic value called "heavy materials." The characteristic value "heavy materials" is not currently available in our database or included in the industry sector characteristic, but we know for a fact that we can infer that the "heavy materials" rule follows this relationship to populate an additional column in the same transaction line in our database.

Derivation Steps

It is important to identify the different types of *derivation steps* that can be created as part of a derivation strategy. Derivation steps are series of steps or tasks that perform specific processes to achieve a specific final outcome. Derivation steps that describe the different functionalities are described as follows:

▶ **Derivation Rule:** performs inference on the values of characteristics based on the values of other characteristics.

▶ **Table Lookup:** performs a search inside the data stored in the operating concern based on conditions. Does not make any modifications to the data; instead, it simply informs whether data has been found that meets certain criteria.

▶ **Move:** performs an assignment to a target field based on a source field or a constant.

▶ **Clear:** performs a delete operation to a specified field based on predefined conditions.

▶ **Enhancement:** uses ABAP programs to create routines to develop more customized applications using both customized and standard user conditions.

Tip
Only characteristics created inside of your operating concern can be manipulated to use in either rules or to generate new values. Also, the profitability segment to which the account assignments will need to be made is determined using the quantity of characteristic values drawn from characteristic derivation.

Steps follow a chain or cause-effect reaction, so if there is an incorrect procedure inside a derivation strategy, the final outcome might not be the most desirable one. Therefore, make sure to review that each process is delivering the information that it is supposed to.

Applicable Object Types

It is important to clearly identify the types of objects for which derivation is applicable:

▸ Manual account assignments, including:

  ▹ Settling orders and projects

  ▹ Direct postings from Financials (FI)

  ▹ Manually created CO-PA line items

  ▹ Manual entry of planning data

You only have to enter a few characteristic values manually. The remaining characteristic values can be entered via characteristic derivation.

▸ Automatic transfer of data from other applications, including:

  ▹ Billing documents

  ▹ Transferring overhead

  ▹ External data transfer

> **Note**
>
> An in-depth explanation of each of the objects listed goes beyond the scope of this book. You should consult additional sources to fully understand their functionality.

Next, we'll explore how to create derivation steps along with the procedure to generate each of them. We will also look more closely at the concepts of the derivation rules and derivation steps by reviewing the general configuration procedures for each of the step types.

5.2.3 Creating Characteristic Derivations and Derivation Rules

Now that we have a good idea of the logic behind derivation, let us begin with a more detailed discussion on how to create a derivation strategy to generate new values using derivation steps.

Creating Derivation Rules

First, let us create a derivation rule following these steps:

> **Note**
>
> Before you start creating objects in the SAP system, remember to rehearse the steps or processes that you want to create on paper and correctly identify them to improve your development efforts.

1. Follow the IMG path **Controlling • Profitability Analysis • Master Data • Define Characteristic Derivation**, as shown in Figure 5.11.

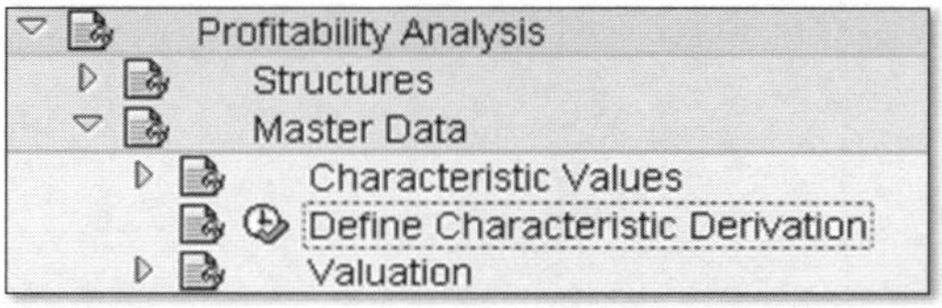

Figure 5.11 Accessing Define Characteristic Derivation

> **Tip:**
>
> When an operating concern is generated, the system produces a standard derivation strategy containing all known dependencies between characteristics. You can display these by choosing **View • Display all steps**. Also, the derivation strategy can be changed by adding more steps, changing previous steps, or deleting, or changing the step sequence

2. The screen **Characteristic Derivation: Change Strategy** appears, as shown in Figure 5.12. Click on the change/modify icon (pencil with glasses).

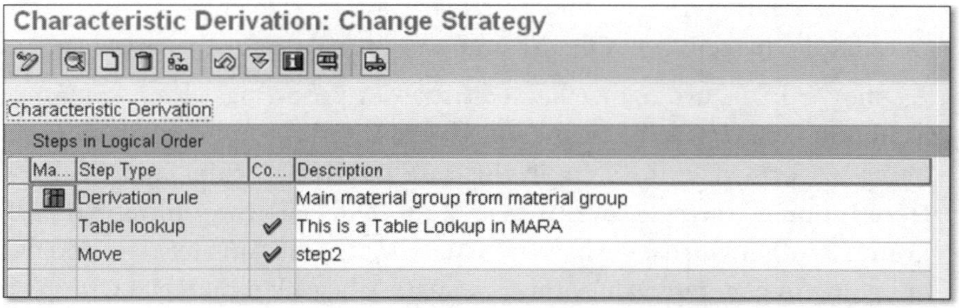

Figure 5.12 Characteristic Derivation: Change Strategy Screen

3. Click on the create icon (white page icon) to start creating a derivation step.

4. In the **Create Step** box that appears, as shown in Figure 5.13, select **Derivation rule** and click on the checkmark icon.

> **Note**
>
> As you can see, there are four additional types of derivation steps that can be created: **Table lookup**, **Move**, **Clear**, and **Enhancement**. We will review the remaining functions in more detail in the following sections.

Figure 5.13 Types of Derivation Steps Available in CO-PA

5. The **Characteristic Derivation: Display Strategy** screen appears after clicking on the checkmark icon in Figure 5.13. For this type of derivation there are some additional options to consider:

   ▸ Under **Maintain rule values**, you enter which values in the target fields should be placed in which characteristic values of the source fields.

   ▸ Under **Characteristics**, you can make additional entries which, for example, make it possible to enter a validity date for the step.

6. As shown in Figure 5.14, characteristic derivation has three columns: **Maintain Entries**, **Step Type** (which identifies the type of derivation being performed in the step, in this case **Derivation rule**), and finally a **Description** of the rule, in this case **Main Material group from material group**. In other words, we have two **Main Material** characteristics and we are going to generate values for a characteristic called **Material Group** as shown in Figure 5.15.

Characteristic Derivation: Display Strategy

Characteristic Derivation

Steps in Logical Order

Maintain Entries	Step Type	Description
⊞	Derivation rule	Main material group from material group

Figure 5.14 Configuration of a Derivation Rule

7. Click on the icon in the column **Maintain Entries** to access the derivation rule filtering options. As shown in Figure 5.15, we have two characteristics — **Material Group Name** and **Main Material Group** (derived characteristic). We will take values from **Material Group Name** to generate user-defined values in the **Main Material Group** characteristic.

Characteristic Derivation: Change Rule Values

Derivation rule   Main material group from material group

Value filter active: Material Group 01

Material Group	Material Group Name	A...	Main Material Group	Main Material Grou...
01	ITEMS WITH MAT'L...	▬	Heavy Materials	Not assigned
02		▬	Heavy Materials	
03		▬	Composite Material	
04		▬	Composite Material|	
		▬		

Figure 5.15 Definition of the Derivation Rule

For example, as shown in Figure 5.15, we have four entries in the **Material Group** column (**01**, **02**, **03**, and **04**), and on the right side we are saying that for material groups **01** and **02** we will derive those values as **Heavy Materials** (shown in the **Main Material Group** column). The same goes for material groups **03** and **04** when we define these two as the **Main Material Group** called **Composite Material**.

There are several steps available when creating **Derivation Tables,** and each of them is defined in a step sequence that controls the order that each rule is applied to the operating concern. For example, step 1 can derive characteristic A, and step 2 uses characteristic A to derive characteristic B and so on.

In addition, you can delete, move, and change your steps. For this, simply select the line that defines the step and perform the process as required, either using the icon menu displayed at the top of the screen shown in Figure 5.15, or using the standard SAP software menu bars.

However, not all of the steps require generating additional values to other user-defined characteristics. As seen previously in Figure 5.13, the second type of step available is the **Table lookup**. As its name suggests, a lookup does not generate additional values, but rather searches inside a database to confirm if certain conditions of values are available.

Let us take a closer look.

Creating Table Lookups

A *table lookup* lets you determine characteristic values by reading them from an SAP table using the target value (the desired value to find inside a table) based on the source fields (location inside the SAP table where you might locate the desired values previously defined in the target value).

To create a table lookup you must perform the following:

1. Access the **Characteristic Derivation** screen shown previously in Figure 5.12.
2. Click on the change/modify icon and the create step icon as previously done for the derivation rule procedure.
3. When the **Create Step** screen displayed in Figure 5.13 appears, select the **Table lookup** option and click on the checkmark icon.
4. The **Enter Table Name** dialog box appears, as shown in Figure 5.16. This required table name is an SAP table name where specific transactions or information is stored.

   As shown in Figure 5.16, we will be searching in the Materials Management (MM) table called **MARA**.

> **Note**
>
> Don't worry about not knowing the names of all of the SAP tables; they are too complicated to remember! You can easily find them online on a variety of websites, such as *http://help.sap.com*, *http://sdn.sap.com* and *www.sapgenie.com*.

5. Click on the checkmark icon to continue.

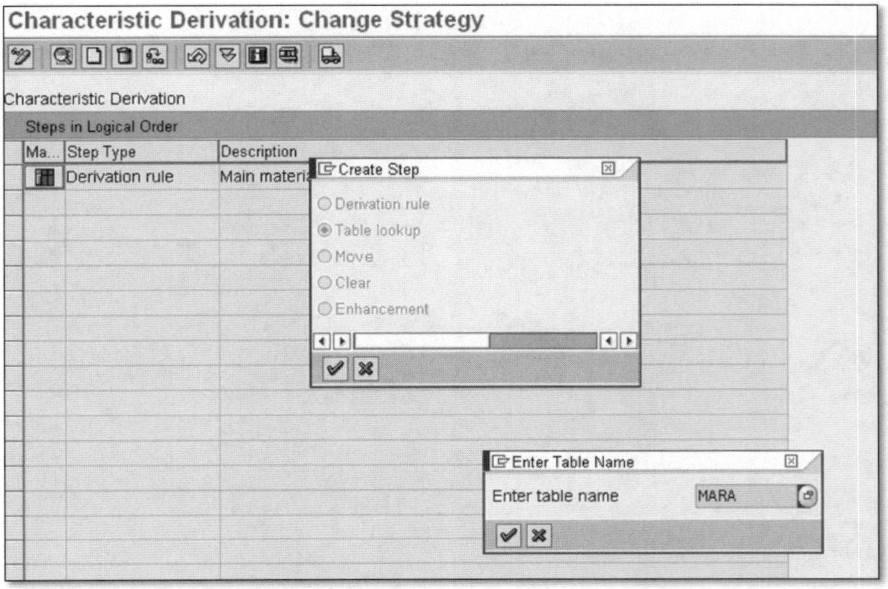

Figure 5.16 Creating a Step for Table Lookup

6. The screen shown in Figure 5.17 displays. Three tabs are available for the table lookup step:

  ▶ **Definition:** lets you define the relationships between the SAP table fields and the fields defined in the operating concern.

  ▶ **Condition:** lets you establish the selection criteria for the data extraction from the SAP tables into the operating concern.

  ▶ **Attributes:** lets you activate the **Issue an error message if no value found** option, to assist during execution if desired.

7. Now, let's suppose we want to look up the base unit of measure and the material group for a particular product number.

8. Select the **Definition** tab. We will use **MATNR Field Name**, which is the material number from the Origin Table **MARA**, and match it with the CO-PA fields called **MATKL** (material group), as shown in Figure 5.17. In the **Assignment of Table Fields to Target Fields** section, you specify where you will store the information once derived by using a condition, which we define on the **Condition** tab next.

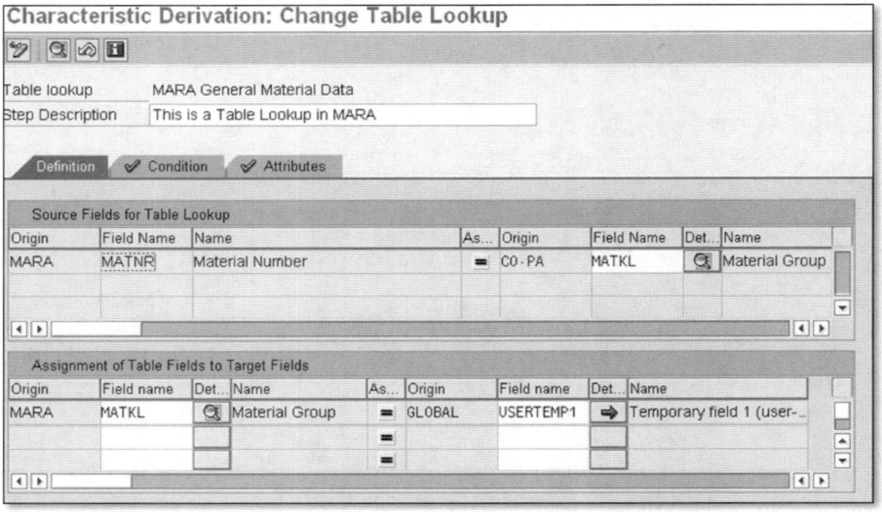

Figure 5.17 Configuring the Definition Tab

9. On the **Condition** tab shown in Figure 5.18, define the CO-PA **Origin** field **Billing Type** (**FKART**) and define the condition greater than (**>**) and the reference **Value B1** with a description of **Rebate Credit Memo**. In other words, we are defining the condition that needs to be satisfied to execute the table lookup step to find any values that meet this criteria.

10. Click on the save icon.

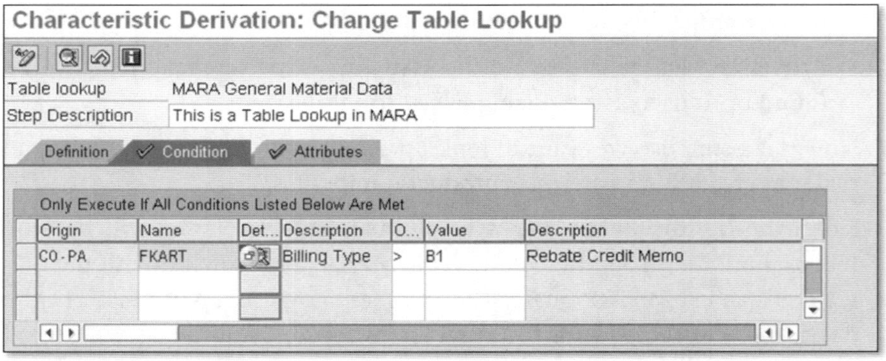

Figure 5.18 The Condition Tab

Next, let us execute the table lookup step we configured, as follows:

1. Go back to the main screen **Characteristic Derivation: Display Strategy**, and click on the new step called **This is a Table Lookup in MARA**, as shown in Figure 5.19.

2. Select the test icon, the icon to the left of the transport (truck) icon, also shown in Figure 5.19.

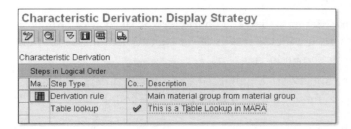

Figure 5.19 Executing the Step Table Lookup

3. Now the screen shown in Figure 5.20 appears, ready to test the characteristic derivation settings. First, however, you must specify the value you want to find in the SAP tables. For our example, we will search for the information of **Product 000011447.**

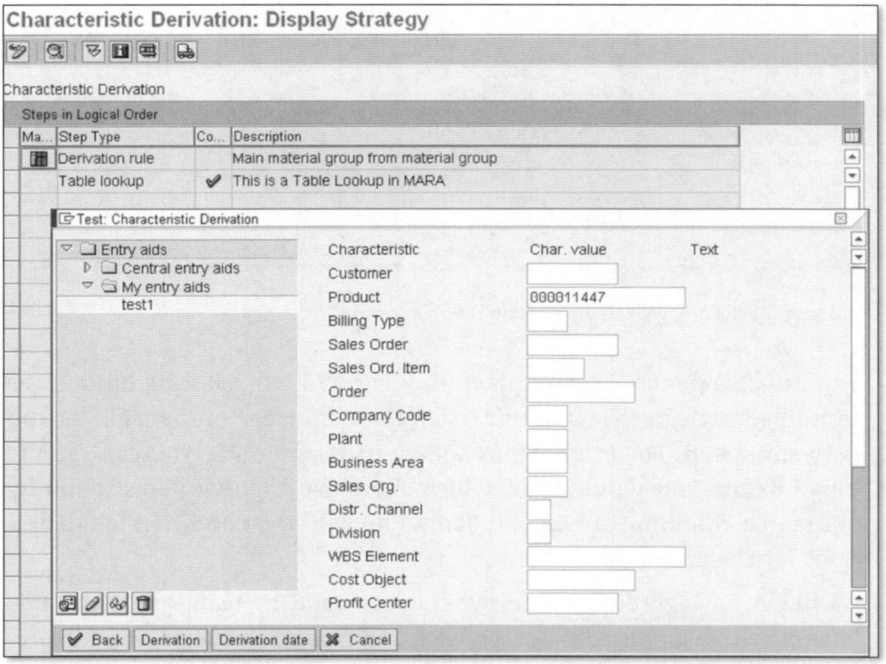

Figure 5.20 Executing your Table Lookup Step

4. Click on the **Derivation** button to start the test.

After clicking on the **Derivation** button, two new buttons appear on the same screen: **Undo Derivation** and **Analyze Derivation**. The first button takes you back to the screen shown in Figure 5.20, and undoes any changes. The second button lets you review the conditions defined in the table lookup step and analyze what this rule has performed.

5. Click **Analyze Derivation** to review the **Characteristic Derivation: Analyze Derivation Steps** screen with the results of the execution of the derivation table lookup step, as shown in Figure 5.21.

6. Notice that step **12** and **17** are highlighted, meaning that data that meets the search criteria defined on the **Condition** tab was found.

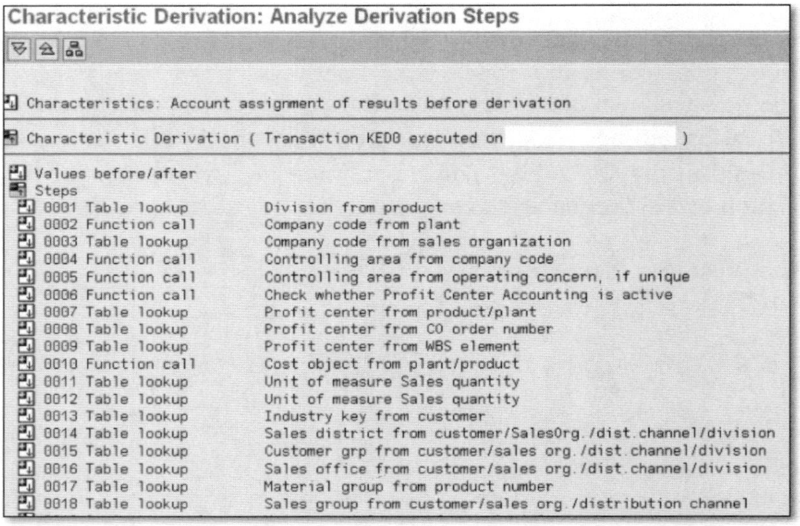

Figure 5.21 Reviewing your Table Lookup Step Execution

7. You can change the display shown in Figure 5.21 by clicking on the tree icon to get a clearer view to understand the influence of the table lookup derivation step. For example, as shown in Figure 5.22, you can see the **Value Before** and **Value After**, which show that the two items found by our search condition are **EA** and **01**, in line with the **Condition** tab definitions for the table lookup.

As shown in Figure 5.22, the two values found by using the step table lookup can be modified if you go back and change the **Condition** tab previously configured.

Characteristic Derivation: Analysis of Derivation Steps				

Source	Field Name	Name	Value Before	Value After
CO-PA	ARTNR	Product number	0000000000000...	0000000000000...
CO-PA	BRSCH	Industry key		
CO-PA	BUKRS	Company Code		
CO-PA	BZIRK	Sales district		
CO-PA	KDGRP	Customer group		
CO-PA	KMVKBU	Sales Office		
CO-PA	KMWNHG	Main Material Gr...	00	00
CO-PA	KNDNR	Customer		
CO-PA	KOKRS	Controlling Area		
CO-PA	KSTRG	Cost Object		
CO-PA	KWSVME_ME	Base Unit of Mea...		EA
CO-PA	MATKL	Material Group		01
CO-PA	SPART	Division		
CO-PA	VKGRP	Sales Group		
CO-PA	VKORG	Sales Organization		
CO-PA	WERKS	Plant		
GLOBAL	DUMMYPRCTR	Dummy Profit Ce...		
GLOBAL	ERKRS	Operating concern	S_GO	S_GO
GLOBAL	PCAACTIVE	Profit Center Acc...		

Sidebar tree:
- Account Assignment
  - Content before derivation
- Characteristic Derivation
  - Values before/after
  - Steps

Figure 5.22 Detailed Result for the Valuation Derivation Step Table Lookup

In the next section, we will explore the move derivation step, and how it can be used to adjust and transfer information stored in one object into another.

> **Note**
>
> Because these functionalities depend largely on the contents or sequence of events to create a derivation strategy, sometimes a table lookup can be used instead to confirm that the status of certain values is different from those that are going to be generated by another step.

Creating a Move Step

As its name implies, a *move step* lets you transfer the contents of any source field or constant to any target field. The **Source field** is where the information is coming from and the **Target field** is where the information will be stored. In addition, the **Constant** value is a default value and can also transfer to a target field, if selected. Figure 5.23 shows the **Characteristic Derivation: Change Assignment** screen, which is used to perform a move step. Notice the differences between this screen and those shown earlier for the derivation rule step and the table lookup step.

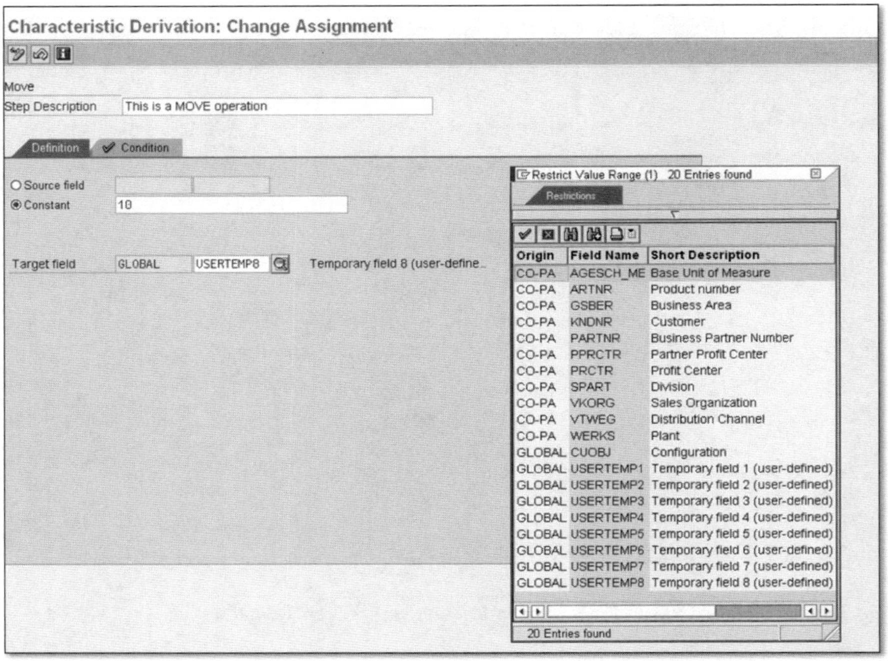

Figure 5.23 Creating a Move Step

The **Definition** and **Condition** tabs on this screen are used to control the behavior of the step. The **Definition** tab lets you specify the data origin — either a **Source field** or a **Constant**. On this tab, you also have to specify the **Target field**, as shown in Figure 5.23. For this you must access the objects available in the default operating concern.

Next, as shown in Figure 5.24, the **Condition tab** lets you limit the transfer of data between two or more objects. For example, the assignment of the **Constant** value **10** to **USERTEMP8**, defined previously as the **Target field**, as shown in Figure 5.23, is determined by the value of the **Controlling Area** (**KOKRS**) to be **0001**.

After configuring the move step, follow the same logic as for any other defined step. That is, select the step, execute it, click on the **Analyze** button, and review your results if successful. Creating derivation steps in CO-PA is similar from step to step, and although there are slight differences in configuration, the process to execute each step is exactly the same.

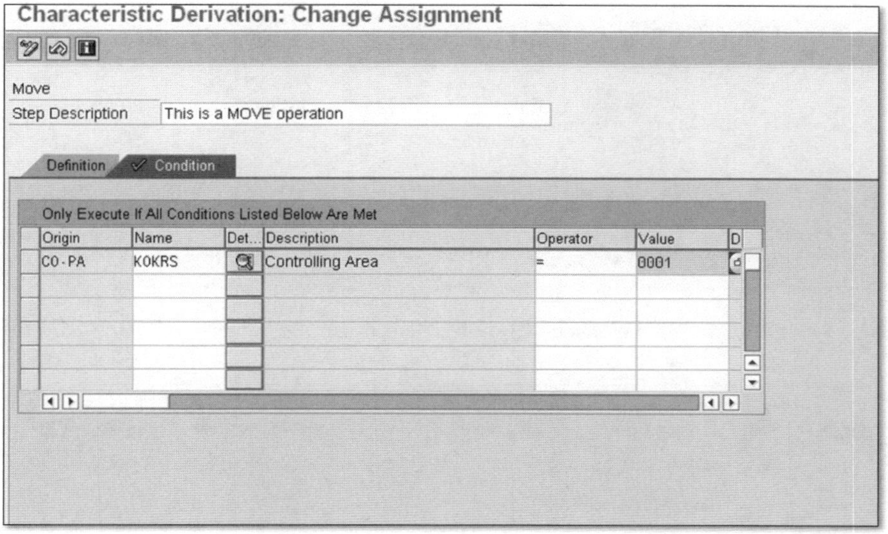

Figure 5.24 The Condition Tab for the Move Step

However, sometimes instead of generating, moving, or storing values into new objects you might want to clear or delete values that currently exist in the database or were previously generated from other steps. This is done using the clear step function that we will review in the next section.

Creating a Clear Step

The *clear* step lets you delete a characteristic value, or, put differently, reset it to "" (blank) for CHAR fields or "0" for NUMC fields:

1. To start, follow the previously discussed procedure to display the **Create Step** dialog box, select **Clear**, and click on the checkmark button.

2. Figure 5.25 shows the configuration screen that displays. As with other steps, a description must be entered, and there is a **Definition** and a **Condition** tab. However, on the clear step's **Definition** tab only one field needs to be defined that identifies the **Field** that has data that you want to clear. In our example, this is **USERTEMP8**.

3. Select the **Condition** tab, shown in Figure 5.26, that lets you specify the requirements the step must have to perform the clear or delete operations. Notice that we have defined the **Controlling Area (KOKRS)** with value **0001** to be the only condition under which to delete data from **USERTEMP8**.

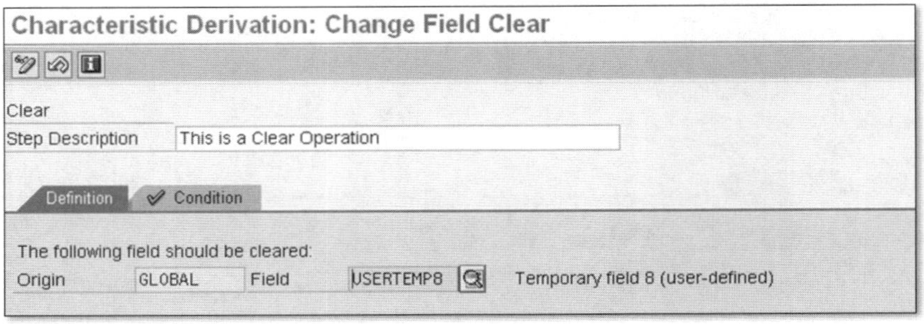

Figure 5.25 Configuring the Change Field Clear Screen

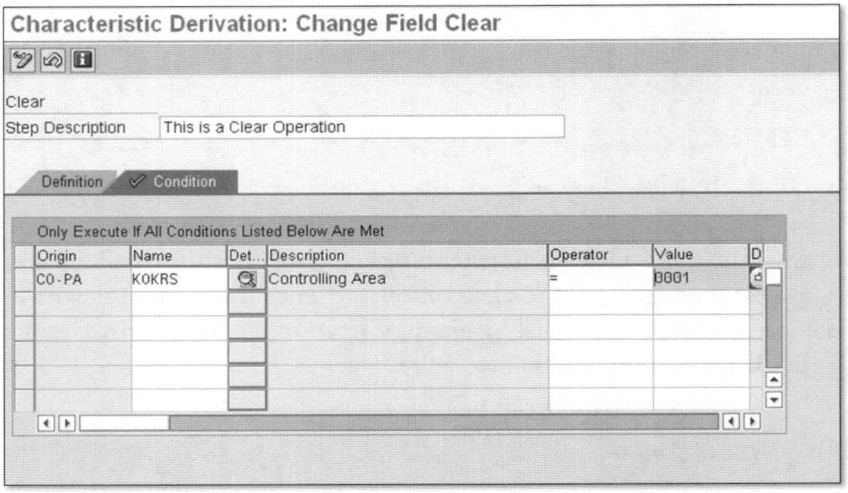

Figure 5.26 Configuring the Condition Tab Screen for the Clear Step

This procedure can be quite useful, especially if you want to empty the fields of an operating concern before you execute another step that will populate it with data.

> **Caution**
>
> We cannot emphasize enough on how careful readers must be when working with this step type. In particular, other objects, such as reports or planning functions, might be value-dependent and final results can be affected by clearing field values.

Finally, you can also define your own step using the enhancement functionality. Enhancements are user-defined ABAP programs that interact with SAP tables to generate more sophisticated procedures.

> **Note**
>
> As we've said before: avoid using ABAP as much as you can. ABAP is not a Best Practice because it requires modification of objects that can be highly sensitive and might be affected after an upgrade.

Creating an Enhancement Step

You can use **Component 003** of customer enhancement **COPA0001** to define your own derivation logic. This enhancement can be inserted anywhere in the derivation strategy, even in more than one place. Note, however, that increasing the complexity of your analysis will also increase the performance requirements of your system. So it is better to use many small steps to complete a sophisticated task rather than generating a few enhancement steps.

As shown in Figure 5.27, an **Enhancement** step using component **COPA0001** is being created. Notice that there are multiple **Source Fields** and multiple **Target Fields** on the **Definition** tab.

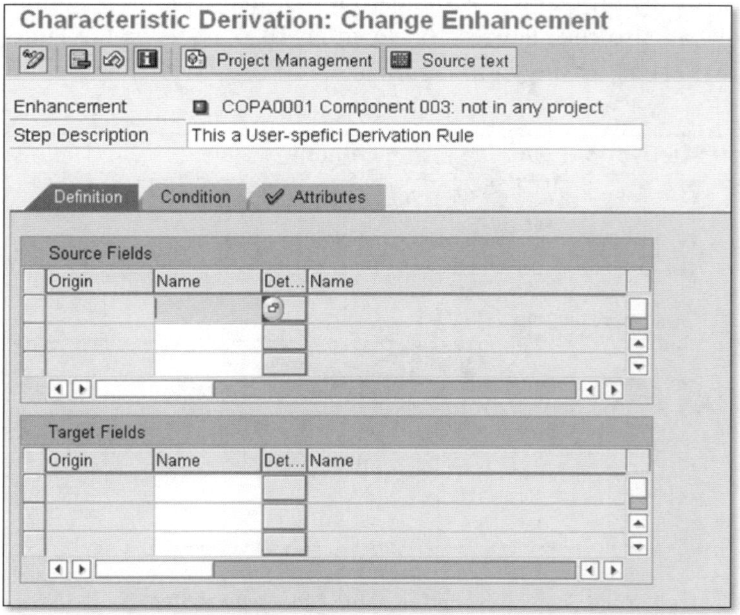

Figure 5.27 Definition Tab of the Enhancement Step

As you can see in Figure 5.28, on the **Condition** tab you can generate multiple conditions to determine when the **Definition** tab options should be executed.

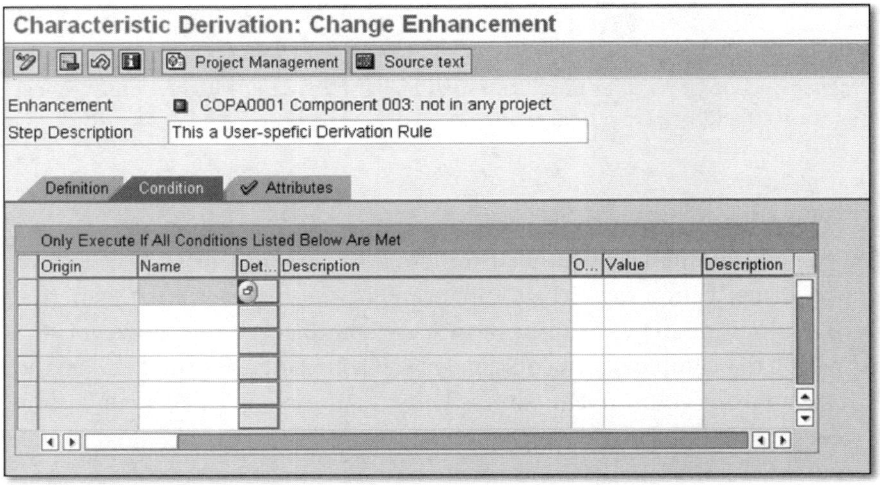

Figure 5.28 Condition Tab of the Enhancement Step

Finally, the **Attributes** tab, shown in Figure 5.29, provides an option to issue an error in case of any problem, as is standard for all step types. In addition, on this tab you can also click **Source text** to enter ABAP code via the **Function Builder** that opens, as shown in Figure 5.30.

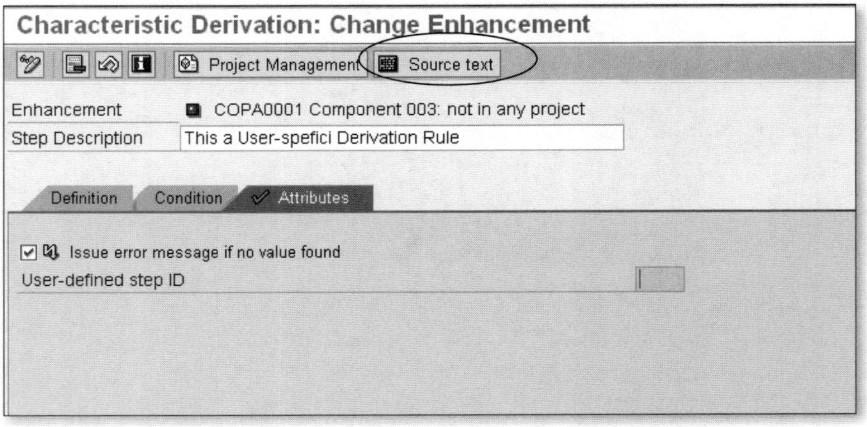

Figure 5.29 Attributes Tab and Source Text Button of the Enhancement Step

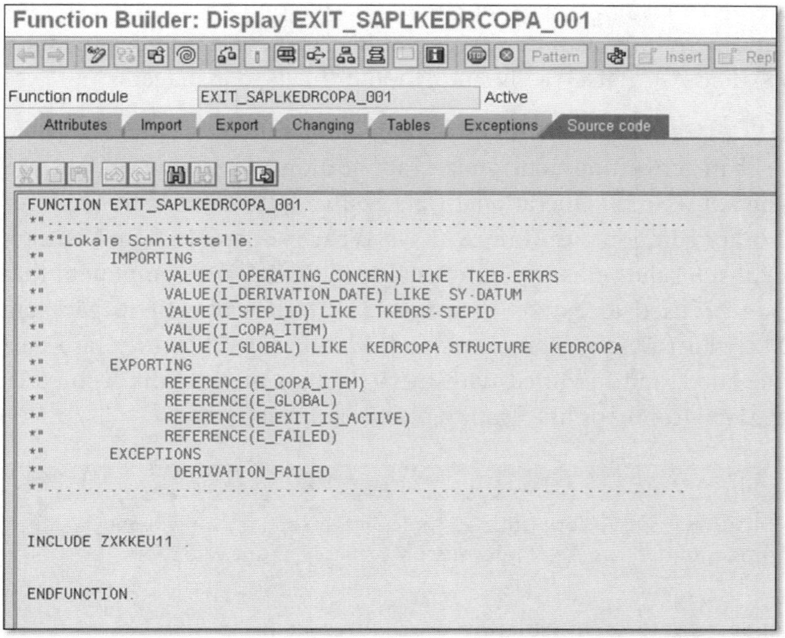

Figure 5.30 The Source Code Tab as Part of the ABAP Function Builder When Using the Enhancement Step

There is one more type of derivation step called customer hierarchy. However, this step is only available if you are using customer hierarchy characteristics in the data structures of an operating concern. For this, you need to create a customer hierarchy step as part of derivation strategy to be able to identify each level of the hierarchy independently.

In the next section we will explore the concept of valuation and how this technique works similar to derivation but is more oriented toward automatic calculations inside CO-PA, based on reference data. Valuation applies if you want to generate more complex scenarios depending on product, price, costs, and material structures associated with volume, sales, and revenue.

5.2.4 Valuation in CO-PA

In this section, we will briefly explore the concept of *valuation*. Valuation is the automatic calculation of values following specific rules for both planning and actual data, but in a costing-based CO-PA environment only. The concept of valuation can be useful for environments with multiple lines of products and materials whose costs and prices are calculated differently depending on the relationship. The alternative to valuation — highly complex relationships in SAP BW or SAP NetWeaver BI, Business Planning and Simulation (BPS), and ABAP itself — is simply too difficult to manage.

Therefore, for large organizations, it is more advisable to use CO-PA valuation rather than generating a customized application to generate similar processes using ABAP, BPS, Operational Data Source (ODS), Business Explorer (BEx) and other components of the SAP NetWeaver BI application. You can, however, consider the valuation functionality in CO-PA as a component that can later on be used to extract data into SAP NetWeaver BI to generate reports. The transformation processes and relationships, however, are best executed, created, and modified with the Valuation menus within the SAP ERP ECC 6.0 environment in a costing-based environment.

> **Note**
>
> Because valuation is such a sophisticated topic, in this section, we will only be able to touch the tip of the iceberg of information available about valuation.

It is quite common to see calculation procedures such as:

▶ The value of marketing commissions is 10 % of total sales value or research.

▶ The development budget is 5 % of the total net revenue.

These types of relationships can be established by using the Valuation menus in costing-based Profitability Analysis to create values that currently do not exist in the SAP ERP ECC 6.0 platform or require further customization. Note, however, that the usage of valuation can significantly increase processing times, reducing system performance and the speed of different transactions inside SAP ERP ECC 6.0.

The concept of valuation in CO-PA is shown in a simplified manner in Figure 5.31. Using input information from the Sales and Distribution (SD) module, there are three main value fields that we are interested in using as reference for further calculations: **Quantity**, **Revenue**, and **Discounts**.

> **Note**
>
> SAP recommends using different value fields for actual and standard costs calculations.

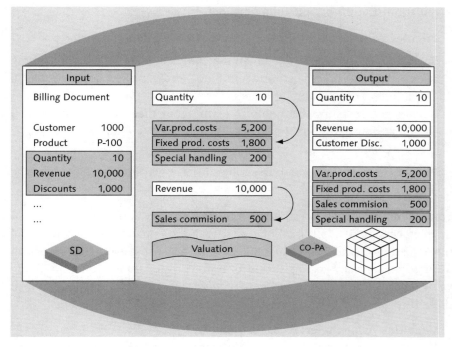

Figure 5.31 The Valuation Concept in CO-PA

With the information in these value fields we can use valuation to generate costs and expenses associated with the values of each of them. For example, the **Quantity** value generates **Var. prod. costs**, **Fixed prod. Costs,** and **Special handling**, and the **Revenue** value generates the **Sales commission**. Once the information has been generated, using different valuation strategies outlined in more detail later, the new values can be stored in CO-PA and used for reporting or planning purposes.

As you can see in Figure 5.31, when CO-PA storage is performed, it affects the profitability segments of the operating concern. From an accounting point of view, valuation can only be implemented using costing-based CO-PA because of reconciliation purposes for both planning and actual data. In addition, you can valuate or revaluate business transactions before their values are posted, once they have been posted, or after they have been posted when performing periodical updates.

Linked with the concept of valuation is the concept of a *valuation strategy*. A valuation strategy is the final link between the valuation methods and the assignment of those methods to specific quantity or value fields coming from the operating concern.

A valuation strategy has the following elements:

▶ **Point of Valuation (PV):** How and how often the data is updated.

▶ **Record type:** The type of document that will be updated, such as incoming sales order (A), direct postings from FI (B), order/project settlements (C), and billing data (F), among others. Discussion of these documents goes beyond the scope of this book; to learn about their characteristics, you should review additional resources, such as *http://sdn.sap.com* and *http://help.sap.com*.

▶ **Plan version** (if applicable): Describes different types of scenarios for the data.

You can define a valuation strategy in relation to the PV, the record type, and the plan version (if applicable). You specify in the valuation strategy which of the valuation methods — valuation using material cost estimates, valuation using conditions and costing sheets, or user exit valuation — to use to fill the value fields and in which order these methods are implemented. Let's look at these three methods, as well as one additional method, in more detail:

▶ **Valuation using material cost estimate**
You can use material cost estimates from Product Cost Controlling (CO-PC) to determine the cost of goods manufactured in Profitability Analysis. The breakdown of these costs in CO-PC is usually more detailed than that required in CO-PA. Consequently, you can assign more than one cost component to the same value field in CO-PA.

Other than the standard cost estimate, the periodic allocation prices or actual cost estimates from material ledger can also be used for valuation. This is particularly useful for period revaluation.

▶ **Valuation using conditions and costing sheets**
This is useful when you need certain data to evaluate a sale but do not yet know the actual values. This makes it possible to calculate such things as sales commission, discounts, cash discounts, or freight costs. You calculate these values by defining conditions, which are stored and processed in a costing sheet. Conditions can be scaled and made dependent on certain characteristic values. To valuate actual data, you need to define special conditions in CO-PA. For planning data, you can also access conditions from Sales and Distribution (SD) directly.

▶ **User exit valuation**
If your requirements for valuation go beyond the techniques supported in the standard SAP system, you can program your own valuation routines.

▶ **Valuation with transfer prices**

Valuation using transfer prices is only possible for plan data. For detailed information about transfer prices and multiple valuation approaches in the SAP system, review the information available at *http://help.sap.com* associated with profit center accounting.

From the design of a complex product pricing strategy, to calculation of sophisticated transfer pricing and commissions, cost-of-sales accounting, information on units sold and discount calculation, and others, CO-PA valuation can be a complex process. While it can be achieved using any one of the four methods we described, we will concentrate on two primary methods: valuation using material cost estimates and valuation using conditions and costing sheets. Detail on the other two methods is beyond the scope of this book.

Working with Material Cost Estimates

A material cost estimate is an approximate value for a set of parameters to perform valuation using estimates of the data stored to support the cost of goods manufactured calculations and decision making. In this section, we will discuss the **Set Up Valuation Using Material Cost Estimate** menu. Figure 5.32 shows the different submenus available in this menu.

Material cost estimates are quite useful, especially when calculating the cost of goods manufactured or to specifically extract information using a set of parameters that control the behavior and determine the data to be read called *costing keys*. Notice in Figure 5.32 that you can assign costing keys to product, material type, and characteristics, and it is possible, for example, to access "the cost values for only product AB or only the costs for product type HEAVY MATERIAL" to valuate your data. So, with this function, you determine which cost estimates from product cost planning should be used to valuate actual or planning data in CO-PA.

We will help you understand how to utilize and understand the logic behind the various menu options; any discussion beyond that, however, is outside of the scope of this book.

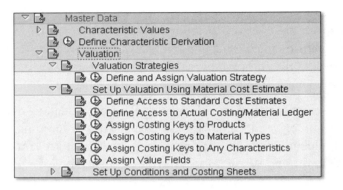

Figure 5.32 Review of the Valuation and Material Cost Estimate Menus

Now, let us explore the steps to creating and defining material cost estimates:

1. First, you need to define the costing keys. To do so, select the **Define Access to Standard Cost Estimates** object, shown in Figure 5.32. Figure 5.33 shows the **Change View "Costing Key": Overview** screen that appears.

2. Click on the **New Entries** button.

3. Enter "This is a Costing Key" into the **Name** column, and specify a **Cstg key** value of "1," as shown in Figure 5.33.

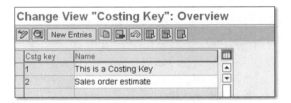

Figure 5.33 Creating a New Costing Key

4. Double-click on **This is a Costing Key** to access the screen shown in Figure 5.34.

   This screen contains a large number of configuration options for the costing key. The main component is the first area called **Determine material cost estimate** that has two options based on CO-PC: **Transf. standard cost estimate** and **Transfer sales order cost estimate**. The first option requires a definition of where the system will find the material cost estimate. With the second option the system uses the cost estimate information stored in the sales order item (already created), simplifying the selection.

Tip

You can only transfer a sales order cost estimate to CO-PA if it was created using material costing. Unit cost estimates cannot be transferred to CO-PA.

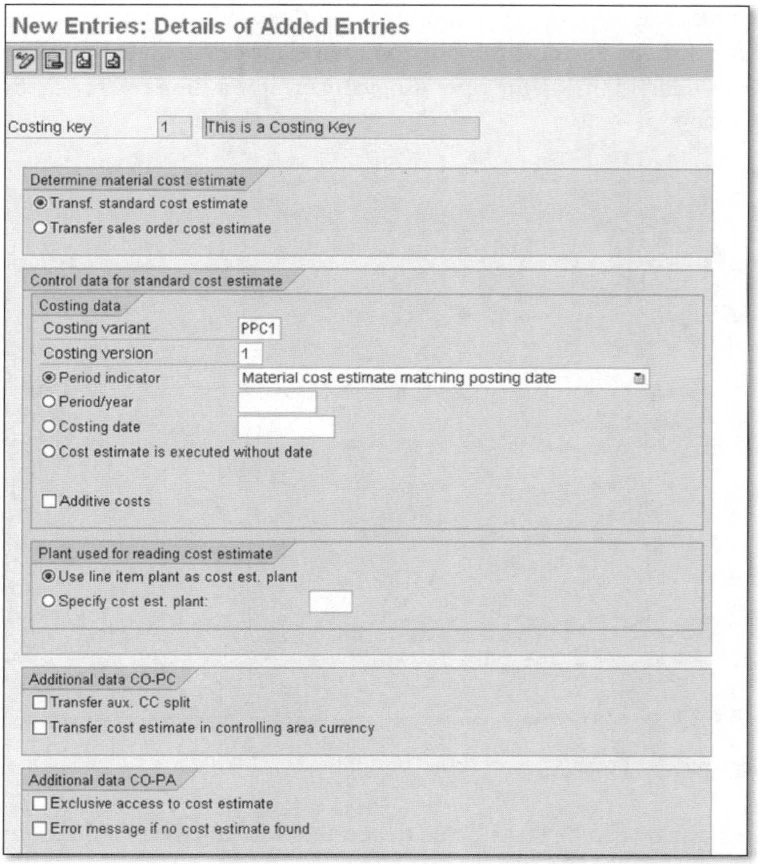

New Entries: Details of Added Entries

Costing key   1   This is a Costing Key

Determine material cost estimate
⦿ Transf. standard cost estimate
◯ Transfer sales order cost estimate

Control data for standard cost estimate

Costing data
  Costing variant   PPC1
  Costing version   1
  ⦿ Period indicator   Material cost estimate matching posting date
  ◯ Period/year
  ◯ Costing date
  ◯ Cost estimate is executed without date

  ☐ Additive costs

Plant used for reading cost estimate
  ⦿ Use line item plant as cost est. plant
  ◯ Specify cost est. plant:

Additional data CO-PC
☐ Transfer aux. CC split
☐ Transfer cost estimate in controlling area currency

Additional data CO-PA
☐ Exclusive access to cost estimate
☐ Error message if no cost estimate found

Figure 5.34 Configuring a Costing Key

5. Review the remaining information presented in Figure 5.34, and then click on the save icon. Remember, you must correctly follow the specifications created in CO-PC to configure how the costing keys will extract the information, but again, this issue goes beyond the scope of this book.

When your sales quantities in CO-PA are valuated using periodic allocation prices or actual cost estimates from the material ledger, which typically occurs at the period end during revaluation, another type of costing keys needs to be configured using the **Define Access to Actual Costing/Material**

Ledger option in the IMG path **Profitability Analysis • Master Data • Valuation • Set up Valuation Using Material Cost Estimate**, shown earlier in Figure 5.32.

This takes you to the screen shown in Figure 5.35, where you can specify to periodically update the information coming from the CO-PC module using a **Valu. Fld Allocation for Periodic Moving Average Price** to calculate the value assigned to a value field inside the operating concern for a time reference, in this case **001/2009**.

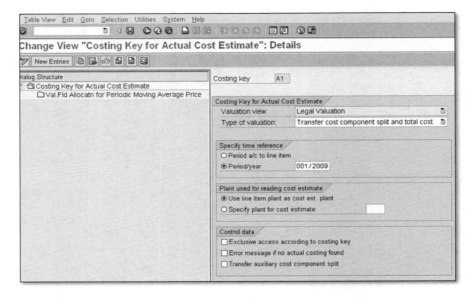

Figure 5.35 Configuring a Costing Key for Actual Cost Estimate

This type of allocation can be transferred depending on the type of valuation:

▶ The complete detail information and totals (transfer cost component split and total cost).

▶ Either total detail or totals depending on what is available (transfer cost component split or total cost)

▶ Only the total cost

What this does is access the information configured inside CO-PC in the **Actual Costing/Material Ledger** menus, as shown in Figure 5.36. That is, we are trying to extract data from CO-PC and use it in CO-PA.

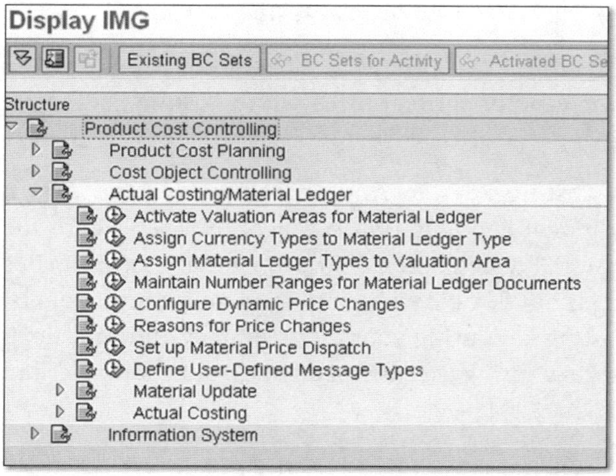

Figure 5.36 Origin of the Data Extracted Using the Costing Keys with Material Ledger

Once you have configured the costing keys information and decided which rules control the data extraction of the different materials from CO-PC, it is time to assign them to our operating concern.

> **Tip**
>
> The system applies the costing keys as long as valuation is active, evaluates the information, and transfers the values as configured.

As shown earlier in Figure 5.32, four types of assignments can be made using the newly configured costing keys:

- **Assign Costing Keys to Products**
- **Assign Costing Keys to Material Types**
- **Assign Costing Keys to Any Characteristics**
- **Assign Value Fields**

You can assign a maximum of three costing keys to control the behavior of products and materials. All of the costing key assignments available in CO-PA valuation require a standard definition of parameters:

- **PV:** Controls how the actual data information will be transferred — real time, periodic, manual, or automatic.
- **Record Type (RecT):** Defines what kind of information will be transferred — incoming sales order, direct postings from FI, order/project settlements, single trans. costing, billing data, and order-rel. project.

- ▶ **Plan Version:** Standard requirement to determine the scenario.
- ▶ **Assignment:** Material, product, or characteristic.
- ▶ **Validity:** Determines the validity period during which costing keys apply to a particular object.

The components **Assign Costing Keys to Any Characteristics** and **Assign Value Fields** require additional configuration settings. In cases where the product-dependent or material-dependent callup of material cost estimates in product cost accounting is not flexible enough to meet your requirements, you can determine the costing keys using your own "strategy" for the "flexible assignment of costing keys" using user-defined tables, table lookups, and customer enhancements.

> **Note**
>
> We will not discuss these flexible assignments in more detail as they are similar to those reviewed in the section on characteristic derivation and derivation steps.

Note, however, that for **Assign Value Fields**, an additional parameter called cost component structure is required that comes from CO-PC. In CO-PC, the cost component structure determines how the results of material costing are updated. The cost component structure groups the costs for each material according to cost component (such as material costs, internal activities, external activities, and overhead). If the material is used in the production of another material, the cost component split (which breaks down the costs according to material costs, internal activities, external activities, overhead, and so forth) remains in the system when the costs are rolled up.

As shown in Figure 5.37, it is possible to determine whether some value fields in the operating concern store cost component structures, such as raw materials, overhead, energy, and fixed or variable costs. The **F/V** column shows whether the cost component is fixed (F) or variable (V).

The concept of material cost estimates is a key strategic and operational challenge by itself, and it requires a high level of organization and is highly company specific. It is recommended to maintain a clear definition and control of the costing keys because they can dramatically affect the profitability decisions over a product or material, especially if three costing keys control the final output of the cost associated. Also, remember that the functionality of valuation must be activated in both the CO-PC and CO-PA modules so that these processes can be executed successfully. Next, let us take a look at working with conditions and costing sheets.

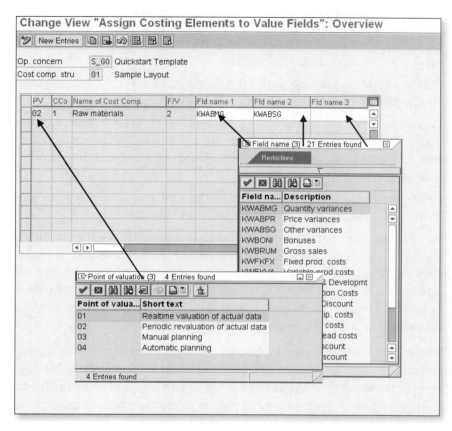

Figure 5.37 Assigning Value Fields in Valuation

Working with Conditions and Costing Sheets

The conditions technique in CO-PA lets you calculate fictitious values that are needed in CO-PA for analyzing contribution margins but are not known at the time the original document is posted. In particular, this makes it possible to calculate sales commissions, cash discounts, other discounts, or freight costs for a sales document that is not yet posted or its complete information is not yet available. This function is useful for planning or estimating future cash flows or profitability by customer or other types of analysis.

Conditions are used to calculate values based on any number of criteria (such as the quantity sold, the product sold, or the customer who bought the product), and you can define CO-PA-specific costing sheets for valuating data in CO-PA. You do this using the same basic functions as those for defining pricing procedures in SD.

To work with conditions, follow this high-level sequence of steps:

1. Identify the line items' characteristics and value fields you want to use for valuation.

2. Define a condition table to select the characteristics, the criteria to generate the valuation, and the validity periods for these rules.

3. Create the condition types and costing sheets to control the rules controlling different calculation procedures, such as prices, surcharge or reduction, base condition type, cash discount from customer master, and other condition types.

4. Define the access sequences that control the relationship between the condition table and the value fields that will store the data.

5. Use pricing reports to define the screen layout for analyzing condition records according to different criteria. However, because they are basically ABAP programs, pricing reports are not discussed because they fall outside the scope of this book. In addition, the options used in valuation can be accessed in the Planning Framework to affect the values of your planning and actual data using a standard layout.

We will now review the concepts behind performing valuation using costing sheets and conditions in more detail. First, Figure 5.38 shows the different components available in the menu **Set Up Conditions and Costing Sheets**. You will recognize several of the components from the previous list.

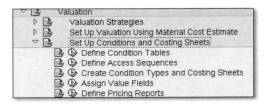

Figure 5.38 Conditions and Costing Sheets Menu

Defining Condition Tables

Condition records in CO-PA are stored in CO-PA-specific *condition tables* whose key consists of specific combinations of characteristic values. Each condition table represents a different combination of characteristics and can be used by any number of conditions. (Different conditions may depend on the same characteristics, such as customer and product, in the same system.)

The key of the condition table consists of those characteristics that make up the key of the condition record. You can use all of the characteristics in Profitability Analysis — in all operating concerns — in the keys for condition tables. Thus if you have, for example, two different characteristics that have the same text in different operating concerns, both of these characteristics appear in the field catalog. The fact that they have the same texts suggests that a double entry exists.

You should only use characteristics from the same operating concern in a condition table. You can use the function "field attributes" to display the corresponding data element for a characteristic in the field catalog. By comparing this data element with the data element stored in table CE1xxxx (xxxx = operating concern) for that characteristic, you can see which operating concern the field belongs to.

To create a condition table, proceed as follows:

1. Specify a number between 501 and 999.

2. Enter a name for the condition table and double-click on the characteristics you want to use for the key.

3. Generate the table.

If desired, you can limit the period of validity of the condition table. If you do, all of the condition records in this table are stored with this period of validity. The table must be a *transparent table* (table type "T").

Steps to define a condition table:

1. As was shown in Figure 5.38, click on the **Define Condition Tables** option. Type the value between 501-999 for the table number.

2. Select **Condition • Create** from the menu to access the screen shown in Figure 5.39 and press **Enter**.

   In this screen, you can select the fields on the right and move them to the left using drag and drop. The end result is shown with **Business Area** and **CustomerHierarchy03**.

3. When you're finished, click on the generate icon (the circle split in quarters) or press [Shift] + [F4].

4. The system asks you to confirm whether you want to generate the condition table. Click on the **Yes** button to confirm and configure the required customization request to generate the object or create it as a local object.

Change Condition Table for Profitability Anal. : Field Overview

Technical view | Other description | Field attributes...

Table 501 Bus. Area/CustHier03

☑ With validity period
☑ with release status

Selected fields	FieldCatlg
Long Key Word	Long Key Word
Business Area	ABC Indicator
CustomerHierarchy03	Aircraft type
	Area
	Billing Type
	Brand
	Business Area
	Business field
	Company Code
	Controlling Area

Figure 5.39 Creating a Condition Table

5. Finally, the system confirms that AXXX table was generated (where the XXX is the table number), and that the reports and screens are marked for generation and activated.

Next, we will look at access sequences, which are components required to execute condition tables.

Tip

Condition tables can only be accessed by the SD application type "V."

Defining Access Sequences

In this step, you define *access sequences* for your condition types in CO-PA. You must assign an access sequence to each condition type for which you create condition records. The access sequence determines the condition tables in which the system should search for valid condition records for the condition type. Thus the access sequence is a sort of directory that tells the system where condition records for that condition type are stored.

To create an access sequence:

1. Access the path **Profitability Analysis • Master Data • Valuation • Set Up Conditions and Costing Sheets • Define Access Sequences**, and click on the execute icon.

2. The screen shown in Figure 5.40 appears. Click on the change/modify icon, and enter a name of "Z112" and a short description of "This is an Access Sequence" for the sequence.

3. In the **Tab** column, specify which condition tables to use to access condition records, and in the **No** column, specify the order in which these condition tables should be read. For example, in Figure 5.40, condition table **502** is the first condition table in the **Access sequence Z112**, as indicated by the entry **1** in the **No.** column.

4. On the left-hand side of the screen, select **Accesses**, and specify the field contents (characteristics) with which they are read.

5. Click on the save icon to save your access sequence.

In our example, the access sequence **Z112** looks for condition records that exist for a certain combination specified in the condition table. If no records are found, the system then looks for a data record for the next condition table, if any, defined in the sequence of events shown in Figure 5.40.

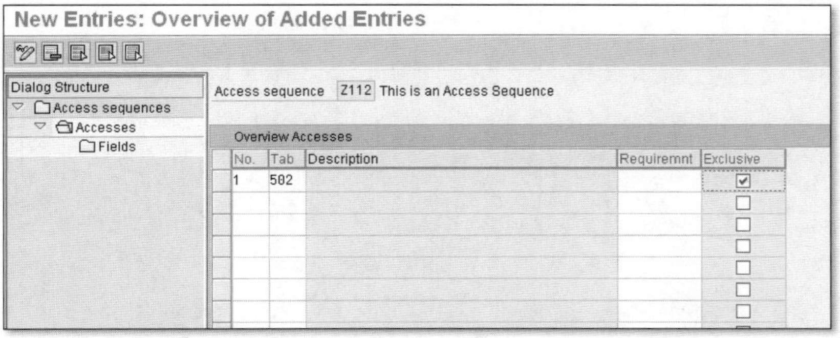

New Entries: Overview of Added Entries

Dialog Structure	Access sequence	Z112	This is an Access Sequence			
▽ ☐ Access sequences						
▽ ⬡ Accesses	Overview Accesses					
☐ Fields	No.	Tab	Description	Requiremnt	Exclusive	
	1	502			☑	
					☐	
					☐	
					☐	
					☐	
					☐	

Figure 5.40 Defining an Access Sequence

You can assign saved access sequences to condition types and create condition records. To be able to make the assignment, when creating your access sequence you must generate a work request in the screen **Cluster Maintenance: Data VVC_T682_KE**.

Next, in the following section, let us look at defining condition types.

Defining Condition Types

If you access the IMG path **Valuation • Set Up Condition and Costing Sheets • Create Condition Types and Costing Sheets**, you will see the information shown in Figure 5.41. There are two areas on the left side:

▶ **Condition types**
Defined in the upper left area, used to generate the calculations of values for prices, surcharges, cash discounts, and others based on different criteria.

▶ **Costing sheets**
Defined in the lower left area, and are part of the **Pricing procedures** used to generate values based on different levels to generate totals.

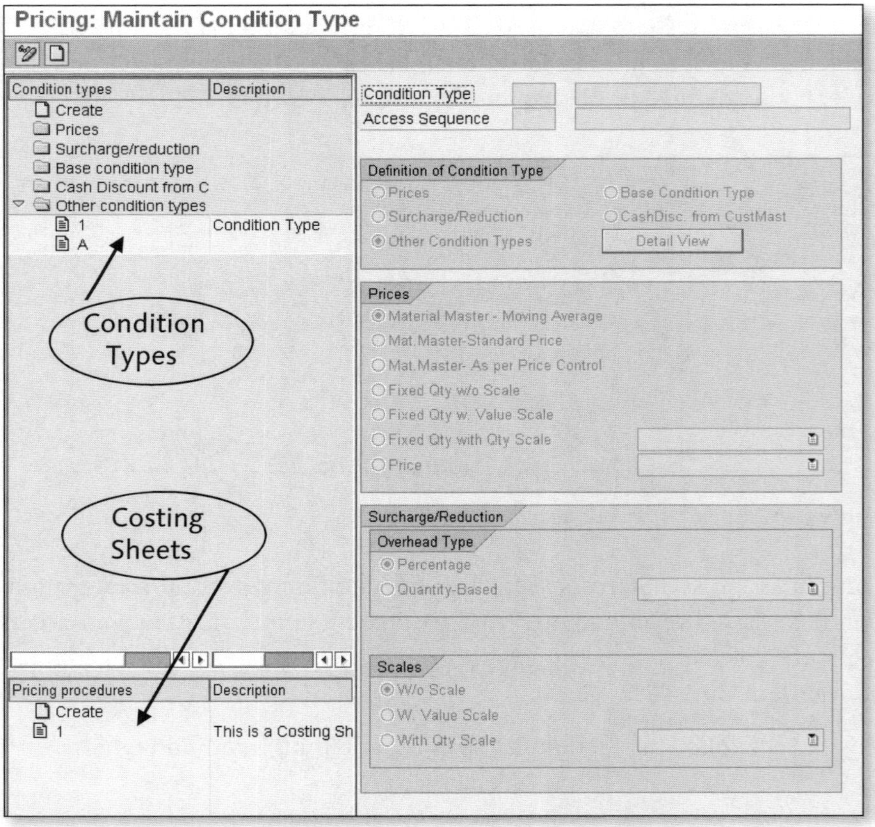

Figure 5.41 Maintaining Condition Types

When working with condition types, you must specify in the upper left area the access sequences that need to be used for the system to find the required characteristics that limit the data extraction to generate the new values. For example, you can generate a condition type that controls the price calculation based on the information coming from MM using moving average based on customer group and material type from the access sequence.

Further, when creating a condition type, you can define the **Overhead Type** as a **Percentage** or a **Quantity-Based** field assigned to specific value fields that will be filled out.

Defining Costing Sheets

To access costing sheets, follow this path: **Profitability Analysis • Master Data • Valuation • Set Up Conditions and Costing Sheets • Create Condition Types and Costing Sheets.** As mentioned previously, to generate costing sheets you must use the lower left area shown in Figure 5.41:

1. Click on the create icon to start the process of generating a pricing procedure associated with the costing sheet.

2. As shown in Figure 5.42, enter "1" as the name for the pricing procedure, and "This is a Costing Sheet" as its description.

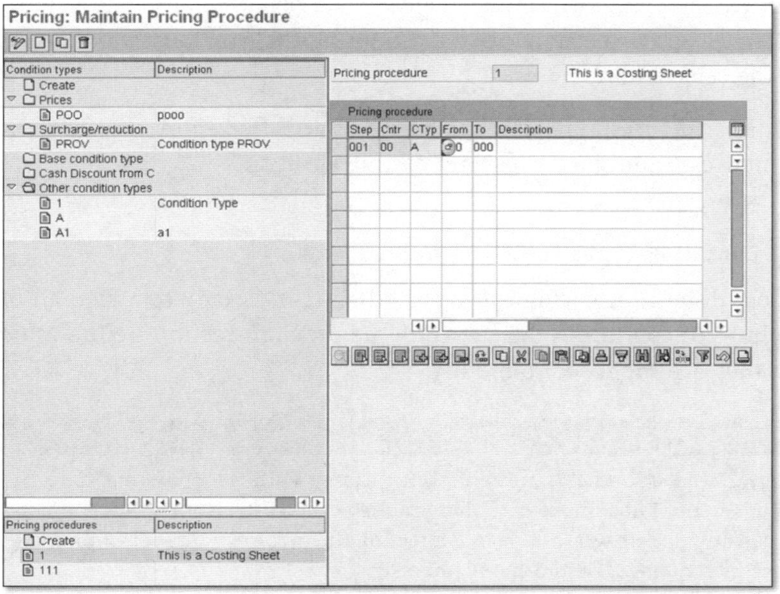

Figure 5.42 Maintain Pricing Procedure Screen

The pricing procedure requires that you specify information in five columns:

- ▶ **Step:** Determines the number in the condition sequence.
- ▶ **Centr:** Condition counter that accesses the step in the pricing procedure.
- ▶ **Ctyp:** The condition type is used for different functions. In pricing, for example, the condition type lets you differentiate between different kinds of discount; in output determination, between different output types, such as order confirmation or delivery note; in batch determination, between different strategy types
- ▶ **From:** Value of which is the basis for percentage surcharges.
- ▶ **To**: Condition step up to which the condition values of the previous steps are totaled. Percentage surcharges are calculated on the basis of the total.
- ▶ **Description:** Lets you provide a description for the process executed in the step.

3. Save your work by clicking on the save icon.

The anticipated costs generated with a costing sheet can be used later in the creation of a valuation strategy (to be discussed shortly). In summary, a costing sheet establishes the link between the different condition types and allows and generates different types of data in a predefined sequence of events. For example, first we can calculate surcharge reductions and cash discounts, then generate the new price considering the previous two components for the selected line items.

The next step is determining which value fields are affected by the different access sequences, condition types, and costing sheets.

Assigning Condition Types to CO-PA Value Fields

You are now done configuring rules and criteria, and ready to assign all of the procedures or conditions developed in the previous sections to the value fields that they are supposed to modify.

> **Note**
>
> Remember, CO-PA value fields are directly associated with the operating concern that contains them. Thus, make sure that you have the correct operation concern set up as current in your system to avoid affecting the incorrect data sets with conditions, access sequences, and other elements.

Also, remember that all of these configuration settings make the calculation automatic, and unless you are aware that a value field is affected by a predefined number of conditions, values, and calculations it is not that easy to see or realize. Also, recall that we are trying to valuate using conditions and costing sheets, meaning that all of the information is not yet posted or not available in the SAP ERP ECC 6.0 system to make the decisions. We are trying to provide a good estimate to make decisions accordingly.

In this IMG Activity, you assign the CO-PA condition types you have defined to the corresponding value fields. This determines which condition types are used to value those value fields. For example, you can assign condition type **DISC** (discounts) to a value field **VVPRD** (price reduction). The field names are filled automatically. However, if two condition types are applied to the same value field, the values of the two conditions are generated and the displayed value is the sum of the two executed procedures. This is true even if the conditions come from different costing sheets in the valuation strategy.

To assign value fields, start out by using the IMG path **Profitability Analysis • Master Data • Valuation • Set Up Conditions and Costing Sheets • Assign Value Fields** to access the screen presented in Figure 5.43.

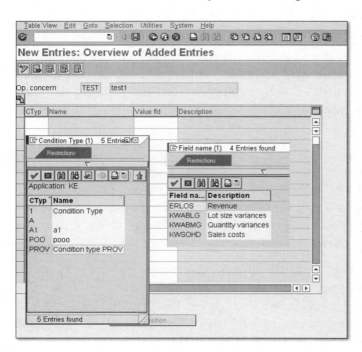

Figure 5.43 Overview of Added Entries Screen

Notice that the assignment requires using a default operating concern, in this case **TEST**. You also need to assign a costing type and then select a value field (in the **Value fld** column), as shown in Figure 5.43.

Notice that in the **Condition Type** window there is a name on the top of the window called **Application: KE**, this notation identifies all applications or components of Profitability Analysis within SAP ERP ECC 6.0. In valuation steps that use a costing sheet (conditions), the application ID determines which application the costing sheet being used comes from. The ID for costing sheets created in Profitability Analysis (actual and plan) is "KE;" the ID "V" is for costing sheets created in the SD. You can only use these costing sheets in planning in CO-PA, but if you want to use product costing or a user exit in a valuation step, do not enter a costing sheet for that step.

By linking condition types and value fields, you complete the automatic calculation of the values that you want to estimate inside the SAP ERP ECC 6.0 platform. Also, remember that because the value fields are directly related to the contents of the operating concern, only those objects created or assigned to the operating concern are visible. For example, in the **TEST** operating concern, only the **Revenue, Lot size variances, Quantity variances, and Sales costs** are available for assignment, as shown in Figure 5.43.

Now you can assign the elements of cost component structure from CO-PC to value fields inside your operating concern. Notice that for each point of valuation it is necessary to maintain value field assignments in CO-PA. With this, it is possible to divide the cost components into fixed and variable parts using as many as required (n:1), and then add them together in the value field.

When valuating multiple cost estimates simultaneously, the values of the cost components within the same cost estimate are aggregated and then entered in one CO-PA value field. The value fields with previous cost estimates are not changed by a later cost estimate. Therefore, a value has to be assigned in Customizing so that the values of different cost estimates are entered in different sets of value fields.

It is possible to assign up to six different value fields from your operating concern to a cost component in the cost component structure. These value fields are identified as fields one through six. Finally, different value field assignments are important, especially when you are interested in applying multiple valuation using different cost estimates.

> **Tip**
>
> Only six cost estimates can be transferred simultaneously from CO-PC to Profitability Analysis.

Valuation Strategies

We have now reviewed both the **Set up Valuation Using Material Cost Estimate**, and **Set Up Conditions and Costing Sheets** options of the **Valuation** menu in CO-PA. The question that arises, however, is what happens if you want to valuate by combining information from both options for more sophisticated scenarios?

The answer lies in *valuation strategies*. Valuation strategies allow not only access to CO-PA application components KE, but also to SD elements using the V application that enable access to condition sheets defined in each environment. Note that this is not allowed for valuation of actual data, because there the SD conditions are transferred directly from the billing document or sales order as defined in the value field assignments of the SD interface. If you use an SD pricing procedure for valuation in planning, the system transfers the values of the conditions to the value fields as assigned in the SD interface.

Under certain circumstances, it may not be possible to use all conditions from SD to valuate data in CO-PA. For example, the access sequences used in the SD pricing procedures may contain condition tables with fields that are not defined as CO-PA characteristics. Consequently, before using an SD pricing procedure, be sure to check whether the fields required by the access sequence are defined as characteristics in your operating concern. Otherwise, the system will not find the condition records, even if they have been maintained in SD.

A valuation strategy requires specifying either a costing sheet (or the appropriate application class), a material cost estimate, a user exit, or a transfer price variant together with the corresponding CO-PA value field.

To work with valuation strategies follow these steps:

1. Access valuation strategies by following this path: **Profitability Analysis • Master Data • Valuation • Valuation Strategies • Define and Assign Valuation Strategy**.

2. Click on the object's execute icon to see the screen displayed in Figure 5.44.

You'll notice that there are several elements that are similar to those we have previously reviewed, such as **Sequence**, **Appl**, **Costg sheet**, **Mat. cstg**, and **Qty field**. In the screen shown in Figure 5.44 you can access the costing sheets, quantity fields, and value fields in CO-PA (KE) or SD (V). In addition, a checkmark in the column **Mat. cstg** informs you that it is possible to perform valuation using a material cost estimate by defining a quantity field.

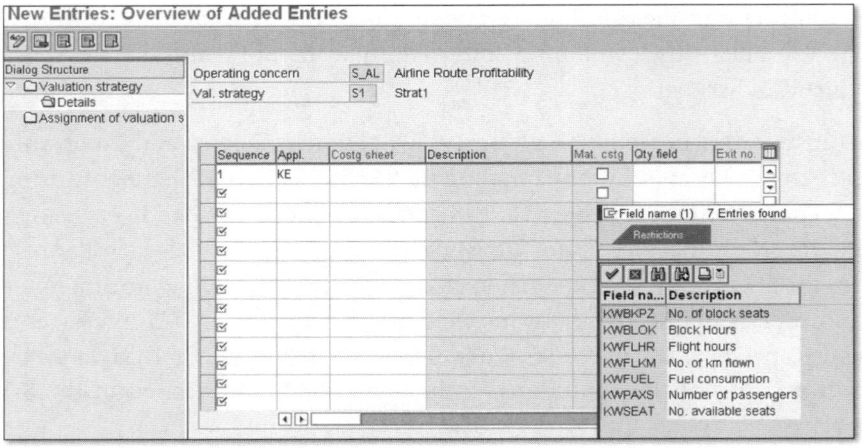

Figure 5.44 Creating a Valuation Strategy

3. Once you have finished configuring the information shown in Figure 5.44, select the next node called **Assignment of valuation strategy** as shown in Figure 5.45.

4. **Assignment of valuation strategy** is where you decide the type of PV (method of update). All application functions that transfer data to CO-PA are assigned to one of these PVs. For external data transfers, PVs 01 and 03 are used for actual and plan data, respectively.

Tip
In CO-PA there are four PVs: 01 real-time valuation of actual data, 02 periodic valuation of actual data, 03 manual planning, and 04 automatic planning.

5. Notice that there are four basic columns in Figure 5.45: **PV** for point of valuation, **Rec.** for record type or document type, **Plan ver.** for plan version to use in planning, and **Val. strat.** to represent the valuation strategy to assign for the process. If a valuation strategy calls for valuation using material costing, the system uses the point of valuation to control which

cost estimate is read and how the cost components are assigned to value fields in CO-PA.

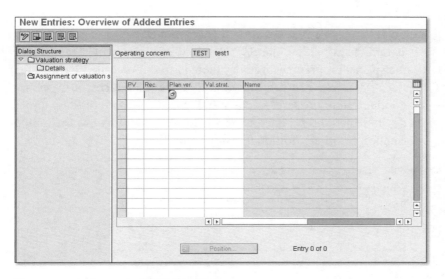

Figure 5.45 Assignment of Valuation Strategy

> **Tip**
>
> The plan version enables you to keep two or more sets of data for the same object. You can maintain and evaluate several plan versions at the same time. For example, you can specify the type of assumption for the forecast (optimistic, pessimistic), when the plan was created (original plan, updated forecast), or how binding the plan is.

6. Determine the record type in the column **Rec.**, shown in Figure 5.45. There are basically five types of record types or document types that CO-PA can affect:

   ▸ **A**: Incoming sales orders

   ▸ **B**: Direct posting from FI

   ▸ **C**: Order/project settlement

   ▸ **E**: Single transaction costing

   ▸ **F**: Billing data

7. In the column **Plan ver.**, select a planning version to use.

8. Finally, select the **Val. strat.** column to assign the valuation strategy that will affect the chosen record types and the previously selected quantity and value fields.

In addition, you can also create your own customizable CO-PA exits with ABAP programs using either the SAP standard enhancement (**Transaction CMOD**) or a special program. Moreover, there is an option called **Variant for TP** (Transfer Prices) in the screen shown in Figure 5.46, which you access by scrolling to the right in the screen shown in Figure 5.44. Both of these topics are outside the scope of this book, however, so you should review the online SAP information or other additional materials on them.

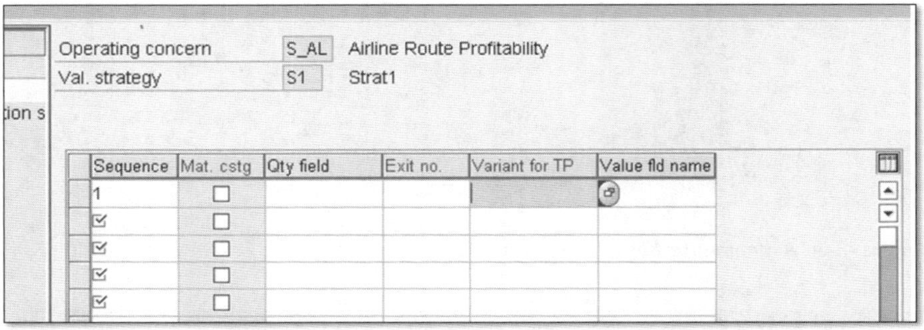

Figure 5.46 Reviewing the Variant for TP Column

> **Note**
>
> Valuation is the generation of different layers of information that are controlled by rules and restrictions. These predefined procedures are ABAP programs that give users flexibility without the need of coding.

To help us summarize the concept of valuation, the logic behind it is simplified in Figure 5.47 in a flow chart that describes each of the steps discussed in this section:

1. First, the **Original Line Items (Raw SAP Data from SAP ERP ECC 6.0)** are identified and it is determined how valuation would be applied.

2. Then, **Condition Tables** are created to predefine the criteria to use to perform the valuation.

3. **Condition Tables** are later on organized in a logic using access sequences that require **Condition Types** to define the table of valuation to perform.

4. **Costing Sheets** take the information from **Access Sequences** and **Condition Types** to control how the conditions are executed.

5. Both **Costing Sheets** and **Condition Types** can be assigned to control the information contained inside the predefined **Value Fields** or **Valuation Strategies**.

6. **Valuation Strategies** allow being more specific about the type of records (billing, sales order, posting from FI, etc.) that are affected by the different conditions specified.

7. **Value Fields** are the ultimate goal of assignment of valuation because they identify the fields that are affected by the different rules or conditions that affect the data and value estimation displayed on the user's screen.

8. Finally, all definitions that affect and are assigned to value fields are automatically executed in the user environment and their effects can be seen in line items as **New Generated Values**.

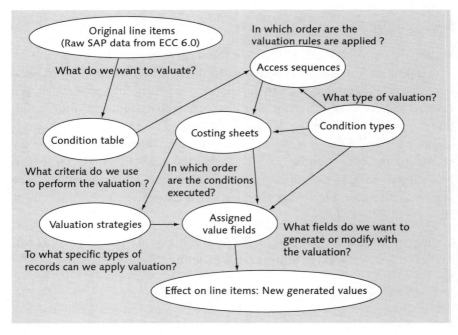

Figure 5.47 Flow Chart for the Concept of Valuation

A final note: valuation and derivation are quite powerful if used correctly; however, avoid using either of these methods if your project does not demand complex selection criteria and multiple relationships of variables.

Also, for simpler requirements, some of the capabilities discussed in the Master Data menu for CO-PA can be performed using the CO-PA planning framework, as we'll discuss next in Chapter 6. For complex implementations that require many relationships, valuation can, however, come in handy (as we said earlier, instead of creating and configuring different large number of objects in the SAP BW/SAP NetWeaver BI environment).

> **Note**
>
> As a Best Practice, we suggest avoiding the use of automatically calculated procedures that run in the background, such as costing keys, valuation, and derivation because it is difficult to identify original values from those generated. For this reason, we feel it is best to work with the CO-PA Planning Framework, which lets you control each component affecting your data. You can also review what went wrong, in case you detect any errors that can be easily corrected using the same objects. More on this in the next chapter.

5.3 Summary

Master data can be used to improve the data manipulation inside CO-PA with automatic calculation procedures. In this chapter, we briefly reviewed how to create hierarchies for use in reporting and planning applications. We covered the creation of derivation rules to generate additional information that can be inferred based on the current data, and we reviewed the concepts of valuation and valuation strategies to generate automatic calculations for estimating the cost of goods sold. Note that the goal of this chapter was to provide you with an overall overview of the functionalities available in the **Master Data** menu, but realize that this doesn't mean you need to use them all.

In Chapter 6, we will explore the CO-PA planning framework, an application similar to SAP NetWeaver BI Integrated Planning (IP) and BPS.

The CO-PA planning framework is the environment that lets you create planning applications without leaving the R/3 or SAP ERP ECC 6.0 environment. CO-PA planning provides powerful functionalities similar to those provided by the Integrated Planning (IP) or the Business Planning and Simulation (BPS) tools in SAP NetWeaver Business Intelligence (BI)/SAP Business Warehouse (BW).

6   Introduction to CO-PA Planning

In this chapter we will review the CO-PA planning framework, the interface created with the OLTP environment for R/3 or SAP ERP ECC 6.0 to create planning applications. Like other SAP system modules, the CO-PA planning framework uses a top-bottom approach to clearly define the data sets used as part of the planning application. We'll start our discussion by giving you an overview of the CO-PA planning framework.

> **Note**
>
> You might not need to implement or use any of the components described in this chapter due to the flexibilities that CO-PA provides to connect to other applications such as SAP NetWeaver BI or SAP BW. Thus, you might only need to transfer a piece of Sales and Distribution (SD) information into CO-PA and then move that information into SAP NetWeaver BI to complete the planning by including Materials Management (MM) information.
>
> Whatever model your team has decided to approach your planning needs, make sure that this model is written down on a piece of paper somewhere, your managers know about it, and that the financial reporting of your firm is protected.

6.1   Overview

Profitability planning is likely a part of any yearly activities for every corporation in the world. Depending on its size, a company must estimate, forecast, or develop scenarios for different areas. Profit and sales planning in CO-PA can also be extended to consider elements such as Materials Requirements Planning (MRP), capacity planning, and any other elements that you can extract information from in the OLTP system, and transfer it into CO-PA and other systems. However, often planning efforts toward quantification or estimation of possible expenses and revenues using data in the SAP system don't become clear until you are actually developing scenarios and sharing them with other people. Also, when working on a project, it is always good to concentrate on "discovering" the system the client requires first and then focusing on the details when the actual application needs to be created. That is, you should simplify the requirements for decision makers, regardless of the complexity of the operations to perform.

> **Note**
>
> CO-PA planning might require you to combine information coming from different data sources from inside and outside SAP systems, and sometimes the best approach is creating an environment that even a young student with basic computer skills could use without major difficulty. However, engineers and scientists are often reluctant to simplify their knowledge into common explanations for laymen, so when collecting requirements, you need not only patience, but you also need to make sure you ask the right questions to collect the correct information.

Planning in Profitability Analysis allows you to plan sales, revenue, and profitability data for any selected profitability segments. You can display the entire planning process of your company in different ways, depending on your business demands, without leaving the SAP ERP ECC 6.0 environment. Some of the applications that can be developed within the CO-PA planning framework can be quite sophisticated and allow addressing the most common requirements without the need to use more complex applications, such as SAP NetWeaver BI Integrated Planning, SAP BW-BPS, SEM-BPS, or others.

You may recall from earlier discussions that CO-PA works and interacts with the OLTP environment (transactional) and the changes performed can be viewed by other users using the regular SAP screens. For example, you can perform adjustments to the purchase order information, run the required processes in the CO-PA planning framework, and the modifications will display on users' screens without them even noticing the processes performed to modify the data.

CO-PA is designed to use revenues and cost data to perform profit and sales planning to produce views that can be assigned to a particular user profile for different roles, such as sales manager, regional manager, sales employee, financial assistants, and others. Distinctions are also often made between the different approaches used, such as central top-down planning and local bottom-up planning

The planning tool in Profitability Analysis offers all of those involved in the planning process a uniform, graphical planning interface that is straightforward. This interface is oriented toward "power users," such as central planning coordinators who model and monitor the planning process, and occasional users (such as sales employees), who only occasionally confirm planning values to make future orders to suppliers, for example.

Because the contents and the level of detail of individual plans vary depending on a person's role and area of responsibility, the CO-PA planning framework allows you to structure planning selectively according to specific planning levels and planning contents. It also allows you to assign the planning structure to individual users. The CO-PA planning structure is represented in a tree hierarchy. From the planning framework, it is possible to execute almost all of the planning functions, from modeling the planning process and monitoring the planning tasks through to manual entry of planning data.

For sales and profit planning, many enterprises have implemented an iterative process consisting of a number of individual planning steps, in which existing planning data is copied, projected into the future, revaluated, adjusted manually, and distributed top-down until they obtain a sales and profit plan that fulfills the enterprise's requirements. For example, automatic methods allow you to produce data automatically for an entire planning application or input data manually into the system. As alternatives to using the standard SAP interface, you can enter planning data locally using Microsoft Excel before loading it centrally into the SAP ERP ECC 6.0 system, or you can enter planning data into the system directly from a corresponding web page.

Another special feature with sales and profit planning is that it is not a "stand-alone component"; that is, it can not only send planning data to other applications but it can also receive planning data from those applications. Accordingly, you have the option, on one hand, of transferring to CO-PA data from Sales and Operations Planning (SOP), from the Logistics Information System (LIS), from internal order planning, and from project planning, and, on the other hand, to transfer planning data to profit center accounting or financial accounting.

Planning is not limited to any specific time frame. This means that you can plan more than one fiscal year at once. In addition, you can plan your data by posting periods or calendar weeks. It is also possible to create and store planning data in different plan versions. This allows you to run planning data versions in parallel (such as an optimistic one and a pessimistic one) for the same object.

The CO-PA planning framework allows you to perform modifications of data behind the scenes for actual and plan data, depending on the origin of the data. It is your job as consultant to determine the best business model to follow to deliver the planning applications to your client and make them simple enough that any person feels comfortable to use them and understand them.

6.2 The Framework of Corporate Planning: Sales and Profit Planning in CO-PA

The ultimate goal of CO-PA is to reflect revenue and costing information from the different components of an SAP system and make this information visible to the decision makers. The most important issue here is having a goal in mind about what you want to achieve, how to achieve it, and what the SAP system has to offer to help you achieve it.

For implementing the CO-PA planning framework, you can either create your own implementation model or follow the ASAP models used in many other implementation projects, but no matter what, it is very important that you have a model in mind. As shown in Figure 6.1, with the CO-PA planning framework, there are always two approaches running parallel to each other. One is strategic planning, and the other the simplified business model that must guide you to clarify the strategy and monitor the implementation.

You start building a simplified business model by collecting the operative knowledge of your business processes stored inside your SAP system. In other words, you need to find out if your system or processes are performing as expected, along with indicators that reflect your strategy is doing things right! To prove this, collect the different elements of your system and specifically select those that deliver the type of information that you need. For example, as shown in Figure 6.1, we will be **collecting the operative knowledge** of the firm by using **Qty** (quantity), **List prices**, **Rebates**, and **Standard costs** to generate our business model.

However, before you conceive your business model, you must link the **departmental goals** to generate an **Operational Budgeting** process, for example. From a strategic point of view, you are not quite clear yet of what you need to do, but your business model thinking tells you that now you need to set up goals and objectives to direct your measures to a common purpose. Finally, the **Strategic Planning** process tells you that linking the strategy and goals will allow you to create planning scenarios directly related to the overall goals of the company.

Using a **Simplified Business Model**, you can deliver what the strategic planning requires because you can combine multiple elements into one model: **Goal-setting**, **Strategy evaluation**, **Simulation**, and **Scenario modeling**. The idea behind this process is to continuously think of ways to slice and dice your final goal because you do not need to achieve your strategy with one single planning model but with multiple small models that interact and perform planning processes independently, with an overall goal in mind.

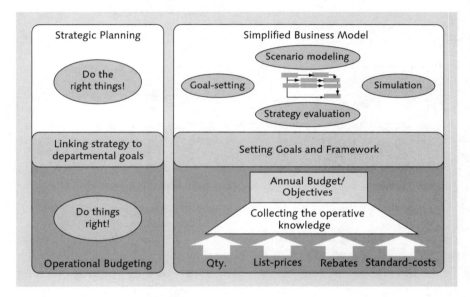

Figure 6.1 The CO-PA Planning Framework

Each of the submodels can be handled with a group or set of indicators that achieve a common purpose and each model can be handled by specific groups of individuals that have access to specific levels of planning, depending on their role in the company. For example, Figure 6.2 provides a general perspective of the concept of planning levels and aggregation, all the way down to a specific set of information that is exactly what our planning applications must deliver to be useful at different levels of our implementation.

Planning at different levels of aggregation means that we can "cascade," for example, the marketing expenses of the overall organization performed by a sales manager, but each of the division managers is limited to plan the expenses based on a specific customer group. If we continue going down in

187

the organization as shown in Figure 6.2, we can plan sales volumes and revenues by customer and product groups that individual sales managers for each division can assign, and at the end generate demand estimates to calculate the cost of goods sold (COGS) by product.

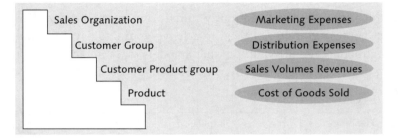

Figure 6.2 Planning at Different Levels of Aggregation

The CO-PA Planning module itself can satisfy most of the planning requirements in most organizations. At the same time, SAP increasingly allows the export of information by creating a data source and performing planning with SAP NetWeaver BI Integrated Planning, SAP BW-BPS, or similar applications outside the traditional SAP ERP ECC 6.0 environment. However, CO-PA also allows interacting in a Microsoft Excel environment, and provides a secure platform to run your simplified planning applications without any need of sophisticated data extraction processes.

The key decision is under what circumstances to stop using CO-PA and instead use the SAP NetWeaver BI environment? Is there a boundary that defines when to stop using one and consider using the other? We will try to answer this question in the next section. Ultimately, however, the decision depends on the required level of complexity of your application and the number of processes that you are interested in performing.

6.3　Planning with CO-PA or SAP NetWeaver BI

When you need to decide which planning environment to use, several elements are required to finalize such a decision. The most important is the level of sophistication of your planning requirements. Table 6.1 provides a relatively simple analysis to help you decide whether CO-PA or the SAP NetWeaver BI platform is the best application to use.

Requirement	Level of complexity	Suggested application	Reason
Need to plan with high volumes of data external to SAP.	High	BI	CO-PA cannot deliver information external to SAP ERP ECC 6.0.
Work with simple operations with data inside the OLTP system.	Medium-Low	CO-PA	Avoid exporting data to perform simple operations available in CO-PA.
Massive data volume with complex multiple planning levels, data transformation, and web interaction.	High	BI or CO-PA	The SAP NetWeaver BI platform allows generating sophisticated reporting and planning operations, and interaction with the enterprise portal. However, CO-PA also allows an interaction with the web environment (but it's not as flexible).
Massive reporting of line-item data that is not included at the segment level.	High	BI or other	CO-PA is not designed to manage this level of detail, and might increase reporting times.
Simple reporting requirements without sophisticated drilldown with data inside the OLTP system.	Medium-Low	CO-PA	CO-PA reporting allows delivering the most common requirements with enough flexibility for low-level planning.
Reporting requirement might increase the number of segment levels, table size, or affect system performance.	High	BI	SAP NetWeaver BI handles high-level data requirements better, especially those that require high-level reporting.

Table 6.1　Comparing CO-PA to SAP NetWeaver BI

Requirement	Level of complexity	Suggested application	Reason
Planning requirements demand simple operations over a low volume of data and characteristics, without the need to share the information on the Web.	Medium-Low	CO-PA	CO-PA planning functions have similar options as those available in SEM-BPS, SAP BW-BPS, and Integrated Planning when planning within the OLTP environment. Summarization levels in CO-PA are good enough to improve system performance.
Planning requirements demand a high level of complexity using data from SAP and non-SAP applications. Summarization levels, Report-Report Interface (RRI), and Report Splitting (RS), discussed in Chapter 12, are not enough to control system performance, and population of segment levels will affect performance.	High	BI	BI is the best platform to integrate, plan, and report data coming from outside an SAP system, but requires multiple object definitions and processes. Complex systems require a detailed level of analysis and performance optimization, and extensive control of the transports moved within and between systems.
Automatic calculations required inside the OLTP system	High	CO-PA	CO-PA allows using valuation strategies to automatically perform calculations inside the OLTP system. Automatic valuation calculations have priority over automatic planning functions in the CO-PA planning framework.

Table 6.1 Comparing CO-PA to SAP NetWeaver BI (cont.)

One of the most important factors that limit CO-PA applications in complex implementations is the reporting of characteristics defined at the segment level with line item data. Drilldown functions in CO-PA are very limited when detailed information is available at the line item level and can only be accessed using Transaction KE23 or the ABAP query tool. However, neither of these tools provide flexible reporting functionalities easily accessible to managers or the end users. This is when SAP NetWeaver BI becomes the best choice. However, CO-PA can be the first choice inside the SAP ERP ECC 6.0

environment for reporting and planning applications that do not demand an extensive level of drilldown functionalities, and satisfies simple slicing-and-dicing of characteristics defined at the segment level that do not require constant modifications to access additional drilldown reporting applications. Generally speaking, if the level of manipulation is high and the number of processes and transformations is high, move to the SAP NetWeaver BI platform immediately.

You can also split your project into pieces, leaving the simple calculations and reporting inside the OLTP environment working with CO-PA, and running the heavy reporting and planning applications in the SAP NetWeaver BI environment using delta updates to transfer the data into SAP NetWeaver BI to extend and finish the transformation. Whichever way you go, your implementation team should be able to make reports and planning applications available to your users depending on their role, and regardless of where they are located.

> **Note**
>
> Splitting projects into pieces works well, especially because not all of the users will require the same level of access and information because their role limits their information need and access. Your implementation team can control which reports are available to end users and can make reports available to a group of users with similar requirements. End users will not even notice if the information comes from SAP NetWeaver BI or the OLTP system.

The level of manipulation required to arrive at a result in CO-PA can be less complex than in SAP NetWeaver BI, because it is simpler to access characteristics that describe a customer or a product in CO-PA compared to having to create complex extraction procedures in SAP NetWeaver BI. Also, complex data manipulation requirements can be eliminated or reduced by using CO-PA assessment cycles that allocate, for example, expenses to profitability analysis characteristics and at the same time allow tracing the method of cost allocation.

Let us now explore in more detail the CO-PA planning framework and its capabilities to deliver customized planning applications within the OLTP environment.

6.4   A First Look at the CO-PA Planning Framework

Applications created with the CO-PA planning framework are quite similar to those delivered in SEM-BPS, SAP NetWeaver BI Integrated Planning, or SAP-BW-BPS. Figure 6.3 provides a general view of the capabilities of the CO-PA planning framework, including manual planning, planning aids, integrated planning, automatic planning functions, and sales and promotions budgets.

There are no real limits to the types of planning possible within CO-PA; as mentioned before, the goal is to quantify revenues and costs of the firm to have an overall view of the operations, whether it is every single component of the balance sheet, or the Profit and Loss (P&L) statements. For example, you can decide to include a planning scenario that controls only how overhead expenses or material management expenses are calculated, and another planning scenario that reflects and plans different strategies that only affect operating profit.

> **Caution**
>
> Whatever your final goal for your planning applications is, remember that you will be interacting within the OLTP system, and thus with real data stored in the SAP ERP ECC 6.0 environment. Therefore, before executing a massive function or modification, be careful to clearly identify the table fields or information that will be modified, and perform multiple tests to make sure that your operations are working as expected.

As shown in Figure 6.3, there are functions that allow you to perform forecasts, revaluations, or valuation-based valuation strategies. However, you do not need to execute or configure all of them at the same time, or use them as part of your planning application. Simply select what is applicable and see every operation as an independent process. For example, you might only be interested in increasing all of your purchase orders by 10%, to be adjusted by inflation using the revaluation function, and then create a forecast using a moving average of the last three periods to have an estimate for a specific company code and controlling areas.

When performing planning, you must also be aware of the type of data that you are working with: plan or actual. For this, you must clearly identify and limit your information when working within the CO-PA planning framework environment using the different planning elements as shown in Figure 6.4. These elements are quite similar to those in SEM-BPS and SAP BW-BPS, and can be described as follows:

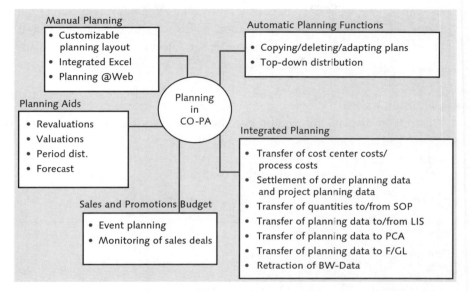

Figure 6.3 Capabilities of the CO-PA Planning Framework

▶ **Planning level**

A *planning level* determines a hierarchy of information that is a general definition of extraction that aggregates or collects specific types of information. For example, you can have one planning level of marketing expenses, another one for operating costs, and another one for balance sheet planning.

▶ **Planning package**

A *planning package* works as a filter of data (in the SAP NetWeaver BI Integrated planning application packages are called filters). Planning packages make the level of planning more specific, such as for a particular fiscal year, business unit, or product line, as long as you have defined the selection criteria to limit the information display and planning operations.

▶ **Planning method**

A *planning method* can be defined as an operation that allows modification of values or display of the data contained inside the OLTP system. For example, the revaluation or valuation functions are planning methods.

▶ **Parameter set**

A *parameter set* allows generating the final specific objects required to perform planning. For example, if you would like to make manual data entries, there is a method that allows you to do just that, and the parameter set defines the layout or environment that will control the data entry.

As you can see, a parameter set is not only an object, but it is also the final element that modifies the information or displays of the data extracted based on the planning level. A parameter set object is controlled by a planning package, which is also required to execute in order for the parameter set to work.

▶ **Definition screen**

This screen displays the required additional definitions to complete the configuration of the parameter set and also displays the final results of your configured methods, either as a spreadsheet or displaying the results of the execution of the method. We will review these functions in more detail later in this chapter.

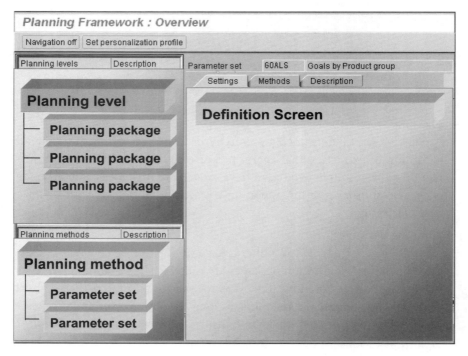

Figure 6.4 CO-PA Planning Framework Components

Figure 6.5 provides an initial overview of the CO-PA planning environment using the IMG Activity menus, with the different components described in Figure 6.4. Also, notice, as shown in Figure 6.5, that there is a graphic indicator that describes the **Status** of the planning package that can be manually controlled; that the different automatic planning functions delivered in CO-PA, which can also be limited by user or application, are all included; and that the definition screen that provides the final display of the operations performed by a specific parameter set is shown.

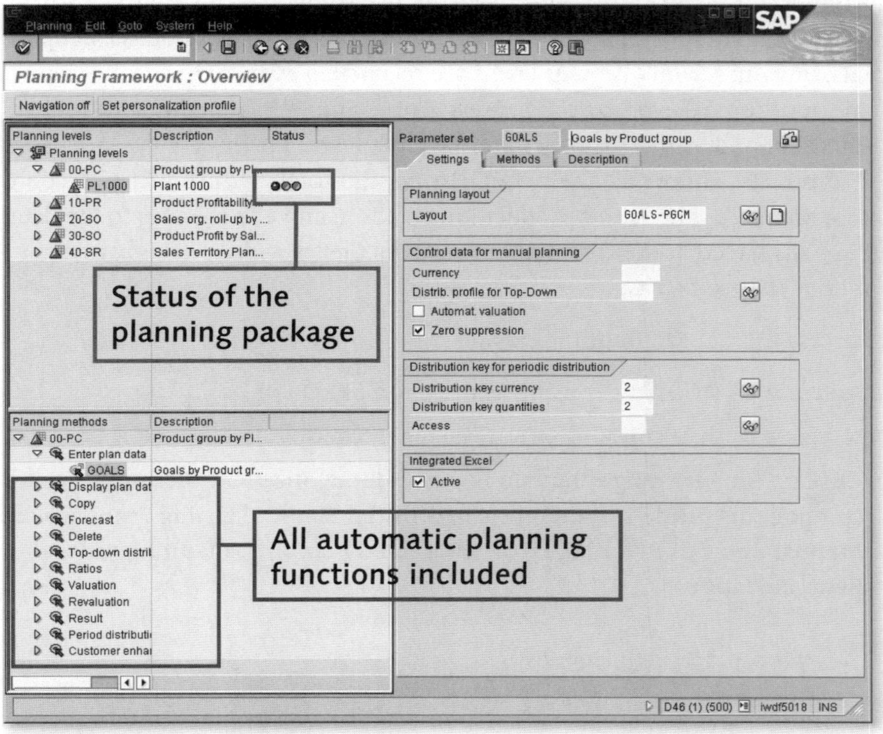

Figure 6.5 General Overview of a CO-PA Planning Screen

Remember, you will make modifications to the data extracted using the operating concern set up as current, and thus the planning levels, packages, and parameter sets created for that particular operating concern. That is, you are not changing any data that you have not chosen to modify or change. This process might be rather tedious but guarantees that the user will plan with specific data within an operating concern, and at the same time guarantees that data will not be changed by accident, and that there is security to control the modifications at any specific time.

Based on Figure 6.4 and Figure 6.5 we can visualize how we can plan at different levels of aggregation within CO-PA. For example, we can plan at the product group, material, or the customer level, but in fact it is possible to plan any profitability segment in CO-PA as long as it has been correctly defined within the operating concern, and make it available following account- or costing-based planning.

An important factor in CO-PA is that the data remains consistent across all levels throughout the planning process, which means that subtotals roll up to totals, or values from different levels are reconciled even if changes are being made at different levels by other users. For example, planned quantities can be first entered at the customer and product level, for three customers and five products. Following the previous rule, the totals by product will coincide with the customer and product information, and any changes to the data will be displayed at the customer and product level with an unassigned customer, if that is the case.

To access the CO-PA **Planning** menu:

1. Access the IMG Activity using Transaction SPRO.

2. Navigate to the **Profitability Analysis** menu shown in Figure 6.6

3. Click on the **Planning** submenu to expand it. Notice that there are several components inside this menu such as **Initial Steps, Planning Framework, Manual Entry of Planning Data, Integrated Planning, Planning Aids**, and **Reorganization**.

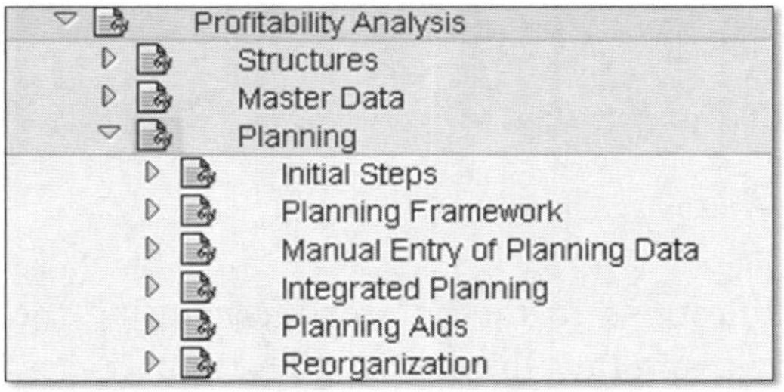

Figure 6.6 Accessing the CO-PA Planning Framework

Now, let us briefly review a common concept required by most financial components in your SAP system: number ranges. Number ranges define how the data will be organized based on a specific set of numbers that control how the different accounts are accessed and what information is displayed in your planning applications.

6.5   Number Ranges for Planning Data

You need to define a number range for updating, for example, plan line items in each of your operating concerns using the path **Controlling • Profitability Analysis • Planning • Initial Steps • Define Number Ranges for Planning Data**. When working with profit planning, the SAP system automatically assigns a number that lies within your selected interval, as shown in Figure 6.7.

> **Note**
>
> To define number ranges, you must have authorization from your system administrator to maintain number ranges. In addition, your operating concern must have been completely defined with characteristics and value fields.

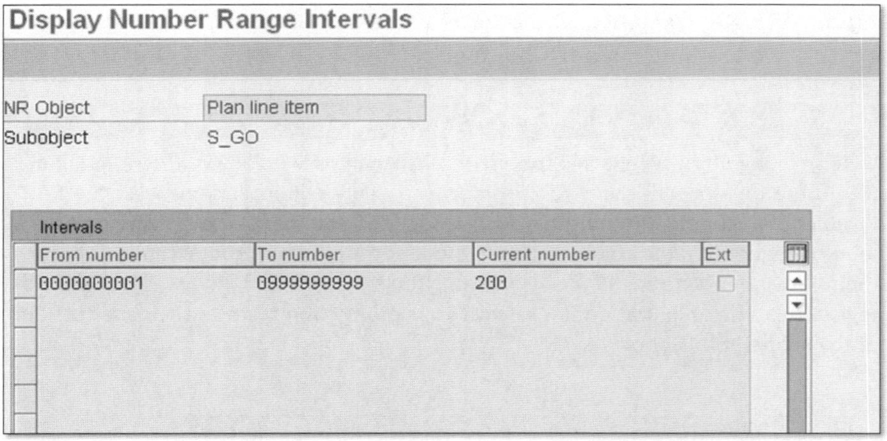

Display Number Range Intervals

| NR Object | Plan line item |
| Subobject | S_GO |

Intervals

From number	To number	Current number	Ext	
0000000001	0999999999	200	☐	

Figure 6.7 Defining Number Ranges

> **Caution**
>
> It is not recommended to transport your predefined number ranges into your production system. Instead, define them manually to avoid any confusion or unexpected changes along the way.

When working with CO-PA planning, you must specify versions to separate data for different purposes. For example, one version can control the data stored inside the operating concern for Sales and Distribution (SD) and another version may control the data that controls the plan data of MM. This definition is achieved using the maintaining versions function, discussed in the next section.

6.6 Maintaining Versions

You also need to define the Controlling (CO) versions you want to use for your operating concern. These versions are valid for all of CO and for all operating concerns. In Profitability Analysis, you can only use versions for plan data. Consequently, the fields **Actual** and **Exclusive use,** shown in Figure 6.9 (you have to scroll to the right to see **Exclusive use**), are not relevant for CO-PA.

Each version has attributes that are only valid for one operating concern, and this information can be accessed following the path shown in Figure 6.8: **Controlling • Profitability Analysis • Planning • Initial Steps • Maintain Versions**.

As shown in Figure 6.9, different checkboxes are displayed, such as **Plan**, **Actual, WIP/RA, Variance**, and other elements that are attributes to the version that we are interested in creating.

Tip
When talking about Work-in-Process/Results Analysis Version (WIP/RA) in Figure 6.9, there are several issues to consider, especially when working with the SAP Production Planning (PP) module. RA is associated with the RA secondary cost element category 31, and these elements are associated with production orders and their movements from Work-in-process items to finished goods. You should review related configuration issues with your production team as they are outside of the scope of this book.

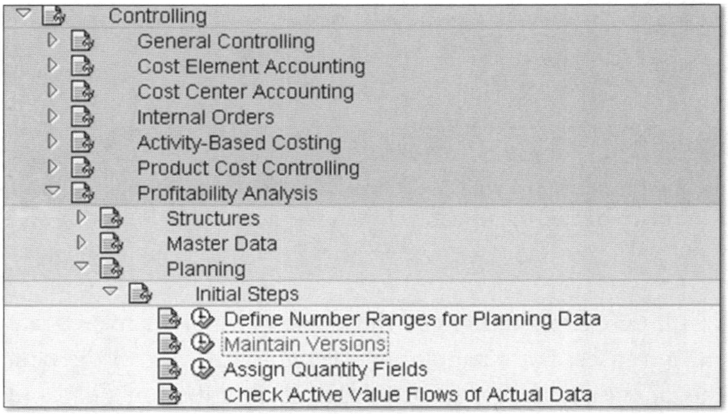

Figure 6.8 Accessing Maintain Versions

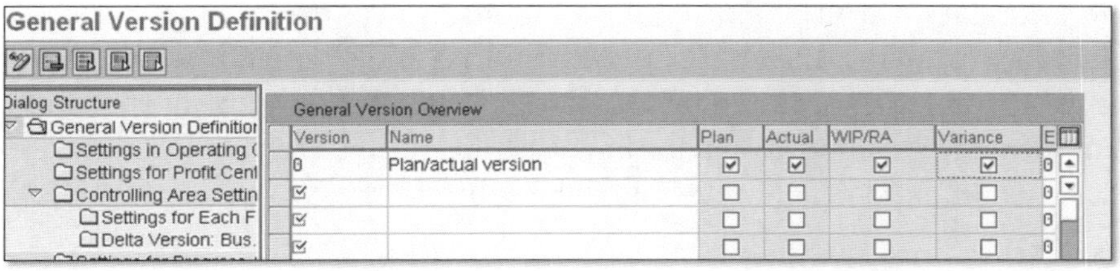

Figure 6.9 Version Attributes

The checkboxes and hierarchy displayed on the left-hand side of the screen shown in Figure 6.9 determine if the version is locked so no changes can be made, the type of currency that should be used to store the data in the version, the company code currency or profit center valuation, the currency type for each version, the exchange rate used to translate foreign currencies to the local currency, and for what date the system should derive characteristics.

If you plan in weeks, you also need to specify which rule is used to distribute the weekly plan values to plan periods. This rule determines how the weekly values are distributed to periods when a week cannot be assigned to one period. Here, as shown in Figure 6.9, we specified that the version handles Plan, Actual, Variance, and we typed "0" and "Plan/actual version" in the **Version** and **Name** columns respectively.

6.7   Planning with the CO-PA Planning Framework

We're now ready to start planning. To access the actual CO-PA planning framework, follow the path in the IMG Activity: **Controlling • Profitability Analysis • Planning • Planning Framework**, as shown in Figure 6.10.

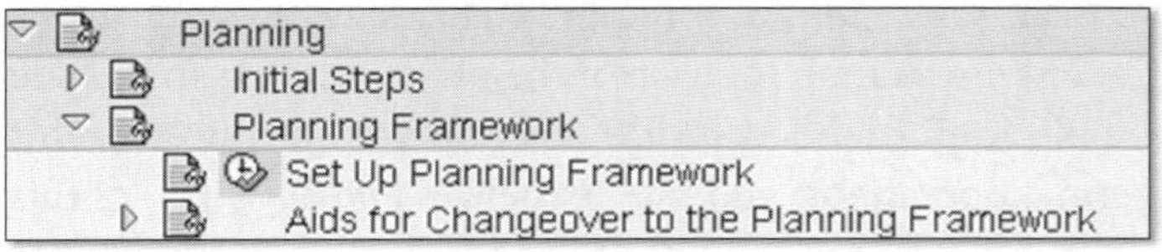

Figure 6.10 Accessing the CO-PA Planning Framework

As shown in Figure 6.11, several components are required to create a planning application using the CO-PA planning framework, including planning levels, planning packages (commonly referred to simply as "packages"), planning methods, and parameter sets. Their main purpose is not only to access the information from the SAP tables but also to control exactly what elements are extracted, the level of detail required, transformation processes to be used, and values required by users. We already looked at the most important elements within this environment earlier in this chapter and they are discussed in more detail in the following subsections.

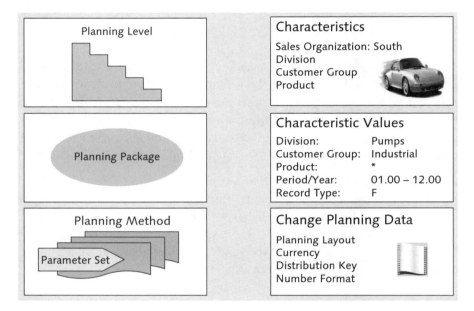

Figure 6.11 Major Components of the CO-PA Framework

6.7.1 Planning Levels

You cannot plan or control every single value of all SAP tables or user-defined fields in your implementation at the same time. However, using planning levels, you can select only the required characteristics and value fields that represent the information for each of the planning areas to include in your planning application, defined inside your operating concern. This lets you plan marketing, operations, and sales expenses and assign all of this information to a common planning application that is simple enough for anyone to use.

To create a planning level, follow these steps:

1. In the screen shown earlier in Figure 6.10, select **Set up Planning Framework** to access the traditional CO-PA **Planning Framework : Overview** screen, shown in Figure 6.12.

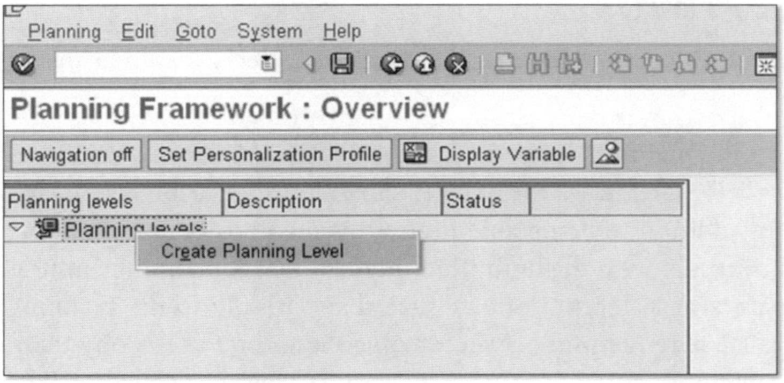

Figure 6.12 Create a Planning Level

2. Review the different elements displayed in Figure 6.12, and notice that there are three columns: **Planning levels**, **Description**, and **Status**. Because none of these elements have been defined yet, no objects are available.

3. Right-click on the **Planning levels** object and select **Create Planning Level**, as shown in Figure 6.12.

4. Another screen appears, shown in Figure 6.13, where you can define the technical name and a description of your planning level. Enter "Level" as the technical name, and "This is a Planning Level" as the description.

5. Click on the checkmark icon to create the planning level.

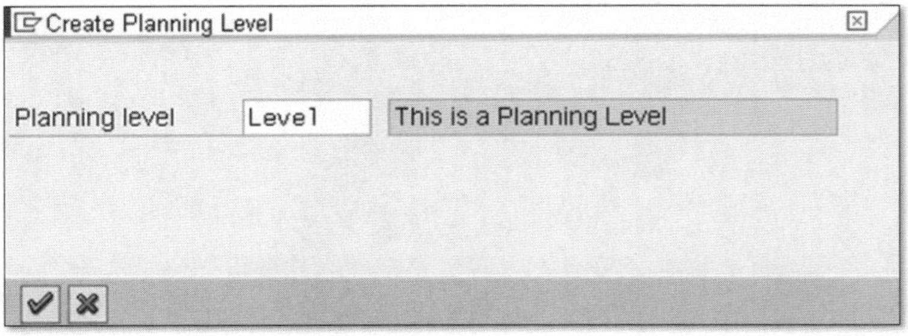

Figure 6.13 Creating a Planning Level

The objects contained in your operating concern are now available for you to plan them. However, you still need to define what type of operations you are interested in performing over those components. To do so, you need to define another component, the planning package, discussed in the next section.

6.7.2 Planning Package

To define a planning package or access any of the objects included in the planning level:

1. Right-click on the planning level we just created and the menu displayed in the upper left portion of the screen shown in Figure 6.14 appears. Notice that in addition to being able to use this menu to **Create Planning Package** (to continue with the definition of your CO-PA planning application), there are also different options related specifically to the planning level, such as **Display Planning Level**, **Change Planning Level**, **Copy Planning Level**, **Delete Planning Level**, and **Transport Planning Level**.

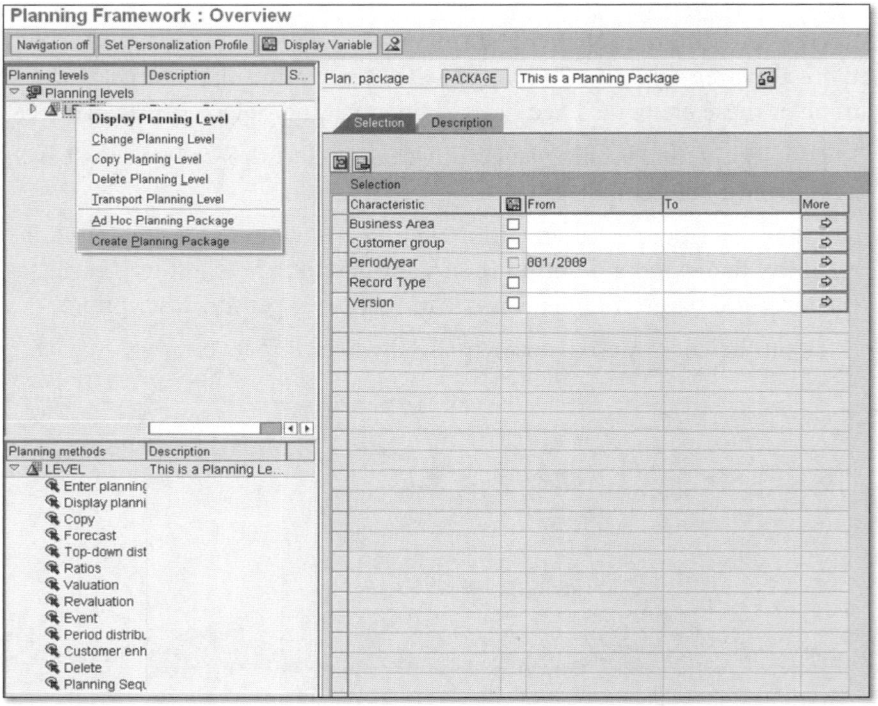

Figure 6.14 Creating a Planning Package as Part of a Planning Level

2. Select **Create Planning Package**, as shown in Figure 6.14, and the screen shown in Figure 6.15 appears. Enter "Package" as the technical name and "This is a Planning Package" as the description of the object.

3. Click on the checkmark icon to create the planning package.

4. Briefly review the different planning methods shown at the bottom of the screen shown in Figure 6.14, which are part of your planning package. Planning methods are predefined processes in CO-PA that can be configured to perform modifications over your data, and they are limited by the settings configured on the plan package's **Selection** tab, shown on the right-side of Figure 6.14.

Notice that the planning methods are attached to your planning level as well, and also notice that the planning package is limiting the display for the elements extracted from the operating concern to starting on **001/2009**. We'll look at planning methods in more detail in the next section.

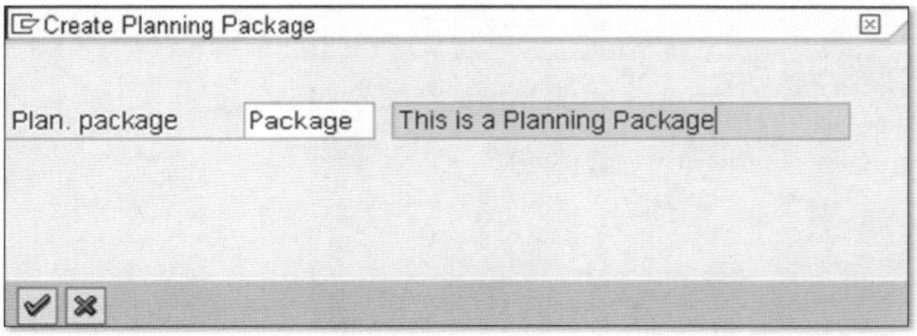

Figure 6.15 Creating a Planning Package

At this point we have configured two key planning elements: planning levels and planning packages. If you want to create additional objects, for example, to manage information for marketing, operations, and sales, then each of them would be a planning level, and the information extracted by each of them is controlled by the selection criteria defined in the planning package. This makes it possible to have marketing as a planning level, and marketing expenses for region A and marketing expenses for region B in two separate planning packages.

Finally, if you review Figure 6.16, you see that each of the columns in the **Planning Framework : Overview** screen now contains objects for the planning level and planning package we created. The **Status** column identifies the completion status of the information, using a graphical indicator. Double-click on this indicator to display the **Set Status** screen, also shown in Figure 6.16. You can configure three indicators:

- ▶ **Open**: specifies that the object is still in the design stage
- ▶ **In processing**: specifies that some work has been done, but changes are still required
- ▶ **Completed**: signals that the planning package is ready for use

You don't have to use the **Status** object all of the time, but it helps with organization, especially when you are working with multiple implementation teams or complex planning applications that might require many packages stored inside the same planning level.

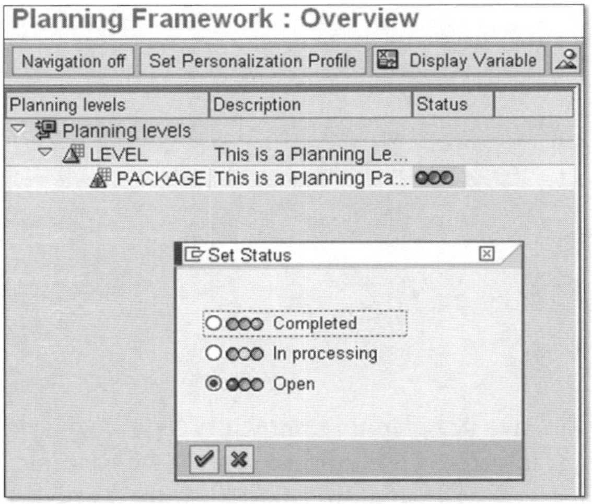

Figure 6.16 Changing the Status of Your Planning Package

Now, let us look at working with planning methods in case you need to perform specific transformations or modifications to your data. Using planning methods can help you avoid modifications of data outside the SAP OLTP environment, and reduce customization efforts.

6.7.3 Working with Planning Methods, Parameter Sets, and Planning Layouts

As was previously mentioned, when working with a planning package you can also see the planning methods that are attached to your planning level.

We will work with the two simplest of the planning methods: **Enter planning data** and **Display planning data**, shown in Figure 6.17. As their names imply, the first allows you to enter and modify planning data, and the second is designed to display the extracted information using the planning package as a filter.

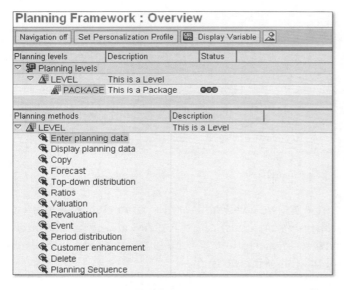

Figure 6.17 Working with the Enter Planning Data Planning Method

To execute any of the planning methods, a planning package must be selected. This object controls what information we want to see when executing these planning methods. The process for working with any of the planning methods available in the CO-PA planning framework is essentially the same, as follows:

1. Select a planning package, (in our example, **PACKAGE**, as shown in Figure 6.17).

2. Select a planning method (in our example, **Enter planning data**).

3. Right-click on the planning method and choose **Create a Parameter Set.**

4. Configure the options of the parameter set that appear on the right side of the screen, as shown in Figure 6.18.

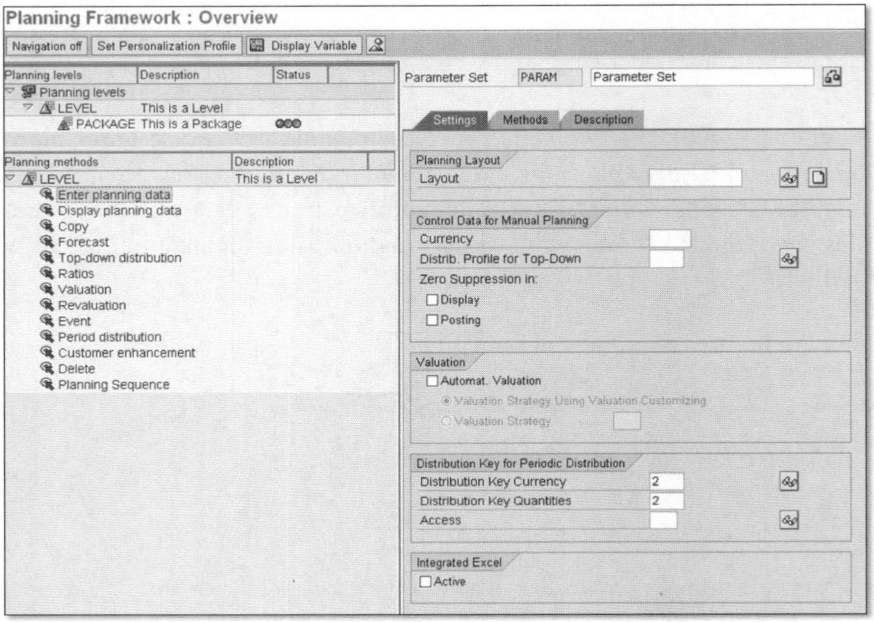

Figure 6.18 Configuration of a Parameter Set

As you can see in Figure 6.18, we have configured a parameter set (required for all of the CO-PA planning methods) called **PARAM** and there are three tabs: **Settings**, **Methods**, and **Description**. For the **Enter planning data** planning method, perform the following steps:

1. Review the different parameter set options shown in Figure 6.18.

2. In the section called **Planning Layout**, select the create icon to define a planning layout. You need to have at least one planning layout to see any data extracted from the SAP tables, and using the information from your operating concern, planning levels, and planning packages on your screen. This is quite similar to SEM-BPS, SAP NetWeaver BI Integrated Planning, and SAP BW-BPS.

3. Specify a name ("Layout") and description ("LAYOUT") for the planning layout, as shown in Figure 6.19.

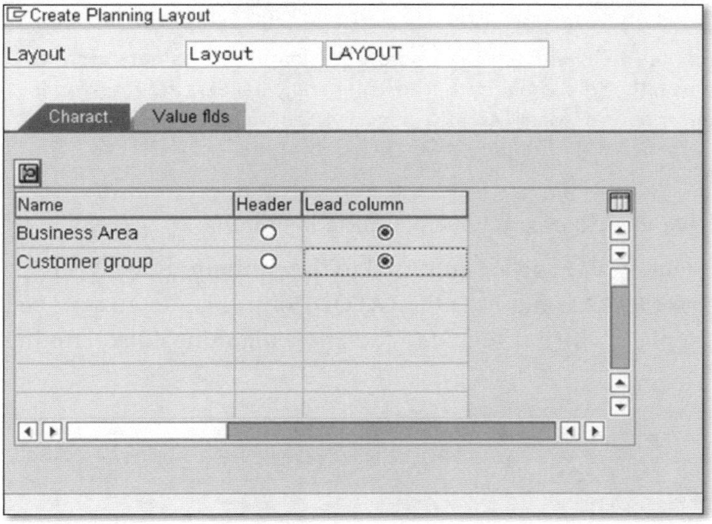

Figure 6.19 Configuring the Characteristics to Include in a Planning Layout

4. Define how you want the characteristics and value fields arranged, using the **Charact.** and **Value flds** tabs respectively. As shown in Figure 6.19, we will use **Business Area** and **Customer group** characteristics as lead columns for our planning layout, and, as shown in Figure 6.20, we will include the value fields **Annual rebates**, **Lot size variances**, **Other variances**, and **Revenue** in our planning layout.

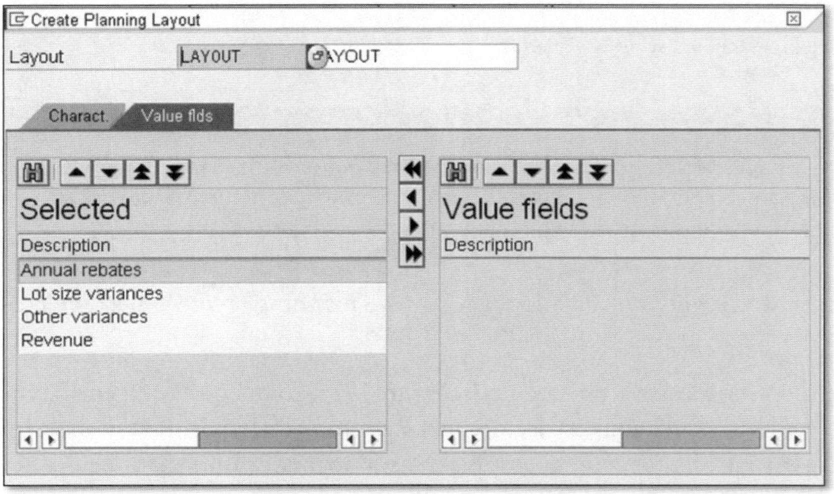

Figure 6.20 Configuring the Value Fields to Include in a Planning Layout

Tip

We are specifying that the characteristics **Customer group** and **Business area** will be leading columns rather than headers because generally headers are reserved for information, such as period, fiscal year, fiscal year variant, and other time-related elements or characteristics that require different levels of hierarchies.

5. Click on the save icon to create your planning layout.
6. As shown in Figure 6.21, you are returned to the configuration screen for the parameter set **PARAM** but now the **LAYOUT** object has been assigned to the parameter set (which is linked to the **Enter planning data** planning method).

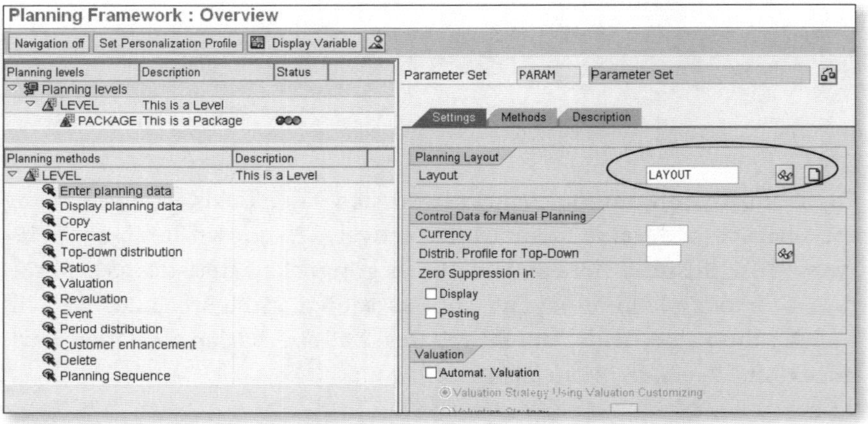

Figure 6.21 Planning Layout Assigned to a Parameter Set

Note

There are several additional options available in the screen shown in Figure 6.21, but they are beyond the scope of this book. You can explore them if you decide to increase the sophistication of your parameter set configuration.

Let us now see how our data looks using the planning layout object we created:

1. Click on the glasses icon, shown in Figure 6.21, to open the screen shown in Figure 6.22. As you can see, **Report Painter** is the environment used by CO-PA to present a general graphical display of your information.

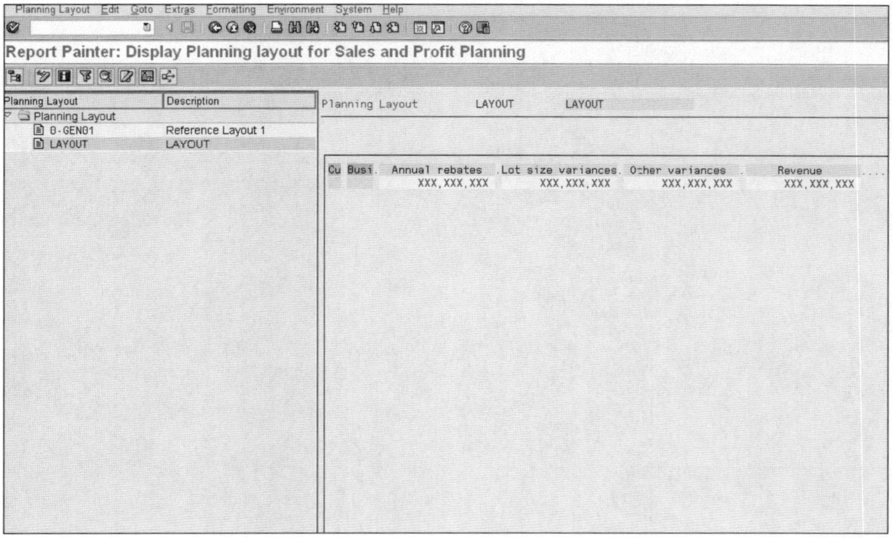

Figure 6.22 Displaying the Structure of Your LAYOUT Planning Layout

2. Review the information shown in Figure 6.22. As we configured earlier, the business area (**Busi**) and customer group (**Cu**) characteristics are the lead columns for our planning layout, and the value fields **Annual rebates**, **Lot size variances**, **Other variances**, and **Revenue** are shown.

3. Click on the back icon located at the top of the screen, as shown in Figure 6.22, to return to the **Planning Framework : Overview** screen.

You now have a general idea of how your Layout "looks and feels." However, we need to make sure that the configuration follows your planning requirements for a particular currency. To do so, let us assign US dollars as the standard planning currency for our parameter set.

1. Return to the parameter set's **Settings** tab, and in the **Currency** field in the **Control Data for Manual Planning** area, type "USD."

2. You can also limit the planning methods associated with our data. To do so, select the **Methods** tab, as shown in Figure 6.23 and select the methods that you want to include as **Permitted methods** as part of your planning application.

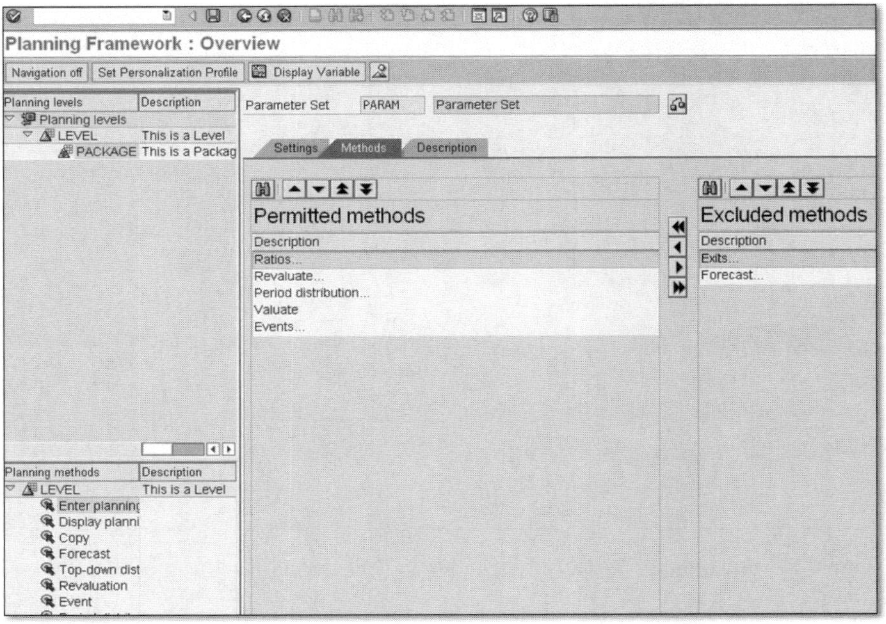

Figure 6.23 Assigning the Permitted Planning Methods to Your Parameter Set

You now have a pretty good idea of how to configure planning methods to develop more sophisticated structures, such as those shown in Figure 6.24. To access this environment:

1. Save your parameter set by clicking on the save icon.

2. Double-click on the **PACKAGE** object.

3. Drilldown to find the **PARAM** parameter set we just configured, right-click on it, and select **Execute Planning Method** to display your LAYOUT planning layout object on the right side of the screen, with all of the desired information, including the characteristics and value fields previously defined, and default header information at the top that describes the type of data that we are modifying.

4. You can now manually enter the information you require. As shown in Figure 6.24, we have entered the values **100**, **1,000**, **2,000**, and **150**, for the key figures **Cash discount**, **Gross sales**, **Marketing division**, and **Quantity discount** respectively. Notice that we chose to provide different value fields in our layout to show that we can add or modify the contents of our layouts to different requirements.

5. Notice that our data is limited in the planning level information to the time frame between **1/2009** and **10/2009**, reflecting that the limitations established by the planning level and planning package are key to displaying the information contained in the parameter set of the planning method and showing it in the Layout.

6. Click on the save icon.

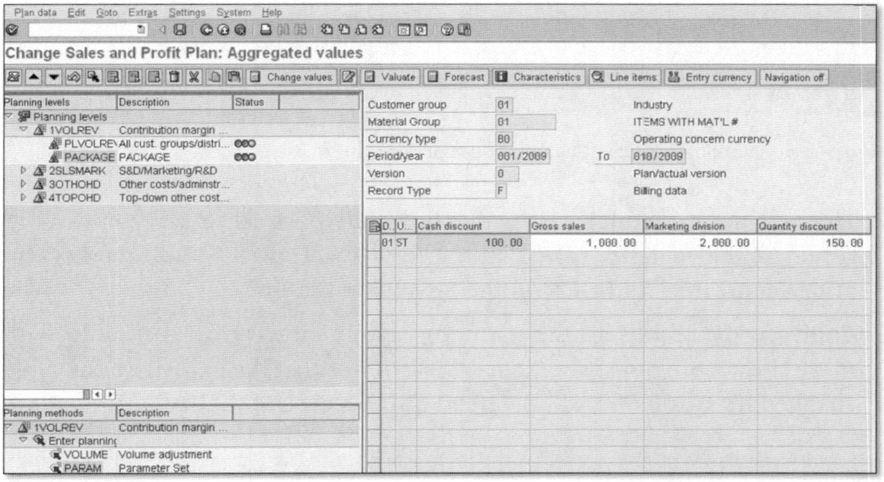

Figure 6.24 Working and Displaying Your Layout and Parameter Set

7. Once you have executed your parameter set you can return to the CO-PA configuration screen by clicking on the back arrow icon located at the top of the screen.

> **Note**
>
> When you perform any modification or addition to the data in the planning layout, the SAP system asks if you want to post (store) your data, and you either accept or decline. Note that there is a different document number generated each time that you save and change your data, and you're provided the number in the message "Plan data was posted with document number 0000000XXX."

Notice that the screen shown in Figure 6.24 contains additional buttons, such as **Valuate**, **Forecast**, **Change Values**, **Line Items**, **Entry Currency**, and **Navigation Off**. These buttons are more or less self-explanatory, and you can explore their usage on your own. However, be careful because some of them change or generate new values based on the information displayed on the screen.

Let's look at one example of this, the **Change Values** button:

1. Position the cursor in a field like **Cash Discount**, and then click on the **Change Values** button. The screen shown in Figure 6.25 appears, where you can revaluate a field either by a percentage or a constant.

ⓒ Change Values			☒
Revaluation factor	10	%	Revaluate
Value			Add values
✔ ☒			

Figure 6.25 Working with the Change Values Screen

2. These values can either be positive or negative, so let us say you want to revaluate the values of cash discount for 10 %. Type "10" into the **Revaluation factor** field and click on the **Revaluate** button.

3. Compare the results in the planning layout shown in Figure 6.26 with those shown previously in Figure 6.24. Notice that the cash discount value changed from 100.00 USD to **110.00** USD because of the 10 % revaluation.

Customer group	01		Industry	
Material Group	01		ITEMS	
Currency type	B0		Operating concern currency	
Period/year	001/2009	To	010/2009	
Version	0		Plan/actual version	
Record Type	F		Billing data	

D.	U...	Cash discount	Gross sales	Marketing division	Quantity discount
01	ST	110.00	1,000.00	2,000.00	150.00

Figure 6.26 Results of the Change Values Button

4. Explore the rest of the buttons available on the screen.

5. If a simple way of revaluation of data values is what you were looking for, save your changes, and click on the back icon to return to the design environment of the CO-PA planning framework.

> **Note**
>
> Using the predefined **Change Values** button might eliminate you having to develop or configure a new planning method. Alternatively, you might expand the revaluation planning method to perform a similar procedure but changing more than just a value at a time.

Now that we have reviewed this functionality, let us explore how to complement our CO-PA planning framework with variables.

6.7.4 Planning Variables

The SAP system lets you create variables to simplify the way information is handled inside your CO-PA planning applications. For example, you can create a variable that has a range stored in it and assign it to a characteristic so you do not need to worry about typing the same information all of the time. Instead, you can call the variable during execution time and the layout will display the required information.

This type of scenario is exactly what we're going to create using the CO-PA planning framework **Define variable** function:

1. Make sure that you are working in the design environment of the CO-PA planning framework shown in Figure 6.27.

2. Click on **Edit • Variable • Define variable**, as shown in Figure 6.27, to access the screen shown in Figure 6.28.

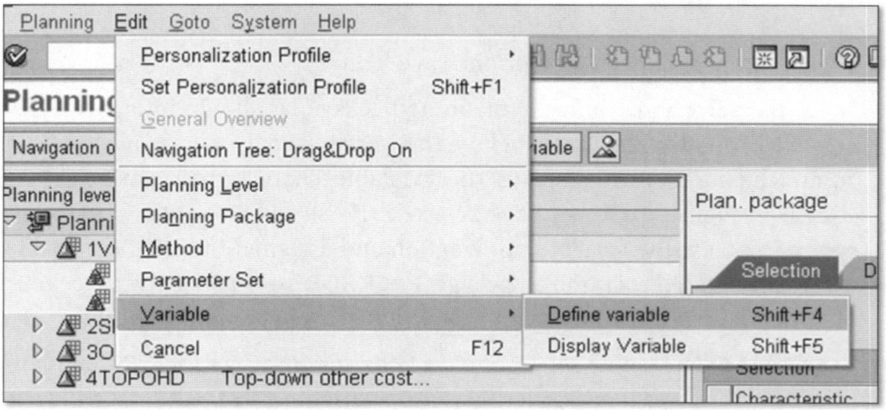

Figure 6.27 Defining a Variable in CO-PA

> **Note**
>
> Before proceeding, know that a CO-PA planning variable is always associated with a specific characteristic.

3. As shown in Figure 6.28, create a variable called **CUST_GRP** assigned to the characteristic **Customer group**, with the value wholesale (**02**) assigned to the column **Value From**. You can now assign the variable **CUST_GRP** to a planning package to extract your predefined data extraction settings into your planning layouts.

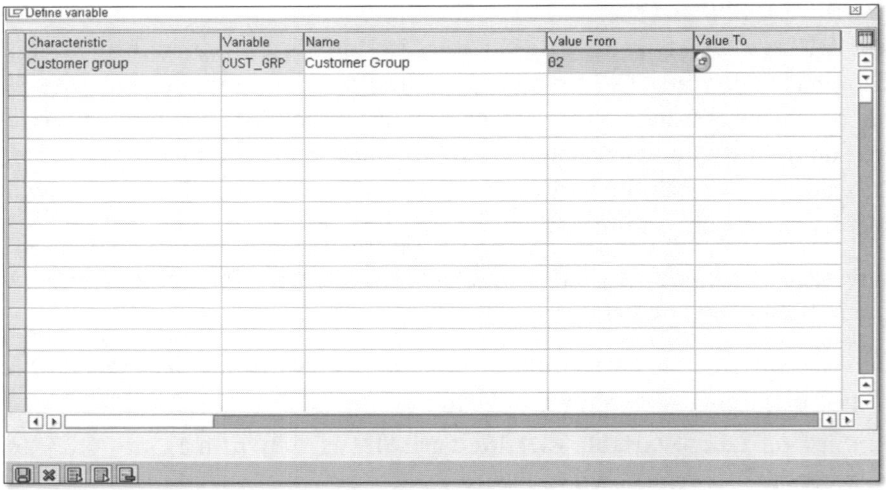

Figure 6.28 Configuring a CO-PA Variable

4. When you're finished, click on the save icon.

5. Go to the **Selection** tab in the planning package, as shown in Figure 6.29, and click on the checkbox below the variable icon, and now you can access the menu that displays the available characteristic variables. As shown in Figure 6.29, we have selected the checkbox next to **Customer group** to access the variable information and assigned the CO-PA variable **CUST_GRP** to the planning package **PACKAGE** so when executing your planning layout the wholesale value will be extracted automatically.

6. Execute the parameter set assigned to the planning method **Enter planning data**, as described earlier. Now the variable **CUST_GRP** controls the behavior of the characteristic **Customer group**, as shown in Figure 6.30, displaying the default value **Wholesale (02)**.

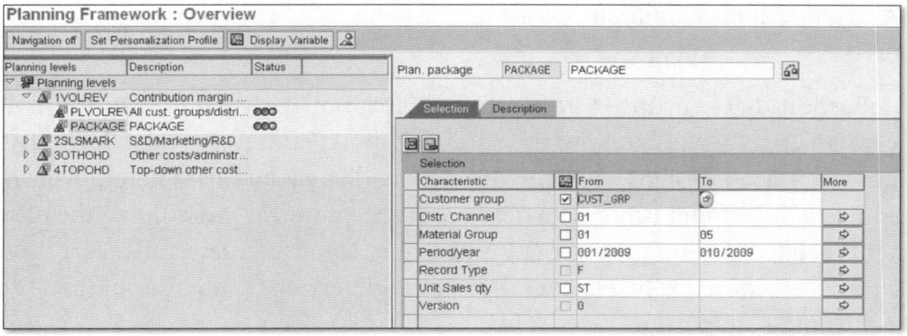

Figure 6.29 Assigning a CO-PA Variable to a Planning Package

Figure 6.30 Using the Variable CUST_GRP as part of your Layout

CO-PA planning variables are useful in complex implementations that require using the same layout, but the information is required by different users in different departments. In our scenario, the PACKAGE object can control the information for the wholesale division, and another planning package using the same layout might require a second variable to display, for example, only the hospitals division, and both users require the same characteristics and key value fields.

> **Note**
>
> We recommend that you explore in more detail the different types of variables that SAP software has to offer using the CO-PA planning framework. You can either use the available *http://help.sap.com* documentation, or interact with the *http://sdn.sap.com* community.

So far we've used the planning method Enter planning data. The alternative would be using the planning method Display planning data. This method provides the same type of capabilities, but users can only review the information, not modify it. This can be useful for managers or end users with few

SAP system skills who require little or no interaction with the data input processes.

A question that remains is how can you create or design more customized layouts? Together, planning layouts and Report Painter provide flexibility and customized designs to improve the data display and data manipulation requirements of end users. The next section explores in more detail the elements related to configuring CO-PA planning layouts from scratch as a way to provide a more extensive overview of the reporting capabilities of the CO-PA planning application.

6.8   The Report Painter and CO-PA Planning Layouts

To get started creating more sophisticated environments using Report Painter without creating planning areas, planning methods, and so on, follow this procedure:

1. Follow the path **Planning • Manual Entry of Planning Data • Define Planning Layout**.

2. Select the **Create Planning Layout** option, and double-click it or click on the **Choose** button. You will manually create a planning layout that you can also modify, display, and later on assign to planning applications.

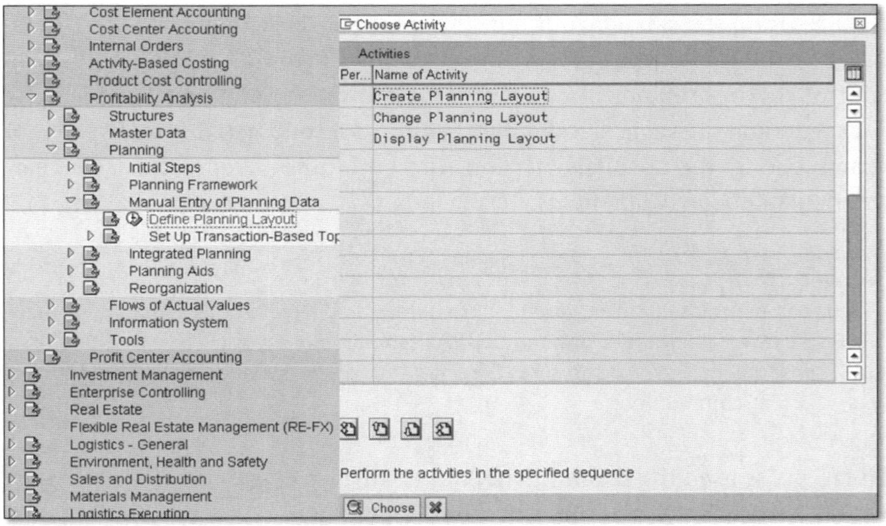

Figure 6.31 Accessing the Define Planning Layout Screen

3. The screen shown in Figure 6.32 appears and the SAP system requires you to provide a technical name, such as "layouttest1," and a description, such as "This is a test layout," for the layout.

4. Once completed, as shown in Figure 6.32, click on the **Create** button.

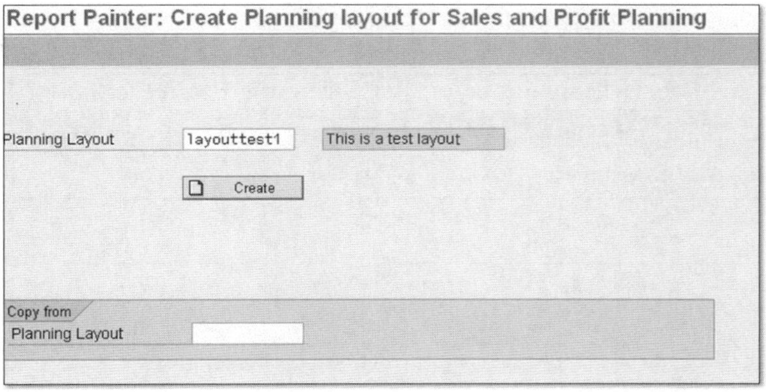

Report Painter: Create Planning layout for Sales and Profit Planning

Planning Layout   layouttest1   This is a test layout

☐   Create

Copy from
Planning Layout

Figure 6.32 Configuring a CO-PA Layout

5. Figure 6.33 presents the initial Report Painter screen to perform sales and profit planning. As you can see, a planning layout is defined as a matrix using rows and columns. You can also use a predefined number format to display your key figure's values and perform calculations with a variable assigned to a column as part of a layout.

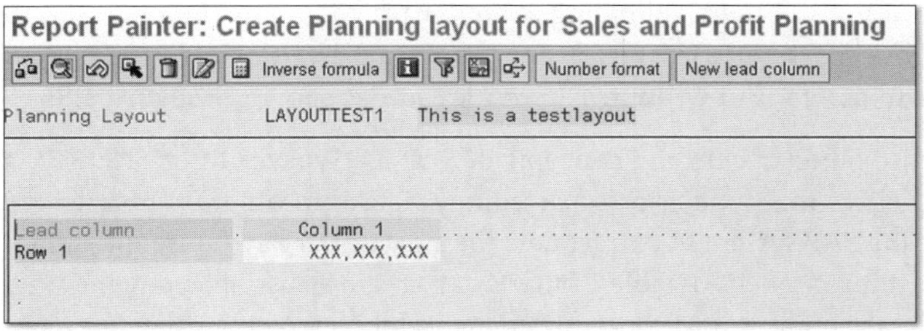

Report Painter: Create Planning layout for Sales and Profit Planning

🔍 🔍 ⟲ 🔍 🗋 📝 ▦ Inverse formula ⅰ 🕎 🖼 ⬚ Number format | New lead column

Planning Layout   LAYOUTTEST1   This is a testlayout

Lead column   Column 1 . . . .
Row 1   XXX,XXX,XXX

Figure 6.33 Basic Planning Layout in the Report Painter

Although this book is not oriented toward a complete explanation of the Report Painter in the SAP ERP ECC 6.0 environment, we'll provide you with some useful hints. So, let's add information to the rows based on predefined characteristics:

1. Select and then double-click on **Row 1** to access the **Select element type** screen, as shown in Figure 6.34. You can now either add a characteristic or a value field with characteristics to **Row 1**. For our example, select **Characteristics** and click on the checkmark icon.

2. Select any of the options available, such as **Industry**, **Customer Group**, or others. For our example, we selected **Industry**.

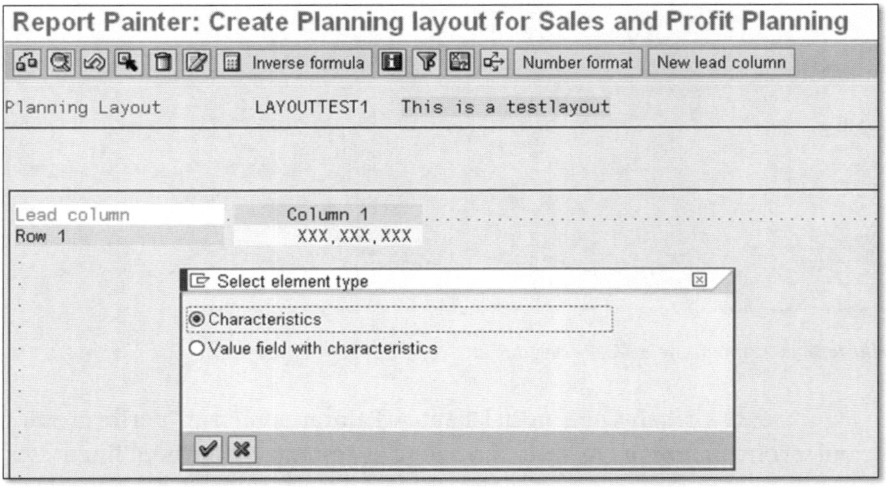

Figure 6.34 Adding a Characteristic to Row1

3. Now, double-click on **Column 1** to perform the assignment and configuration of a value field, following a similar procedure as the one used to assign the characteristic. We are going to create a value field called **Gross sales** and assign it to **Column 1** in our layout, as shown in Figure 6.35.

4. For those familiar with the concepts of SAP NetWeaver BI or SAP BW, a value field is the same as a restricted key figure. In other words, we are telling the SAP system to extract data for a particular key figure that might not exist inside the SAP tables, but we can create a customized name with specific selection criteria to restrict the values extracted. That way not everything is extracted at once, which improves system performance. In the case of the information shown in Figure 6.35, we are defining the value field gross sales to those values that have **Record Type=F**, **Version=0**, and **Period/year** between **1/2009** and **12/2009**. It is possible to include additional characteristics to improve the restriction of the information that describes a value field. To do so, use the **Available characteristics** displayed on the right-hand side of the screen.

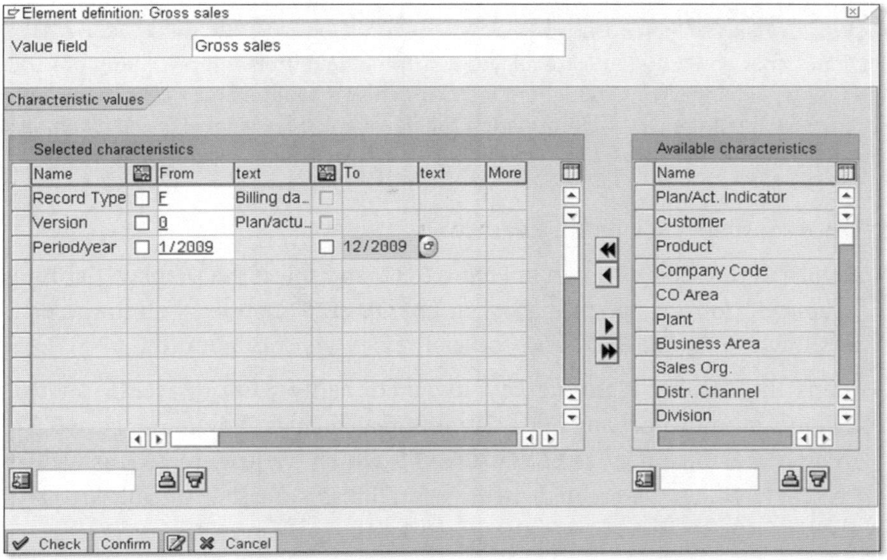

Figure 6.35 Configuring a Value Field

5. Once you're satisfied with the characteristics and the selection criteria restrictions that describe your value field, click on the **Check** button to review any inconsistencies and make any corrections.

6. Finally, click on the **Confirm** button to complete the assignment of the gross sales value field to **Column 1**.

7. Now, as shown in Figure 6.36, the final results of the assignments to the initial row 1 and column 1 display. You'll see that the characteristic **Industry** and the value field **Gross sales** are the only elements displayed in the planning layout **LAYOUTTEST1**.

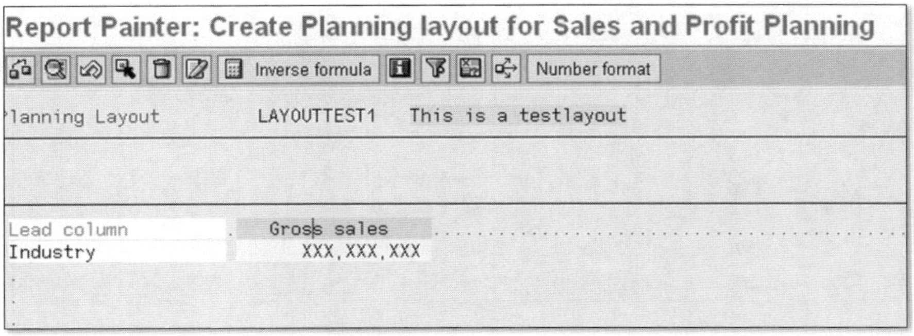

Figure 6.36 Final Results of the Characteristic and Value Field Assignments

> **Note**
>
> It is not enough that you create a layout with the definition and restriction of values. Any planning layout configured following the procedures shown has to be created thinking of the type of information that is, or will be, available in the planning levels, planning packages, and parameter sets where it is be assigned.

8. Once satisfied, click on the save icon.

9. Return to the screen shown in Figure 6.31, and select the **Display Planning Layout** option. The planning layout **LAYOUTTEST1** appears on the screen, as shown in Figure 6.37, and you can review its configuration.

   Using the **Display Planning Layout** functionality you can access, review, delete, and transport any of the layouts available, as shown in Figure 6.37. In our case, this includes **LAYOUTTEST1**, which we just created, as well as **LAYOUT**, which we created earlier. You'll also see other default SAP layouts.

Explore the rest of the available functionalities in this part of Report Painter for sales and profit planning. There are formatting functionalities to add more rows and columns, limit the number range displayed, add attributes and formulas, and other elements that are important to explore.

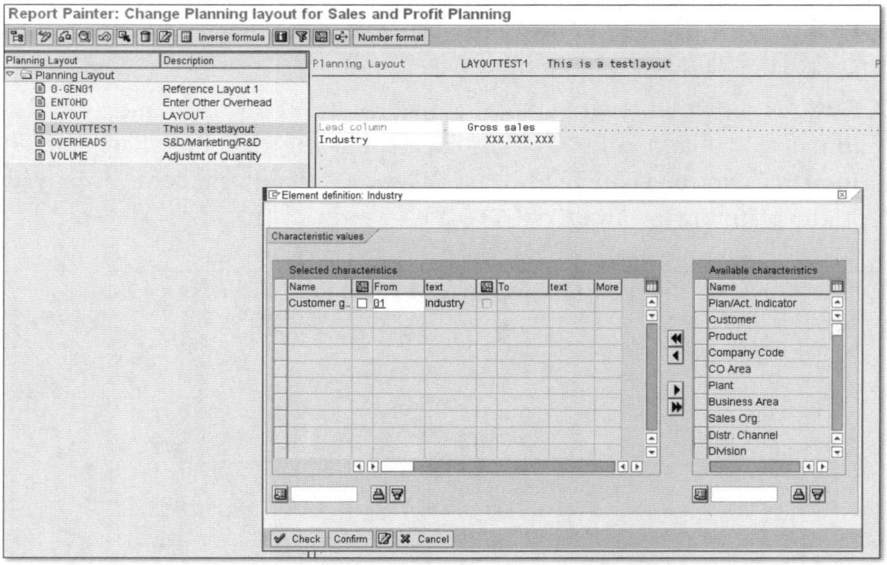

Figure 6.37 Displaying the Newly Created LAYOUTTEST1

In the next section, we will explore in more detail how to control and assign the objects configured in the CO-PA planning framework to users, and roles and functions using planning profiles.

6.9   Planning Profiles

Users plan, use, and monitor information differently depending on their role in the organization. For this reason, a CEO will not require or maintain the same volume of data as a shop floor employee who needs to keep track of production orders. With this example in mind, think of planning profiles as ways to divide the areas of responsibility in your SAP implementation based on the roles of users. Generally, there are three types of users in any SAP implementation, as shown in Figure 6.38, and described in the following list:

▶ **Power Users**
Generally, top-level managers, network and system administrators, project managers, team leaders, or developers that control or limit the information displayed or used by super users or end users.

▶ **Super Users**
Users that may have a medium- to low-level usage of the application. Super users have authorization and usage limitations placed on them that only power users are allowed to change.

▶ **End Users**
Generally, the final customers of any SAP system. End users perform data input operations and execute functions created by power and super users.

In Figure 6.38, the arrows represent the level of influence and relationships between the different types of users. For example, P**ower Users** can modify information available for themselves, end users, and super users, while **Super Users** can modify information for themselves and end users, but are limited by the objects that power users have set up. Finally, **End Users** cannot perform any modifications over the objects assigned to them and they just use the objects available and associated with their user IDs inside the SAP system.

The concept of planning profiles goes along with these classifications because there can be planning applications or views intended only for each of these types of users, depending on their authorizations and roles. For example, if you want certain users to work with specific levels, methods, etc., you can use a planning profile to limit their work and display capabilities:

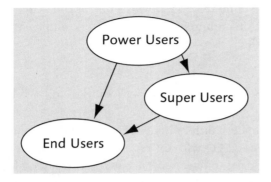

Figure 6.38 Roles and Relationships of an SAP Implementation

1. Make sure that you are working in the design environment of the CO-PA planning framework shown earlier in Figure 6.18.

2. As shown in Figure 6.39, select **Edit • Personalization Profile • Create Personalization Profile**.

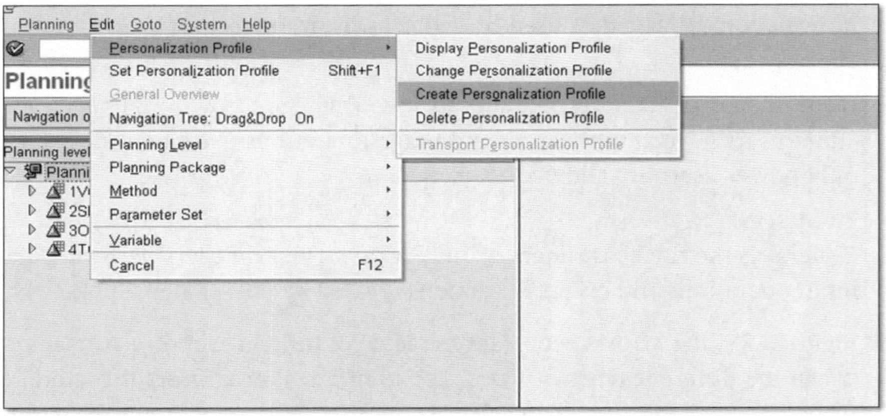

Figure 6.39 Creating a Personalization Profile

3. The screen shown in Figure 6.40 appears. The SAP system requires the initial configuration of the technical name, "USER25," and the description associated with this name, "End-User Profile." The USER25 planning profile is used to assign all of the different end users of the planning application and to limit their modification capabilities.

4. Once you are satisfied with the configuration settings in the **Create Personalization Profile** screen shown in Figure 6.40, click on the create icon (the white page icon), to generate your planning profile.

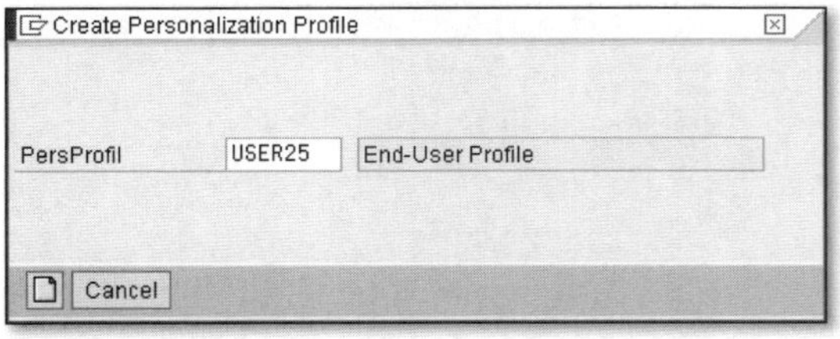

Figure 6.40 Configuring a Personalization Profile

5. As shown in Figure 6.41, the **USER25 End-User Profile** has been created. Notice that on the right side there are two tabs: **User List** and **Authorizations**. Also, notice on the left-hand side the planning levels available in your operating concern. You can use the checkboxes to select only those objects contained in the planning levels that you want to include as part of your profile, as shown in Figure 6.41.

On the right-hand side notice that the **USER25** planning profile has been assigned to the User IDs **MS2006**, **MWBWTST**, and **MXJWW2**, which must be created inside the SAP system by a system administrator.

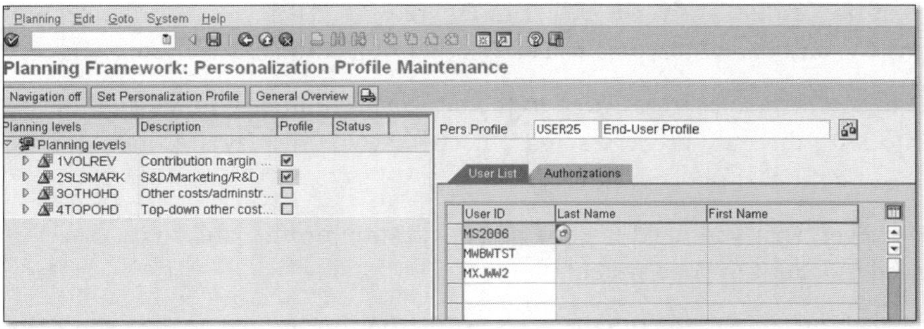

Figure 6.41 Assigning Users and Objects to Your Personalization Profile

Tip
The person who creates the planning profile and assigns users will become the administrator of the profile.

6. Select the **Authorizations** tab, as shown in Figure 6.42.

7. To allow access or execution rights to any of the objects, select the checkbox next to the name of the appropriate function. For example, if you want to allow a user to create a planning level, select the checkbox next to **Create Planning Level** and the object **Root node, object tree** will be displayed.

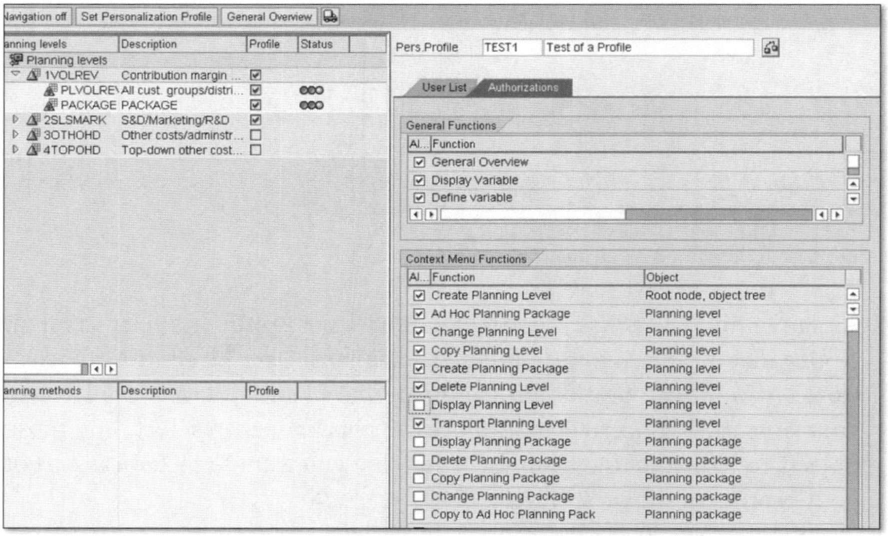

Figure 6.42 Configuring Authorizations of a Personalization Profile

8. Save the profile. You can always can go back to modify the assignments of the profile, as shown earlier in Figure 6.41. Also, you can change, display, and delete the profile as any other object in an SAP system.

Once users have been assigned to the personalization profile, when they log into SAP, the only processes and objects that will display are those configured by the planning administrator.

However, first you need to set a personalization profile, and to do that you need to load it in your system:

1. Click on the **Set Personalization Profile** button located at the top of the screen shown in Figure 6.41 and Figure 6.42, or use [Shift] + [F1].

2. Now the screen shown in Figure 6.43 appears, asking you to select the name of your personalized planning profile (**PersProfil**). In this case we have a profile called **TEST1** and we want to review the status and functionalities (which we can do because we are the administrators of this profile).

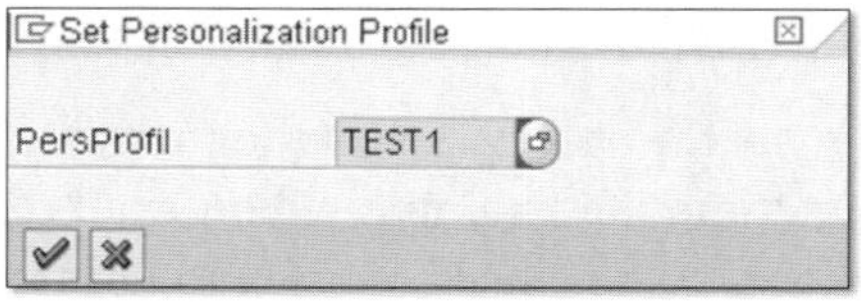

Figure 6.43 Set a Personalization Profile

3. Click on the checkmark icon.

4. Review the information in the screen that displays, shown in Figure 6.44, and notice that only the two planning levels previously selected in Figure 6.42 are displayed.

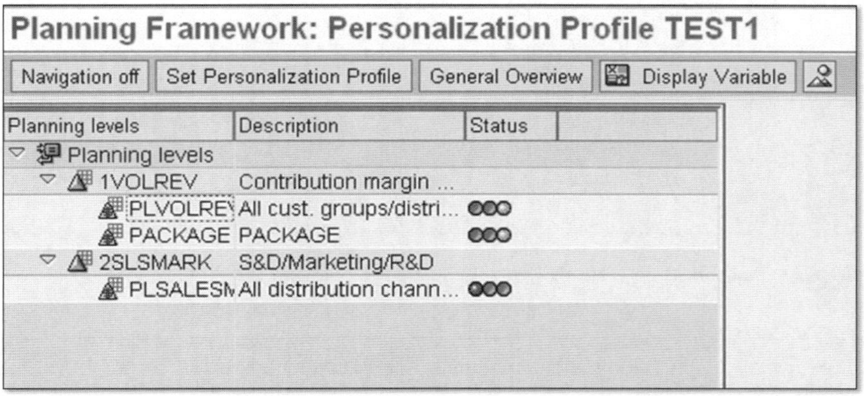

Figure 6.44 Reviewing the Newly Created Personalization Profile TEST1

Now let us review the authorization settings previously configured (shown in Figure 6.42), and how they work from a user's and administrator's point of view:

1. Review Figure 6.45, where we are trying to modify the contents of a pre-defined planning package, and see that all of the options have been grayed out. In other words, the user is not allowed to modify the package, all they can do is execute it and access any planning layouts associated with this package.

2. Now, in comparison, review the information presented in Figure 6.46, which shows the screen from an administrator's point of view, where all of the functions are available.

Note
If you find options that are unavailable or you can't perform a function, always make sure that you know that you are working in the correct environment before thinking that there is a bug in the system or something to that effect.

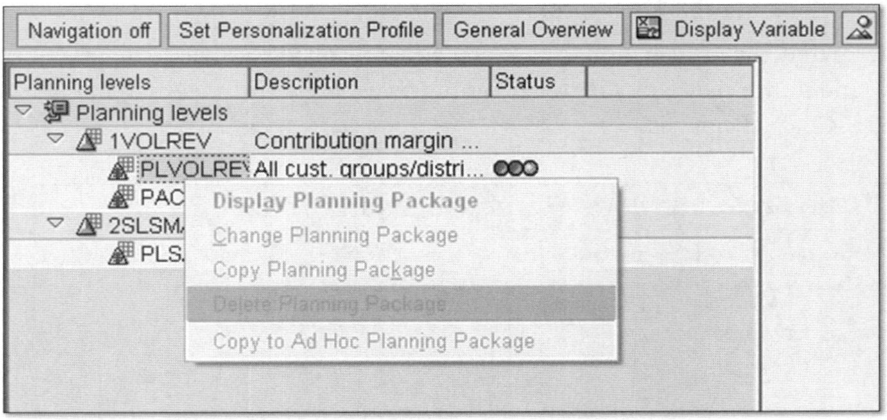

Figure 6.45 Authorization Options Control End-User Options in the Profile TEST1

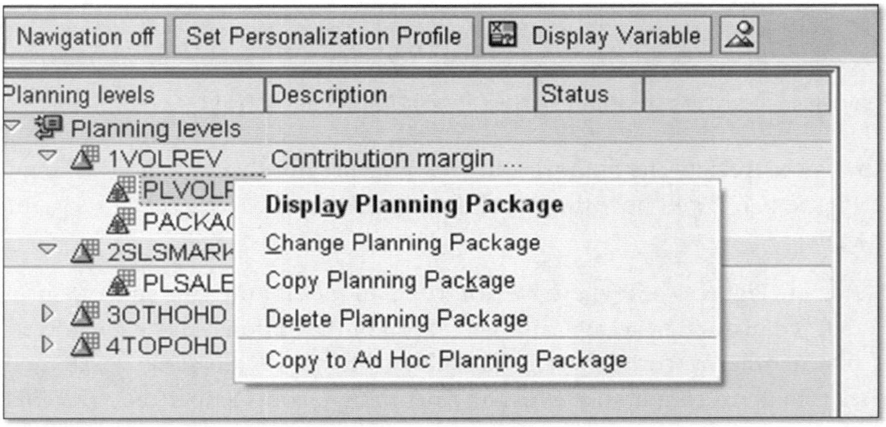

Figure 6.46 General View Without Planning Profiles

You have now learned how to generate and work with a planning profile, which is a useful tool when working with multiple users with different levels of expertise, data input, and requirements. We were also able to perform modifications in the behavior of specific objects inside the CO-PA planning framework, which means that our profile is working and doing what it is supposed to do. We recommend that you experiment more with this application, assigning users to profiles and testing their environments with their IDs to make sure you understand the concepts behind all of this.

6.10 Summary

In this chapter, we have provided a general overview of the components that define the CO-PA planning framework. Think of the CO-PA planning framework as a simple environment to develop sophisticated applications without leaving R/3 or SAP ERP ECC 6.0 and without the generation of cubes, extractors, or using information that is not as current. The CO-PA planning framework provides direct access to the data in its original format, allows performing transformations, and sharing data with different users.

In Chapter 7, we will explore in more detail additional functionalities available in the CO-PA planning framework and we will review the configuration options required to create a planning application. In addition, we will explore components such as ratios, key figure schemes, planning functions, and additional planning methods.

This chapter explores more practical components of the CO-PA planning framework, such as forecasting, planning profiles, valuation and ratio planning, ratio schemes, and others that enhance the ability to modify data within the OLTP environment. These planning components complete the configuration steps required to generate a CO-PA Planning application.

7   CO-PA Planning: Configuration

In Chapter 6, we reviewed the general concepts behind the CO-PA planning framework, and briefly discussed some of its components. In this section, we will move forward to the configuration steps that really define a planning application, and explore how to configure basic planning methods. In addition, we will review elements such as *key figure schemes* that can be used to improve performance, *ratios*, a sophisticated tool to create formulas and add them to a report, and *planning sequences*, which let you automate running multiple planning methods consecutively. Let's get started.

7.1   Basic Planning Methods in the CO-PA Planning Framework

Most of the CO-PA planning methods shown in Figure 7.1 are predefined ABAP programs that run behind the scenes, and that require certain parameters to perform the desired processes. In this section, we will explore the most important of these planning methods, including **Display planning data**, **Copy**, **Forecast**, **Valuation**, **Revaluation**, **Ratios**, and **Delete**.

In Chapter 6, you already learned how to work with the basic planning method: **Enter planning data**, to use if you want to configure a layout and input data manually. However, this is not always desirable because business applications require data transformation to deliver real planning applications, and these processes will post the data directly into the SAP database in real time. Planning applications and data volume can also affect system performance if they are not carefully configured.

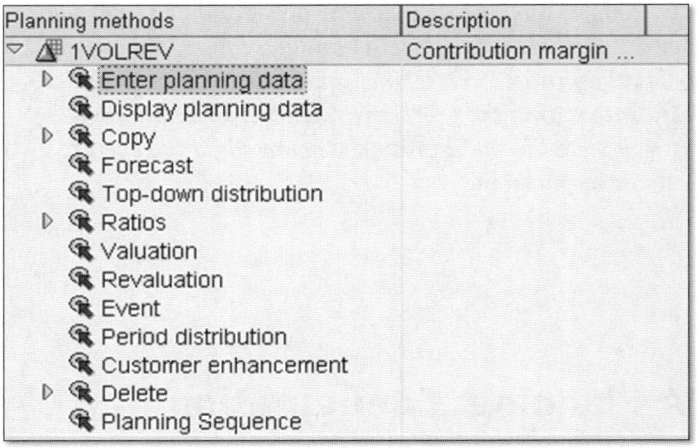

Planning methods	Description	
▽ ◫ 1VOLREV	Contribution margin ...	
▷ ◈ Enter planning data		
◈ Display planning data		
▷ ◈ Copy		
◈ Forecast		
◈ Top-down distribution		
▷ ◈ Ratios		
◈ Valuation		
◈ Revaluation		
◈ Event		
◈ Period distribution		
◈ Customer enhancement		
▷ ◈ Delete		
◈ Planning Sequence		

Figure 7.1 The CO-PA Planning Methods

As a Best Practice, use CO-PA planning methods to extract and modify data within the OLTP system, and limit the usage of custom ABAP programs for highly sophisticated requirements that cannot be delivered with standard SAP functions. You do not want to affect sensitive data because of a mistake in the definition of your ABAP coding.

Now, let us get started with our discussion of the most important planning methods available in CO-PA.

7.1.1 Enter Planning Data

We already explored this functionality in Chapter 6, so we will not discuss it in this section.

7.1.2 Display Planning Data

Display planning data provides similar functionality as Enter planning data, but you assign a planning layout, such as the planning layout LAYOUT shown in Figure 7.2, to extract information for display purposes only. Manual input of information is not possible. Depending on the role of your users, you may allow them to use the Enter Planning Data or Display Planning Data planning method.

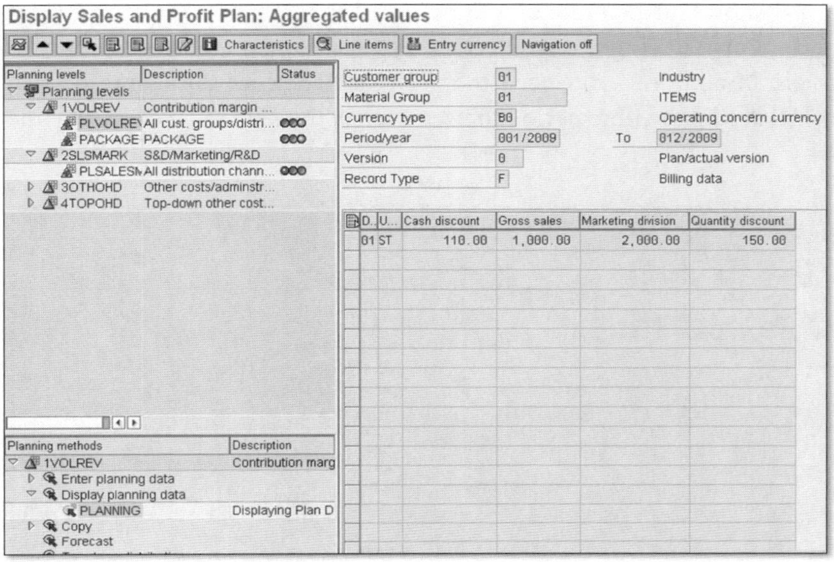

Figure 7.2 Using the Display Planning Data Planning Method

7.1.3 Copy

The Copy planning method is one of the most important functions because it simplifies any operations that perform similar processes based on predefined selection criteria.

Tip

In any client or project interview, you will likely be asked about your knowledge of the Copy function. Knowing this function in either CO-PA, SEM-BPS, BI-BPS, or any other module that performs similarly is sure to be a big plus for you in the interview process.

Three different copy operations exist:

▶ **Copy values**
Replaces the previous value with the new value.

▶ **Add**
Adds the new value to the existing value. Be careful with this operation; you might ending up having double of everything.

▶ **Subtract values**
You can remove values that already exist in the target based on predefined selection criteria.

Figure 7.3 shows an example of a Copy function in CO-PA. On the **Settings** tab, in the **Copy** area, you can select the type of copy operation to apply to your data. In addition, you need to specify a **Reference data** time period, which will define the time period to use to select the data to be copied by the system.

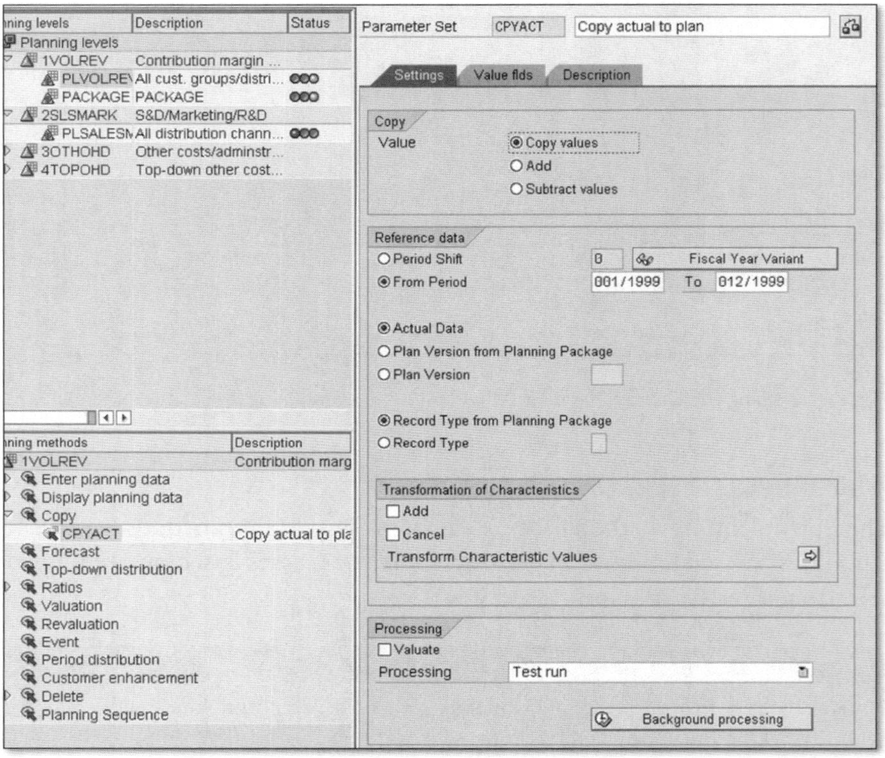

Figure 7.3 Working with the Copy Planning Method

To access the Copy planning method:

1. Click on the **Copy** planning method, shown in Figure 7.3.

2. Right-click to create the associated parameter group called **CPVACT**. The screen displayed on the right-hand side of the screen in Figure 7.3 appears.

3. In the **Processing** area, you can select **Test run** from the dropdown box to copy information that we have now as actual data and generate an exact copy of those values in order to generate our plan data, and later on make modifications.

4. Save your new parameter set **CPYACT.**

Now, you need to execute the planning method, following this procedure:

1. Select and right-click on **CPYACT**, then select **Execute Method**, as shown in Figure 7.4. Because we are running the test run environment, the system will let us know if any problems are encountered during execution of the planning method.

Tip

It is important to make sure the procedures and processes you want to execute are doing exactly what they are intended to do. That is, it is not enough that the system tells you that the execution was performed successfully; you need to verify that the processes are the correct processes for your data transformation requirements. Review this on your own with several tests to make sure your functions are doing what they are supposed to do. Do not transport or assume that your objects are working successfully until you have manually verified the calculations and their effects on the test data, even if you successfully executed the planning method.

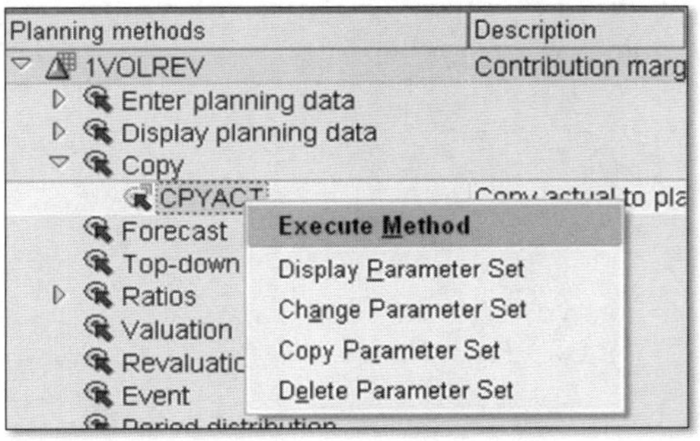

Figure 7.4 Executing the Copy Parameter Set

2. The screen shown in Figure 7.5 displays, showing the results of the test run. It appears that the parameter set executed successfully.

3. Right-click on the **CPYACT** planning method and select **Change Parameter Set**.

4. In the **Processing** area, select **Update Run** from the dropdown list. Once executed, this will complete the posting and update the SAP tables in the OLTP system.

5. Right-click on **CPYACT** and select **Execute Method** again.

Parameter Set	CPYACT	Copy actual to plan						

Date/Time/User		Number	Planning level	Plan. package	Method	Parameter ...	Processing
⊙ 02/22/2007		1	1VOLREV	PLVOLREV	ACOP	CPYACT	Test Run

Type	Message Text
⊙	Editing has been completed successfully

Figure 7.5 Screen Output of the Status of the CPYACT Copy Parameter Set

---

Tip

Before you execute the function, you can take a screenshot or write down the values so you can evaluate the final result of the processes.

Figure 7.6 presents the current (before) status of the data included in planning layout and the different characteristic and value fields selected to which to perform the change. The Copy planning method, as defined in Figure 7.3, copied all of the data between **01/2009** and **12/2009**.

Customer group	01		Industry
Material Group	01		ITEMS
Currency type	B0		Operating concern currency
Period/year	001/2009	To 012/2009	
Version	0		Plan/actual version
Record Type	F		Billing data

	D.	U...	Cash discount	Gross sales	Marketing division	Quantity discount
	01	ST	100.00	100.00	100.00	100.00

Figure 7.6 Data Status Before Executing the Copy Operation

Figure 7.7 shows the status after executing the Copy planning method, indicating that changes were made to the original data in the **Cash discount**, **Gross sales**, and **Quantity discount** columns displayed in Figure 7.6.

Take your time to analyze and understand the Copy planning method. It is very difficult to avoid using this planning method while developing your planning applications with the CO-PA planning framework. For that reason, the Copy planning method is considered one of the most important planning methods in the SAP system.

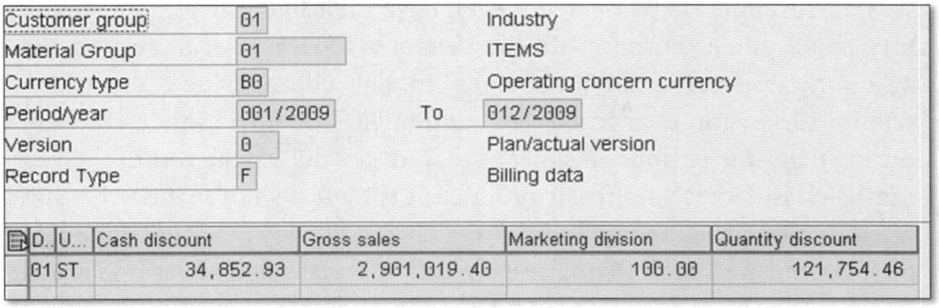

D.	U...	Cash discount	Gross sales	Marketing division	Quantity discount
01	ST	34,852.93	2,901,019.40	100.00	121,754.46

Customer group: 01 — Industry
Material Group: 01 — ITEMS
Currency type: B0 — Operating concern currency
Period/year: 001/2009 To 012/2009
Version: 0 — Plan/actual version
Record Type: F — Billing data

Figure 7.7 Data Values After Executing the Copy Operation

> **Tip**
>
> You can reset the system to the status before a planning method was executed by using the following path: **Edit • Undo Planning Function**.

7.1.4 Forecast

If you are interested in working with planning applications, you will want to generate scenarios that describe the future performance of selected values. The Forecast planning method provides a practical and scientific way to estimate your data into the future, using a predefined mathematical algorithm.

> **Note**
>
> Because this is a book designed to present the functionalities of the CO-PA planning framework rather than provide a complete view of financial, mathematical, and other types of analysis, we will limit our discussion of the Forecast planning method to a brief overview.

When working with forecasts in general there are three types of models:

▶ **Constant**
Used for time-series data in which values do not change much over time. For example, for a supermarket, the sales of frozen pizza is a constant value during the fiscal year, thus if the retailer knows that they will sell around 10 pizzas per day, all of the deliveries from the supplier must be planned using a constant model. In other words, the retailer in this scenario would want 10 packs of pizza available to the public at all times.

▶ **Seasonal**
Also called cycles, their behavior might depend on external factors, such as demand or period of the year. For example, for no other day of the year is turkey sold more than for Thanksgiving Day in the USA. For retailers,

seasonal products like this might even have their own category for inventory management purposes. In the case of a supermarket or retailer that sells turkeys, for example, a seasonal model will describe the expected sales of turkey for a particular year, and might also affect its classification during that time period. This means that turkey during the rest of the year can be classified as a nonbasic product (it is ok if it's not in stock because sales are slow; and it could be controlled with a constant model, for example), but during Thanksgiving season, turkey is classified as basic-seasonal. In other words, the retailer must have turkey in stock during this time if he wants to also sell tomatoes, spices, lettuce, gravy, and other things that people buy to go along with the turkey. They also need to control the product availability of the complimentary products, using turkey as a product that generates dependable demands.

▶ **Trend**
Trend is a rather complex model because it is a combination of the constant and seasonal models. It uses alpha, beta and gamma factors as ways to smooth the models' behavior. This model is the most common and you do not have to use all of the parameters.

In addition, the Forecast planning method requires a parameter set object and a forecast profile that has an alphanumeric name that uniquely identifies it. This forecast profile is a group of parameters with which you can project future values in a time series. You can use the same forecast profile again and again, saving you time, to manage the behavior of one or more key figures based on a forecast strategy.

Generally you should create a separate planning package to store the forecast data, because this planning method requires reference data from before the periods chosen inside the planning package. Once executed, the Forecast planning method reads the information available at the segment level of the operating concern to perform the forecast of a value field.

Tip

A forecast strategy is the same as a forecast model or mathematical algorithm that controls the behavior of the data values generated. There are at least 20 mathematical algorithms designed to create a forecast time series that can be as simple as a first-order equation and moving average, or as complex as the seasonal and Winters methods. The Winters Methods (part of the Winters-Whitney Methods) are considered to be one of the most mathematically accurate forecasting algorithms for time series and seasonal data.

Not all of the models require the smoothing factors available in the Forecast planning method, but they are available depending on the mathematical needs and complexity of your time series extracted from the OLTP system.

To successfully apply and develop your Forecast planning method, you need to perform additional configuration:

1. Go to the CO-PA planning framework, as shown in Figure 7.8, and review the information stored in your planning package for the dates, in this case between **1/2009** and **12/2009**, because this information will be used as a reference to forecast the values for 2010.

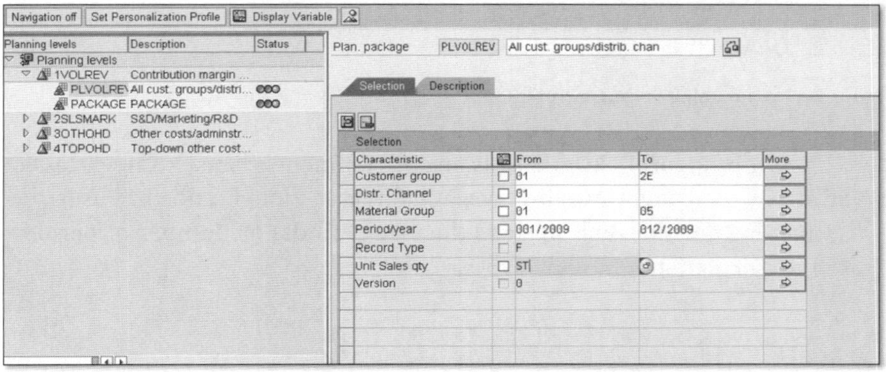

Figure 7.8 Reviewing the Planning Package for Defining the Reference Data for Forecasting

2. Next, we need to work with the maintain forecast profiles function, following the path **Profitability Analysis • Planning•Planning Aids • Maintain Forecast Profiles,** as shown in Figure 7.9.

3. Now you can configure the forecast profile, which is similar to a planning profile but creates a planning strategy associated with an algorithm that generates the planned values. As shown in Figure 7.10, different parameters are required, depending on the forecast strategy. For example, we will select the **Moving Average** forecast strategy, which only requires the parameter **Hist. periods** (number of periods). Define three periods, then complete the information as shown in Figure 7.10.

> **Note**
>
> When you configure your Forecast planning method, the historical periods (**Hist. periods**), **Periods/season**, and **Weighting group** determine the number of periods used by the forecast strategy to generate the data. For example, for generally stable data values, using the last three periods of the year is enough, but for very complex behavior maybe the last twelve periods might help with estimating the next six periods.

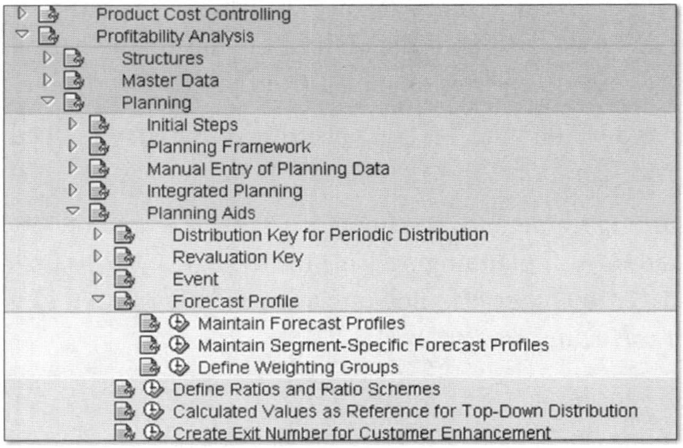

Figure 7.9 Maintaining Forecast Profiles

4. As shown in Figure 7.10, there is an SAP-defined forecast strategy called **FSC** that it is using a **Moving average** forecast model, and that uses the parameter **3** for the **Hist. periods** (history periods) or number of periods used to calculate the moving average.

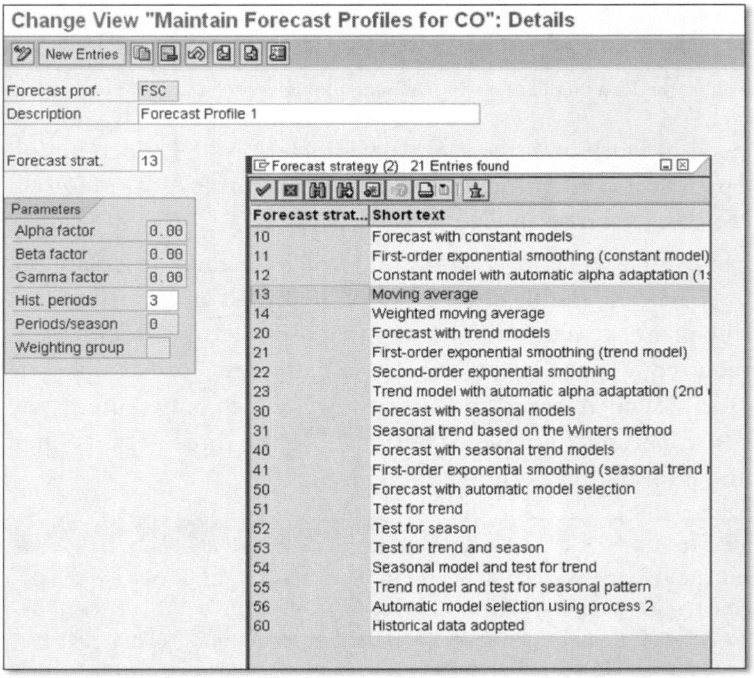

Figure 7.10 Creating a Forecast Strategy and a Forecast Algorithm as Part of a Forecast Profile

5. Now, you can use the **FSC** profile as part of the Forecast planning method as shown in Figure 7.11, under **Planning methods**. Also, notice that we are using as reference data the actual data from **01/2009** until **12/2009** to generate the new forecasted data using the moving average algorithm.

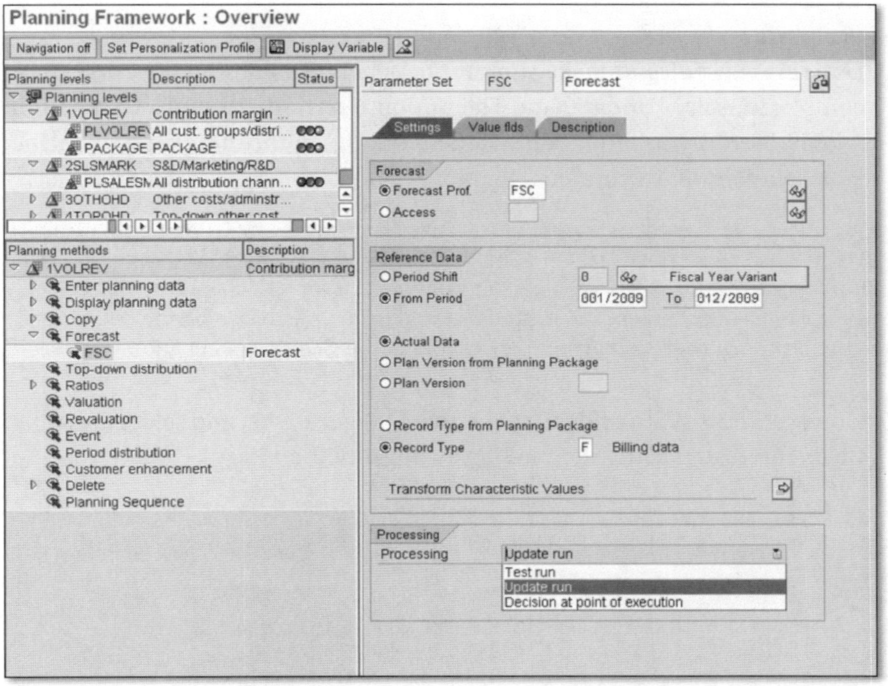

Figure 7.11 Assigning the FSC Planning Profile to your Forecast Planning Method

The key elements, as we will configure them on the **Settings** tab, shown in Figure 7.11, include:

▶ **Forecast Prof. (Forecast Profile)**
This has been set to FSC to access the moving average of the previously defined strategy.

▶ **Reference Data**
This is the data the SAP system will use to perform the forecast:

  ▶ **From Period**
  The time period to use as reference to generate the new data for the time periods limited in the planning package, or 1/2010 to 12/2010.

  ▶ **Actual Data**
  This specifies that we will perform a forecast of actual data only.

▶ **Record Type**

This lets you select the data type. F means that only billing data will be included in the forecasted periods. Other types of documents are reviewed later on in Chapter 8 when transferring data into CO-PA from other SAP modules.

▶ **Processing**

Use **Test run** twice to make sure not to generate values with errors. Once completed, select **Update run**. The option **Decision at point of execution** is only used if you think you will be working online and you will decide later whether to execute this function.

Tip

You do not use the Forecast planning method to estimate characteristics values but to estimate key figures. Characteristics are maintained based on the definitions of the planning levels and planning packages in the CO-PA planning framework.

---

6. Now, select the **Value flds** tab as shown in Figure 7.12, and select the value fields forecasted using the moving average method.

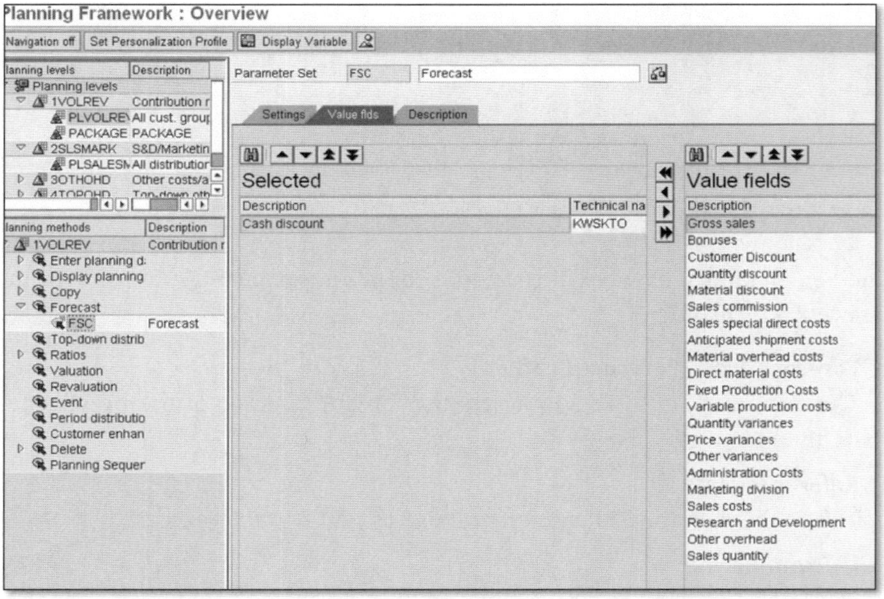

Figure 7.12 Adding the Cash Discount Value Field in the Value Field Tab

Notice that on the right side is the list of the different **Value Fields** available. Select the ones you are interested in and click on the left arrow to add them to the **Selected** region on the left. As shown in Figure 7.12, the **Cash discount** value field is the only selected key figure, to be forecast using the moving average, and the configurations created on the **Settings** tab displayed in Figure 7.11, such as **Record Type F**, **Actual Data**, and **Forecast Profile FSC**.

7. Select and right-click on **FSC Forecast** on the left.

8. Click on **Execute Method**, as shown in Figure 7.13.

The SAP system now generates a general check over the information presented and provides the information shown in Figure 7.13, informing you if any errors were detected during the execution of the planning method. Based on the same figure, we can conclude that our Forecast planning method has been correctly configured and executed. However, we still need to see if the data was generated as expected because regardless if the execution was successful, the configuration might be still incorrect.

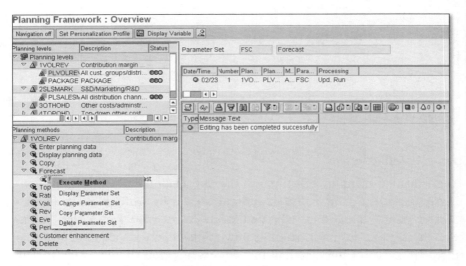

Figure 7.13 Executing the Forecast Planning Method

Remember, we wanted to generate data between 1/2010 and 12/2010 using 2009 data for the same time range as reference, and only for the **Cash discount** value field. With this information in mind, and knowing that the planning method ran successfully, let's see if any data was available for the selection criteria.

As shown in Figure 7.14, using the CO-PA planning framework, and the Display Planning Data planning method, we see that for the time period **1/2010** to **12/2010** the **Cash Discount 34,852.92** was generated based on the information previously contained in the 1/2009-12/2009 data range. This means that our Forecast planning method was successfully executed because previously there was no such data in the system (notice that the other value fields contain no data values).

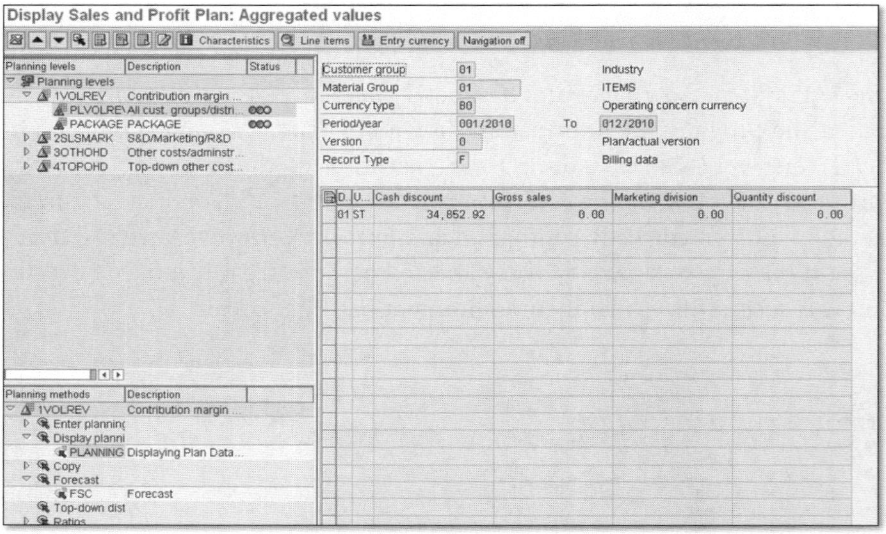

Figure 7.14 Reviewing the Forecast Planning Method Generated Values

7.1.5 Valuation

The Valuation planning method uses the information defined previously in Master Data using the path **Valuation Strategies in Profitability Analysis • Master Data • Valuation • Valuation Strategies • Define and Assign Valuation Strategies**. This information is now available in the Valuation planning method as part of the planning framework, and you simply assign it. The steps configured in your valuation strategy will be applied to the data in the planning framework. Refer back to Chapter 5 for the concepts behind this planning function.

7.1.6 Revaluation

In this section, you will learn about the Revaluation planning method, which you can use to change values during planning by specified percentages. In comparison with the Valuation planning method, Revaluation requires a planning aid called *revaluation keys*. As is the case with other planning methods in CO-PA planning framework, there are additional objects required to complete the definition and control the behavior of the data selection and generation in Revaluation. That is, Revaluation requires you to work with either **Maintain Revaluation Keys**, or with **Maintain Segment-Specific Revaluation Keys** if you want to affect particular characteristics and value fields contained inside your operating concern and defined as a segment.

Follow this procedure to create revaluation keys and use them in your planning applications:

1. Follow the path **Revaluation Keys object Profitability Analysis • Planning • Revaluation Key • Maintain Revaluation Keys**, as shown in Figure 7.15, and click on the execute icon next to **Maintain Revaluation Keys**.

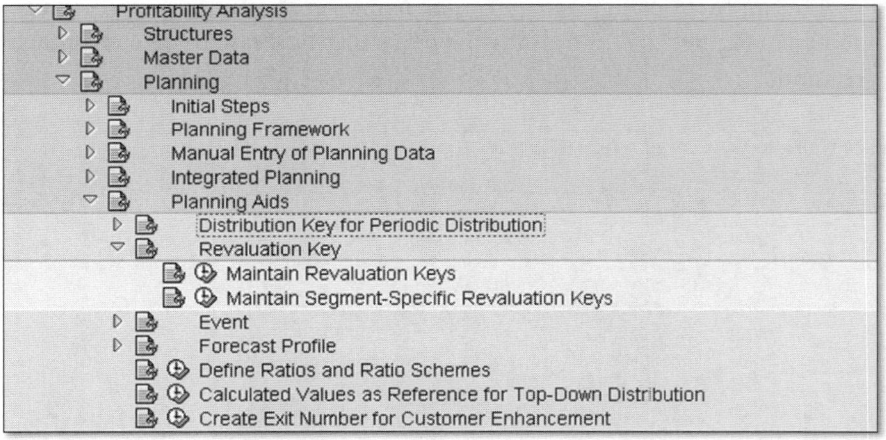

Figure 7.15 Accessing the Maintain Revaluation Keys Function

2. The screen shown in Figure 7.16 is displayed. Notice there are two nodes: **Revaluation Keys**, which defines the name of the object that will carry the value fields and the percentages, and **Assign factors**, where we create the assignment of value fields and percentages.

3. Select the change/modify icon (the pencil with glasses), and click on **New Entries**. Give the revaluation key a technical name of "RV" (in the **Rev** column) and a **Name** of "This is a Revaluation Key" as shown in Figure 7.16.

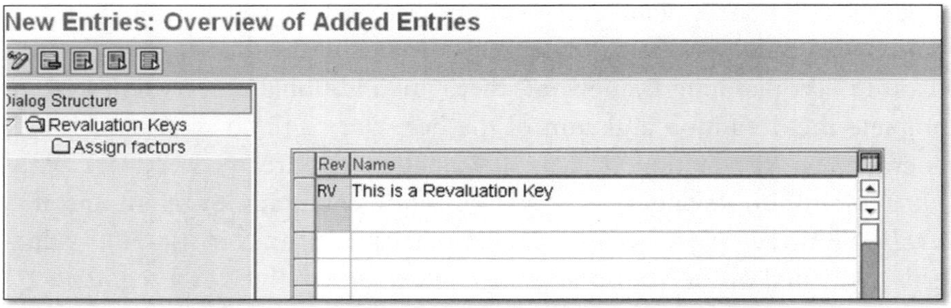

Figure 7.16 Configuring a Revaluation Key

4. Now, select the **Assign factors** node on the left-hand side of Figure 7.17 to define which key figures will be included as part of revaluation key **RV**, as shown in the same figure.

5. Assign the value fields that you want to increase by a specific percentage by finding them using their technical names in the **Field Name** column, shown in Figure 7.17, and typing the percentage increase in the **Percentage** column.

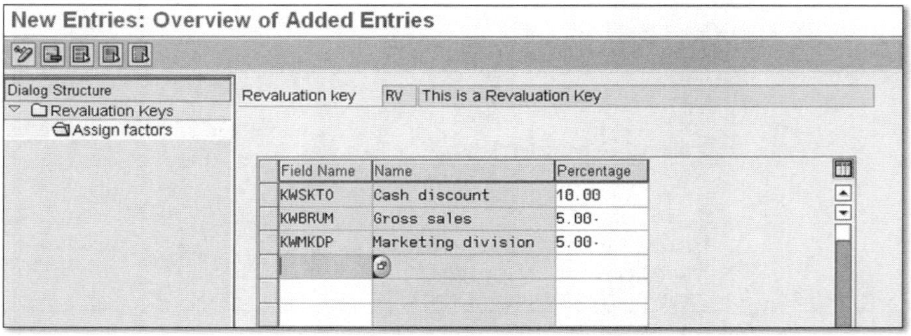

Figure 7.17 Configuring the Value Fields and Percentages of the Revaluation Key RV

As shown in Figure 7.17, we want to work with the following value fields:

▶ **KWSKTO (Cash discount)** increased by 10 %

▶ **KWBRUM (Gross Sales)** reduced by 5 %

▶ **JWMKDP (Marketing division)** reduced by 5 %

Notice that the notation for the SAP system to create a reduction is **5.00-**, with the minus sign at the end, as also shown in Figure 7.17. To make a percentage increase, just the number is entered (without a sign).

6. Once you are satisfied with your changes, save them.

At this point, you have completed the definition of your revaluation key RV. Now, let us suppose that we want to adjust the current data values with the percentages previously defined. For this, we need to work with the Revaluation planning method in the CO-PA planning framework and configure another parameter set to access the information contained in the RV revaluation key.

First, let us review the current status of your data for the period from 01/2009 to 12/2009 in your SAP system, as shown in Figure 7.18. This is what the data looks like before executing the Revaluation planning method.

D.	U...	Cash discount	Gross sales	Marketing division	Quantity discount
01	ST	34,852.93	2,901,019.40	100.00	121,754.46

Figure 7.18 Data Before the Revaluation is Executed

Next, we will review the **Settings** tab of the Revaluation planning method and its parameter set. As shown in Figure 7.19, perform the following:

1. In the **Revaluation** section on the **Settings** tab, assign the **Revaluation key RV** that we just created.

2. In the **Processing** section, select **Test run** to avoid postings for the time being.

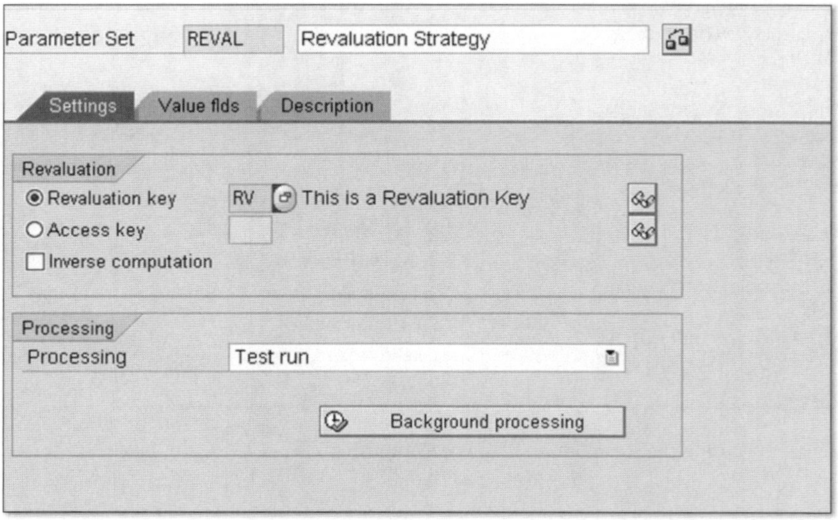

Figure 7.19 Configuring the Revaluation Key Parameter Set

3. Select the **Value flds** tab to select the value fields **Gross sales**, **Cash discount**, and **Marketing division**, as shown in Figure 7.20. Use the left arrow to move selected value fields from the **Value fields** area to the **Selected** area.

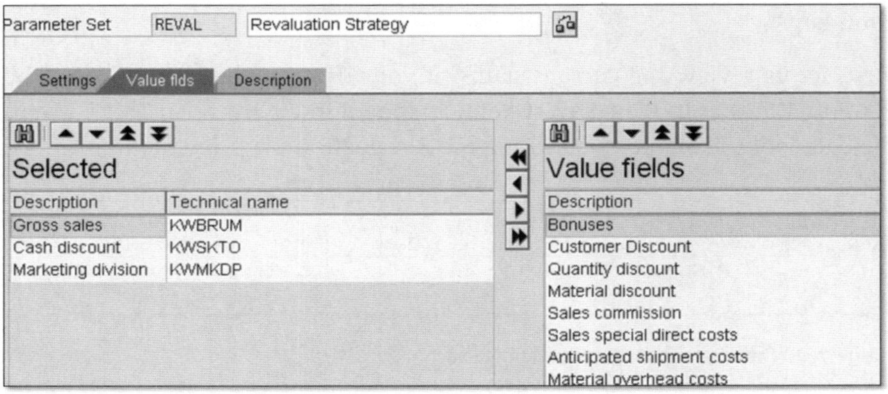

Figure 7.20 Adding Your Value Fields to the REVAL Parameter Set

4. Save your work, and go back to the CO-PA planning framework and identify the parameter set that you defined, in this case **REVAL**, and execute the Revaluation planning method as shown in Figure 7.21.

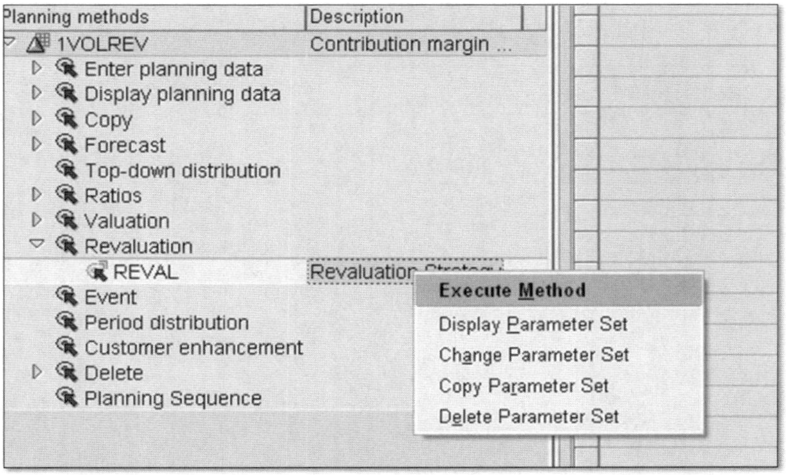

Figure 7.21 Executing the Revaluation Planning Method

To make sure that what you thought you created (the Revaluation planning method) is actually being executed inside the SAP system, review your data values using a parameter set in the Display Planning Data planning method with the same layout, as shown in Figure 7.22.

D. U...	Cash discount	Gross sales	Marketing division	Quantity discount
01 ST	38,338.24	2,755,968.47	95.00	121,754.46

Figure 7.22 New Values After Executing the Revaluation Planning Method Using the Revaluation Key RV

Compare your original and modified data values shown in Figure 7.18 and Figure 7.22 respectively, to see how effective your design and configuration are:

▶ **Cash discount**: 38,338.24 is 10 % more than 34,852.93.

▶ **Gross sales**: 2,755,968.47 is 5 % less than 2,901,019.4.

▶ **Marketing division**: 95 is 5 % less than 100.

Now you can be confident that you have successfully configured the Revaluation planning method and you can use the same revaluation key with other planning packages and planning levels.

The flexibility of an SAP system often allows more than one correct way of delivering the same result. Thus, you can generate the same data values you generated with revaluation keys with an alternative planning method called Ratios. Ratios are typically used when more sophisticated calculations are required as part of your planning efforts that demand working with the division and the multiplication operations.

7.1.7   Ratios

The Ratios planning method lets you valuate a plan version using average prices from a reference version or reference actual data. This means that you can store your price plan and quantity plan separately and then use these prices to valuate the quantity plan. Ratios can be used both in manual planning and in automatic planning.

Ratios are another example of CO-PA planning methods that require additional definitions external to the CO-PA planning framework. Ratios are quite popular among managers because they are the calculation of indexes that divide a numerator by a denominator and sometimes followed by multiplication.

For example, for just-in-case situations, if we define the equation A/B, A is the numerator, and B is the denominator. A ratio is a division, and sometimes we may find relationships, such as A/B*C. A ratio is the quotient of two value fields, such as sales revenue divided by quantity. In this section you will define ratios used as part of your planning applications with the Ratio planning method.

Ratios can be used in four ways (using an example of a formula with three fields):

▶ If you change one value of a formula of three fields and the other two can either be entered or cannot be entered, or are not even in the layout, the system cannot decide which of the two fields should be calculated.

▶ If you change one of the fields and only one of the other two fields can be entered manually, the system assumes that it should calculate the field that cannot be entered manually, regardless of which calculation type was chosen.

▶ When you change two of the fields, the system calculates the third field.

▶ If you change all three fields, the system calculates sales as quantity * price and overwrites the manually entered value.

You must assign at least one access-level characteristic to each ratio in a ratio group. Access-level characteristics determine for each ratio which combination of characteristics the system should use to access the valuation. This makes it possible, for example, to calculate the average price for a product group. The calculation types for the ratios are not involved in this function.

You need to define the ratios separately and place these in a ratio scheme before you can use them to valuate your plan data. The ratio scheme determines which ratios are selected in which order.

With an "access-level characteristic," you can specify the planning level (the combination of characteristics) at which the ratio should be used for valuation. This makes it possible, for example, to plan individual products and valuate these using the average price at the product group level. Ratios, ratio schemes, and access-level characteristics are defined in customizing.

Depending on the industry, the calculation of ratios will vary depending on the performance indicators required to be reported to management. For example, if you are in the automotive industry, you are interested in knowing about cost reduction efforts, inventory flow, and production indicators, such as cycle time and downtimes of machinery, and all of them can be defined as ratios. In the retailing industry, it is more important to know inventory turnover, delivery times, profitability by product line, and sales per square foot. If you are in the financial sector, you probably want to know the profitability by client segment, number of transactions per day by product line, and number of new mortgage loans approved; because all of them are core indicators that reflect the health of the business.

Regardless of where your CO-PA implementation is taking place, you must clearly define and understand your ratios before creating them, making sure that they measure exactly the relationships that you want to monitor.

> **Note**
>
> The useful and simple calculations performed by the Ratio planning method are a must in any SAP implementation, and therefore you must remember them.

Now let us start working with ratios, creating quantity discounts:

1. Follow the path **Planning • Planning Aids • Define Ratios and Ratio Schemes** to start configuring ratios and ratio schemes, as shown in Figure 7.23. A ratio is one object, and a ratio scheme is a collection of objects with specific relationships. Ratio schemes reuse the information in the ratio objects they contain.

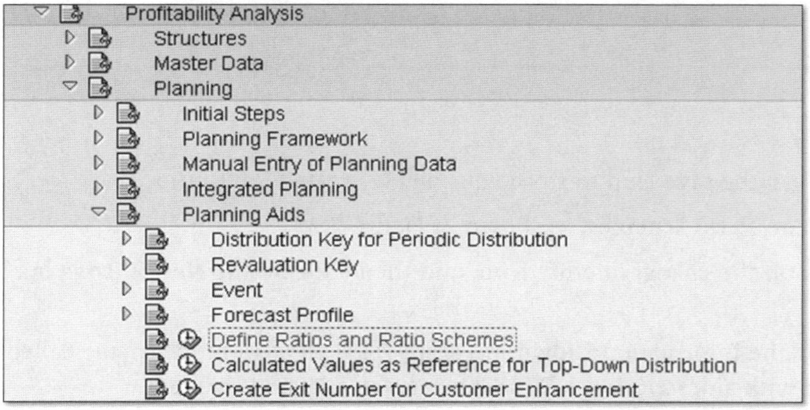

Figure 7.23 Accessing the Define Ratios and Ratio Schemes Object

Part of the ratio definition is the calculation type, which is only relevant in manual planning, but not for ratio schemes. Calculations, such as price = revenue/quantity, revenue = quantity * price, or quantity = revenue/price depend greatly on a number of factors, such as which fields are changed or which fields can or cannot be manually entered.

2. Click on the change/modify icon.

3. Click on the **New Entries** button to create the ratio with the configuration information shown in Figure 7.24. The ratio is called **Rat1**, and has two components: **Numerator KWSKT0** and **Denominator KWMGRB**. In addition, the **Rat1** ratio uses **Calc. type 1** (calculation type 1), which requires recalculating the ratio. Now you can assign the ratio **Rat1** to a group of specific ratios called a ratio scheme.

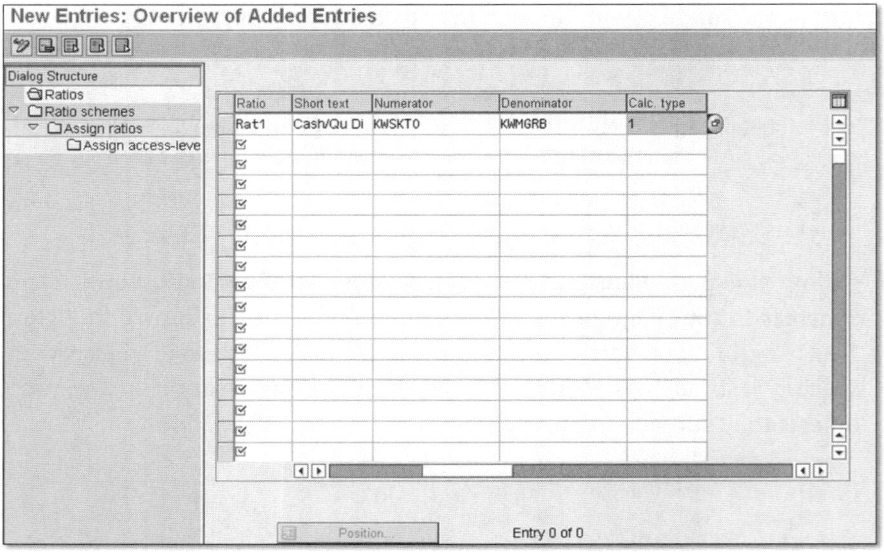

Figure 7.24 Creating Ratio Rat1

4. Click on the save icon to store your newly created **Rat1** ratio.

5. Click on **Ratio Schemes**, as shown in Figure 7.25.

6. Click on the change/modify icon, and then click on the **New Entries** button.

7. Using the information shown in Figure 7.25, create a ratio scheme called **TEST** with a description of **This is a test for a Ratio Scheme**.

8. Click on the save icon.

9. Select the line of the newly created **TEST** ratio scheme to assign ratios inside of this object.

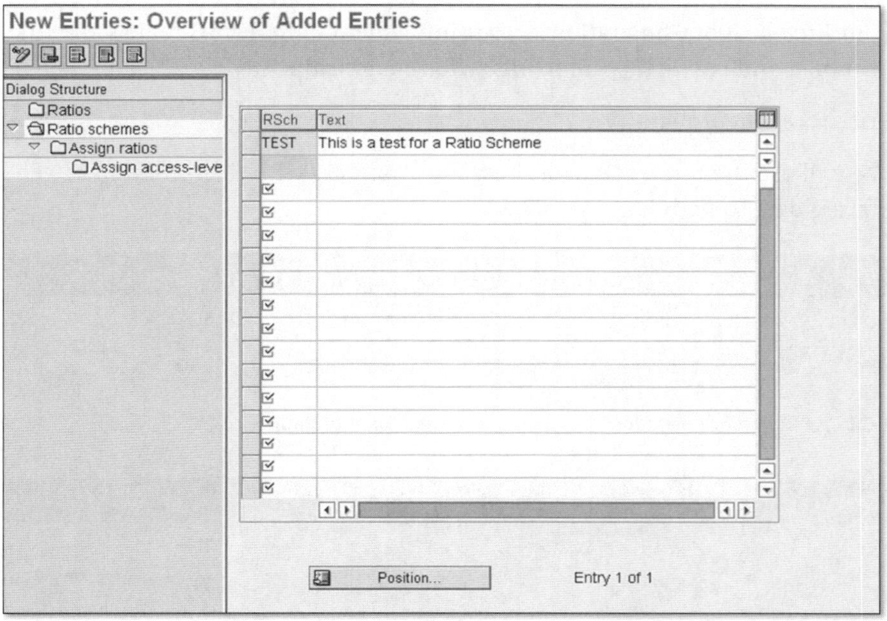

Figure 7.25 Creating a Ratio Scheme

As shown in Figure 7.26, you are assigning two ratios to the ratio scheme **TEST**. One of them is **RAT1 Cash Disc/Quant Disc** (cash discount/quantity discount) and the other is **FPROD Prod. Fixed costs/pc.** Thus, the **TEST** ratio scheme is an umbrella object that carries the information of several ratios, so the SAP system can access a common element to execute different functions.

10. Save your changes.

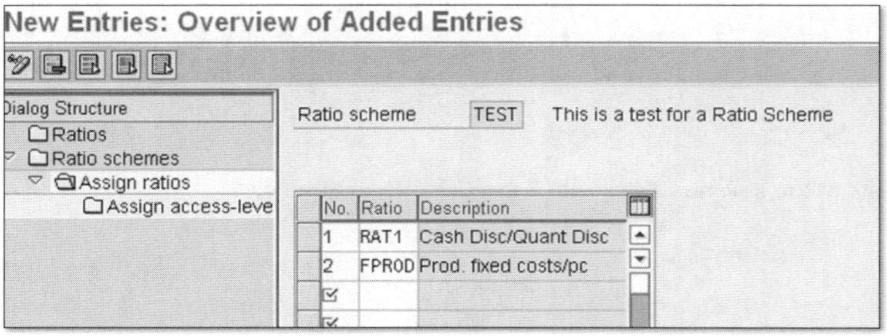

Figure 7.26 Assigning Ratios to a Ratio Scheme

Next, we need to define the level of detail at which the reference data is selected during the calculation of ratios, using access-level characteristics. Access-level characteristics can be simple or sophisticated, depending on your final goal of using ratios in your implementation. Let us review the first example, and create the following ratio relationship:

Price = revenue/quantity

We will use the reference data shown in Table 7.1 with the intention of generating data to populate Table 7.2.

Product	Customer	Quantity	Revenue
P1	C1	10	100
P1	C2	20	260

Table 7.1 Reference Data for the Price = Revenue/Quantity Ratio

Product	Customer	Quantity	Revenue
P1	C1	11	???
P1	C2	22	???

Table 7.2 Goal of the Ratio Price = Revenue/Quantity Generation Ratio

▶ **Strategy 1**
Using access-level characteristics, you can estimate the values of revenue in different ways. In strategy 1, you use two characteristics relationships, product and customer, to estimate the values of revenue, as shown in Table 7.3. This leads us to ratio calculation strategy 1: revenue is calculated based on the price for each individual customer from Table 7.1 as reference, and then multiplied by the quantity in Table 7.2.

Product	Customer	Quantity	Revenue
P1	C1	11	110
P1	C2	22	286

Table 7.3 Results of the Revenue Ratio with Ratio Calculation Strategy 1

The calculation logic using product and customer as access-level characteristics for the ratio revenue values displayed in Table 7.3 is as follows:

```
110 = 11 * 100 / 10
286 = 22 * 260 / 20
```

▶ **Strategy 2**
Alternatively, you can calculate revenue by using the product characteristic as the only access-level characteristic assigned to the ratio revenue, leading us to ratio calculation strategy 2: quantities are valuated using an average price for all customers because only the characteristic product is used to estimate the values of revenue. The results of this change in logic are presented in Table 7.4.

Product	Customer	Quantity	Revenue
P1	C1	11	132
P1	C2	22	264

Table 7.4 Results of the Revenue Ratio with Strategy Ratio Calculation 2

The ratio calculation procedure using strategy 2 is as follows:

```
132 = 11 * ( 100 + 260 ) / (10 + 20 )
264 = 22 * ( 100 + 260 ) / (10 + 20 )
```

The difference in the results, shown in Table 7.3 and Table 7.4, by simply changing the number of characteristics assigned in the access-level characteristic, is significant. In general, the number of characteristics assigned greatly depends on the logic behind your ratio calculation. Based on this information, you can see that the calculation of ratio schemes can be a sophisticated issue, depending on the number of characteristics involved.

For our purpose, define access-level characteristics as follows:

1. Define **Customer group** and **Material Group** as the access-level characteristics for our **TEST** ratio scheme, as shown in Figure 7.27.

2. Assign the **TEST** ratio scheme to the **Ratio** planning method as shown in Figure 7.28.

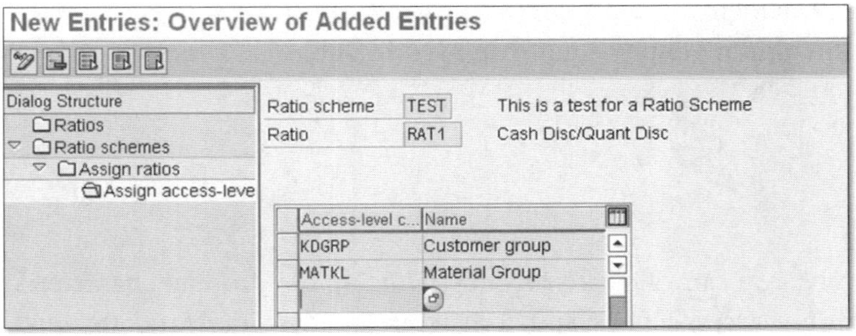

Figure 7.27 Configuration of the Access-Level Characteristics

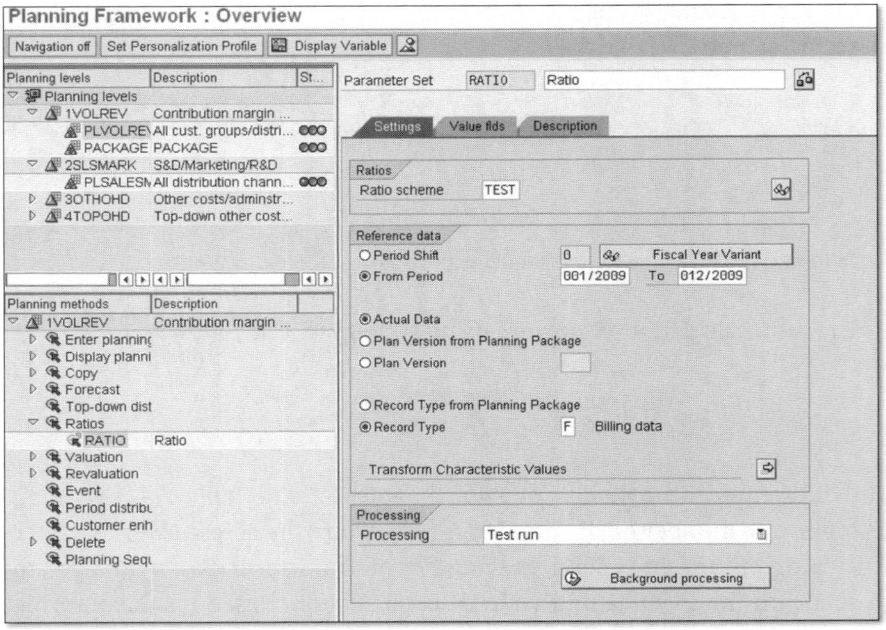

Figure 7.28 Assigning the TEST Ratio Scheme to the Ratio Planning Method

Creating Your Own Ratio Calculation Formulas

Although ratios are an easy function to master, you can alternatively create your own calculation formulas using Report Painter and adding them to your layout as an additional column, limiting characteristics in that way.

As an alternative to creating ratios, use this procedure:

1. Follow the path **Planning • Manual Entry of Planning Data • Define Planning Layout** and choose **Change Planning Layout**. Figure 7.29 shows the information from our previously created **LAYOUT** planning layout in the **Report Painter** environment.

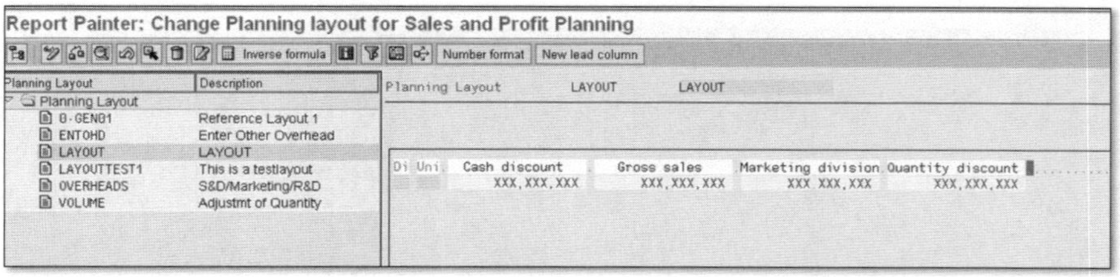

Figure 7.29 Creating a Ratio in a Planning Layout

2. Start creating an additional column as part of the layout by clicking on the end of the column called **Quantity discount**, and selecting the element type **Formula**, as shown in Figure 7.30.

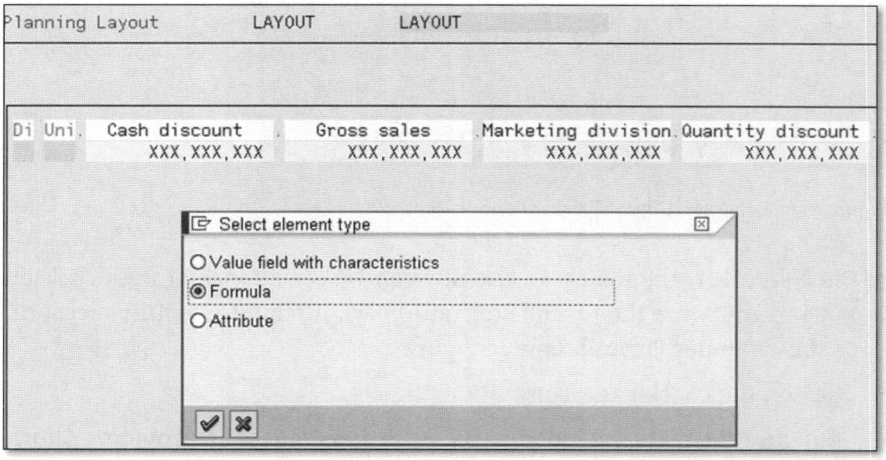

Figure 7.30 Creating a Ratio as a Formula Object

3. Click on the checkmark icon to enter the Report Painter formula editor, shown in Figure 7.31. The formula editor contains different components:

   ▸ **Formula Table**
   Describes the relationships or formula calculations of the value fields available.

255

▶ **Formula Components**
Displays the components available to include as part of the **Formula Table** using an **ID** identifier. For example, **X001** identifies the **Cash discount** value field. There are also other components that help to design a formula such as multiplication (*), division (/), parenthesis, individual numbers, and others.

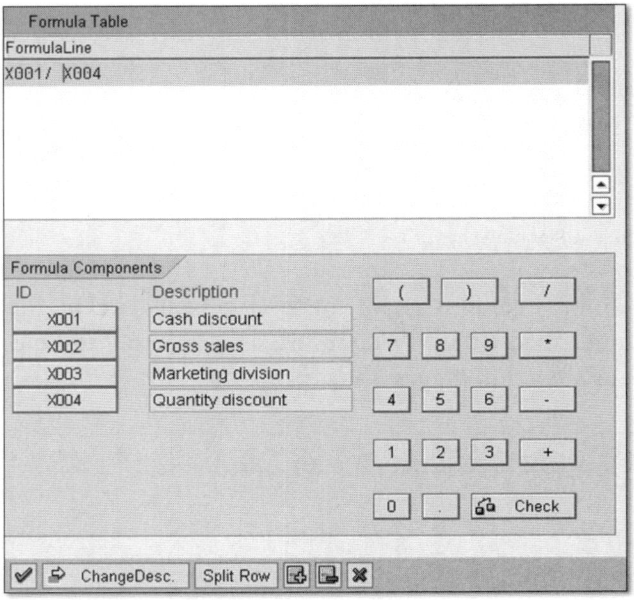

Figure 7.31 Using the Report Painter Formula Editor

4. Click on **X001**, then click on the division (/) operator, and then click on **X004** to configure the formula (or ratio) Cash discount/Quantity discount, as shown under **FormulaLine** in Figure 7.31.

5. Click on the checkmark icon.

6. Configure the name and identifiers of the new object by providing **Short**, **Medium**, and **Long** texts, as shown in Figure 7.32.

7. Click on the checkmark icon.

As shown in Figure 7.33, you now have an **Alternative Ratio** calculation as part of your **LAYOUT** planning layout.

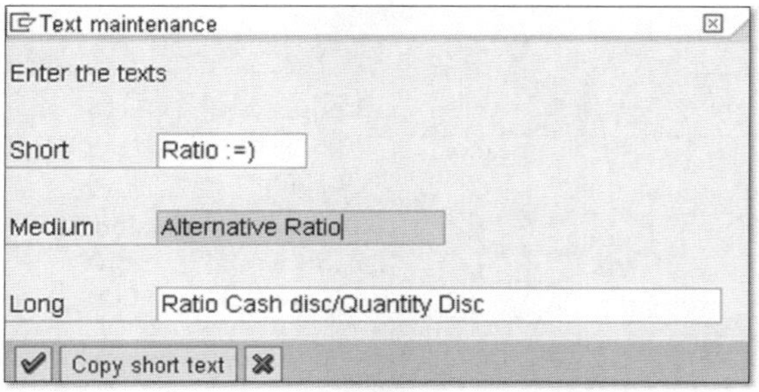
Text maintenance
Enter the texts
Short
Ratio :=)
Medium
Alternative Ratio
Long
Ratio Cash disc/Quantity Disc
Copy short text

Figure 7.32 Configuring the Names for the New Formula Object

> **Note**
>
> More complicated ratios are better delivered using the Ratio planning method in combination with segment-level characteristics.

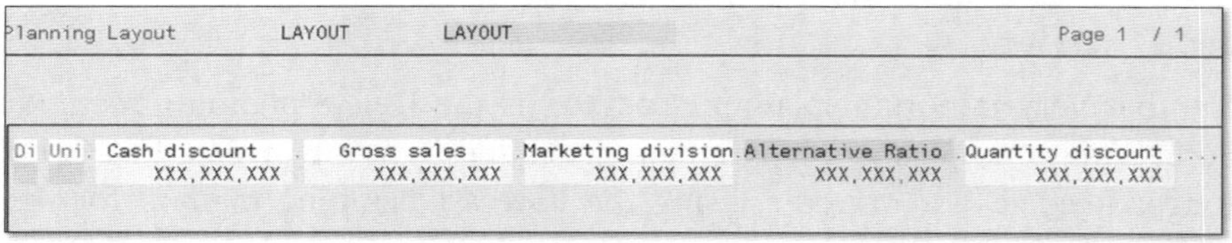
Planning Layout
LAYOUT
LAYOUT
Page 1 / 1
Di
Uni
Cash discount
Gross sales
Marketing division
Alternative Ratio
Quantity discount
XXX,XXX,XXX
XXX,XXX,XXX
XXX,XXX,XXX
XXX,XXX,XXX
XXX,XXX,XXX

Figure 7.33 Reviewing your Formula Object in Your Planning Layout

If you now run the planning layout LAYOUT, the ratio **Alternative Ratio** displays a value of **0.29**, as shown in Figure 7.34, after performing the same procedure used by the Ratio planning method. As you can see, there is more than one way to deliver and achieve the same information.

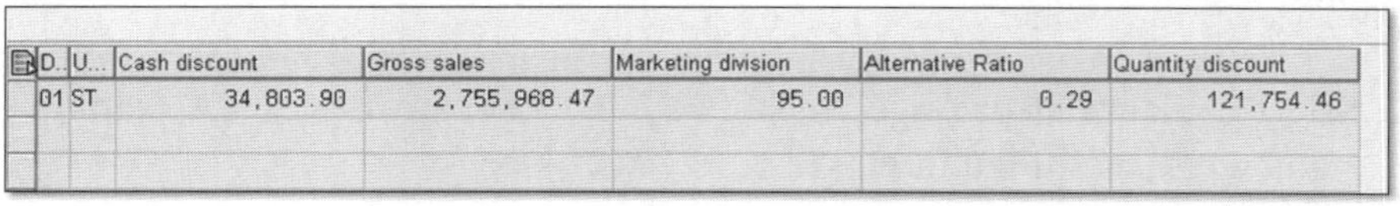
D.
U...
Cash discount
Gross sales
Marketing division
Alternative Ratio
Quantity discount
01
ST
34,803.90
2,755,968.47
95.00
0.29
121,754.46

Figure 7.34 Reviewing the Alternative Ratio Information After Executing the LAYOUT Planning Layout

In summary, review Figure 7.35 for a final look at the ratio concept. On the right side of the figure, you see that you require a **Reference version** of data that you will use to calculate the **Ratio R1=Q1*R2/Q2**. This relationship is maintained in the generation of the **Current plan version**, shown on the left side of Figure 7.35. Notice that we are using two access-level characteristics, product and customer, to make the calculation.

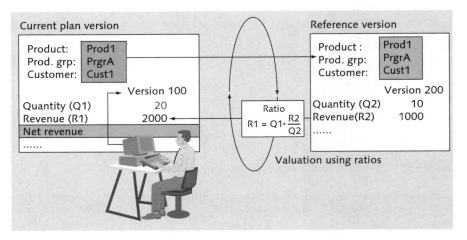

Figure 7.35 Valuation Using Ratios from a Reference Version

7.1.8 Delete

Another very important planning method is the Delete planning method. Sometimes you need to remove data generated by error or data that is no longer needed. For example, using the Forecast planning method for the cash discount value field, we generated data for the period between 1/2010 and 12/2010. We now want to get rid of this information, following this procedure:

> **Note**
>
> By now you should know how to navigate the CO-PA planning framework to access the screen shown in Figure 7.36. If not, go back to previous activities to review this information.

1. Select a planning package, such as **PLVOLREV**, in the CO-PA planning framework, as shown in Figure 7.36.

2. Select the **Delete** planning method, and create a **Parameter Set** called **DELEFSCT**, using the information shown in Figure 7.36.

3. Specify the date when the data to be deleted was generated. In our case, we want to delete the data generated on **02/24/2007**.

4. In the **Processing** section, select **Update run**.

5. Select the **Value flds** tab and select the **Cash discount** value field in order to delete *only* the data for that particular object.

6. Save your work, and execute the planning method.

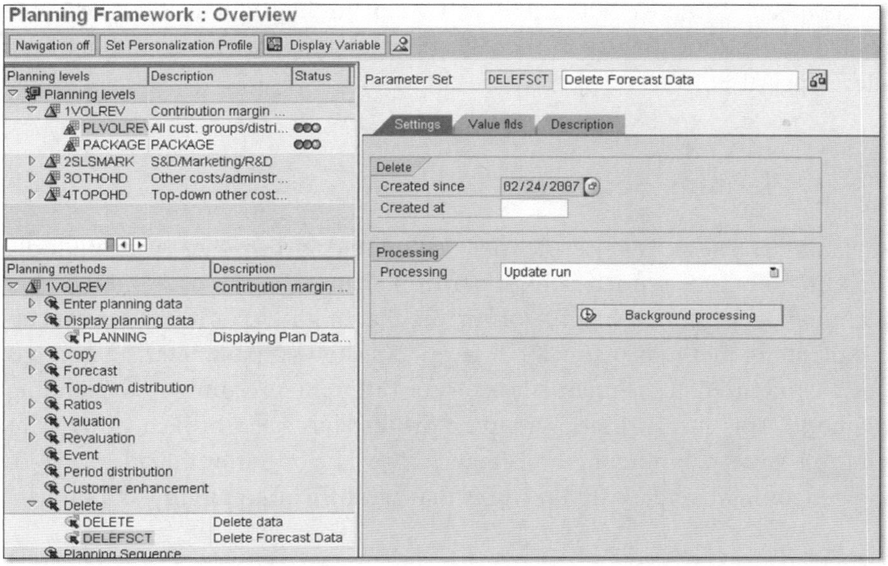

Figure 7.36 Deleting the Forecasted Data Created on 02/24/2007

7. You should receive confirmation that the run was successfully completed. Otherwise, you can review any issues on the right side of the screen.

8. Go back to the display planning area layout for the **01/2010** to **12/2010** data range established in the planning package to verify that the data for **Cash discount** for the forecast time periods has been erased from the SAP database, as shown in Figure 7.37.

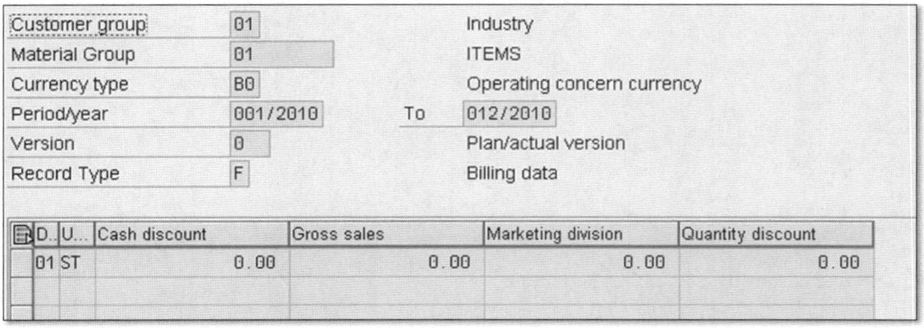

Figure 7.37 Confirming the Deletion of Your 2010 Data

Note

Exercise extreme caution when using the Delete planning method to avoid deleting data that is still required in the SAP system.

In the next section, we will briefly explore planning sequences, a more controlled and automatic way of managing complex operations by subdividing these operations into small pieces.

7.2 Planning Sequences

A *planning sequence* is a user-defined sequence or process that runs multiple planning methods sequentially to perform changes to the data limited by a planning package. This helps avoid errors that might occur if you are executing planning methods manually. Figure 7.38 shows a parameter set that has been configured to sequentially execute different preconfigured planning methods. This means that a complex process has been broken down into multiple small planning methods that change data one after the other, avoiding generating complex architectures that are difficult to modify and update.

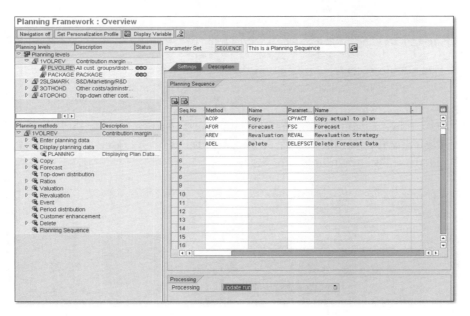

Figure 7.38 Creating a Planning Sequence

For example, based on the information we have previously developed, you may want to use a planning sequence to execute multiple operations, using the following specific logic:

1. Copy actual data from a referenced plan data.

2. Perform a forecast of the actual data.

3. Revaluate the actual data by specific percentages to reflect adjustments for inflation.

4. Delete the data of previously forecasted years.

For the planning sequence to work properly, you must select a planning method to execute at each part of the sequence, and then associate the parameter set linked to that planning method. For example, in **Seq. No 1**, shown in Figure 7.38, the planning method **ACOP (Copy)** is the first to run, using the parameter set **CPYACT (Copy actual to plan)** contained in the planning method. The same logic applies to the rest of the objects included in the planning sequence.

In this respect, the goal of the CO-PA planning framework is to visualize complex operations as a planning sequence to simplify a controlled data transformation process.

> **Note**
>
> The CO-PA planning framework has a submenu called **Integrated Planning** that was not discussed in this section. This submenu allows interaction with other components of the SAP system, such as Materials management (MM), Financials (FI), and SAP NetWeaver Business Intelligence (BI).

7.3 Summary

The CO-PA planning framework is a powerful and important tool available in CO-PA that helps you avoid increasing the complexity of your implementation and at the same time provides interaction with data input and transformation. Planning with CO-PA allows you to create sophisticated and powerful applications without leaving the traditional OLTP environment of SAP, and without the need to create complex objects that interact with SAP NetWeaver BI 7.0 or SAP Business Warehouse (BW) to use SEM-BPS or BW-BPS. This is because the CO-PA planning framework lets you perform operations very similar to those performed in these environments.

However, the CO-PA planning framework has limitations depending on the data volume and based on the types of data transformation required. For example, if you need to interact heavily with the Enterprise Portal Applications (EP), you should use the capabilities available in the SAP NetWeaver BI environment. On the other hand, if you simply require data manipulation, the planning methods in CO-PA provide solutions for most requirements.

Using CO-PA as a consolidation tool to access information from different SAP modules is one of its most important capabilities. In this chapter, we will briefly explore some of the options contained inside the Flows of Actual Values menu and how to configure some of the structures required for this functionality.

8 Flows of Actual Values: Transferring Actual Data into CO-PA

Profitability Analysis is not just about connectivity to a few tables in R/3 or SAP ERP ECC 6.0, it is also about determining whether the overall transactions from a company, business unit, controlling area, profit center, or all of them are profitable for the corporation. For this reason, to evaluate revenues, expenses, investments, and costs in CO-PA, we need to transfer actual data from other components of the transactional system into CO-PA. We'll look at how to do this in detail in this chapter.

> **Note**
>
> This chapter will provide a brief introduction on how to connect to modules such as Financials (FI), Controlling (CO), Materials Management (MM), Sales and Distribution (SD), and others, but because there are quite a few functionalities available in the transactional system of SAP, the information in this chapter cannot go into a lot of detail. Many of the concepts involved require further study that, unfortunately, goes beyond the scope of this book.

8.1 Overview

Figure 8.1 provides a general overview of the power of CO-PA to consolidate data without leaving the transactional system of SAP, that can be uploaded into profitability segments created inside the operating concern. Processes described in this figure provide an overview of the possible data and the consolidation power of CO-PA, similarly to that of SAP Business Warehouse (BW)/SAP NetWeaver Business Intelligence (BI) to connect to different sources of data inside the transactional system.

As shown in Figure 8.1, some of the components that you can access by using CO-PA flows of actual values include **Overhead Cost Controlling**, information from **Cost centers**, **Cost objects** from **Product Cost Controlling** (PC), **Revenues** from **SD**, **Cost Element Accounting**, **FI** information, and more.

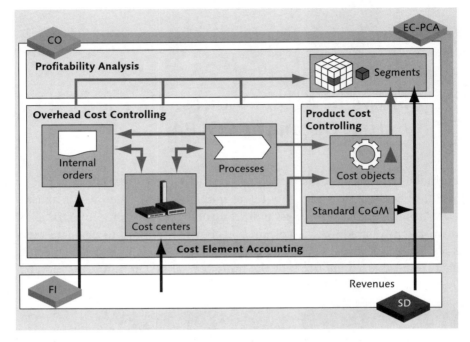

Figure 8.1 Reviewing Actual Data Flows Available in CO-PA

To enhance your understanding of the information and data available for the integration and transfer of actual data inside the CO-PA profitability segments, review Figure 8.2. It provides a more detailed breakdown of the data elements involved to generate Profit and Loss (P&L) information. For example, you can see that you can extract sales order information, such as sales quantity, rebates, and sales revenue by transferring billing documents from SD, or that you can generate direct costs values by making direct postings from FI, and so on.

The processes shown in the model presented in Figure 8.2 occur within the transactional system of SAP. Therefore, you combine data already consolidated inside CO-PA with other platforms such as SAP BW/SAP NetWeaver BI and Customer Relationship management (CRM) environments, as shown in Figure 8.3, to perform extraction and retraction.

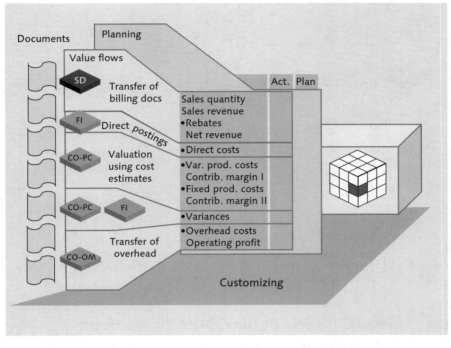

Figure 8.2 Integrated Business Model to Collect Revenue and Costs

> **Note**
>
> Extraction and retraction are extensively covered in two ASAP "how-to" papers called "How-to CO-PA Extraction" and "How-to CO-PA Retraction." You can access these papers in the SAP Marketplace or at *http://sdn.sap.com*.

Figure 8.2 and Figure 8.3 identify just how much information can be connected to CO-PA using the menu Flows of Actual Values, and how this information can be directed into other systems, such as SAP NetWeaver BI/SAP BW. As its name implies, flows of actual values is the component that controls how actual values are accessed and included into the characteristics and value fields that define profitability segments. However, sometimes you might need to connect to other systems using SAP NetWeaver BI technologies instead.

Let's now take a general look at the CO-PA Flows of Actual Values menu.

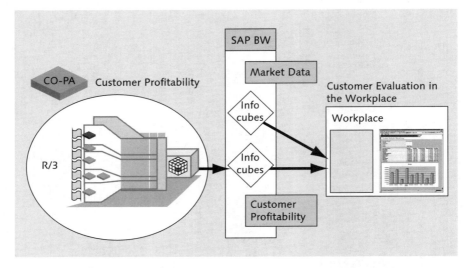

Figure 8.3 Data Flow into the SAP BW/SAP NetWeaver BI Environment Using CO-PA as a Data Source Environment

8.2 General Review of the CO-PA Flows of Actual Values Menu

As shown in Figure 8.4, the **Flows of Actual Values** menu is displayed by following this path: **Profitability Analysis • Flows of Actual Values**. As we've said before, the idea of CO-PA is integration with other SAP system modules to calculate a company's value every period, using transactional data to present revenues and costs as accurately as possible. In the **Flows of Actual Values** menu, you can see the different components, such as **Transfer of Incoming Sales Orders**, **Transfer of Billing Documents**, **Order and Project Settlement** (internal orders and projects), **Direct Posting from FI/MM**, **Settlement of Production Variances**, **Transfer of Overhead**, **Multiple Valuation Approaches/Transfer Prices**, **Periodic Adjustments**, and others.

A detailed explanation of each of these items is beyond the scope of this book; however, it is within the scope of this book to explain to you how to get this information and incorporate it into your reports and planning applications to calculate revenue and costs to create cash flows for each time period within a fiscal year.

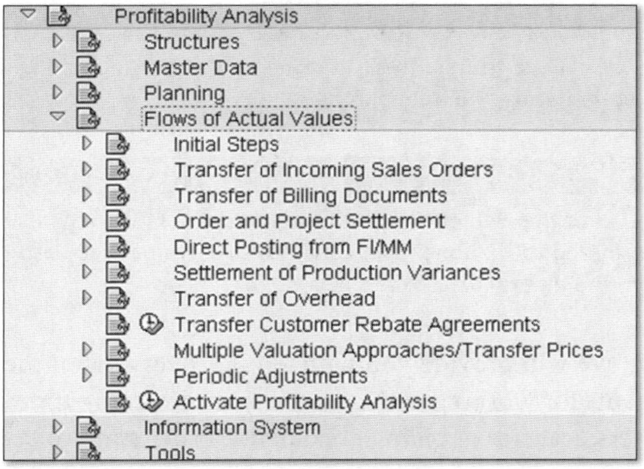

Figure 8.4 Reviewing the Flows of Actual Values Menu of CO-PA

A general procedure can be described as follows, regardless of the type of component to extract:

1. Any of the actual value components shown in Figure 8.4 can be added to your operating concern. To do so, you need to associate each component with value fields or characteristics, or create user-defined objects to accept the information. Remember that value fields can be of type value or quantity to store a currency or a number.

2. Define number ranges to filter the information to transfer into CO-PA. You can define number ranges in the **Initial Steps** submenu inside the **Flows of Actual Values** menu of CO-PA, as shown in Figure 8.4. When doing so, you must define value field groups representing the possible combinations of value fields in an operating concern. These value fields groups are used to specify the following:

   ▸ Which value fields should be made available to users entering or displaying a line item

   ▸ In what order these value fields should be displayed

   ▸ Whether specific value fields can be filled

   ▸ Whether specific value fields have to be filled

   ▸ Whether specific value fields may only be displayed

3. Select the fields and components you want to transfer.

In the following sections, we will provide you with a quick overview of the most important components for working with actual values, including transfer of incoming sales orders, transfer of billing documents, order and project settlement, direct posting from FI/MM, settlement of production variances, and transfer of overhead.

8.3 Transfer of Incoming Sales Orders

Sales orders are the source of revenue for the SAP system coming from the SD module based on the transfer of billing documents. As shown earlier in Figure 8.2, notice that sales order information is extracted based on four components: **Sales quantity**, **Sales Revenue**, **Rebates**, and **Net Revenue**.

All revenues, sales deductions, and other values (such as transfer prices) are defined as conditions in SD. You assign these conditions to the corresponding CO-PA value fields, with limitations, to transfer billing documents to CO-PA. Now let us review how to access and configure CO-PA to accept incoming sales order information:

▶ To transfer condition types for sales revenues and sales deductions to CO-PA, you need to make sure that the condition types are linked to an account in FI that is also defined as a cost element of category "11" (revenue element) or "12" (sales deduction) in CO. These condition types must be assigned to a CO-PA value field. Condition types linked to FI accounts that are defined as cost elements of another category are not transferred to CO-PA, even when the condition type has been assigned to a CO-PA value field.

▶ Condition types such as "VPRS" (cost) that are defined as statistical in SD are always transferred to CO-PA if they are assigned to a value field.

▶ All condition types that you want to transfer to CO-PA must be active in the SD pricing procedure. Inactive conditions in a billing item are not transferred. If all of the conditions in a billing item are inactive, that item is not transferred to CO-PA. Conditions do not need to be active, however, to be transferred with sales order items, because the transfer of incoming sales orders is always statistical.

It is also possible to transfer conditions from MM to update billing data in pooled payment in the Information Systems (IS) retail system. These are transferred according to the same rules as SD conditions. Conditions from SD are always transferred to CO-PA with "+" signs, with the exception of credit memos and returns. The reasons for this is that the signs for revenues are handled differently in the different applications of the system. For example, revenues are positive in SD, while they are negative in FI. Consequently, CO-PA accepts all of the values as positive, and then subtracts deductions and costs from revenues in IS.

> **Note**
>
> Note that the indicator transfer +/– is not used to compare the different use of +/– signs between FI or SD and CO-PA. If you activate the indicator, shown later in this section in Figure 8.7, only the positive and negative values for the condition in question will be balanced. This guarantees that the sum of the negative and positive condition values is displayed as a correct total value in the value field assigned to that condition.

> **Tip**
>
> In order to perform transfer conditions from the billing document the same definitions must be established for the value fields in Profitability Analysis and both pricing and condition types must be defined in SD.

To transfer incoming sales orders:

1. Follow the path **Flows of Actual Values · Transfer of Incoming Sales Orders**, as shown in Figure 8.5.

2. Notice that there are three elements: **Assign Value Fields, Assign Quantity Fields**, and **Activate Transfer of Incoming Sales Orders**.

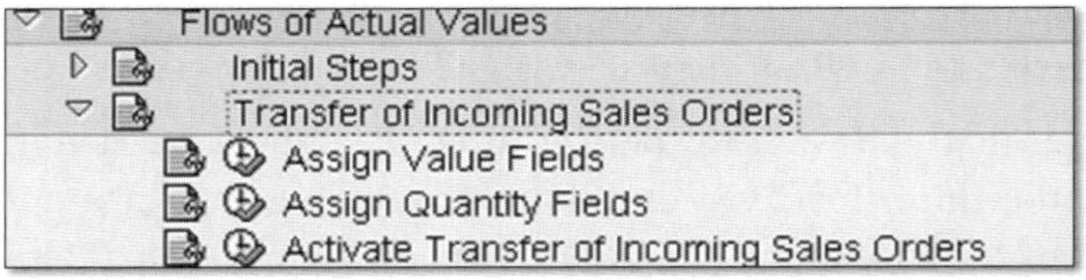

Figure 8.5 Reviewing the Transfer of Incoming Sales Orders Menu

Following SAP theory, there are two types of key figures:

► **Amount**
Refers to data stored in a currency format, such as gross sales, net revenue, and operating costs, that describes monetary transactions.

► **Quantity**
Refers to information, such as material levels, number of complaints, number of parts in storage, and inventory levels, basically everything that reflects nonmonetary transactions.

As shown in Figure 8.5 you can extract both of these key figure types using the functions **Assign Value Fields** and **Assign Quantity Fields**, respectively.

Assigning Value Fields

Let us review an example to assign value fields:

1. Click on the object **Flows of Actual Values · Transfer of Incoming Sales Orders · Assign Value Fields**, as shown in Figure 8.5.

2. Review the screen shown in Figure 8.6 and notice that you can connect to three systems, SD, MM, and CRM.

3. Click on the line **Maintain Assignment of SD Conditions to CO-PA Value Fields** to display the screen **New Entries: Overview of Added Entries**, shown in Figure 8.7.

> **Tip**
>
> In the screen shown in Figure 8.7, you access the value fields defined in SD and link them with value fields defined inside your operating concern. Remember that there are default value fields inside CO-PA, but that you can create your own user-defined value fields using the path **Profitability Analysis · Structures · Define Operating Concern · Maintain Value Fields**.

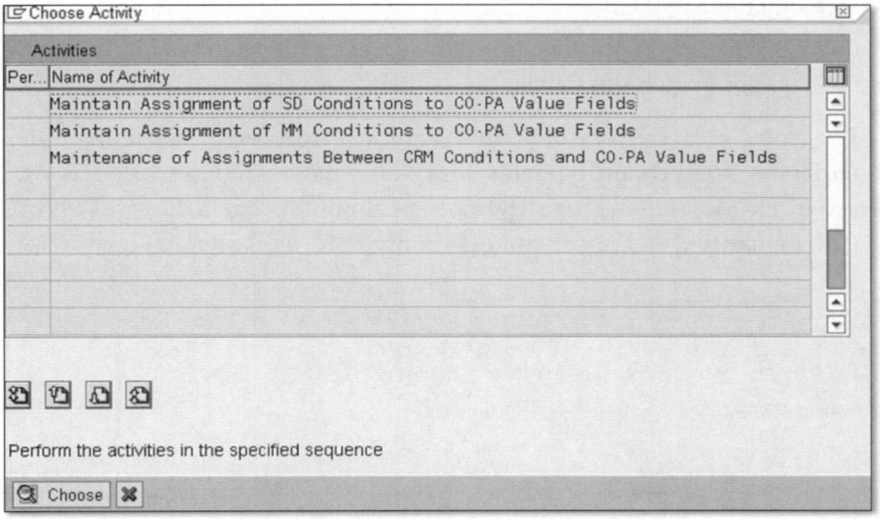

Figure 8.6 Assigning SD, MM, or CRM Components to CO-PA

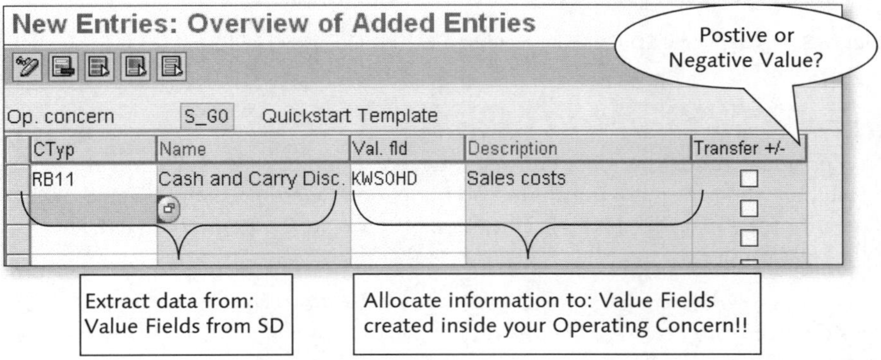

Figure 8.7 Assigning SD Fields to CO-PA Value Fields in the Operating Concern S_GO

4. In the column **CTyp,** enter the technical name of the SD value field you want to extract and on the right-hand side, make sure that **Val. fld** matches the value field contained inside your operating concern. In our example, the operating concern is **S_GO** and we are matching the SD field **RB11 (Cash and Carry Disc)** to the value field **KWSOHD (Sales Costs)** in our operating concern. You can name and assign value fields any way you want; the example in Figure 8.7 is there just to show you the assignment procedure.

271

Assigning Quantity Fields

Following the same logic as we just did with assigning value fields, let's now look at assigning quantity fields:

1. Select the object **Flows of Actual Values • Transfer of Incoming Sales Orders • Assign Quantity Fields**, and, using the operating concern **S_GO**, assign **FKIMG (Billed Quantity)** in the column **SD qty field** to **KWSVME (Sales Quantity)** in the column **CO-PA qty field**, as shown in Figure 8.8.

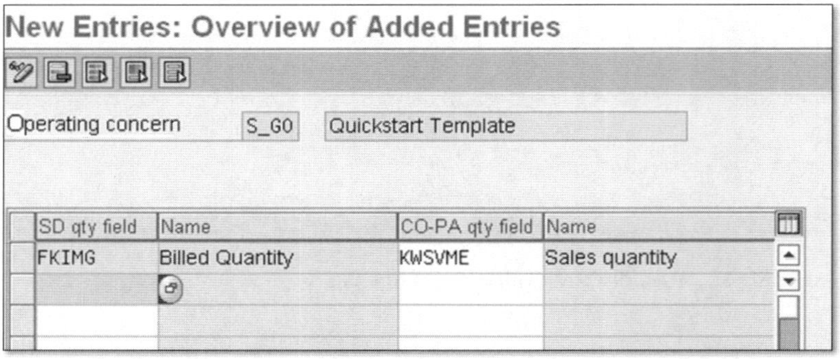

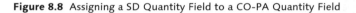

Figure 8.8 Assigning a SD Quantity Field to a CO-PA Quantity Field

> **Tip**
>
> When you activate your data transfer between SD and CO-PA, you can determine whether sales orders are transferred on the period when they were created or the period of the planned delivery. This information is stored in the schedule lines in the sales order.
>
> Also, sales orders are transferred to CO-PA with the record type "A" and sales orders from projects receive the record type "I" when transferred during the project settlement. Both need to be displayed in separate columns from billing documents in the information system. In addition, incoming sales orders are only updated in costing-based Profitability Analysis. Only documents that are likewise represented in FI can be posted to account-based Profitability Analysis.

Activating the Transfer of Incoming Sales Orders

The last object available in the **Transfer of Incoming Sales Orders** menu, shown earlier in Figure 8.5, is **Activate Transfer of Incoming Sales Orders**.

Follow these steps to complete the activation of your actual data flows from SD into CO-PA:

1. Click on **Flows of Actual Values • Transfer of Incoming Sales Orders • Activate Transfer of Incoming Sales Orders**. This opens the **Active Flag for Transfer of Incoming Sales Orders** screen shown in Figure 8.9, which contains the same table we accessed in Chapter 4 when we activated CO-PA. This means that any changes you make in this screen will also affect any configurations we discussed in Chapter 4, so be careful!

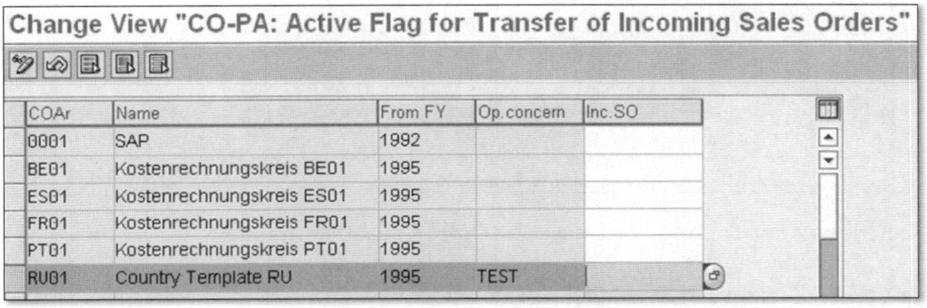

Change View "CO-PA: Active Flag for Transfer of Incoming Sales Orders"

COAr	Name	From FY	Op.concern	Inc.SO
0001	SAP	1992		
BE01	Kostenrechnungskreis BE01	1995		
ES01	Kostenrechnungskreis ES01	1995		
FR01	Kostenrechnungskreis FR01	1995		
PT01	Kostenrechnungskreis PT01	1995		
RU01	Country Template RU	1995	TEST	

Figure 8.9 Active Flag for Transfer of Incoming of Sales Orders into CO-PA

> **Tip**
>
> The transfer of incoming sales order is performed based on the controlling area. Also, the column **Inc. SO** (which stands for "Transfer of Incoming Sales Orders") next to the operating concern assigned with the controlling area describes the activation status.

2. To activate the incoming sales order as shown in Figure 1.10, start by selecting the line of the desired controlling area, in our example, **RU01 Country Template RU**, and review the assigned operating concern (**TEST**).

3. Click on the **Inc. SO** field associated with the **RU01** controlling area to select the type of data transfer and pick the flag value (a number between 1 and 3), as shown in Figure 1.10.

4. Click on the checkmark icon to save your changes.

Next we'll look at transfer of billing documents, which is closely related to transfer of incoming sales orders.

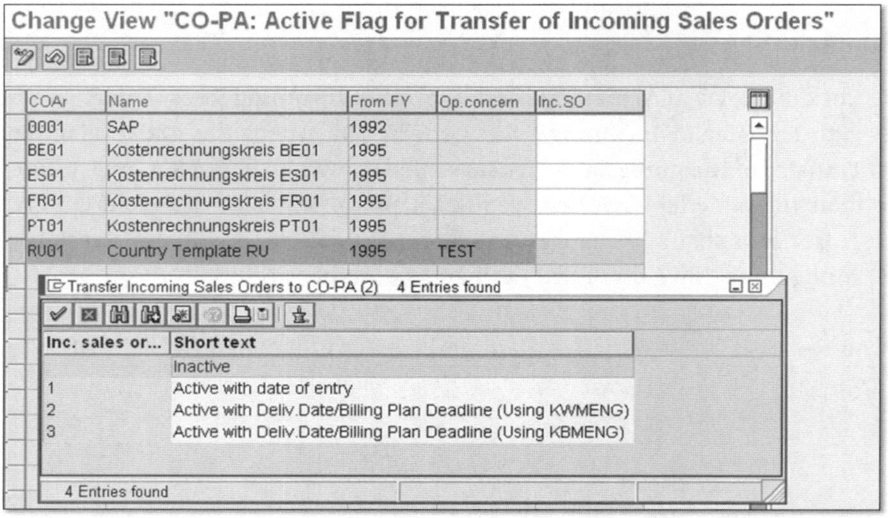

Figure 8.10 Activating Your Incoming Sales Order Actual Data Transfer

> **Note**
>
> Before selecting any of the values shown in Figure 1.10, you should call your SD, FI/CO, and Sarbanes-Oxley team leads to ask for advice on when a sale is recognized in your system. The problem is that a "sale" is a tricky term that can be recognized by your company when the sale order was created, when the product was delivered to the client, when it was shipped from the plant to the client, when the company received payment, and so on. Your selection in the screen shown in Figure 1.10 depends on this information.

8.4   Transfer of Billing Documents

In this section, you'll learn how to define how billing document items (record type "F") for sales from stock are transferred to Profitability Analysis. In costing-based CO-PA, you need to assign condition types and quantity fields from SD to the value and quantity fields in CO-PA. In account-based CO-PA, the system only transfers the posting lines available in FI.

> **Note**
>
> Almost every single component in transfer of actual values follows the PA transfer structure procedures discussed in the previous sections. For this reason, we will briefly review the menus in the following sections without going into much detail, because they all follow the same logic.

Now, to transfer the information coming from billing documents and postings from FI, you must assign condition types to the desired value fields in CO-PA. These assignments transfer the real conditions (postings in FI, such as revenues, sales deductions, and cost-of-sales accounts) and must be defined as CO-relevant accounts (cost or revenue elements).

Similar to transfer of incoming sales orders, there are two functions available when transferring billing documents from the transactional system: **Assign Quantity Fields** and **Assign Value Fields**. To access these functions, follow the path: **Controlling • Profitability Analysis • Flows of Actual Values • Transfer of Billing Documents**, as shown in Figure 8.11.

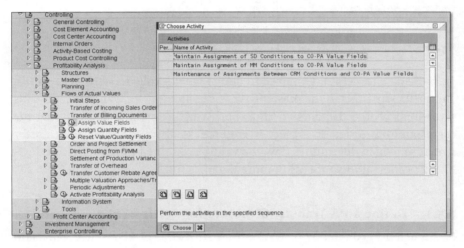

Figure 8.11 Transfer of Billing Documents

The screen shown in Figure 8.11 is very similar to the screen shown earlier in Figure 8.6 (for transfers of sales orders) because we are accessing the same object but with a different record type ("F" for billing documents, rather than "A" or "I" for sales orders).

In addition, you can see in Figure 8.11 that there is a function object called **Reset Value/Quantity Fields**, which is used to reset a quantity or value field, depending on the billing type. This means that the condition value set in the field is replaced by the value 0. This makes it possible to post only the revenue and quantity in Profitability Analysis (i.e., for returns) while retaining the freight costs of the original billing document. To do so, you would set "RE" as the billing type and reset the value field "freight costs."

Next, we'll look at order and project settlement.

8.5   Order and Project Settlement

Production orders and project system information can be accessed in the **Order and Project Settlement** menu, as shown in Figure 8.12. Two functions are available to transfer actual and plan data for orders and projects with Record Type "C":

▸ **Define PA Transfer Structure for Settlement**

▸ **Assign PA Transfer Structure to Settlement Profile**

Figure 8.12 Reviewing the Order and Project Settlement Menu

To settle data to CO-PA, you need to define what is called a *settlement profile*, and then assign this to the master data of the objects you want to settle. This settlement profile contains an allocation structure, which defines how the corresponding order or project is credited. It also contains a PA transfer structure, which determines how the values are settled to value fields in CO-PA. Let's look at this process in more detail.

8.5.1   Define a PA Transfer Structure for Settlement

In this activity, you define the PA transfer structures used to settle actual and planning data for orders and projects. To be able to transfer order and project system information, you first define a PA Transfer Structure to assign the original cost elements on the order or the project to lines (assignments) that are later assigned to value fields in Profitability Analysis.

To create the PA transfer structure, follow these steps:

1. Click on the **Define PA Transfer Structure for Settlement** object shown in Figure 8.12.

2. The screen shown in Figure 8.13 appears.

3. Click on the **New Entries** button, and type an abbreviation and name for your PA transfer structures. For example, as shown in Figure 8.13, we have three structures **CO**, **E1**, and **FI** with their respective descriptions.

4. Next, select a structure in the **Structure** column, for example, **CO**.

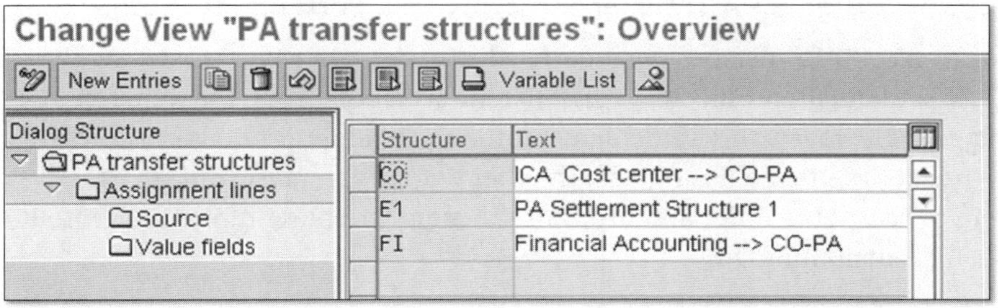

Change View "PA transfer structures": Overview

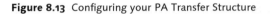

Structure	Text	
CO	ICA Cost center --> CO-PA	
E1	PA Settlement Structure 1	
FI	Financial Accounting --> CO-PA	

Dialog Structure
- ▽ 🗀 PA transfer structures
  - ▽ 🗀 Assignment lines
    - 🗀 Source
    - 🗀 Value fields

Figure 8.13 Configuring your PA Transfer Structure

5. Then, to perform an assignment, first select the **Source** object on the left side of the screen and add your source fields (the SAP ERP ECC 6.0 or R/3 fields from where the data is extracted).

6. Next, select the **Value fields** object on the left side of the screen and specify the value fields that will receive the data in CO-PA coming from the previously defined source fields. You need to assign a CO-PA quantity field (quantity/value indicator "2") to an assignment line for the billed quantity. Now the billed amount of the settlement information is transferred from CO-PA to an assigned field.

7. Now, select the **Assignment lines** object on the left side of the screen. In that object, you must select the quantity billed/delivered indicator for a particular assignment line, such as CO, E1, and FI to be transferred to CO-PA. These assignment lines are then used to transfer the cost elements to CO-PA value fields:

   For each assignment line, enter into the order/project the cost element(s) or the cost element group to be assigned; you should usually activate the "costs/revenues" option as the source. The "variances on production orders" option is only relevant for the settlement of production orders. In the latter case, you should define a separate operating concern. The "accounting indicator from Service Management (SM) orders" option is only relevant for the settlement of service orders.

After completing the definition of your PA transfer structure, you are ready to assign it to a settlement profile that contains all of the relevant information required for settling CO orders, sales orders, projects, and production orders. This functionality is explained in the following section.

8.5.2 Assign a PA Transfer Structure to a Settlement Profile

From the CO-PA perspective, you need to assign your PA transfer structure to a settlement profile to access the information from the different CO objects. However, this settlement profile must allow profitability segments to be set as settlement receivers. In other words, you must configure the system to accept the order and project settlement structure information into its final destination: CO-PA.

Because the settlement profile is usually entered automatically in the Master Data menu of the specific objects being settled, such as internal orders, sales orders, and/or projects, a settlement profile must be specified as default. You can perform this in each of these components by object type:

▶ For internal orders, you can do this when you maintain order types.

▶ For sales orders, you do this when you maintain requirement classes.

▶ For projects, you do this when you maintain project profiles.

Settlement profiles are highly dependent on other modules or functionalities within SAP, such as Project System (PS) and CO. We won't discuss this configuration item further. Instead, let us move on to briefly review the functionalities available to transfer direct postings from FI/MM.

8.6 Direct Posting from FI/MM

Direct postings from FI or MM can be configured in CO-PA to identify revenues and costs for record type "B." The revenue component of MM appears when there is inventory that can appreciate, such as oil and gold. In addition, you can transfer expenses, such as gifts to customers, special promotions, or samples. Note that these are not costs, because they are never billed to a client as part of a sale, but rather expenses of your operations. This is a delicate topic, however, and you should review the financial regulations in your country to understand how this type of expense is handled.

As shown in Figure 8.14, there are two components in the **Direct Posting from FI/MM** menu: **Maintain PA Transfer Structure for Direct Postings** and **Automatic Account Assignment**. These components let you transfer direct primary postings from FI and MM to profitability segments.

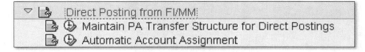

Figure 8.14 Direct Postings from FI/MM

You can use these MM extraction settings under the following circumstances:

► When you post special direct costs from sales, such as transport insurance for a certain delivery, and would like to assign these primary costs directly to a profitability segment.

► When you post an invoice for promotional events and you want this invoice to appear statistically in the responsible marketing cost center, and at the same time assign it to a profitability segment in Profitability Analysis. In this case, you would assign the invoice to both a cost center and a profitability segment.

► When you create automatic postings in MM and you want these revenues and expenses from the revaluation of material stocks to be automatically posted to Profitability Analysis. This instance also requires that you define "Automatic assignment to a profitability segment."

Additional considerations are required in MM to perform the actual transfer of data into CO-PA. You should consult with your MM team lead or responsible consultants to assist you with this MM-specific information. Let's now look in detail at the two components available under direct posting from FI/MM.

> **Note**
>
> Other configurations are possible to allow the transfer of material ledger information into CO-PA. Unfortunately, they go beyond the scope of this book as they depend on activation of the Product Costing Module (CO-PC) and configuration of the S and V price components.

8.6.1 Maintain PA Transfer Structure for Direct Postings

As shown in Figure 8.15, when you access the **Maintain PA Transfer Structure for Direct Posting** component, you access a screen similar to the one previously shown in Figure 8.13. However, the configuration options inside of each of these objects differ, and in this case are specific for FI/MM information.

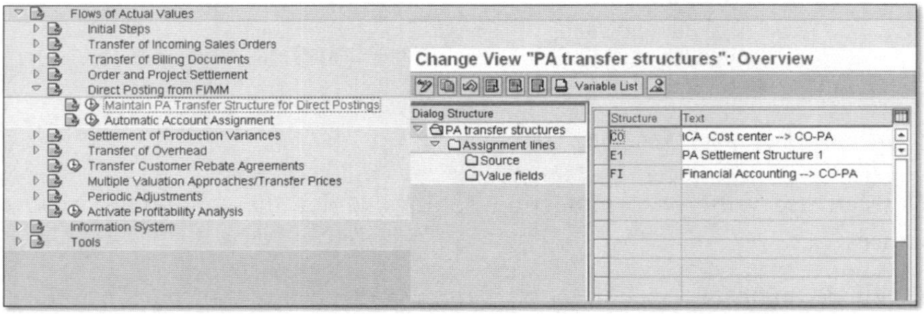

Figure 8.15 Accessing FI/MM PA Transfer Structures

In this activity, you define the PA transfer structure FI to post costs and revenues directly to profitability segments in CO-PA. Similar to how you configured the previous transfer structures, in this functionality you specify how the different cost elements and posted amounts are matched with specific components within the CO-PA operating concern:

1. Define the PA transfer structure "FI."

2. Divide your cost elements according to how you want to group them in Profitability Analysis, and create assignment lines accordingly. The indicator for quantity billed/delivered is not relevant for the PA transfer structure FI and therefore should not be activated.

3. For each assignment line, enter the cost element or the cost element group to be assigned. As the source, activate the "costs/revenues" option.

4. For each assignment line, enter the value field (or, if the costs are split into fixed and variable portions, both value fields) into which costs/revenues are imported.

Automatic postings created in MM can be transferred to CO-PA using automatic assignment. This configuration is briefly discussed in the next subsection.

8.6.2   Automatic Account Assignment

Automatic account assignment executes an automatic procedure to identify profitability segments automatically posted, such as those generated for MM. These automatic postings can be passed on to CO-PA by means of an automatic assignment to a profitability segment, depending on the characteristics found in FI. For this reason, if the information identified in the FI documents is not very detailed, the posted values are transferred to CO-PA at an aggregated level, which can also become a drawback. This functionality might be advisable for certain accounts and business transactions only, such as the following:

▶ The transfer of price differences that are posted in purchasing due to differing order prices or differing prices in invoice receipt (as period costs).

▶ The transfer of expenses or revenues that arise due to a revaluation of material stocks (as period costs).

▶ The transfer of inventory differences (as period costs).

Now, let us review how to work with the function automatic account assignment:

1. Follow the path **Profitability Analysis • Flows of Actual Values • Direct Postings FI/MM • Automatic Account Assignment**.

2. As shown in Figure 8.16, in the left area of the screen, you now see the **Default account assignment**, **Detail per business area/valuation area**, and **Detail per profit center** hierarchy.

Change View "Default account assignment": Overview									
New Entries									
Dialog Structure	CoCd	Cost Elem.	BArIn	Cost Ctr	Order	PrfSeg	Profit	Ac...	Acct assignmt detail
▽ ◻ Default account assignment	0001	400000	◻			◻		1	Valuation area is mandatory
◻ Detail per business area/valuation area	0001	410000	◻	SC-1		◻		1	Valuation area is mandatory
◻ Detail per profit center	0001	415000	◻	SC-1		◻		1	Valuation area is mandatory
	0001	417000	◻	SC-1		◻		1	Valuation area is mandatory
	0001	604000	◻	SC-1		◻		1	Valuation area is mandatory
	0001	893020	◻	SC-1		◻		1	Valuation area is mandatory
	0001	894020	◻	SC-1		◻		1	ⓐluation area is mandatory

Figure 8.16 Accessing Automatic Account Assignment in FI/MM

3. As also shown in Figure 8.16, you can define the company code (**CoCd**), cost element (**Cost Elem.**), cost center (**Cost Ctr**), and account assignment detail (**Acct assignmt detail**). Notice in this case that we are using Cost Ctr **SC-1** that is also dependent on the controlling area and the information stored in it. In this case, **SC-1** is an SAP default MM cost center.

4. Select the profitability segment indicator (**PrfSeg**), shown in Figure 8.16, to transfer postings from the different cost element accounts displayed and move that information into CO-PA. Selecting this indicator means that first the profitability segment is found using substitution for automatic postings, and then the corresponding posting is transferred to CO-PA.

Generally, a profitability segment is automatically found and updated in Profitability Analysis when the corresponding sender document is created (such as when you enter FI documents with direct assignment to Profitability Analysis, or when you create sales orders or billing documents).

Therefore, it is not desirable to have the system find a profitability segment for all of the accounts relevant to profits by assigning accounts in this customizing step.

5. Make sure that the account for automatic postings is assigned in the PA transfer structure "FI" with a cost element account, using the **Source** object displayed earlier in Figure 8.15.

6. Click on the line for cost element **400000** displayed in Figure 8.16, and select the **Detail per business area/valuation area** object in the hierarchy displayed on the left-hand side of the screen, as shown in Figure 8.17. Here you can configure the detail by cost center, order, profit center, and others.

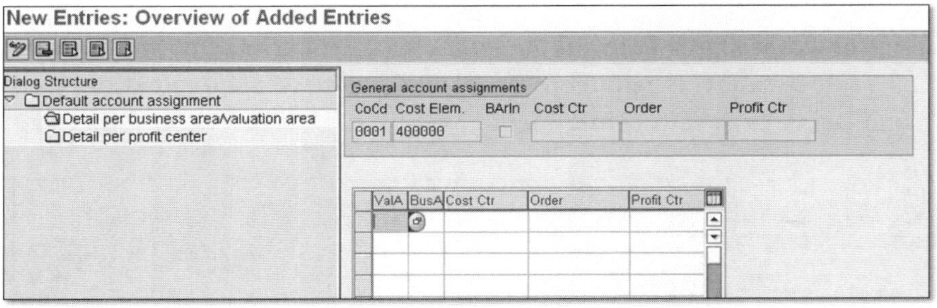

Figure 8.17 Detail Per Business Area/Valuation Area

7. Also, you can configure the detail more simplistically by profit center, as shown in Figure 8.18. In this case, you can define **General account assignments** for company code (**CoCd**), cost element (**Cost Elem.**), cost center (**Cost Ctr**), order (**Order**) and profit center (**Profit Ctr**).

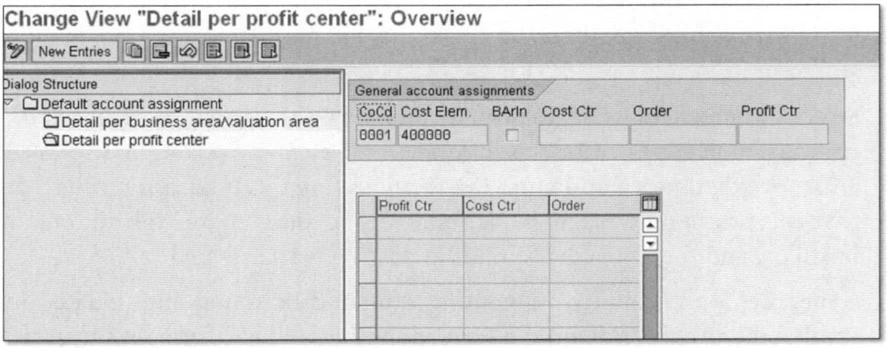

Figure 8.18 Detail Per Profit Center

Whether you will use **Detail per profit center** or **Detail per business area/ valuation area** will depend on the type of postings you need to extract. You must analyze your data postings to decide which is more appropriate. Next, let's look at the settlement of production variances function.

8.7 Settlement of Production Variances

If you have information coming from the **Production Planning module (PP)** and if your company plans to produce actual products or goods, there might be differences because of scrap, shop floor delays, material defect delays, reprocessing, and others. When variances are calculated in CO-PC, production variances are determined and stored. When you settle production orders, you can transfer these variances — differentiated by cost element and variance category — to value fields in CO-PA, using the **Settlement of Production Variances** functionality.

As shown in Figure 8.19, you need to configure two objects: **Define PA Transfer Structure for Variance Settlement** and **Assign PA Transfer Structure to Settlement Profile**.

> **Note**
>
> It is highly recommended to define separate PA transfer structures for different allocation types.

Figure 8.19 Reviewing the Settlement of Production Variances Menu

Follow these steps:

1. Click on the object **Define PA Transfer Structure for Variance Settlement** as shown in Figure 8.19. The configuration of this PA structure is similar to that reviewed in Section 8.6.

2. Decide how the variances and assignment lines in the PA transfer structure are defined, using the procedure explained in Section 8.3. The value fields are moved to CO-PA once the assignments are completed.

3. Select the indicator for the quantity billed/delivered in the assignment line that is used for transferring the quantity of the production order that has

been delivered to the plant to CO-PA. As before, you must assign a CO-PA value field under the value fields object shown previously in Figure 8.13, and in the assignment line for the delivered quantity (quantity/value indicator "2"). When the production order is settled to CO-PA, the delivered quantity is transferred to the assigned field.

4. For each assignment line, enter the cost element(s) or the cost element group from which the production variances are settled, and select a variance category as the source (such as price variances for materials input). If, instead of a variance category, you select the costs/revenues option as the source, all variances of the entered cost element are settled to the production order.

5. For each assignment line, enter the value field (or, if costs are split into fixed and variable portions, both value fields) into which the appropriate variance category is imported.

6. Save your work and return to the IMG Activity environment, and click on **Assign PA Transfer Structure to Settlement Profile**. Here you need to link the previous configuration to a **Settlement profile** object, as shown in Figure 8.20.

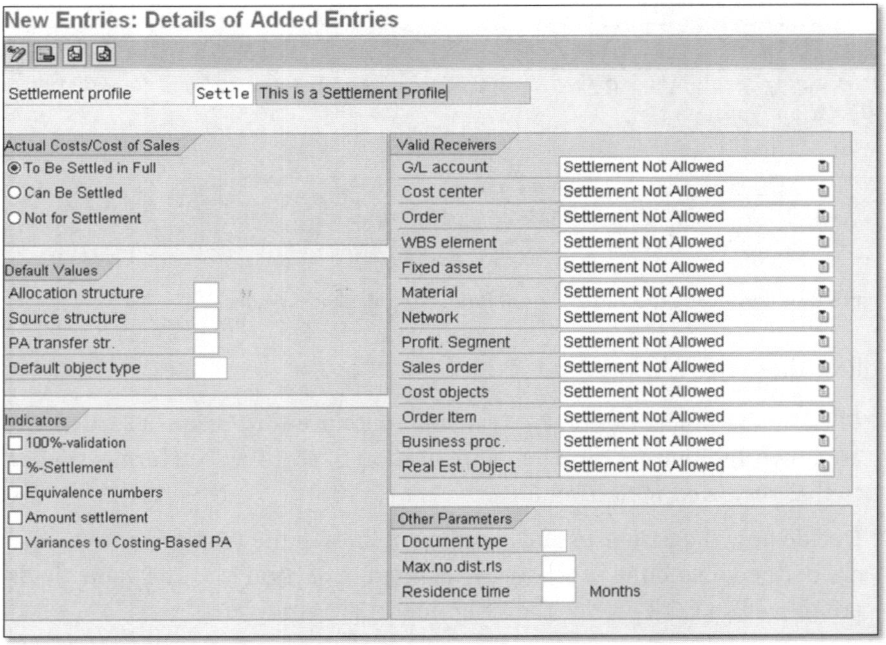

Figure 8.20 Creating a Settlement Profile

Similar to order and project management, the settlement profile contains all relevant information needed for settling CO orders, sales orders, projects, and production orders. From a CO-PA perspective, the settlement profile must allow profitability segments to be set as settlement receivers in order to settle production variances.

For this, assign the PA transfer structure (**PA transfer str.**) in the **Default Values** area, shown in Figure 8.20, and change the status of the profit segments in the **Valid Receivers** area to allow settlements. Because the settlement profile is usually entered automatically in the master data of the object being settled (internal order, sales order, or project), you need to specify the desired settlement profile as a default, as follows:

▷ For internal orders, you can do this when you maintain order types.

▷ For sales orders, you do this when you maintain requirement classes.

▷ For projects, you do this when you maintain project profiles.

There are more options available as you can see in Figure 8.20, to allow receivers from other sources, including **G/L account**, **Cost center**, **Order**, **WBS element**, **Fixed asset**, **Network**, **Profit. Segment**, **Cost Objects**, **Business proc.** (business processes), and others. These are elements that go beyond the scope of our discussion, however.

In the next section, we will very briefly review the options available in the Transfer of Overhead menu.

8.8   Transfer of Overhead

As shown in Figure 8.21, the **Transfer of Overhead** component of CO-PA is a rather large submenu within the **Flows of Actual Values** CO-PA menu. Because overhead within FI and CO can involve information and data coming from cost centers and process costs, direct and indirect allocations, project settlements, actual cycles, and many more, this topic could be a chapter or more on its own, and a discussion beyond showing you the available menu options is beyond the scope of this book.

If you require using this complex functionality, interact with people in financial accounting or with the controllers in your company to review how these elements can be configured.

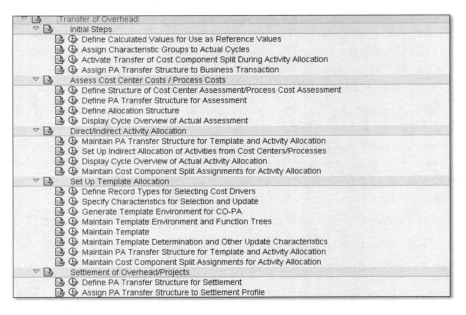

Figure 8.21 Overview of the Transfer of Overhead

Note

Another component we were unable to discuss is the integration between CO-PA and material ledger using CO-PC. We recommend that you review this functionality if integration between MM and CO-PA is a requirement for you when working with the COGS from the material master. In addition, you should review the presentation ML46C available in the SAP Service Marketplace for more information on integrating material ledger with CO-PA.

8.9   Summary

The information in this chapter is difficult to explain without reviewing and exploring other components external to Profitability Analysis because flows of actual values is an integrator component between the data coming into CO-PA from other modules, such as FI and CO. However, we can say that a PA transfer structure is a standard component that requires configuration in order to link the information coming from the source system to CO-PA operating concern components.

The aim of this chapter was to make you aware of the Flows of Actual Values menu and familiarize you with it. You are encouraged to analyze carefully when to use it, as there might be alternative ways to access the same information in SAP, depending on your reporting environments. For example, you can access the same information in SAP BW/SAP NetWeaver BI, or you can access specific components to consolidate the data within the SAP ERP ECC 6.0 or R/3 reporting environment.

Next, Chapter 9 introduces you to the concepts of CO-PA reporting, including basic profitability reports, line item reports, forms and working with Report Painter.

In this chapter, we will explore the general reporting functionalities of CO-PA, which will give you an overview of its main capabilities, as well as its role within the overall SAP environment. Typically, CO-PA fulfills most overall requirements for reporting in most implementations without the need to create objects within the SAP NetWeaver Business Intelligence (BI)/SAP Business Warehouse (BW) environment.

9 CO-PA Reporting: Basics

The ultimate goal of any SAP ERP implementation is the generation of reports to keep track of key information and to share it with different users or interest parties. However, there are several tools available within and outside of the SAP system to achieve such a goal.

In this chapter, we explore CO-PA reporting basics to understand the concepts behind R/3 or SAP ERP ECC 6.0 reporting and how CO-PA is a useful tool for the generation and combination of data coming from different sources inside and outside the SAP environment. The analysis you can perform using CO-PA reporting is multidimensional because CO-PA provides dynamic sorting and rearranging of data within a single report.

Furthermore, in this chapter, the concept of market segments or profitability segments will become clearer as a way to suppress or limit characteristics related to customers, products, time, and others for a particular level of information or user role. In addition, you will see how market segments allow access to the information stored in your operating concern related to quantities, revenues, discounts, surcharges, product costs, margins, period costs, and other predefined value fields that are extracting data coming from different SAP tables. Let's get started by looking at some CO-PA reporting scenarios.

9.1 CO-PA Reporting Scenarios

Reporting must have a purpose, a strategy, and a general framework under which all functionalities are created. The following three types of reporting are typical scenarios involving CO-PA, the more powerful tools of SAP NetWeaver BI and SAP BW, as well as legacy systems and third-party tools:

▶ Reporting data within SAP R/3 or SAP ERP ECC 6.0 and sharing it with the SAP NetWeaver BI/SAP BW platform from a single CO-PA data source.

▶ Reporting data with CO-PA from several systems, data sources, or processes, and also sharing it with SAP NetWeaver BI/SAP BW.

▶ Reporting data using a combination of SAP data and data coming from legacy systems or other third-party tools.

The first scenario is shown in Figure 9.1. In this case, CO-PA is used in profitability reporting to move reporting tasks from an R/3 or SAP ERP ECC 6.0 system into an independent system using the operating concern as the data source or interface to create the link between the SAP transactional system and the OLAP reporting environment. For such a scenario, the R/3 or SAP ERP ECC 6.0 system operates as an OLTP system, which runs the operational business, while the SAP NetWeaver BI/SAP BW system serves as an OLAP system. By diverting the performance-intensive reporting tasks to a separate system, the following strategic advantages can be gained:

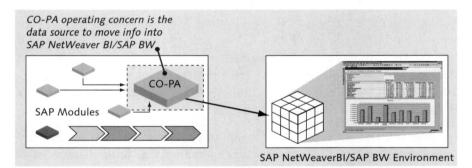

Figure 9.1 Reporting CO-PA data outside the OLTP Environment

▶ Reporting does not affect the response times of operational business transactions in the OLTP system.

▶ Each system can be optimized to perform its specific tasks: You can tune the R/3 or SAP ERP ECC 6.0 system to efficiently perform OLTP-typical parallel updates and single-record accesses, whereas the SAP BW system can be adjusted to handle complex search requests that involve summarizing large sets of hits. Competing updates are bundled via cyclic replication, thus eliminating any interference with the queries.

▶ OLTP transactions do not influence the response times of reporting.

▶ Besides the technical advantages, the efficiency of reporting is further increased by uniformly reporting across all functional areas and R/3 or SAP ERP ECC 6.0 applications.

The second scenario, illustrated in Figure 9.2, involves situations where there are multiple environments with several SAP systems that represent, for example, slightly different methods of profitability analysis for various countries or business units. For this scenario, it is essential to gain a cross-system view, such as the one shown in Figure 9.2. Here, the results from different organizational subunits are combined into a single InfoCube in SAP NetWeaver BI/SAP BW that contains the same reporting levels and calculations of contribution margins.

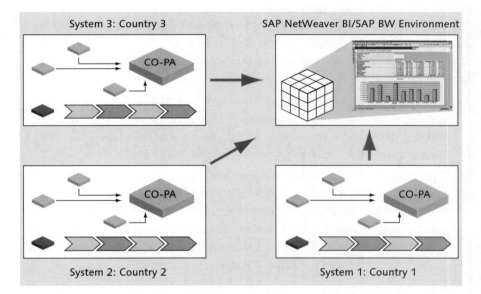

Figure 9.2 Integrating Several Systems with CO-PA Into a Common Reporting Environment

CO-PA provides the necessary functions to create classification groups to analyze your business processes according to sales between affiliated companies and customers. This classification of internal and external customers enables you to report your group profit by analyzing profits from external customers as well as profits from affiliated companies.

In addition, there are several recommendations to consider when working with the scenario presented in Figure 9.2:

▶ You should valuate quantities sold with the group cost estimate in parallel with value fields in CO-PA to eliminate intercompany profits.

▶ The data prepared in CO-PA can easily be extracted into SAP NetWeaver BI/SAP BW. The integration of CO-PA and SAP NetWeaver BI/SAP BW also allows you to harmonize heterogeneous operating concerns as previously described.

▶ If a business unit (affiliate, division, country) stores sales data in CO-PA at a more detailed level than other units, appropriate presummarization can be carried out when the data is transferred.

▶ If a division system stores a detailed cost component split for the cost of goods sold (COGS) while group-level reporting is carried out in less detail, cost of sales can be aggregated from the split during data transfer.

The third typical scenario for the implementation of CO-PA with an SAP NetWeaver BI/SAP BW installation is when affiliated companies, or portions of your company, operate systems other than R/3 or SAP ERP ECC 6.0, and their data has to be consolidated in your reporting of group profitability, as shown in Figure 9.3. The structure presented in Figure 9.3 has certain implications to consider:

▶ External data transfer into the R/3 or SAP ERP ECC 6.0 system is recommended when financial accounting and management accounting are updated simultaneously. In this case, the integrated business model of CO-PA will assure the consistency of your profitability data.

▶ If there is no need to integrate your data into R/3 or SAP ERP ECC 6.0 accounting, SAP Netweaver BI/SAP BW can provide an excellent cross-system view when data is loaded directly into SAP BW. The powerful staging mechanisms within SAP NetWeaver BI/SAP BW provide extensive support for importing external data, data quality management, and subsequent bulk updates of the imported data.

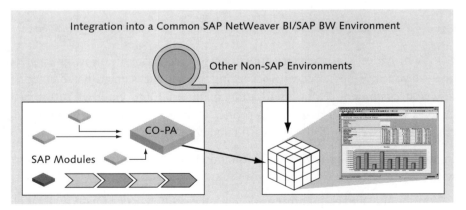

Figure 9.3 Integrating SAP Data with Legacy and Other Non-SAP Environments

All of this shows that CO-PA can be a logical system to integrate into high-level reporting environments, such as SAP NetWeaver BI/SAP BW; however, CO-PA has very similar and powerful capabilities that allow it to be a reporting platform by itself. This not only saves development time, the CO-PA reporting tool also operates in real time, and allows interfacing with Microsoft Excel. In the following section we will explore in detail the menus and options available to access the information contained in your operating concern objects to create reports in CO-PA.

9.2   Working with Reports in CO-PA

To access the reporting functions of CO-PA, you need to work with the **Information System** menu, as shown in Figure 9.4 However, because there are quite a few functionalities, we will explore only the most common.

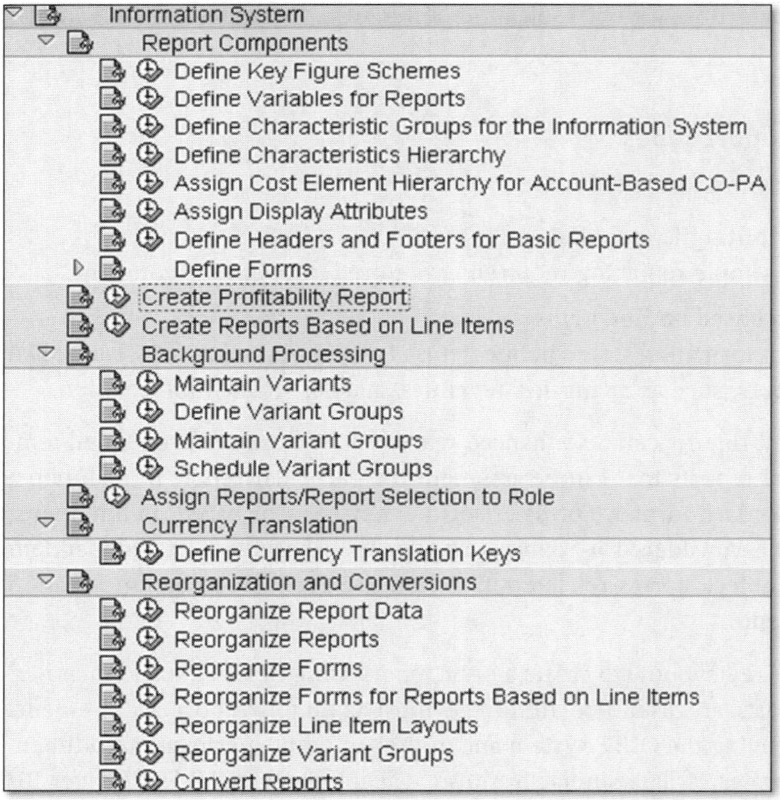

Figure 9.4 Reviewing the Information System Menu of CO-PA

You can then explore the remaining items on your own. CO-PA reporting will be covered in two chapters — Chapter 9 and Chapter 10. When you're done with these two chapters, you will know how to do the following:

▶ Work with reports

▶ Work with forms, and understand the difference between reports and forms

▶ Link a form to a report

▶ Perform basic drilldown operations in CO-PA

▶ Work with line item lists, key figure schemes, characteristic groups, and hierarchies

▶ Improve the performance of your reports with frozen data and summarization levels

▶ Define headers and footers

In the next section, we will look at the different report types available in CO-PA.

9.2.1 Report Types

CO-PA uses two kinds of reports:

▶ **Basic profitability reports**
Deliver simple reporting requirements stored in operating concerns.

▶ **Reports based on line items**
Extract information stored in line items of different transactions, controlled by headers, such as quantities, revenues, and cost-related information.

In addition, reports can be enhanced with *forms*. Forms are predefined template-based reports that can be assigned to a particular report to maintain a desired standard format. Forms are also either basic or based on line items, and can be considered a report component rather than an independent reporting object. Forms-related options are also available in the Information System menu.

Now let us review how to create a basic report using CO-PA data. Remember, these reports are useful to fulfill the most common report requirements without leaving the OLTP system and at the same time perform multidimensional analyses of data similar to those available in the SAP NetWeaver BI/BW platform.

9.2.2 Creating a Basic Report

To create a basic report in CO-PA, follow these steps:

1. In the **Information System** menu, click on the execute icon for the **Create Profitability Report** object as shown in Figure 9.5.

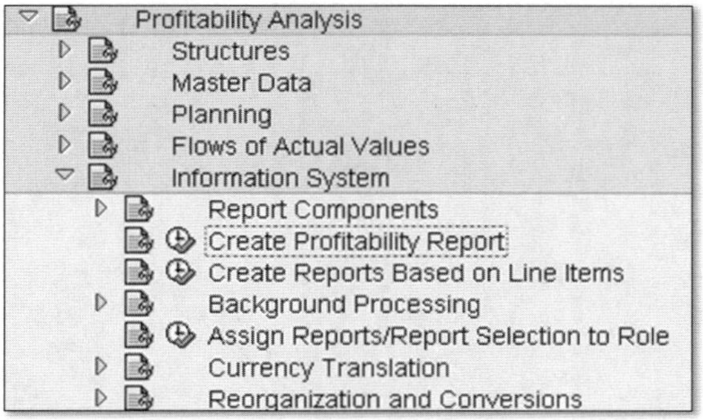

Figure 9.5 Identifying the Two Types of Report Creation Objects in the Information System Menu

2. In the **Choose Activity** screen that displays, as shown in Figure 9.6, click on the **Create Profitability Report** option.

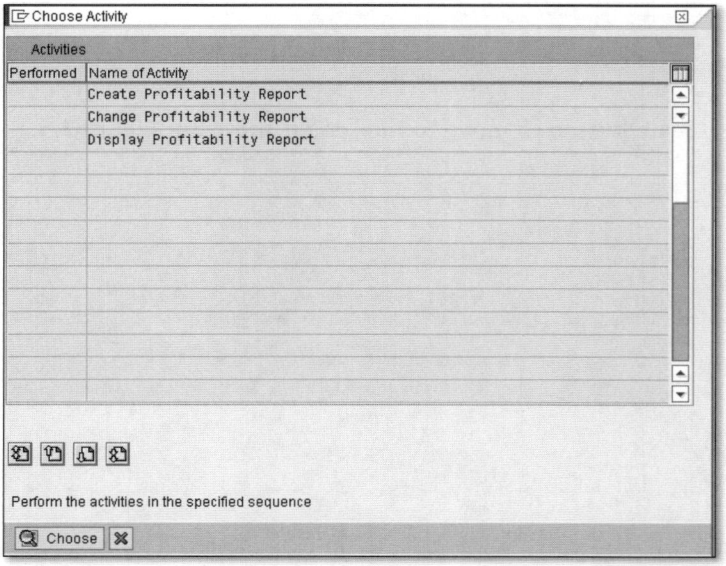

Figure 9.6 Accessing the Create Profitability Analysis Report Activity

3. The screen called **Create Profitability Report: Initial Screen** appears. Enter a name ("Report1") and a description ("This is a PA Report"), as shown in Figure 9.7.

4. In the **Report Type** area, verify that **Basic report** is selected. Alternatively, **Report with Form** lets you build a report following a previously created form that is used like a predefined template.

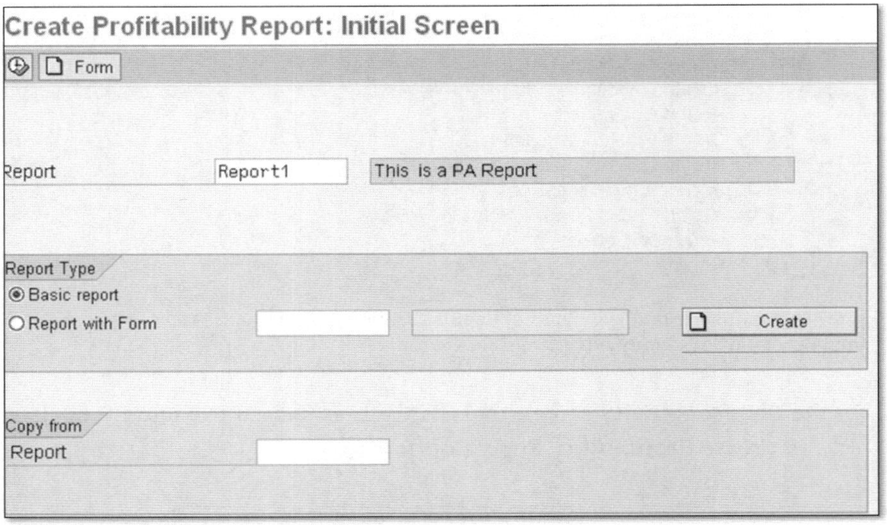

Figure 9.7 Create Profitability Report: Initial Screen

5. Click on the **Create** button to move to the screen shown in Figure 9.8.

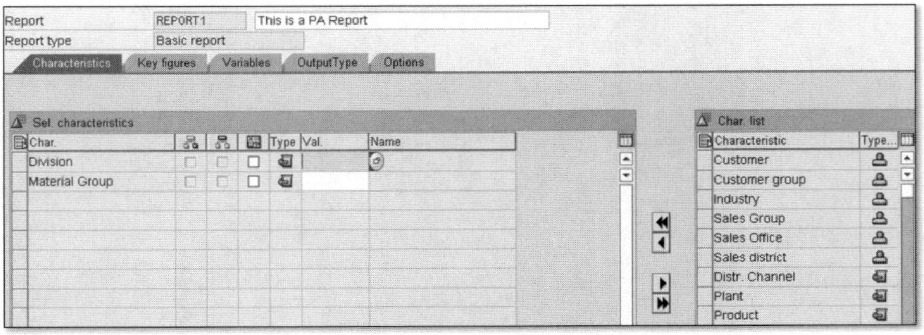

Figure 9.8 Reviewing the Configuration Tabs for a Report Object

This screen contains the following tabs: **Characteristics**, **Key Figures**, **Variables**, **Output Type**, and **Options**. These tabs let you select the elements that will be included in your report. Use the arrows to move items to be included in the report to the left (**Set characteristics** area) or items that you do not require to the right (**Char. list** area). Note that the first two columns next to the **Char.** column in the **Set characteristics** area identify if the characteristic is part of a node or a hierarchy.

6. Use the corresponding tab to limit which characteristics and key figures will be included, leaving the **Variables**, **Output Type**, and **Options** tabs alone for now. We will be using gross sales, sales costs, sales quantity, material costs, bonuses, cash discounts, and customer discounts as key figures for 2009 data, and some characteristics such as division, material group, version, and record type.

7. Click on the save icon and return to the **Create Profitability Report: Initial Screen**, which shows that your report has been created, and is ready to execute.

8. To start executing and simultaneously testing your report, click on the clock with the checkmark icon.

9. The screen **Selection: This is a PA Report** appears. Fill out the requested information, as shown in Figure 9.9, and click on the clock with the checkmark icon.

Selection: This is a PA Report		
⊕		
Report selections		
Period from	001/2009	1. Period 2009
Period to	012/2009	12. Period 2009
Plan/Act. Indicator	1	Planning data
Version	0	Plan/actual version
Record Type	F	Billing data

Figure 9.9 Executing Your New CO-PA Report

10. If any errors occurred during the execution of your report, the affected fields in the screen shown in Figure 9.9 are displayed in red, requesting you to review your data selections to match with the available information. If successfully executed, you should see information similar to that shown in Figure 9.10, depending on your configuration. Notice that there are four regions on this screen:

▶ **Navigation**
Allows you to perform drilldown in the report using characteristics to change the values displayed in the chart and in the upper portion of the screen.

▶ **Key figures**
Displays the value fields values, limited by the characteristics information, and the data graphed in the chart is based on these values. For example, in the screen shown in Figure 9.10, you see the key figure information, based on the characteristic **Division**. To change the display to the key figures based on the characteristic **Material Group**, double-click on **Material Group** in the left area of the screen, and the displayed values and chart will be adjusted accordingly.

▶ **Detail**
Shows the key figure detail, based on the defined navigation characteristics, complemented with totals information.

▶ **Graphical area**
Displays charts that can be customized by users, using the information available in the **Navigation** and **Key figures** regions.

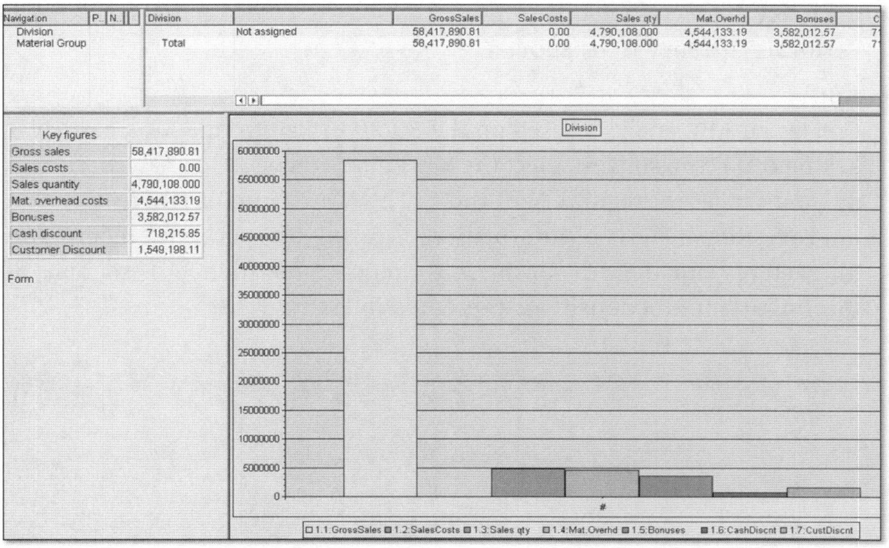

Navigation	P.	N.	Division		GrossSales	SalesCosts	Sales qty	Mat.Overhd	Bonuses	C
Division				Not assigned	58,417,890.81	0.00	4,790,108.000	4,544,133.19	3,582,012.57	7
Material Group			Total		58,417,890.81	0.00	4,790,108.000	4,544,133.19	3,582,012.57	7

Key figures	
Gross sales	58,417,890.81
Sales costs	0.00
Sales quantity	4,790,108.000
Mat. overhead costs	4,544,133.19
Bonuses	3,582,012.57
Cash discount	718,215.85
Customer Discount	1,549,198.11

Form

Division

☐ 1.1:GrossSales ☐ 1.2:SalesCosts ☐ 1.3:Sales qty ☐ 1.4:Mat.Overhd ☐ 1.5:Bonuses ■ 1.6:CashDiscnt ☐ 1.7:CustDiscnt

Figure 9.10 Reviewing Your Newly Created CO-PA Report

Menu of Icons Available in a Report

Every report you create lets you perform additional functions using the menu of icons located at the top of the report, as shown in Figure 9.11.

Figure 9.11 A Report's Icon Menu

Each of these icons is described in the following list, going from left to right, based on Figure 9.11:

▶ **Report Parameters**
Displays the general information of the report definitions, such as characteristic values, key figures, user that created the report, dates, and duration to generate the report, all as a way to monitor performance.

▶ **Export**
Lets you export the report to Microsoft Excel (you will see the letters XXL) as a table or pivot table. If successful, the system will suggest to **Save data in the spread sheet**. To keep the file, you have to save it in Microsoft Excel, and then click on the checkmark icon in the SAP system. Otherwise, the temporary file will be closed and you return to the SAP environment.

▶ **Currency**
Performs currency translation.

▶ **ABC**
Creates an ABC analysis based on the 80/20 or Pareto rule for a particular key figure. To do so, you select the key figure you want to analyze, and set up your ranges for regions A, B, and C. This is a *very* important feature that improves the analysis of information, focusing on specific elements, and interacting with the SAP Business Graphics application. An example of this important functionality is presented in Figure 9.12.

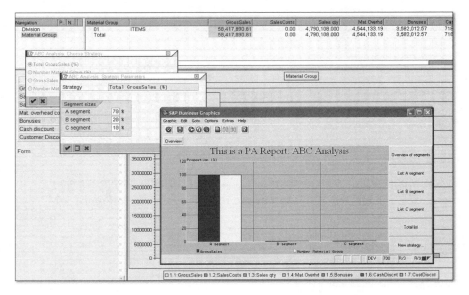

Figure 9.12 Reviewing an ABC Analysis Using the Upper Menu

▶ **Attributes**
Displays any information attached to a characteristic.

▶ **Number Format**
Lets you change your data display of the decimal and factoring places in your report, and activate or deactivate your unit of measure as shown in Figure 9.13. For example, you can display 10 instead of 10,000 or 1 instead of 1,000, to simplify your data analysis.

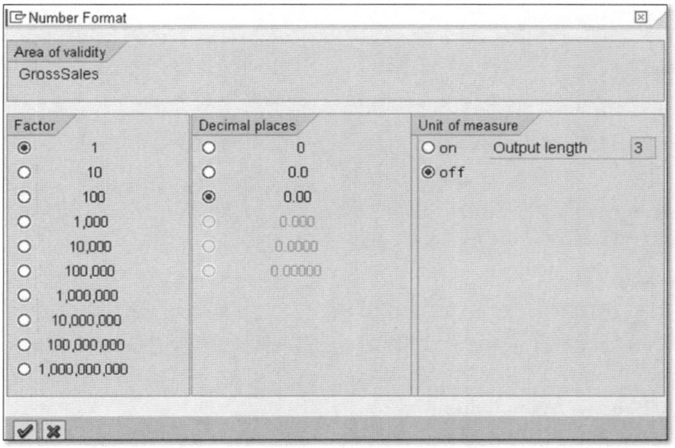

Figure 9.13 Working with the Number Format Icon

► **Display**
  Lets you display any comments available in the report.

► **Maintain or Create Comments**
  Lets you add headers (comments) attached to your report, depending on your needs. You can use Microsoft Word, SAP editor, binary document, and other formats, using the **Type** dropdown list shown in Figure 9.14.

Figure 9.14 Creating a Document Header

CO-PA Report Menu Options

Now let us explore the **Save data** and **Save layout** options on the **Report** menu available inside the CO-PA reporting environment, as shown in Figure 9.15. (The other menu options are standard for most SAP applications.) With these two functionalities, a user can create frozen data with reference to a time period without the need to execute a real-time report. The advantage is that retrieving frozen data with a predefined set of parameters is faster than real-time reporting because the latter demands a larger number of system resources.

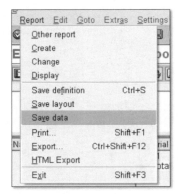

Figure 9.15 Reviewing the Report Menu Options

When you execute the **Save data** functionality, you see the last date and time when the layout was saved. You can then choose to retrieve the data for this timeframe or extract the **Current data** (latest), as shown in Figure 9.16. The **Save layout** option is used to maintain the same screen definition so that each time you want to access your report the same format will be maintained.

Tip
When executing the **Save data** option, the screen shown in Figure 9.16 only appears if the selection criteria are exactly the same as those of the saved data. This means if you run your report with different selection criteria values, the screen shown in Figure 9.16 would not appear because you are executing another part of the database (for the first time). In this scenario, time delays might occur, depending on the data volume.

Figure 9.16 Executing Your Profitability Report with Frozen Data

CO-PA Report Edit Menu Options

We will now explore the **Edit** menu, which lets you perform functions, such as **Cumulative curve**, **Classification**, **Ranking list**, **Condition**, and others, to control the data display and analysis of your reports, as shown in Figure 9.17.

Some of the options might be unavailable (grayed out) because they are used exclusively in reports based on line items, and also specifically to work with *hotspots*. Hotspots are dynamic links inside your report that control the data display of your report. Consider them the main delimiter of data display.

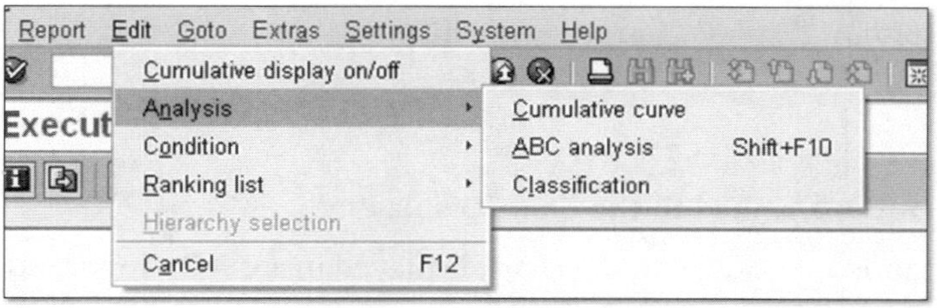

Figure 9.17 Working with the Edit Menu

In addition, you can review the information contained in the line items of the report if you need further information for specific transactions associated with your report data by clicking on **Goto • Line Items**. As shown in Figure 9.18, you can also define exceptions to complement the display capabilities of your data based on a range.

That is, you can define, for example that if the value for gross sales is above 1,000 USD, it will display as green, and if it is below 1,000 USD, it will display as red.

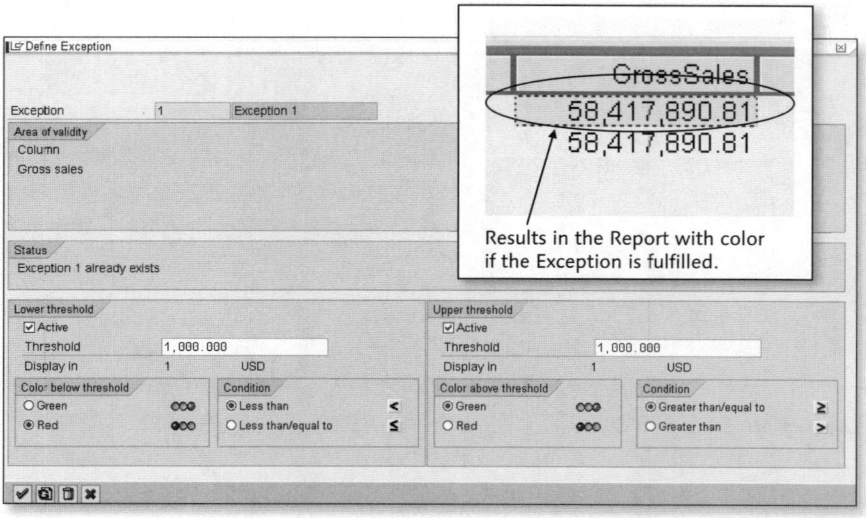

Figure 9.18 Working with Exceptions

Explore on your own the additional options in the menus, such as:

- **Switch on and off the totals**
- **Percentage/absolute**
- **Zeros on/off**
- **Restrict the column display/Characteristic display**
- **UNDO**

CO-PA Report Options Linked to the Chart Display

Several functionalities are linked to the chart displayed in a CO-PA report, as shown in Figure 9.19. You can access them by double-clicking on the chart. Some of the functionalities available include: specifying the color for a particular data series, changing patterns, determining axis, displaying error bars, formatting a specific data series, showing data values, defining value ranges for data display, displaying data labels, and others. You can also select the legend and change the chart type to meet your requirements. If something goes wrong along the way, undo your changes. You can undo them back to the last saved version of the layout.

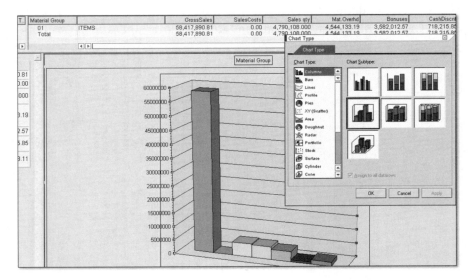

Figure 9.19 Working with Charts

As you can see, the capabilities for data analysis for CO-PA are quite powerful, and you do not have to leave the traditional R/3 or SAP ERP ECC 6.0 environment to design and create flexible reports.

Transporting CO-PA Reports

In Figure 9.20 you can see several reports that can be transported, including any attached subobjects, such as forms, or key figure schemes, and for a specific language if desired. Now, all this information, which exists inside the objects you see in Figure 9.20, can be moved to another system by using a *transport request*. To do so, you click on the truck icon located in the **Change Report: Settings** screen shown in Figure 9.20. Finally, your report(s) are always available to be accessed by and assigned to a user, according to his authorizations and roles, and in the change report mode (accessible by clicking on the change/modify icon), you can review and access the different reports created.

Change Report: Settings

Report	Description
▽ 📁 Report	
⬚ REPORT1	This is a PA Report
⬚ SG0B01	Saless/sales revenues/discou
⬚ SG0B02	Target Achievement
⬚ SG0B03	Price History
⬚ SG0B04	Development of Customer Sal
⬚ SG0B05	Analysis of Operating Profit
⬚ SG0B06	Analysis of Incoming Orders
⬚ SG0B07	Analysis CM II

Figure 9.20 Reviewing the Change Report Screen

This ends our discussion on how to create a basic CO-PA report, and some of the key functionalities to be aware of when working with this type of report. Next, we will discuss the more specific line item CO-PA reports that do not provide charts, or any type of graphics, because they are focused on displaying transaction data.

9.2.3 Creating Reports Based on Line Items

In this section, we will create reports based on line items, or change or display existing line item reports. In comparison with basic reports that display the characteristics and value fields you specify using a standard layout, line item reports are best suited to searching for trends in data classified by various characteristics.

Line item reports are also called form reports because they allow you to display the characteristics and key figures according to your requirements and without using a standard layout. Now, let us create a line item CO-PA report with these steps:

1. Access the menu path **Information System • Create Reports based on Line Items** as previously shown in Figure 9.5, and perform the same configuration steps done for the basic report.

2. Move the characteristics to the selected characteristics screen. When you work with line items you can use the following characteristics:

   ▸ All of the characteristics in the segment level, plus those excluded from the segment-level characteristics.

   ▸ The creation of date of line item.

   ▸ The name of the person who created the line item.

3. Select the key figures you want to analyze. You can choose from the value fields of your operating concern and any key figures defined in a key figure scheme (which we will review in Chapter 10).

4. If required, specify restricting values for the variables defined for the report. Select **Enter at execution** if you want users to be able to enter or replace these variables when they execute the report.

5. Select the output type that you want to use to display the report, and an HTML template:

   ▸ If you select **Graphic report output**, the report may consist of several information areas (header and navigation area, graphic area, drilldown, and details list). You can use an HTML template to include individual graphics in the report header. For this output type, you can use drag and drop for functions such as navigation and drilldown switch.

   ▸ If you select the output type **Classic drilldown**, your reports are displayed as drilldown lists.

▶ The **Object list** enables you to display reports using the ABAP list viewer. This is a particularly useful output type if you want to display several characteristics in the lead column.

▶ If you select the output type **XXL** (spreadsheet), you can display reports in Microsoft Excel.

6. Among the settings under **Options**, you find print layout settings and performance settings for executing a report. When specifying the latter, you need to decide whether current data should be read or whether the system should read the data from the last time the summarization level was built up.

> **Note**
>
> Not all of these steps may be possible or required because they will depend on the report and the form concerned. In addition, because basic reports and line item reports also allow working with variables, characteristic groups, key figure schemes, and additional elements, all of these items must be defined beforehand so you can have access to them during your report design.

Another important element when working with line item reports is hotspots, which, as we've mentioned before, are objects that you can click on inside the report that change the data display. Line item reports are mostly geared toward the analysis of data and review of system transactions; therefore, using hotspots is very important for drilldown. However, line item reports can also display any chart or graphic as part of the report, but you need to create these items separately using 3D and a portfolio graph option, and saving the report with a .dat file extension.

Because you create line item reports using a similar procedure to that of creating basic reports — you execute them by clicking on the execute icon, and access the data contained in your characteristics — we will go directly to presenting an example of a final result of a line item report, as shown in Figure 9.21.

Notice in Figure 9.21 that a line item report is essentially a more simplified version of a basic report, showing two characteristics, **Material Group** and **Division,** to control the data display for the **GrossSales** value field. Also, notice that you can display totals for the information contained inside of the value fields displayed in columns.

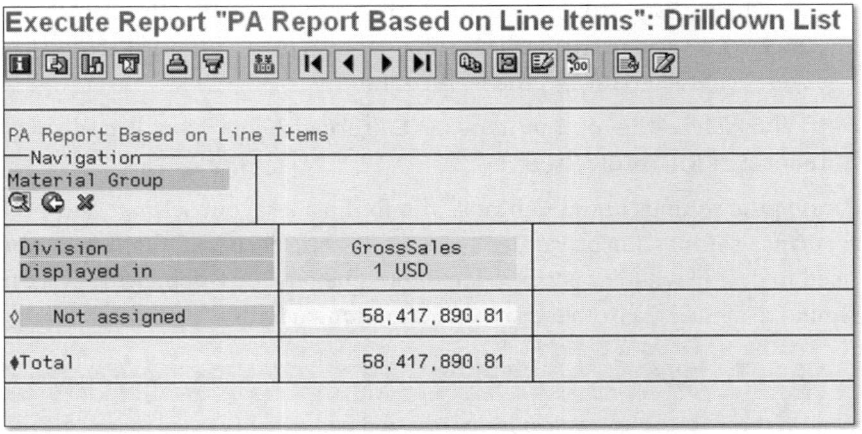

Execute Report "PA Report Based on Line Items": Drilldown List

PA Report Based on Line Items
Navigation
Material Group

Division Displayed in	GrossSales 1 USD
◊ Not assigned	58,417,890.81
♦Total	58,417,890.81

Figure 9.21 Reviewing a Line Item Report

The report shown in Figure 9.21 also contains one hotspot that controls the drilldown navigation display, so we'll use it to improve our analysis:

1. Click on the **Division** characteristic (step 1 in Figure 9.22).

2. Click on the **Material Group** characteristic to perform the switch of the display of the Hotspot (step 2 in Figure 9.22).

3. See the final result of the Hotspot and data display, adding the display of the **ITEMS Material Group** (step 3 in Figure 9.22).

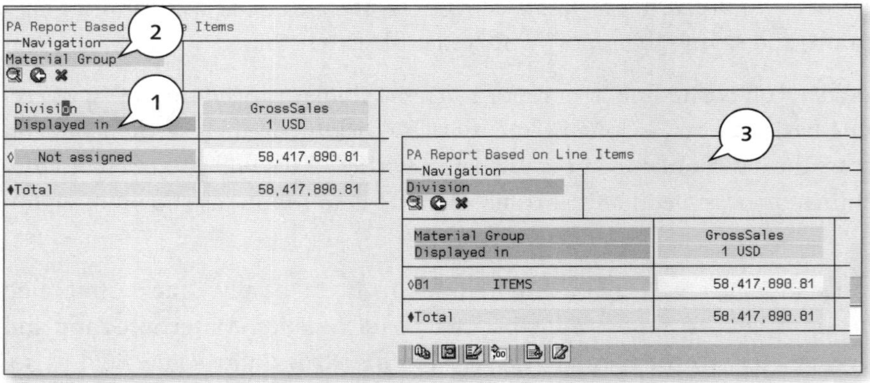

PA Report Based on Line Items
Navigation
Material Group

Division Displayed in	GrossSales 1 USD
◊ Not assigned	58,417,890.81
♦Total	58,417,890.81

PA Report Based on Line Items
Navigation
Division

Material Group Displayed in	GrossSales 1 USD
◊01 ITEMS	58,417,890.81
♦Total	58,417,890.81

Figure 9.22 Working with Hotspots to Change the Data Display

Play around and explore other options and different alternatives to your data display by adding more characteristics and value fields. If you access the **Edit** menu, as shown in Figure 9.23, you'll see that different options from those available with the basic report are now available because they are for exclusive use with line item reports.

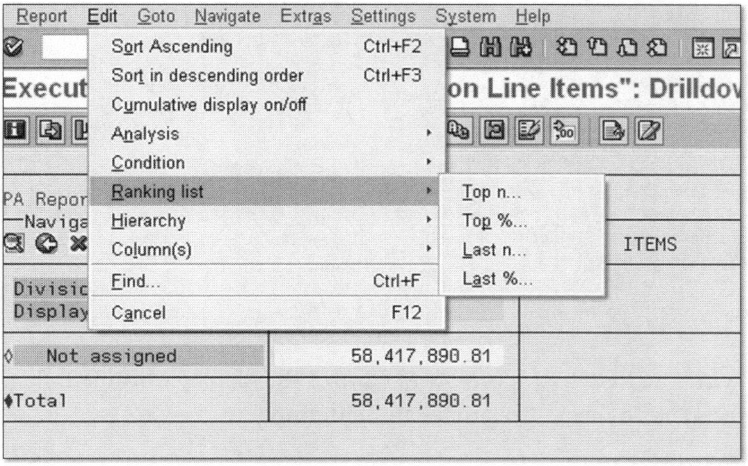

Figure 9.23 Reviewing the Line Item Report Additional Options in the Edit Menu

In the next section we will review the concept of forms and how to interact with reports based on a common template. These types of components are useful for large implementations where different departments or business require maintaining a standard reporting template.

9.3 Working with Forms

You have probably already noticed that there is a **Form** button in some of the screens we have worked with while creating reports, for example, the screen shown in Figure 9.7. You'll see this button when you first start creating a basic or line item report, and clicking on this button lets you create forms used by basic or line item reports. Alternatively, you can access this functionality by following the path **Information System • Report Components • Define Forms • Define Forms for Profitability Reports** or **Define Forms for Reports Based on Line Items,** as shown in Figure 9.24.

Either way, you are taken to the screen shown in Figure 9.25. The form object accesses an alternative environment of Report Painter created for forms to define a standard template based on a value field (key figure) structure that other reports may follow to maintain standard reporting values. When a report follows a form, only the **Characteristics**, **Variables**, **Output**

Type, and **Option** tabs are available, but not the **Key Figures** tab because that information is controlled by the template of the form.

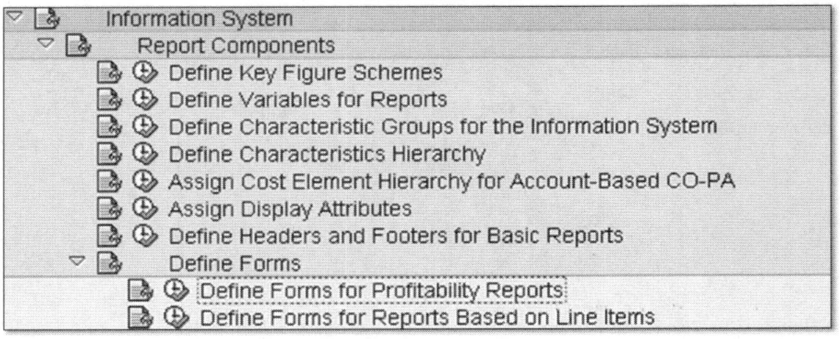

Figure 9.24 Accessing the Forms menu

Forms work with key figure structures and control the display of value fields. There are three types of structures that can be defined:

▶ Two axis (matrix)

▶ One axis with key figure

▶ One axis without key figure

These configurations let you create flexible reporting templates that can be maintained around different business areas, allowing users to only modify the characteristics needed to limit the data displays, but the information generated is exactly the same. You can also generate a form as a copy from another form and use it as a reference. When creating a report using a form, at least one characteristic must be used to limit the data extraction of the template.

For our example we will define a matrix form for a basic report:

1. Click on the option **Define Form for Profitability Reports** following the path **Information System ・ Report Components ・ Define Forms ・ Define Forms for Profitability Reports**.

2. Provide a name of "Form1" and a description of "This is Form1" for the form. Notice that when creating forms, we are accessing a Report Painter environment, as shown in Figure 9.25.

3. Select **Two axes (matrix)** to define the structure of your form.

4. Click on the **Create** button.

5. As shown in Figure 9.26, you can see a standard template with a **Lead colum** with different rows and columns. Because this is a matrix, double-clicking on each of the columns and rows defines what data is extracted to each of those locations.

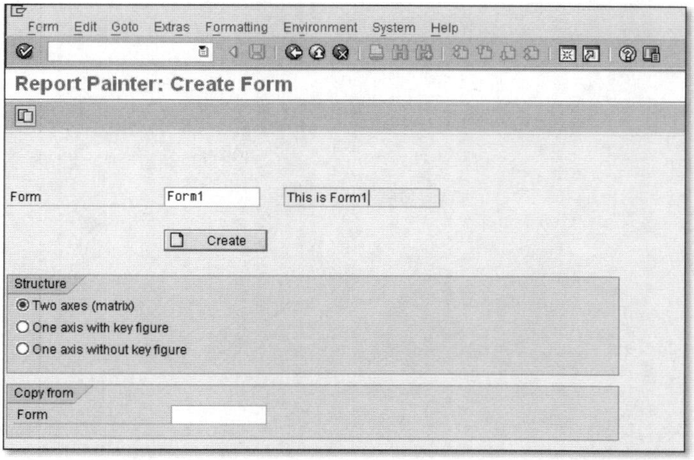

Figure 9.25 Creating a Form Name and Description

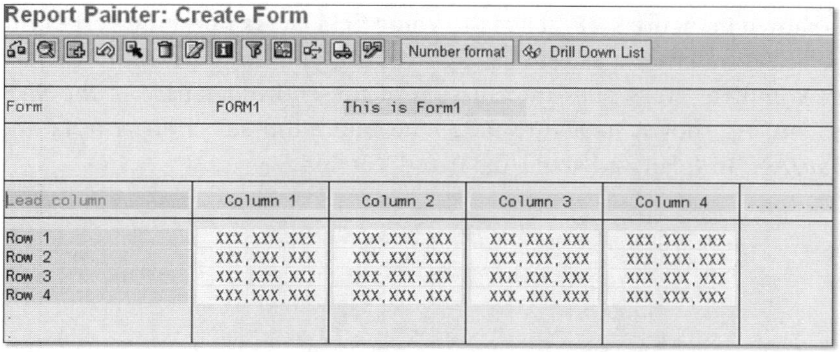

Figure 9.26 Reviewing Matrix Form1

6. Double-click on **Row 1** and you'll see that you can create characteristics, value fields with characteristics, key figure scheme elements, and predefined elements as types.

7. Select characteristics and select and limit the characteristics values. As shown in Figure 9.27 we are selecting **Material Group** with a default value for **ITEM**.

8. Once you have completed defining the restrictions and selection criteria for your characteristic, click on the **Confirm** button located at the lower bottom of Figure 9.27.

9. Double-click on a column, select the **Value Field with Characteristics** option, and click on the checkmark icon.

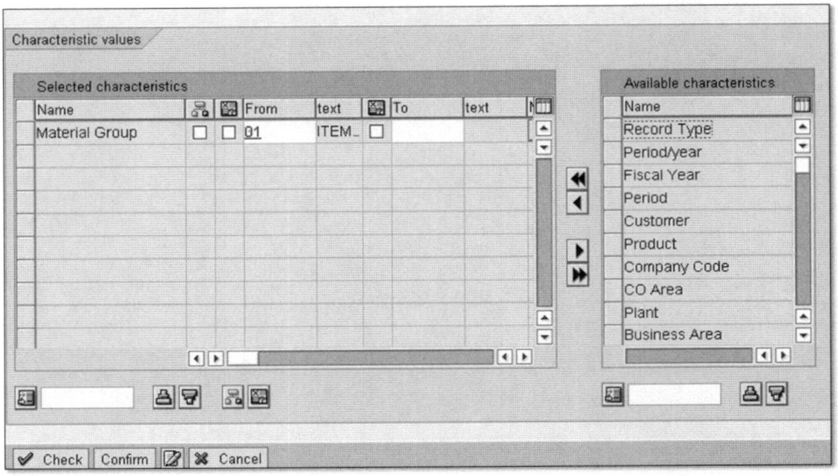

Figure 9.27 Restricting a Characteristic in a Form

10. As shown in Figure 9.28, select the **Value field Gross sales**, then establish the selection criteria as required. Of course, you do not want to extract the complete gross sales information of the entire database in the SAP system. As shown in Figure 9.28, the minimum selection criteria are **Plan/Act. In** (plan and actual data) and **Version**.

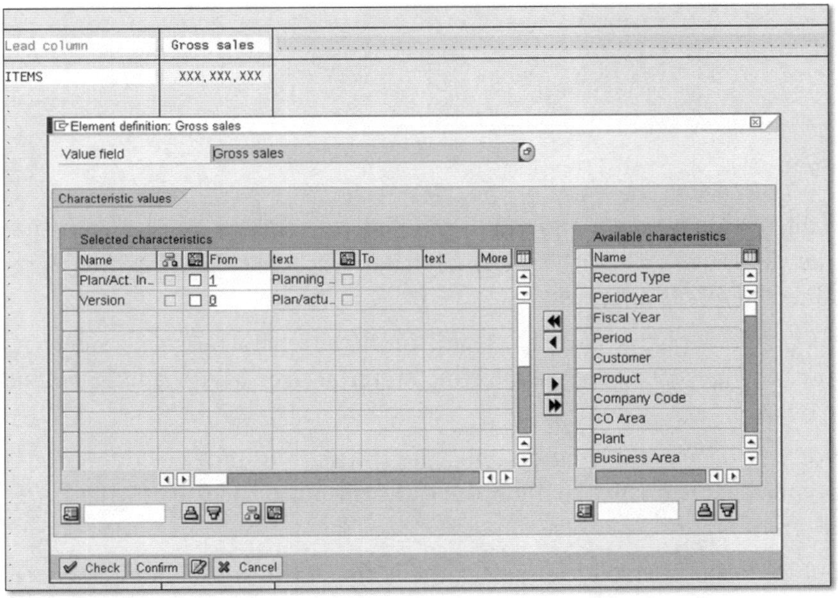

Figure 9.28 Creating a Value Field in a Form

11. Click on the **Confirm** button.

> **Note**
>
> You can also click on the **Check** button before clicking on the **Confirm** button to make sure that everything was created correctly.

12. Save your form.

Now you must assign the form to a basic report:

1. Return to the **Profitability Analysis · Information System · Create Profitability Report** function. However, this time instead of choosing the **Basic report** option, select the **Report with Form** option, and assign the **FORM1** form we just created. Also, create **Report3** as shown in Figure 9.29, and type "Report Using Form1" as a description.

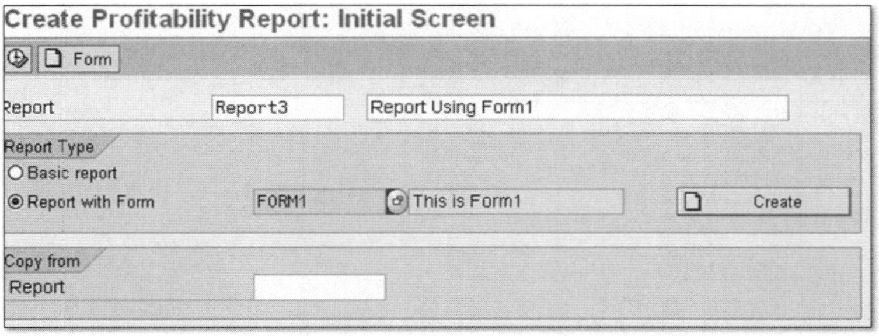

Figure 9.29 Assigning a Form to a Report

2. Click on the **Create** button.

3. Notice that there is no **Key Figures** tab available as before, and you must select at least one characteristic on the **Characteristics** tab. In this case, as shown in Figure 9.30, we will leave the **Val.** Column empty to extract all of the information. You can change and modify the options displayed in Figure 9.30 at any time, but for now we'll leave them as they are.

4. Save your new report based on a form.

5. In the appropriate screen, select the newly created **REPORT3** report as shown in Figure 9.31, execute it (by clicking on the clock with the check-mark icon), and click on the **Yes** button to extract the latest information.

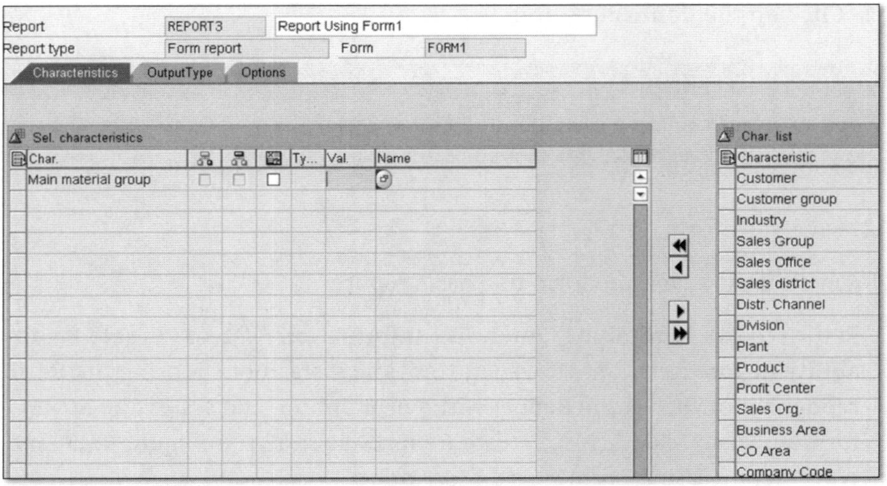

Figure 9.30 Reviewing the Configuration Tabs of a Form-based Report

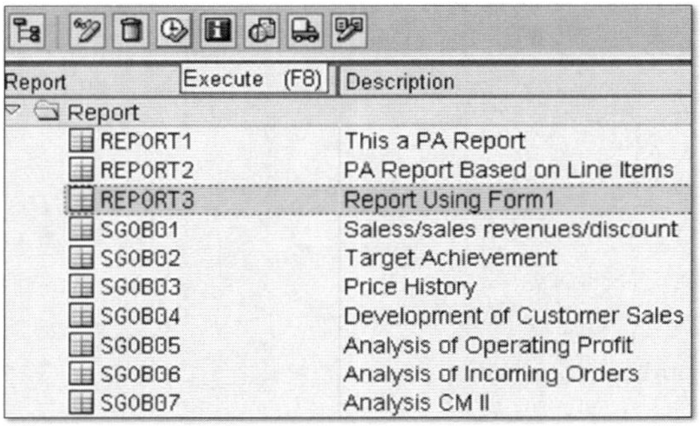

Figure 9.31 Select and Execute Your Form-based Report

6. Now the report is executed and displayed, as shown in Figure 9.32. Notice at the bottom of the screen, the report confirms that this report is based on **Form1**.

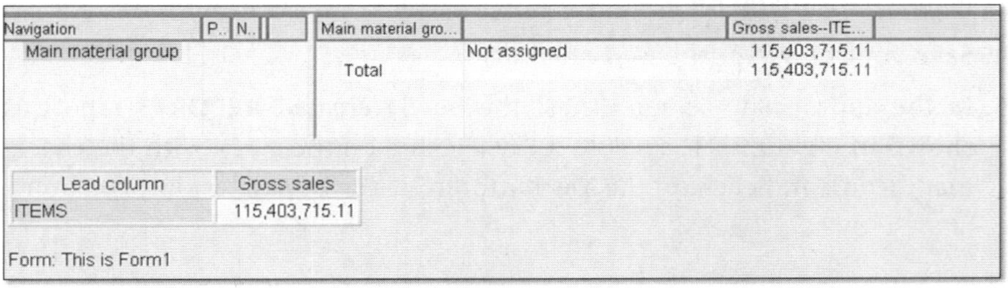

Figure 9.32 Working with a Form-based Report

This was a simple example; if you want, you can now explore more complex ways to improve forms and report generation on your own. Finally, be aware that you can create forms based on line items following the same logic.

9.4   Summary

This chapter introduced you to the concepts of CO-PA reporting, and how similar some of the functionalities are to SAP NetWeaver BI/SAP BW. You also saw that Report Painter, a standard SAP reporting functionality used in other modules of SAP, also works within the CO-PA environment. You learned about basic reports and reports based on line items, and you also learned how to create forms and how to use them when creating reports.

There are additional functionalities that we will discuss in the Chapter 10, such as frozen reports, variables, and formulas. All of these elements increase the sophistication and power of the reports generated within CO-PA and it is compared with many functionalities available in SAP BW/SAP NetWeaver BI.

We are now moving on to advanced topics in CO-PA reporting. This chapter is not appropriate for end users, unless there is a strong interest in becoming a super or power user that allows handling and configuring objects, such as summarization levels, frozen reports, key figure schemes, formulas, and others.

10 CO-PA Reporting: Configuration

In the previous chapter we reviewed the concepts of basic and line item reports, forms, and general configuration options available in CO-PA. In this chapter, we will explore in more detail further configuration settings available in the Information System menu. Some of the elements we will discuss are how to configure headers and footers if you want to provide additional information attached to your report or form, creating key figure schemes, variables, configuration of frozen reports, working with the Formula Editor, and more. Let's start our discussion by looking at how to predefine headers and footers.

> **Note**
>
> Most of the elements discussed in this chapter can be used in both forms and reports. Thus, we will not specify for which component the configuration object is applicable.

10.1 Predefining Headers and Footers

You're probably aware that a header and footer in a report allow you to include additional information, such as addresses, page numbers, descriptions, or comments you want to attach to the report and make available to the user either at the top (header) or bottom (footer) of the report, and printed on each page. We'll now review in more detail how to include these two elements as part of a report using the Report Painter environment with CO-PA.

To start creating headers and footers in CO-PA reports, follow these steps:

1. Access the header and footer definitions by following the path **Information System • Report Components • Define Headers and Footers for Basic Reports**, shown in Figure 10.1.

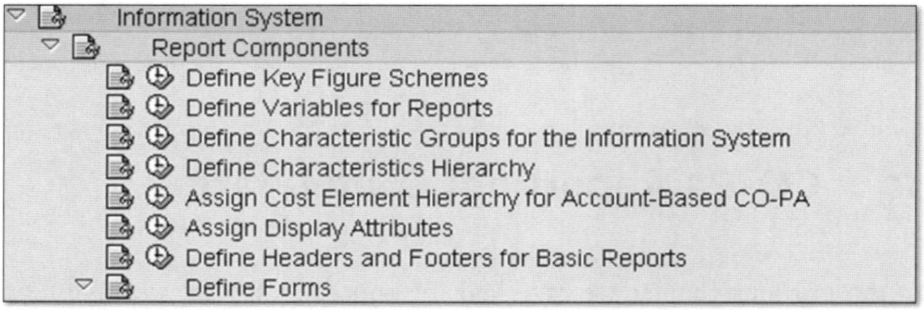

Figure 10.1 Creating Headers and Footers in the Information System Menu

2. Alternatively, when creating a basic report, as discussed in Chapter 9, access the **Output Type** tab, as shown in Figure 10.2. In the **Layout** area, select the checkbox next to **Headers** or **Footers** (or both of them if you need to) and click on the respective change/modify icon(s) to define the contents of each of these objects.

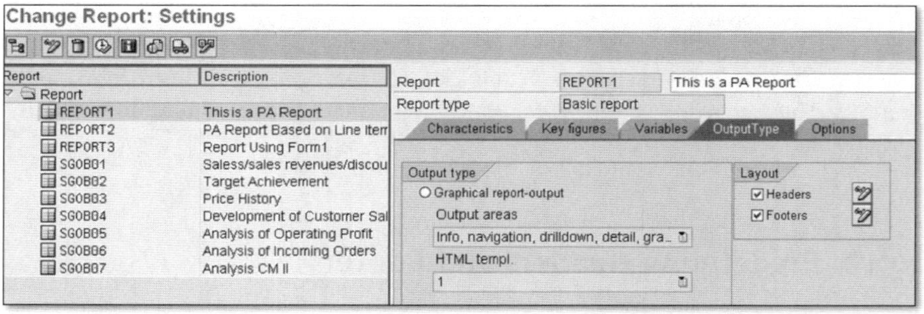

Figure 10.2 Creating Headers and Footers in the Change Report: Settings Screen

Both types of objects have a common menu, as shown in Figure 10.3. The buttons on this menu, in order from left to right, are: add line, cut, paste, delete line, delete variable (**Variable**), insert frames (**Frames**), insert general variables (**Gen. variables**), and insert text variable for selection parameters (**Sel. parameters**).

Figure 10.3 Header and Footer Menu

Now let us explore the functions of the last three buttons displayed in Figure 10.3 (**Frames**, **Gen. variables**, and **Sel. parameters**), starting with **Frames**.

10.1.1 Frames

A *frame* is a text variable with a width and height specified, as shown in Figure 10.4, that you can predefine to be maintained in all of the pages of a report. It is a line that defines the division of information or contains information details needed to comply with certain formatting requirements for a particular report. For example, to define settings similar to those shown in Figure 10.4 as part of your report, proceed as follows:

1. Double-click on a line in the report and click on the **Frames** button to add the frames object to your report.

2. Modify the formatting options by double-clicking on the frame object and configuring your settings. For our example, in the **Formatting** area, change the character length to "10" for **Width** and "1" for **Height**, as shown in Figure 10.4.

3. Click on the checkmark button to save your settings.

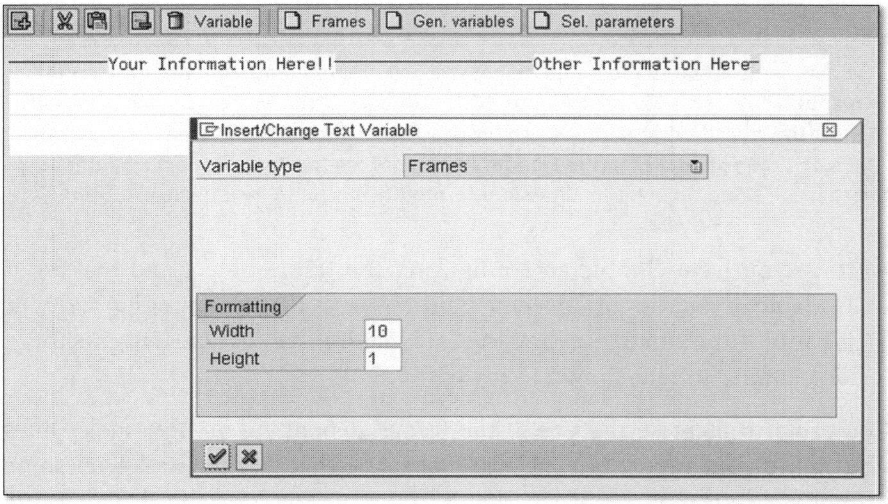

Figure 10.4 Adding a Frame Object to Your Report

4. As shown in Figure 10.4, you are creating multiple lines, some blank, some with text. For example, you can see the text **Your Information Here!!** and **Other Information Here** as part of the the header section, and you can add as many lines as required to your report.

5. Once you have created your lines as shown in Figure 10.4, you can type a header description, such as "This is your Header with ---------Frames!!------."

6. Save your work, and go back to the **Change Report: Settings** screen, as shown in Figure 10.5, and, on the **Output Type** tab in the **Layout** area, select the **Headers** checkbox option to display the newly created frame object when executing your report.

7. Save your changes.

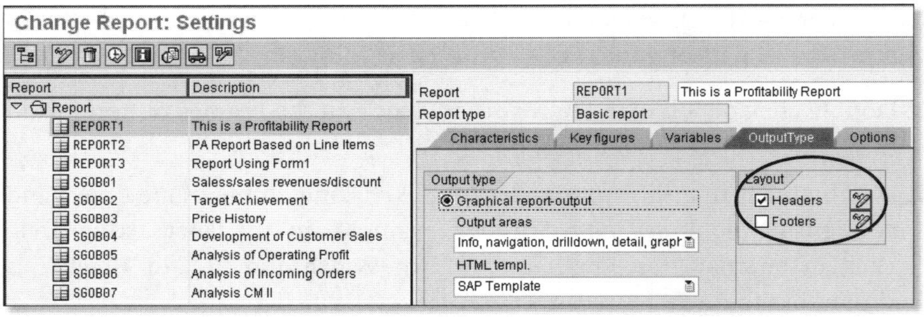

Figure 10.5 Displaying the Frame Object in the Header of REPORT1

> **Tip**
>
> Remember, to modify the frame object you just created, you can either click on the **Output Type** tab shown in Figure 10.5 and access the **Headers** change/modify icon, (the pencil with glasses), or you can follow the path **Information System • Report Components • Define Headers and Footers for Basic Reports**. Both paths access the same object and allow you to modify or create headers and footers.

8. Once you have completed configuring the frame object and making it available to your report, execute your report as discussed in Chapter 9. At the top of the report, review the information we just created; it should look similar to that shown in Figure 10.6.

You can also increase the size of the frame, depending on how many lines you add to your report header. Just make sure that you test and print some samples of your report to verify that it fits your paper size and that all of the required information is displayed according to the required format.

```
This is a PA Report

This is your Header with ─────────Frames!!──────────────────────



  ┌Navigation┐
  Division
  ⊞ ↻ ✖
```

Material Group	⊠	GrossSales 1 USD	SalesCosts 1 USD	Sales qty 1 ST	Ma
Displayed in					
◊01 ITEMS		58,417,890.81	0.00	4,790,108.000	4
♦Total		58,417,890.81	0.00	4,790,108.000	4

Figure 10.6 Executing Your Report and Reviewing the Frame Object

Likely, you will be interested in adding more information to your headers, such as a page number, page count, date, and other types of descriptive information. This is the function of the general variables (**Gen. variables**) button discussed in the next section.

10.1.2 General Variables

General variables are objects that either store, generate, or format data depending on report settings, such as page number or additional description. To add a variable to a report, use this procedure:

1. Access the headers menu again following the path **Information System • Report Components • Define Headers and Footers for Basic Reports**, as shown earlier in Figure 10.3.

2. Add a new line and type the description "Page Number is:" as shown toward the top of the page in Figure 10.7. This description is specified before you create the general variable.

3. Click on the **Gen. variables** button.

4. The screen **Insert/Change Text Variable**, as shown in Figure 10.7, appears.

5. Select **General text variable** from the **Variable type** dropdown list.

6. From the **Variable Name** dropdown list, select **Page Number**.

7. In the **Formatting** area, leave the **Width** as **5**.

8. Click on the checkmark icon to attach the **Page Number** variable object to the report as part of your frame object, after the description **Page Number is:**.

9. In Figure 10.7, you see a **0** after the text **Page Number is:**. This is where the general variable will display the page number of the report.

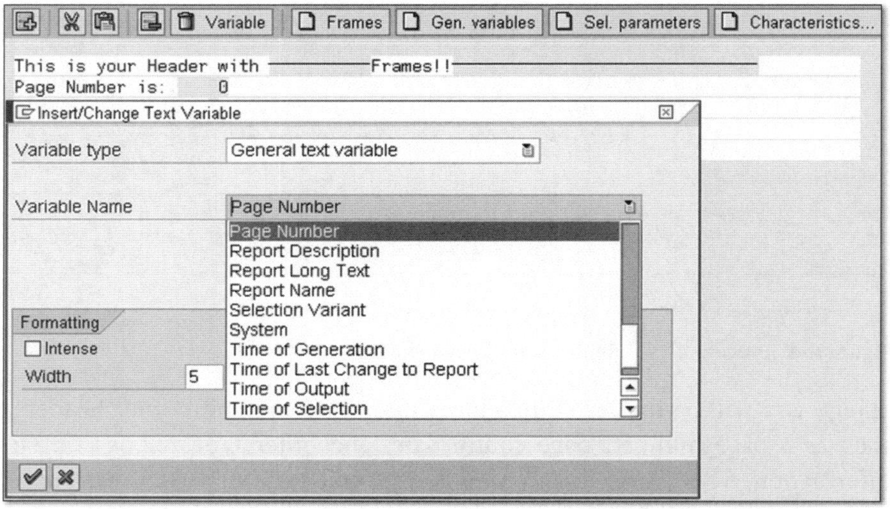

Figure 10.7 Creating a General Variable for Your Report

> **Tip**
>
> To delete any of the general variables, position the cursor on the desired object to delete, and click on the **Variable** button (with the trash can next to the word **Variable**). The system prompts you to confirm your deletion. Click on the checkmark icon to remove the variable from your report.

If you wish, you can experiment with the many types of variables available, adding different ones to your report. Also, sometimes it is useful to display information related to the characteristics included or attached in your report; for example, you might like to make sure you are reporting only billing data or a specific category within a material group. This type of information might be meaningful for your users to have and adding it is done using of the selection parameters (**Sel. Parameters**) function we discuss in the next section.

10.1.3   Selection Parameters

Before we look at selection parameters, let us quickly review what we have done so far. We have created a frame object using several lines that define a region on the header. This object allows writing or attaching information to clarify the contents of the report for your users. Next, we created a variable that provides the page number of the report (to organize reports that have more than one page). Now, we will provide an additional functionality to display information related to data classification based on the characteristics used in the report, using selection parameters.

Let us say that we want to add a variable for selection parameters to display the value of the record type characteristic that is already stored in the report. This way, users will always know that the report is generated based on the type of data being displayed. To create a selection parameter variable, follow these steps:

1. Access the headers and footers configuration settings, using the path shown earlier in Figure 10.3.

2. Create a new line and type the description "The Record Type is:" (the result of which is shown in Figure 10.8).

3. Click on the **Sel. Parameter** button to display the **Insert/Change Text Variable** screen, as shown in Figure 10.8. Notice that the **Variable type** is **Text variable for selection parameters**.

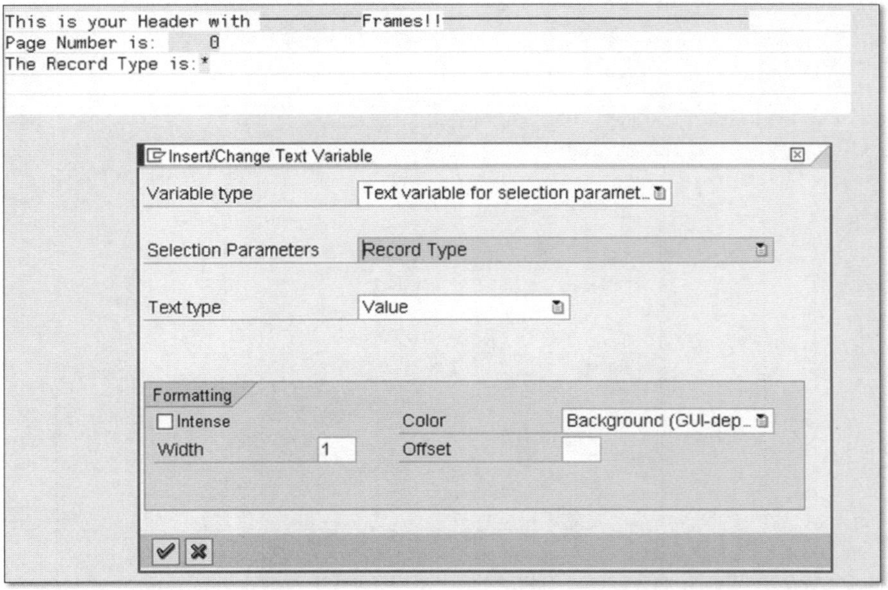

Figure 10.8 Creating a Sel. Parameter Object in Your Report

4. From the **Selection Parameters** dropdown list, choose the **Record Type** characteristic, as shown in Figure 10.8

5. Select the **Text type** to be **Value**.

6. Remember to control the **Width** field information, depending on the expected length of the data to be displayed. In this case, as shown in Figure 10.8, we chose a **Width** size of **1** because the **Record Type** displays only one letter.

7. Click on the checkmark icon to complete the creation of your frame, and then click on the standard save icon to store your configuration.

8. As shown in Figure 10.8, you now see an asterisk after the text **The Record Type is:**. This means that a new object has been added to your report, where the record type value will be displayed.

9. Create another selection parameter in another line. As shown in Figure 10.9, add the **Material Group** characteristic, and the description "We are working with" before the **Sel. Parameter** object. However, this time define the width as **15** to be able to display the complete description. As you can see, the selection parameters is just another type of variable added to your report.

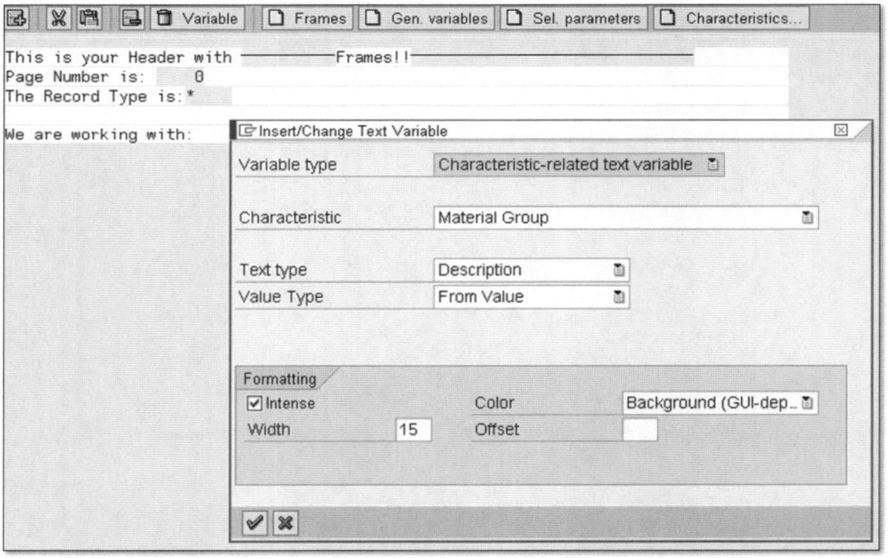

Figure 10.9 Adding the Material Group Selection Parameter

10. Save your changes and see the results by executing your report, as shown in Figure 10.10. Notice the header information at the top of the screen, and the information extracted using your predefined selection parameter variables **Page Number** and **Record Type**.

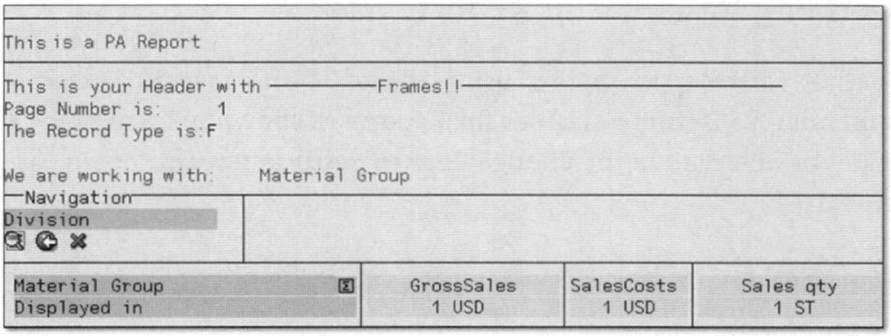

Figure 10.10 Reviewing Your Header Report with Variables and Descriptions

10.1.4 Footers

What about footers? It is simple, all of the information we just reviewed for headers applies to footers, also; the only difference is that the information displays at the bottom of the report! To access the footer information, select the **Footers** checkbox on the **Output Type** tab, as shown in Figure 10.11, and with the change/modify icon access the **Maintain Footers** area where you can configure your footer information.

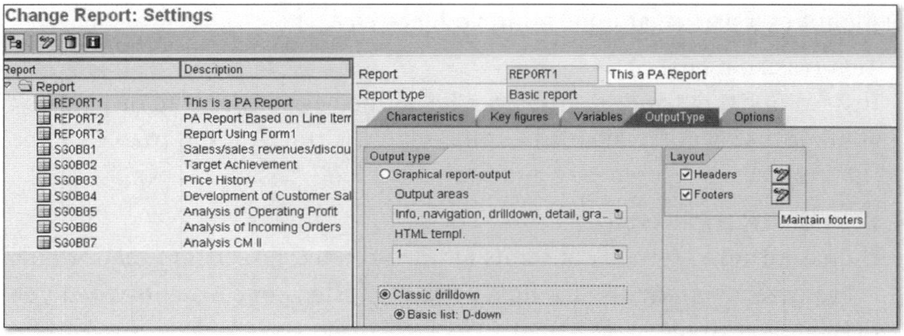

Figure 10.11 Adding Footers to Your Report

You now have a general idea of how variables work inside your CO-PA reporting environment. You can also define variables that control more than just the information displayed in your headers and footers. For example, you can define variables that control characteristic values, hierarchy nodes, texts, formulas, and other information. This is our main topic of discussion in the next section, so let us begin!

10.2 Defining Variables in Reports

You can define variables in reports using the path **Information System** • **Report Components** • **Define Variables for Reports** as shown in Figure 10.12 or access the **Variables** tab in the **Change Report: Settings** screen, shown earlier in Figure 10.11.

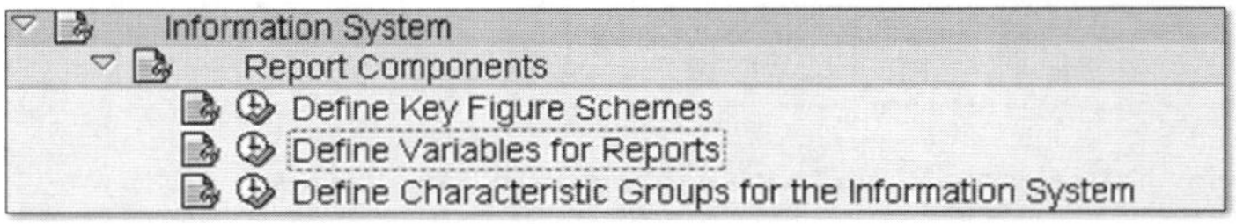

Figure 10.12 Reviewing the Variable Access Path in the Information System Menu

Generally speaking, in an SAP system there are several types of variables that are used to simplify or automate data extraction. In CO-PA the following types of variables are available:

► **Characteristic value** (variable type 1)
A unique value within a characteristic (field name).

► **Hierarchy node** (variable type 2)
Identifies a particular node within a hierarchy.

► **Text** (variable type 3)
Instead of being fixed text, text can be defined as a variable to display text content that is not available before a report is run. A text variable can be used to make a reference to another text.

► **Formula** (variable type 4)
If, in a formula, certain constants are determined just before the formula is evaluated, you can use formula variables instead of constants when you define the formula.

► **Hierarchy** (variable type 5)
You can assign a variable to extract a specific hierarchy variable stored in the system.

► **Hierarchy node/Characteristic value** (variable type 6)
A combination of a variable node (variable type 2) and a characteristic value (variable type 1). When executing a report, you can either enter a hierarchy node or different characteristic values.

In addition to the variable types discussed above, another element called *replacement type* is required to complete the definition of the variables.

Replacement type defines how a CO-PA variable will be replaced by a value, automatically or manually:

▶ **Automatic replacement path** (replacement type 1)
For variables of types 3 and 4, you can create an automatic replacement path. You define the replacement path using the following entries: source field (field name), from/to flag, characteristic value/text flag, offset, and length.

▶ **Replacement by manual entry** (replacement type 2)
The contents of the variable are determined by the entry you make when carrying out the transaction.

▶ **Replacement by user-exit** (replacement type 3)
The content of the variable is defined by a user-exit. User-exits can be found and are maintained in the module pool SAPLXYEX. The function modules are called EXIT_SAPLKYP1_001, EXIT_SAPLKYP1_002, and EXIT_SAPLKYP1__003. You also need to create the corresponding includes ZXYEXU01, ZXYEXU02, and ZXYEXU03 as local objects.

▶ **Replacement by SAP-Exit** (replacement type 4)
The contents of the variable are determined by a path prescribed by the SAP system. These variables begin with a number and cannot be maintained.

▶ **Replacement by a fixed value** (replacement type 5)
The contents of the variable are determined by the entry in the field fixed value.

▶ **Replacement by user parameters from the GPA area (only online)** (replacement type 6)
Relevant for variable type 1 (characteristic value). The variable is automatically replaced by the Get parameter value of the entered field.

▶ **Replacement by a reference** (replacement type 7)
Relevant with variable type 5 (hierarchy). The hierarchy display in the report list can be controlled using this variable when using a hierarchy node in the form. At the same time, the hierarchy node of the formula is used for the hierarchy display of the report list. Prerequisite: A hierarchy node variable (variable type 2) with replacement type 2 (entry) is used for the hierarchy node in the form. The name of the node variables must agree with the name of the hierarchy variables (variable type 5, replacement type 7). This hierarchy variable is offered in the report definition with the hierarchy selection. Example: Global hierarchy node variable &KNOTEN used in the form (variable type 2, replacement type 2). In addi-

tion, a global variable &KNOTEN is defined with variable type 5, replacement type 7. The variable &KNOTEN can be highlighted in the report definition using the hierarchy selection. Then the report list is displayed in accordance with nodes entered when executing the report.

As you can see, not only the variable type is a configuration decision issue, but also how the values of the variable are handled. For our example, we will limit the discussion to a standard user so we define the most basic of the variables and replacement types: a **Characteristic value** variable that extracts data from a characteristic during execution time with manual **Entry** as the **Replacement type**, as shown in Figure 10.13.

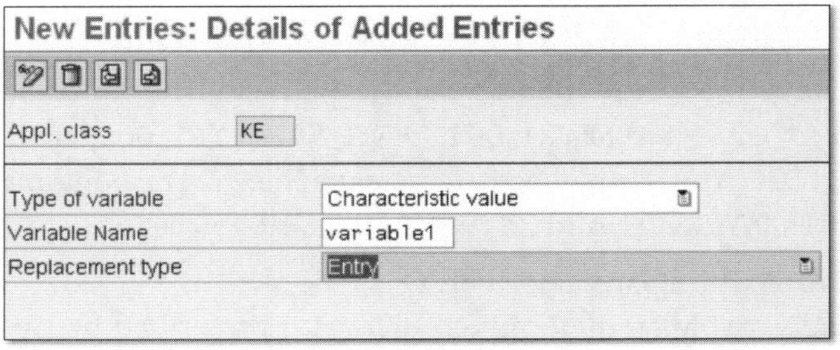

Figure 10.13 Creating a Characteristic Variable with Manual Entry Replacement Type

Follow these steps to create the sample variable, **variable1**:

1. Access the screen shown in Figure 10.13, using the path **Information System • Report Components • Define Variables for Reports**.

2. Notice the nonmodifiable field **Appl. class** with the text **KE**. This identifies that the variable will be for Profitability Analysis use only.

3. Select the **Type of variable** to be **Characteristic value,** as shown in Figure 10.13, specify a **Variable Name** of "variable1," and select the **Replacement Type** to be **Entry**.

4. Press **Enter** to move to the next configuration portion of the screen. Do not save at this point yet; otherwise the system prompts you with an error that it is waiting for the definition of the characteristic to use.

5. The system changes the screen display, as shown in Figure 10.14, and grays out (blocks) the fields **Type of variable** and **Variable Name**.

6. Type the technical name "MATKL" in the **Field Name** to specify that you want to use the material group characteristic for variable with the technical name **&VARIABLE1**.

7. Leave the rest of the options seen in Figure 10.14 as they appear in the figure, and type the description "**Material Group**." That way you'll know that you are working with that characteristic attached to **variable1**.

Appl. class	KE	
Type of variable	Characteristic value	
Variable Name	&VARIABLE1	
Field Name	MATKL	
Replacement type	Entry	
Default value	Set / Get parameter	
Optional entry	Required entry	
Parameter/selectopt.	Parameters	
Short text	Matl Group	
Description	Material Group	
Text	Material Group	

Figure 10.14 Completing the Configuration of &VARIABLE1 for Material Group

8. Save your work, and go back to the **Change Profitabiliy Report:Specify Profit. Segment** environment.

9. On the **Characteristics** tab, in the **Set characteristics** area, notice the checkbox in the third column from the left in the line **Material Group,** as shown in Figure 10.15. This checkbox enables access to predefined CO-PA variables (such as the one created in the previous steps). Select this checkbox to access the **VARIABLE1** variable we just created.

Change Profitability Report : Specify Profit. Segment		
Report	Description	Report	REPORT1	This is a PA Report
Report		Report type	Basic report	
REPORT1	This is a PA Report			
REPORT2	PA Report Based on Line Item	Characteristics Key figures Variables OutputType Options		
REPORT3	Report Using Form1			
SG0B01	Saless/sales revenues/discou			
SG0B02	Target Achievement	Sel. characteristics		
SG0B03	Price History	Char. Ty... Val. Name		
SG0B04	Development of Customer Sal	Material Group		
SG0B05	Analysis of Operating Profit	Division		
SG0B06	Analysis of Incoming Orders			
SG0B07	Analysis CM II			

Figure 10.15 Adding &VARIABLE1 to your REPORT1

10. As you can see in Figure 10.16, after selecting the checkbox in the variable column in the line **Material Group**, we are able to attach a variable to the characteristic **Material Group**. Because we only have one variable at the moment, select the line for **VARIABLE1**. Also, notice that in this line, you see the settings you specified in the screen shown in Figure 10.14.

11. Click on the checkmark icon to accept the selection and attach it to the characteristic **Material Group**.

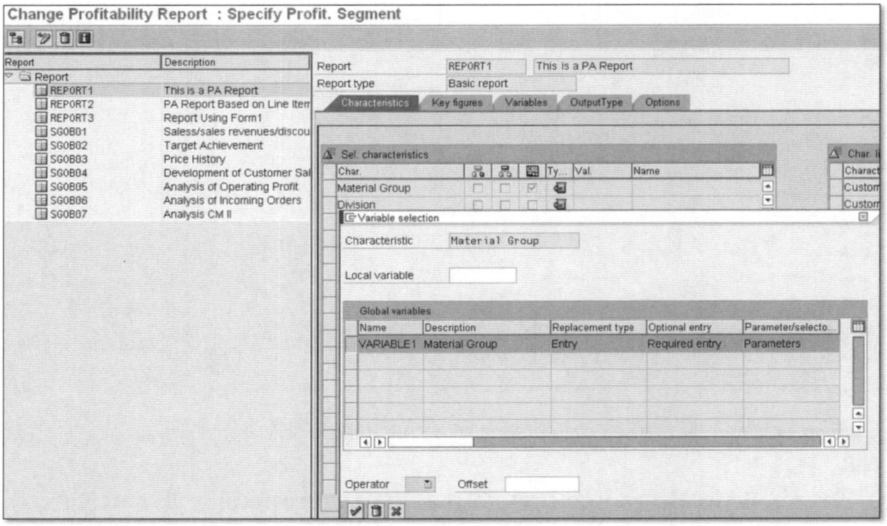

Figure 10.16 Adding VARIABLE1 to Your CO-PA Report

12. As shown in Figure 10.17, variable **VARIABLE1** has been added to **the Material Group** characteristic and it is grayed out to disallow any other information input (unless you want to change the variable, which you would do by clicking on the checkbox again).

13. Notice also that the description of the variable is visible in the column called **Name** in Figure 10.17, and currently shows **Material Group**, the name we previously configured in the screen shown in Figure 10.14. You could have chosen a different name if you wanted the variable name to be different from the characteristic name.

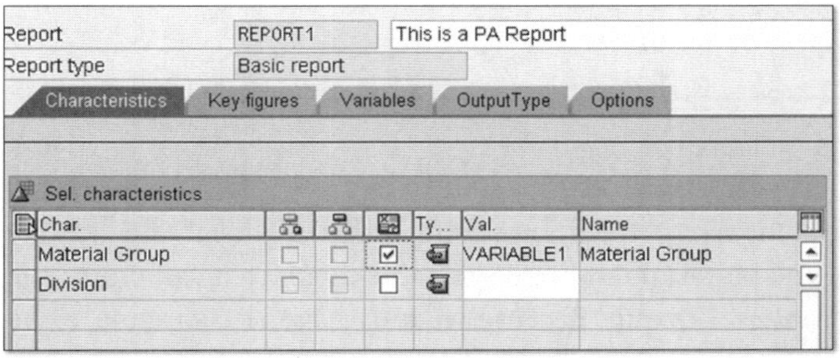

Figure 10.17 Assigning Variables to Your Report

14. Save your report to update all of the configuration settings, and execute it again.

15. Notice that in the **Report selections** area in the screen **Selection: This is a PA Report**, shown in Figure 10.18, the **Material Group** characteristic displays without any type of definition. We'll change this to take advantage of the VARIABLE1 variable.

Selection: This is a PA Report

Report selections	
Material Group	
Period from	
Period to	
Plan/Act. Indicator	☑
Version	0
Record Type	F

Figure 10.18 Executing Your Report

16. Go back to the **Change Profitability Report : Variable Entry** screen, as shown in Figure 10.19, and select the **Variables** tab.

17. Notice that all of the required data values to input before each report are also variables and that for your variable **Material Group** (VARIABLE1), the **Entry at Execution** column checkbox is checked and grayed out to inform you that a variable is attached and that it cannot be removed.

    Remember, VARIABLE1 was set up to be a required entry, meaning you cannot omit inputting a value to this characteristic when executing your report. However, the other variables shown in Figure 10.19, **Period from**, **Period to**, **Plan/Act Indicator**, **Version**, and **Record Type** are not required during execution. Therefore, you can uncheck any of the checkmarks in the **Entry at Execution** column to remove the associated variable, but *not* **Material Group**.

18. Also, notice that there is a question mark (**?**) in the **Variable Value** column. This means that the value is required, and before executing the report, this field must be either defaulted in the screen shown in Figure 10.19, or typed in at run time. Otherwise, the system will not allow the report to run and an error message appears to inform you about this situation.

19. Remove the variables **Version** and **Record Type** by clicking on their respective checkboxes in the **Entry at Execution** column.

Change Profitability Report : Variable Entry

Report			
Report	REPORT1	This is a PA Report	
Report type	Basic report		

Characteristics | Key figures | Variables | OutputType | Options

Variable Name	Variable Value	Name	Entry at Execution
Material Group			
Period from			☑
Period to			☑
Plan/Act. Indicator	?		☑
Version			☑
Record Type			☑

Figure 10.19 Reviewing the Variables Tab

20. Type a default value of "AA-001" into the **Variable Value** field for the **Material Group** variable (VARIABLE1), as shown in Figure 10.20. This value will appear as the default during execution of the report.

Change Profitability Report : Variable Entry

Report			
Report	REPORT1	This is a PA Report	
Report type	Basic report		

Characteristics | Key figures | Variables | OutputType | Options

Variable Name	Variable Value	Name	Entry at Execution
Material Group	AA-001		☑
Period from			☑
Period to			☑
Plan/Act. Indicator	?		☑
Version			☐
Record Type			☐

Figure 10.20 Creating a Default Value for Your Material Group Variable

21. Save your changes.

22. Execute the report again and compare the screen shown in Figure 10.21 with the one shown earlier in Figure 10.18. In the **Report selections** area, **Material Group** now displays **AA-001** as the default value that is required to execute the report and will extract all of the information from the other three characteristics if nothing else is defined, but always specifically extracts information for **Material Group**. Also, notice that the characteristics **Version** and **Record Type** that we removed earlier don't display anymore.

23. Notice that VARIABLE1 now carries a default value of **AA-001**, as shown in Figure 10.21.

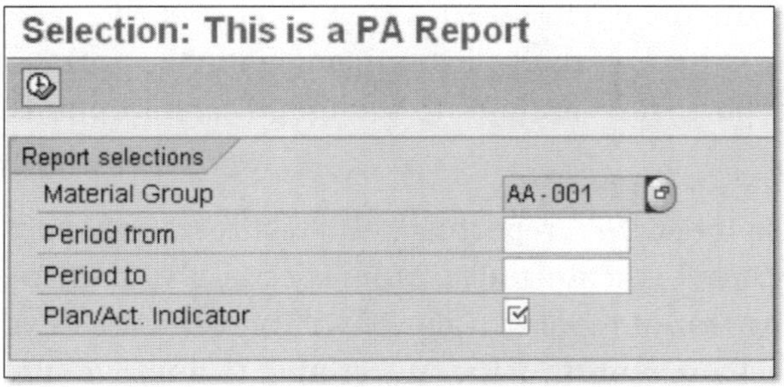

Figure 10.21 Reviewing Your Default Value for Your VARIABLE1

This completes our discussion of configuring variables for CO-PA reports. Beyond this, you've probably already explored the remaining tabs available in the **Report Change: Settings** screen that we have worked on in this chapter and in Chapter 9. Notice, however, that in the **Output type** section of the **Output Type** tab, you can control how your report is displayed, using **HTML**, **Classic drilldown**, the traditional **Object list (AVL)**, or **Excel (XXL)** format, as shown in Figure 10.22. To switch between the different displays for your report, select the appropriate radio button. For example, in Figure 10.22, the configuration is set to **Graphical report-output** using the **Output areas** dropdown list for further configuration.

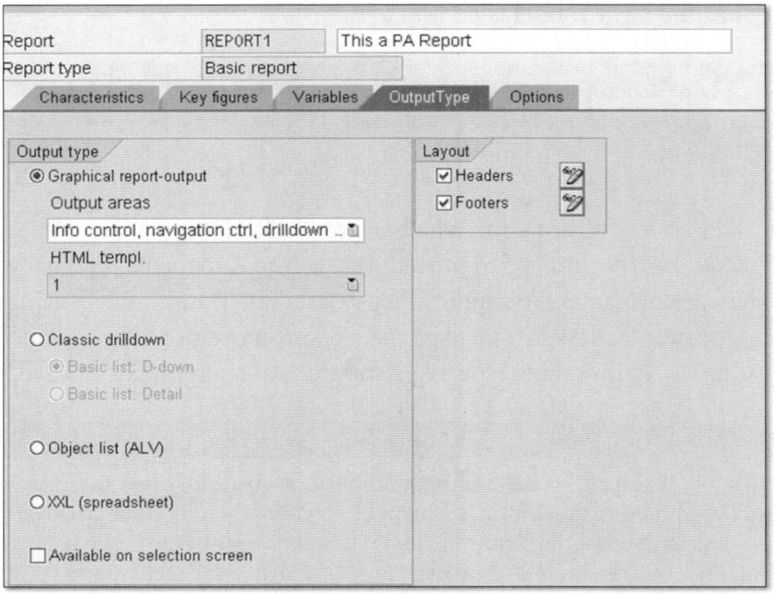

Figure 10.22 Reviewing the Output Type

Overall, remember to configure the environment that will most likely make your users feel comfortable when working. Experiment with the various options and execute your reports several times to see the different options and capabilities.

In the next section we will explore CO-PA reporting Best Practices, and as part of this, work with more advanced functionalities. More specifically, in Chapter 9, we worked on creating frozen reports; now we will move to the next level and explain how to run these reports in the background to improve system performance. We will also look at the configuration of key figure schemes and other techniques useful to improve your reporting efforts.

10.3   CO-PA Reporting: Best Practices

We have created reports, forms, headers, footers, and variables, and modified the data selection process, so what's next? Best Practices! System performance should always be on your mind at each step of implementing any SAP module. Having a project leader who is aware of the importance of this concept and is knowledgeable about it is considered priceless. Unfortunately, in many projects, the project leader works on multiple projects and is under pressure to deliver his projects; therefore, system performance is often not considered until the basic model is completed.

> **Note**
>
> Some terms introduced and briefly discussed here will be explained in more detail in Chapter 12.

This section addresses decisions for which a project leader should consider using Best Practices or recommended procedures in CO-PA reporting that truly improve system performance and simplify data extraction. In addition, by using Best Practices, project leaders can manage their teams more productively and avoid generating ABAP programs by using standard SAP components instead.

> **Note**
>
> Most people know that ABAP is the SAP programming language and that it can be used to create applications to perform a variety of functions. However, alternative intermediate ways to perform the same functions without requiring ABAP coding are often available. For this reason, ABAP by itself is not an SAP Best Practice, and it is not recommended unless your system requires so many fixes that it is justified. This, however, increases the risk that all of your work might be lost in future upgrades.

You don't necessarily have to apply everything written in this section, but you should keep these Best Practices in mind and see if they are useful in your implementation.

Let us now start our review of the suggested Best Practices of CO-PA:

- Do not include too many characteristics in your reports because this practice reduces system performance and increases extraction time. A good rule of thumb is to limit your characteristics to six or less per report.
- Use Report-Report Interface (RRI) and Report Splitting (RS), to be discussed in detail in Chapter 12, to link and have access to several reports, use line items for reconciliation, to improve performance, to remove unnecessary characteristics, and to simplify reporting.
- Use frozen data for reports that take a long time to execute.
- Use mass print settings when you need hard copies.
- Study value fields and determine any dependencies required to be added to your report. For example, if you set up a single field called "Net Revenue" without including the components that generate this value field and the information is posted, the SAP system would not allow breaking down the data later on to identify how the number was calculated. In other words, once data has been posted to a particular value field, there is no way to identify the components that generated the value in the first place.
- Use key figures schemes to manage groupings of value fields across reports and ensure consistency.
- Improve system performance with summarization levels.

Some of these procedures are reviewed further in Chapter 12 because they are more suited for advanced users. For this chapter, we will focus our attention on extensively explaining the concepts of frozen reports, key figures schemes, and summarization levels. Frozen reports were briefly reviewed in Chapter 9, but here we will expand the discussion to generate pre-calculated reports running in the background with an ABAP program without any type of coding!

10.3.1 Creating Frozen Reports

We already worked with frozen reports in Chapter 9, however, in this section we will expand on their practical usage. First, let's take a quick refresher of the concepts and procedures. Remember that extracting data directly from an OLTP SAP database might be time consuming and require a lot of memory, slowing down the generation of a report or form, especially when thousands of lines of data need to be extracted. For this reason, it is practical to have selection parameters stored and associated with previously generated data that does not require generation of data from scratch, but rather exists "hidden" in the memory for a particular report, with predefined selection parameters, and for a particular time and date.

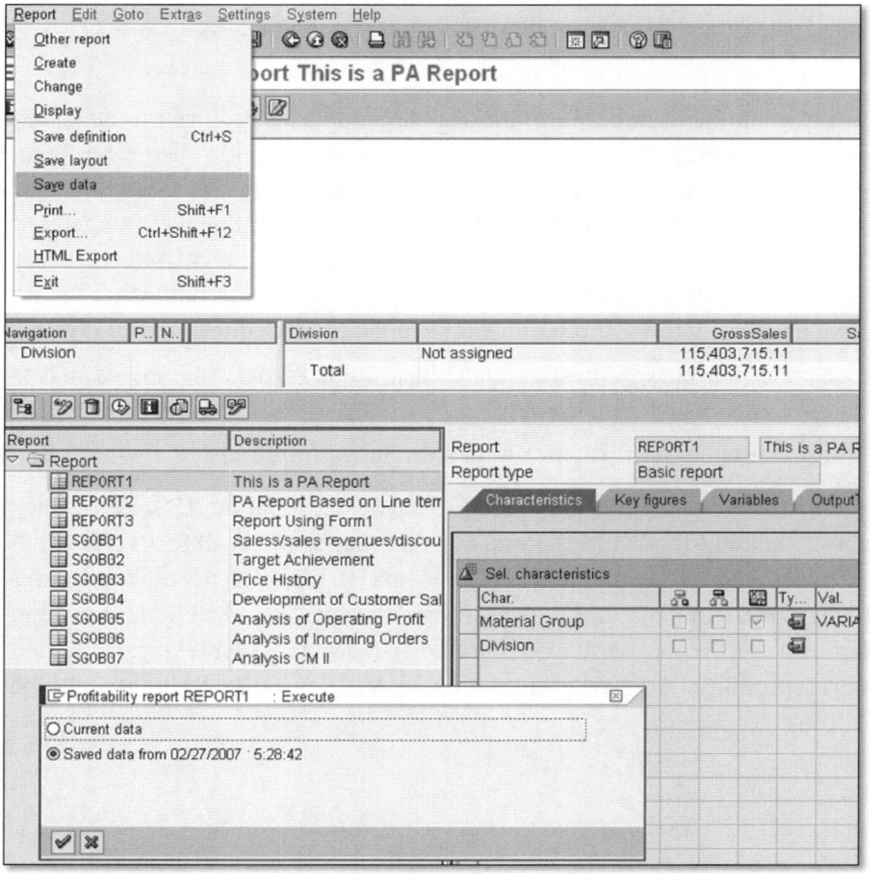

Figure 10.23 Creating and Accessing Frozen Data

This process is what is called *freezing data* in CO-PA and this data can be reused at any time. Users have the choice to access this frozen data or perform a new extraction to obtain the latest data with the desired selection criteria. In addition, remember that after generating a report, you can select the path **Report • Save data**, as shown in Figure 10.23, to freeze the current settings for the generation of your report without spending time and resources to run it again, especially if you have a large volume of data to extract.

Using this function, your data is saved in memory and you can retrieve it the next time your selection parameters exactly match those of the data stored and associated to your report.

To expand your understanding of this process, we will this time update the data in the background running a variable.

To create a variable that controls the frozen data associated with a report, follow these steps:

1. Follow the path **Profitability Analysis • Information System • Maintain Variants**, as shown in Figure 10.24, and click on the execute icon next to **Maintain Variants**.

2. The screen **Background Processing for Drilldown Reports** appears, as shown in Figure 10.25. Notice that there are two field elements required, a report and a variant.

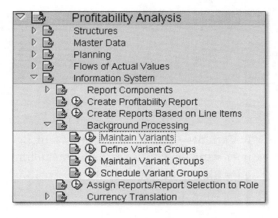

Figure 10.24 Accessing the Maintain Variants Option

3. In the **Report** field, type the technical name of the report that has frozen data. Based on what we did in Chapter 9, and as shown in Figure 10.25, "REPORT1" is the object we are looking for.

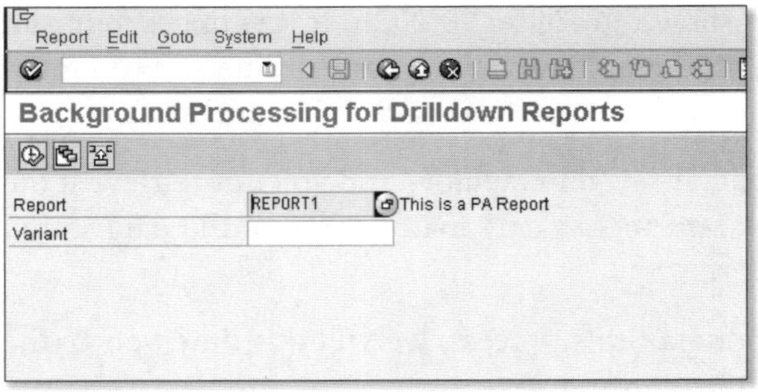

Figure 10.25 Accessing the Maintain Variants Screen

4. In the **Variant** field, shown in Figure 10.25, you need to enter the name of the variable (**Variant**) that you are associating with the frozen data stored in the **REPORT1** report and that controls its execution in the background. We still need to create this variable, so follow the path **Edit • Variant**, shown in Figure 10.26.

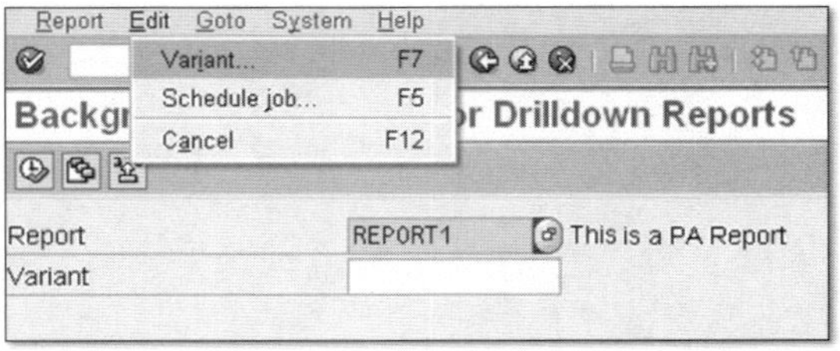

Figure 10.26 Creating a Variant Variable

5. As you can see in the screen **ABAP: Variants – Initial Screen**, shown in Figure 10.27, you are not only creating a variable, you are actually interacting with an ABAP program associated with the variant that we are creating (**Variant1**).

6. Type "Variant1" in the **Variant** field.

7. In the **Subobjects** area, select **Values**.

8. Click on the **Create** button.

9. The screen **Maintain Variant: Report** displays to initiate the configuration of the **VARIANT1** variant, as shown in Figure 10.28.

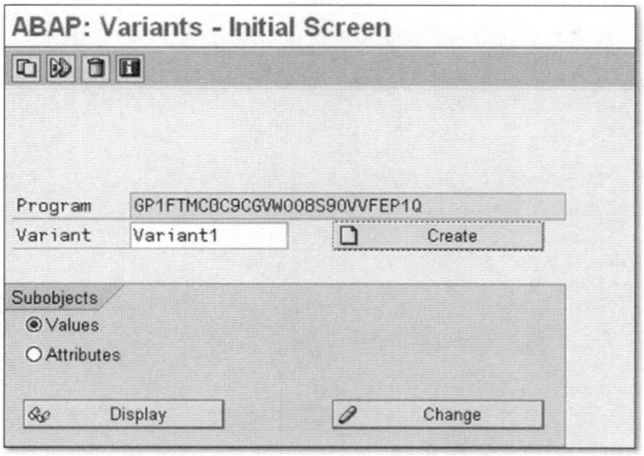

ABAP: Variants - Initial Screen

| Program | GP1FTMC0C9CGVW008S90VVFEP1Q |
| Variant | Variant1 | ☐ Create |

Subobjects
- ⦿ Values
- ○ Attributes

| ⚙ Display | ✎ Change |

Figure 10.27 Creating a Variant

10. Notice that we have the **Report selections** coming from our REPORT1, and we can even modify these selections! Remember, we have configured information for **001/2009** until **012/2009** for **Planning data 1.**

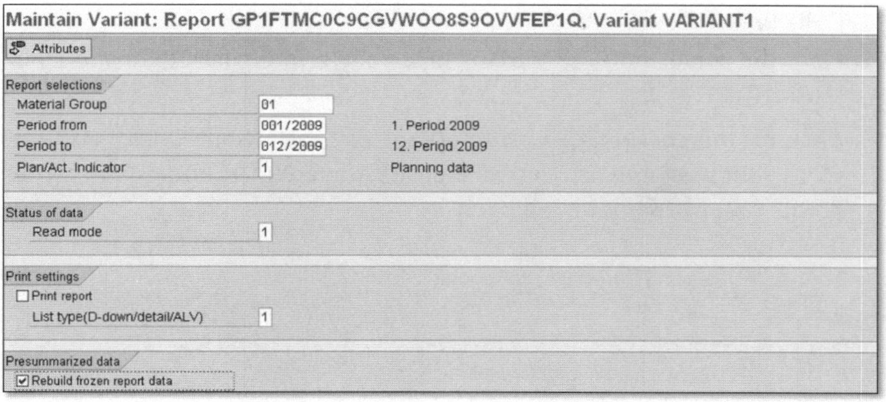

Maintain Variant: Report GP1FTMC0C9CGVWOO8S9OVVFEP1Q, Variant VARIANT1

⚙ Attributes

Report selections
Material Group	01
Period from	001 / 2009	1. Period 2009
Period to	012 / 2009	12. Period 2009
Plan/Act. Indicator	1	Planning data

Status of data
| Read mode | 1 |

Print settings
☐ Print report
| List type(D-down/detail/ALV) | 1 |

Presummarized data
☑ Rebuild frozen report data

Figure 10.28 Configuring Variant1 to Use Predefined Selection Criteria and to Access Frozen Data

11. Select the checkbox **Rebuild frozen report data** to allow the variant to access any frozen data stored in your REPORT1, and click on the **Attributes** button.

12. The screen **Variant Attributes** appears, as shown in Figure 10.29. Notice the **Variant Name** field is grayed out, meaning that the technical name has been already created and cannot be changed. Complete your definition by typing the description "This is a Variant" into the **Meaning** field, as shown in Figure 10.29.

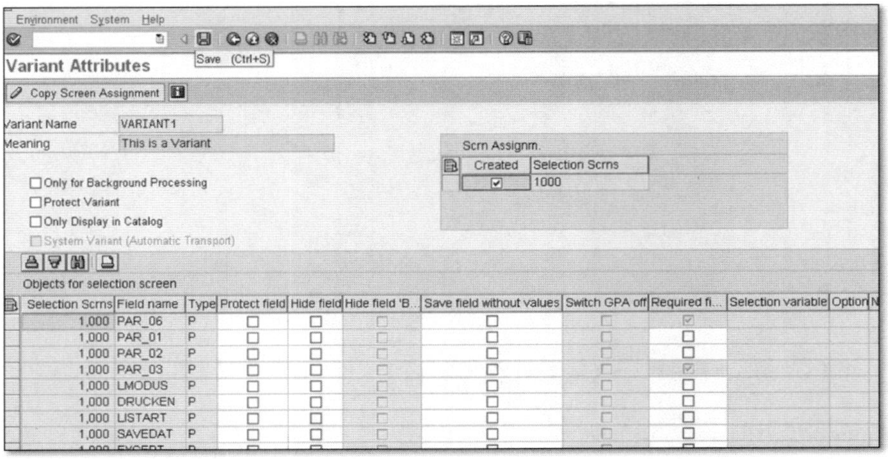

Figure 10.29 Configuring the Variant Attributes

13. Click on the save icon to save the values of VARIANT1.

14. Go back to the screen shown in Figure 10.30 by clicking on the back icon or using Transaction KE3Q.

15. Place the cursor into the **Variant** field shown in Figure 10.30 and enter "VARIANT1."

16. Click on the checkmark icon to accept your selection. Once you complete your assignment, you have an ABAP variant running with a predefined report without coding!

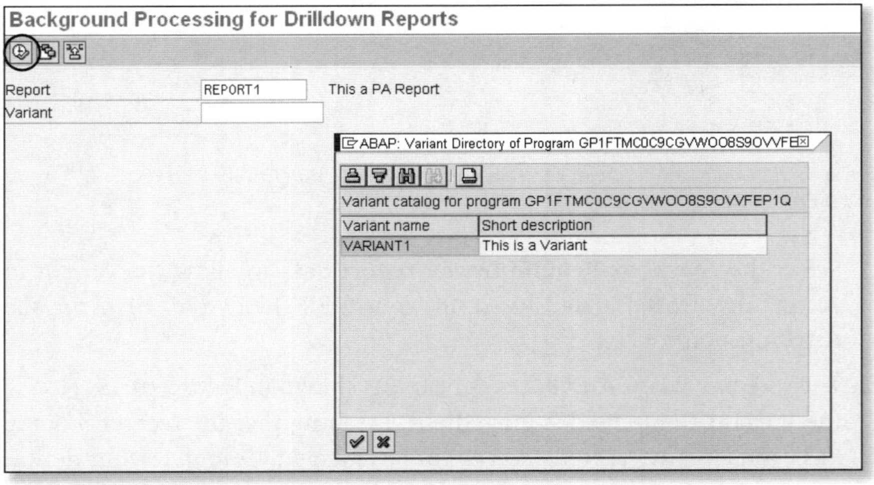

Figure 10.30 Assigning VARIANT1 to REPORT1

17. Click on the execute icon, and the following message appears at the bottom of your screen, **Report data for REPORT1 saved**. This means that the variable **VARIANT1** is now carrying frozen data that belongs to REPORT1 running with an ABAP Program!

Now we need to perform some additional steps to allow the variable to execute in the background:

1. Return to the IMG Activity and follow the path **Profitability Analysis • Information System • Background Processing • Define Variant Groups**.

2. Click on the **New Entries** button, and the screen shown in Figure 10.31 appears. Notice that the **Application Class** again is **KE**, for Profitability Analysis, and that we are working with **Table Name CE1S_GO**, associated with the operating concern where the data exists.

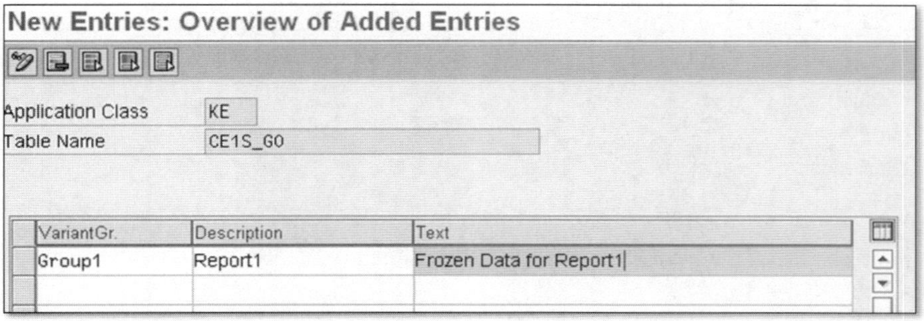

	VariantGr.	Description	Text	
	Group1	Report1	Frozen Data for Report1	

New Entries: Overview of Added Entries

Application Class   KE
Table Name   CE1S_GO

Figure 10.31 Creating a Variant Group

3. Create the Variant Group (**VariantGr.**) "Group1," with **Description** "Report1," and **Text** "Frozen Data for Report1," as shown in Figure 10.31.

However, we still need to maintain the variant groups, so perform these steps:

1. Go back to the IMG Activity and follow the path **Information System • Maintain Variant Groups** to access the screen shown in Figure 10.32.

2. Select the **Operating concern** associated with your report information, in this case **S_GO**.

3. Select the **Type of Profitability Analysis** to be performed inside your operating concern (in this case **1**, for costing-based; otherwise you would select 2 for account-based).

4. Select the **Variant group GROUP1**.

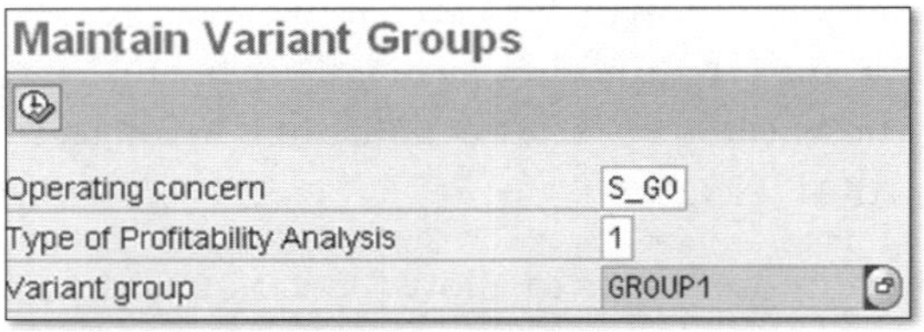

Figure 10.32 Maintaining Variant Groups

5. Click on the execute icon.

6. Click on the **New Entries** button. Notice that the information you just defined is displayed and grayed out, and that you are directly interacting with **Table Name CE1S_GO**, as shown in Figure 10.33.

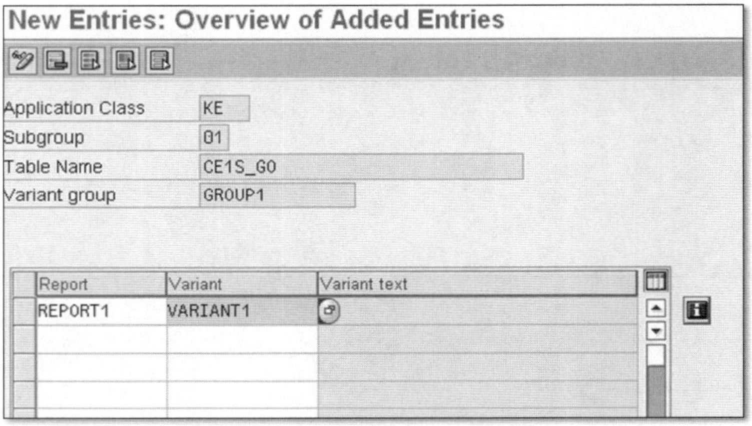

Figure 10.33 Linking REPORT1 to VARIANT1 with Variant Group GROUP1

7. With this configuration, you are saying that **VARIANT1** controls the info in **REPORT1**, so click on the save icon to complete the link.

Now you need to schedule these variants to interact with each other, executing the report extraction in the background:

1. Follow the path **Profitability Analysis • Information System • Background Processing • Schedule Variant Groups**.

2. At this point, as shown in Figure 10.34, you are ready to execute a job by typing the following parameters:

   ▶ **Operating concern**: "S_GO"

   ▶ **Type of Profitabiliy Analysis**: "1" (costing-based)

▶ **Variant group:** "GROUP1"

▶ **Report name(s):** not needed because we have it associated with the variant and a variant group.

▶ **Job name:** the description used as an identification for your frozen data execution program. In this case, "We are freezing data!!!" sounds good.

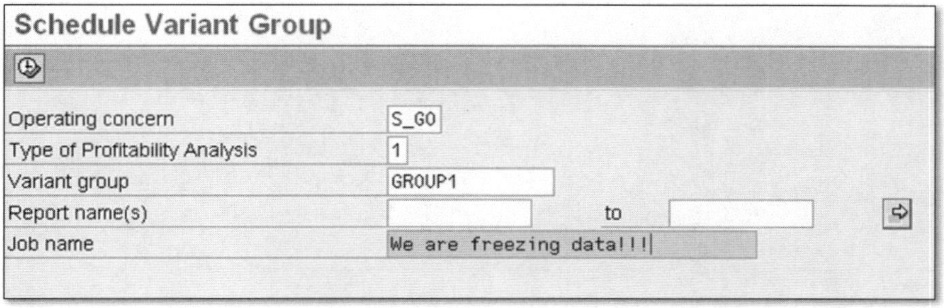

Schedule Variant Group		
⊕		
Operating concern	S_GO	
Type of Profitability Analysis	1	
Variant group	GROUP1	
Report name(s)		to
Job name	We are freezing data!!!	

Figure 10.34 Scheduling Variant Groups

3. You are now ready to extract your data in the background without users knowing that you are updating the frozen data. To start, click on the execute icon shown in Figure 10.34.

4. The screen shown in Figure 10.35 appears and you are ready to schedule VARIANT1 for execution, using the job called **WE ARE FREEZING DATA!!!**. The only thing missing is configuring the frequency of the data collection, and we want to perform this in a controlled way.

5. Click on the **Start condition** button, and the **Start Time** window appears, shown in Figure 10.36.

6. Either click on the **Immediate** button, also shown in Figure 10.36, to initiate the execution right away, or select how you want to schedule the variant to collect the data periodically, using the **Date/Time**, **After job**, **After event**, **At operation mode**, or any other button available to control the frequency of the execution.

7. For our purposes, click on the **Immediate** button and then click on the save icon.

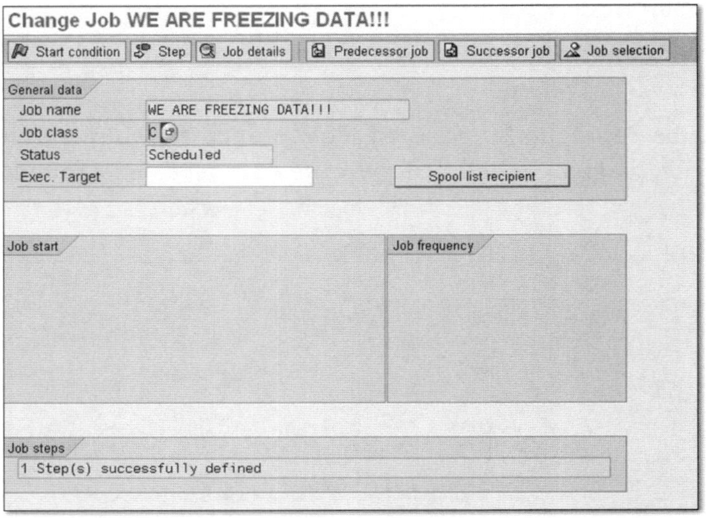

Figure 10.35 Preparing to Schedule the Frozen Data Collection in the Background

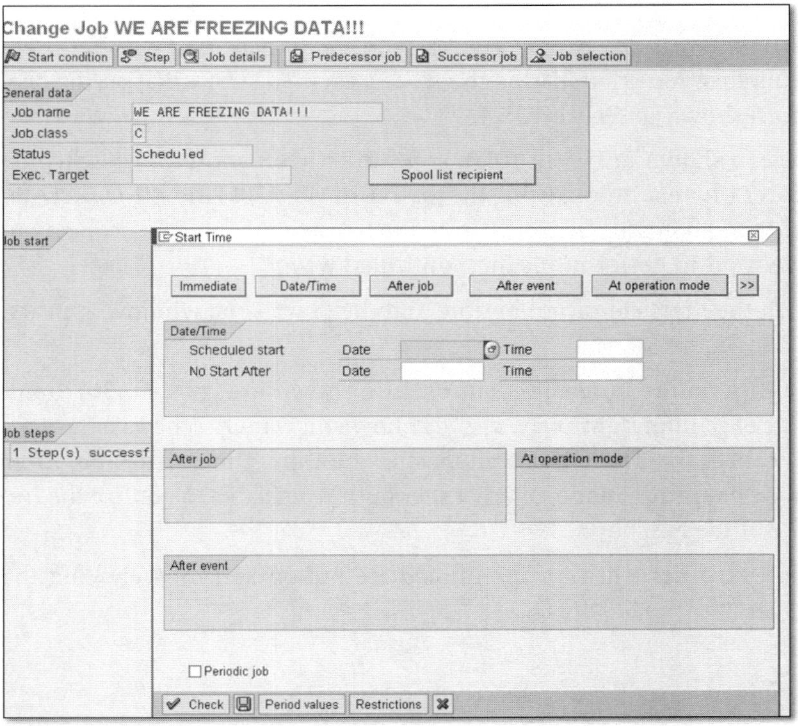

Figure 10.36 Configuring the Frequency of Execution of Frozen Data Collection with VARIANT1

8. Completely exit all screens and return to the **Profitability Analysis •
   Information System • Create Profitability Report** to access the **Change
   Profitability Report** screen, shown in Figure 10.37.

Change Profitability Report : Specify Profit.	
Report	Description
▽ ☐ Report	
▽ ☐ REPORT1	This is a PA Report
☼ VARIANT1	This is a Variant
☐ REPORT2	PA Report Based on Line Items
☐ REPORT3	Report Using Form1
☐ SG0B01	Saless/sales revenues/discount
☐ SG0B02	Target Achievement
☐ SG0B03	Price History
☐ SG0B04	Development of Customer Sales
☐ SG0B05	Analysis of Operating Profit
☐ SG0B06	Analysis of Incoming Orders
☐ SG0B07	Analysis CM II

Figure 10.37 Accessing the Change/Report Environment

9. Identify **REPORT1** and notice that **VARIANT1** is linked to this report as a
   hierarchy, as shown in Figure 10.37. This means there is a scheduled process running behind the scenes associated with this particular report.

10. Execute the report and you will see the same message on the screen the
    last time VARIANT1 was executed to collect frozen data.

Overall, this process allows users to access information fast, does not require
them to know how the data was generated, and, most important, it improves
system performance using a predefined ABAP program, without any coding
required. This is a good way to control and share information between different users in the system without overloading the system at the same time. Some
of these variants can be scheduled to run late in the evening so users have new
information early the next day, for example, or the data can be updated every
day, depending on your scheduling configuration using the scheduler.

In summary, in this section we reviewed and explored the concept of collecting and generating frozen data with a variable. This variable can be controlled and associated with a report to collect frozen data in the background,
and make it available to users of a particular report. Performing a new freeze
of data overwrites the previously saved copy, thereby updating stored frozen
data. Unfortunately, each report can only have one version of frozen data
stored in the background unless you want to generate real-time data each
time you refresh your report. Next let's look at the concept of key figure
schemes in more detail.

10.3.2 Key Figure Schemes

As explained at the beginning of this section, *key figure schemes* are groupings of value fields that are set up once and can be used several times across reports. There are two ways to access key figure schemes, either using the path **Profitability Analysis • Report Components • Define Key Figure Schemes** or using the Transaction KER1.

In a key figure scheme you can define any number of interrelated key figures, referred to as *elements* of the key figure scheme, that establish the relationship. Key figure schemes work as formulas that carry out automatic operations and the results are stored in a variable that can be used as part of a report or form, and behave similarly to regular value fields. Now let us create a key figure scheme using the following example:

1. Follow the path **Profitability Analysis • Report Components • Define Key Figure Schemes**, as shown in Figure 10.38, to start creating a new key figure scheme.

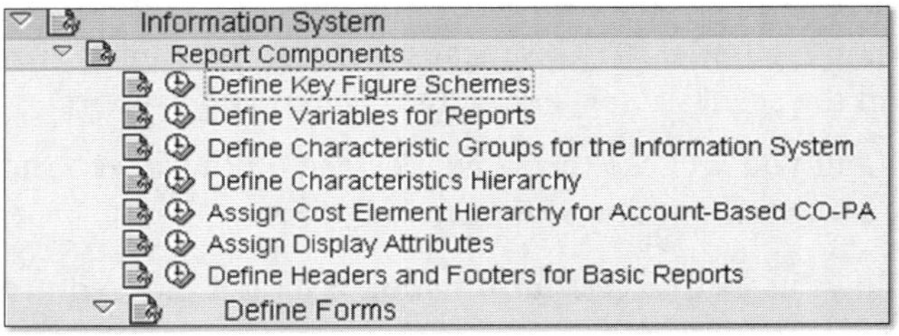

Figure 10.38 Creating a Key Figure Scheme

2. Click on **New entries**.

3. Verify that the **Key figure scheme** level is selected in the **Dialog Structure** on the left of the screen, as shown in Figure 10.39.

4. Enter a number between 01 and 8999 in the **KF** column (we entered **01**), and a suitable text, as also shown in Figure 10.39, in the **Medium-length text** column (we entered **Detailed**).

5. When you're done working with the key figure scheme, in this case **01 Detailed**, you need to configure key figure scheme elements. In the **Dialog Structure** on the left side of the screen, select **Elements of the key figure scheme**.

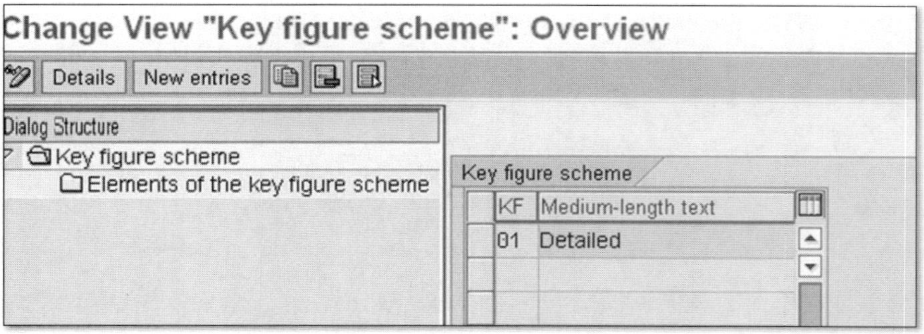

Change View "Key figure scheme": Overview

Details | New entries | 📋 🖺 🖺

Dialog Structure
▽ 🗀 Key figure scheme
　　🗀 Elements of the key figure scheme

Key figure scheme

KF	Medium-length text	⊞
01	Detailed	▲
		▼

Figure 10.39　Creating a Key Figure Scheme

6. In the screen that displays, shown in Figure 10.40, there are two functions you can use to define the content of a key figure as part of a key figure scheme:

▷ To define an element that simply represents the addition and subtraction of different values, click on **Basic formula**. The system then displays a list of all of the elements available to create your formulas and select all of the value fields that you want to use in the element. This formula will then become available when you define the next element of the scheme, and will therefore appear in the list of elements under Choose entries.

▷ If you want to define a more complex formula, click on **Formula editor**. Here you can link constants and any elements of the scheme using standard mathematical operators (+, −, *, /) as well as your own ABAP functions. For a detailed description of the functions available in the formula editor, see the section "Information System" in the online documentation for Profitability Analysis at *http://help.sap.com*. Using the function "check key figure scheme" (accessible by clicking on the icon represented with two squares joined with a line), you can check all of the elements of the scheme for syntactical errors.

In addition, clicking on the "overview list" icon (the mountains with the sun icon), you can obtain an overview of all of the formulas in a key figure scheme and also print the key figure scheme.

7. In the column **Elmnt**, add the element number and in the column **Medium-length text**, add descriptions, as shown in Figure 10.40.

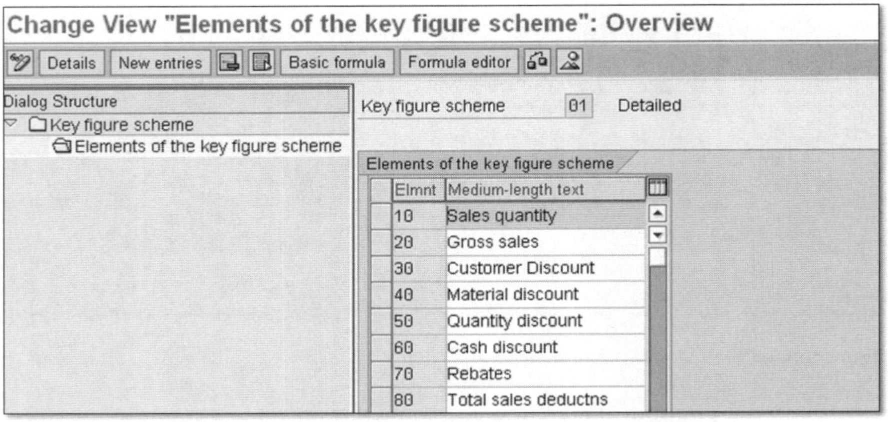

Figure 10.40 Adding Elements of the Key Figure Scheme to Your Key Figure Scheme

8. Double-click on the element **165 Contrib. margin I**, shown in Figure 10.41, to review it as one of the components of the **Key figure scheme Detailed (01)**.

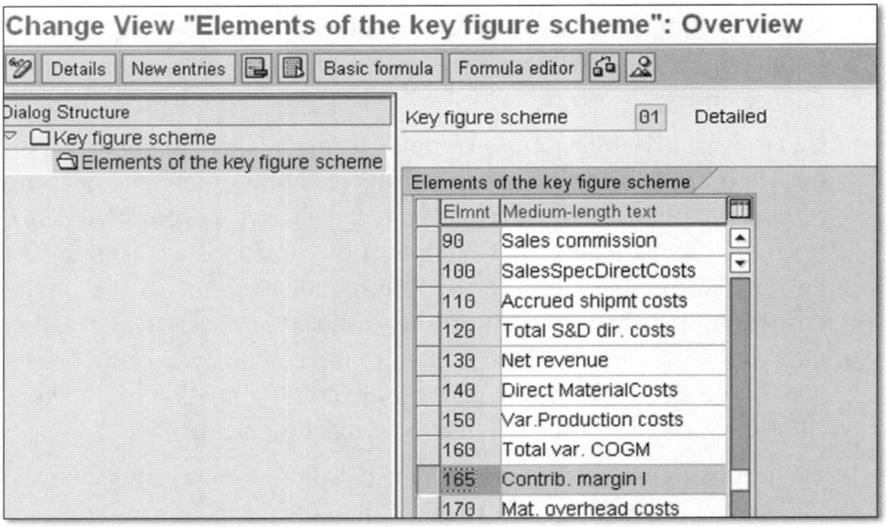

Figure 10.41 Working with Contrib. margin I

9. The screen shown in Figure 10.42 appears. Note that the element is now in design mode.

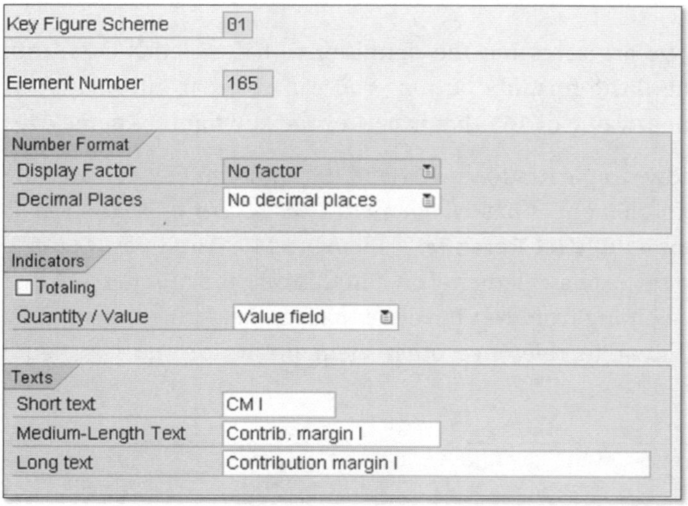

Figure 10.42 Reviewing the Configuration Settings of an Element of a Key Figure Scheme

10. Notice that the different components that form an element as part of a key figure scheme, as shown in Figure 10.42, are as follows:

▸ **Key Figure Scheme**: has a number, in this case **01**.

▸ **Element Number**: also has a number, in this case, **165** (the identifier for Contrib. Margin I).

▸ **Number Format**: includes the **Display Factor** and the number of **Decimal Places**.

▸ **Indicators**: the **Totaling** indicator is a special function that is only used with formulas containing user-defined calculations. The **Quantity/Value** indicator identifies whether the format is for a **Quantity field** or a **Value field**, that is, whether the result of the calculation is a quantity or a value. The system will normally determine this automatically. You should set the indicator manually if you want to divide a value using a formula and then interpret it as a quantity.

▸ **Texts**: as with most SAP applications, there is a short, medium, and long text to describe the element.

To clarify the concept: an element can be a stand-alone value that carries a negative or positive value extracted from a value field, and later used by another element as part of a formula. For this, CO-PA provides two environments for formula editing, which you can access using the **Basic formula** and **Formula editor** buttons.

Basic Formula

In Figure 10.43, we are accessing the definitions of the element Contrib. Margin I using the **Basic formula** button. You can see that information is based on the element value of **165** that is part of the key figure scheme **01**.

You can also see how simple it is to understand the equation that controls the key figure scheme element. That is, **Element 165** (Contrib. Margin I) is defined as **Element +130 (Net Revenue) – Element 160 (Total var. COGM)**. Now you see why we need an element code, in this case the number **130** that identifies the data coming from **Net Revenue** that can be defined as an independent value field or to reference other elements inside the key figure scheme.

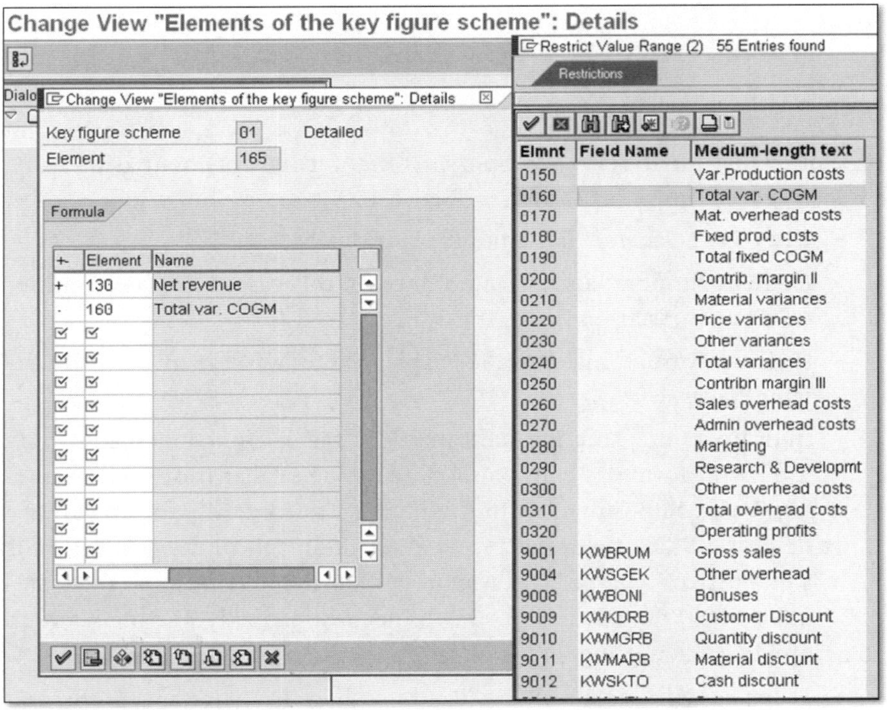

Figure 10.43 Working with the Basic Formula environment

When working with **Report Painter,** we are creating formulas without overloading the system because here values are calculated internally as if they were actual value fields with data stored.

Now, let us review in more detail the functionality accessed using the **Basic formula** button to better understand how the elements inside the key figure scheme work. Notice the positive (**+**) or negative (**–**) sign in the first column in Figure 10.43, then you see the **Element** number as part of the equation, and of course the **Name**.

If you click on a field in the **Element** column, you can either directly enter the element number, or, using the dropdown list that appears, access the **Restrict Value Range** window that is displayed on the right side of the screen shown in Figure 10.43. There you will see three columns: **Elmnt** (for the element code, using the coding system you already know), the **Field Name** (it's technical name), and **Medium-length text** (the name of the element). In this portion of the screen, you identify the element for each line to be added individually, and whether the element is part of a key figure scheme following the previously displayed code numbers. To make a selection, double-click an element or select an element and click on the checkmark icon.

Notice the other element codes further down in this area of the screen, for example **9001** with a **Field Name** of **KWBRUM**, and **Medium-length text** of **Gross Sales**. These are the value fields from the regular SAP tables that are part of our operating concern!

Formula Editor

In addition, for more sophisticated users and complex formulas you can use the Formula Editor, which works similar to the formula creation environments of SAP NetWeaver Business Intelligence (BI), SAP Business Warehouse (BW), and BEx. In this environment, you first get the original value fields that you require, then create a formula assigned to an element, and then you can use this information to generate different new values and access them as regular value fields. As you can see, this lets you use value fields and create system-friendly formulas easily, without any coding in ABAP!

To access the Formula Editor:

1. Select the **Formula editor** button shown earlier in Figure 10.42. As shown in Figure 10.44, the Formula Editor environment is a sophisticated environment more suited for developers and not for users new to the SAP system, or advanced computer systems in general.

2. Notice that the formula and other information of element **165** (**Contrib. margin I**) now appears in a different format that is more appealing to developers.

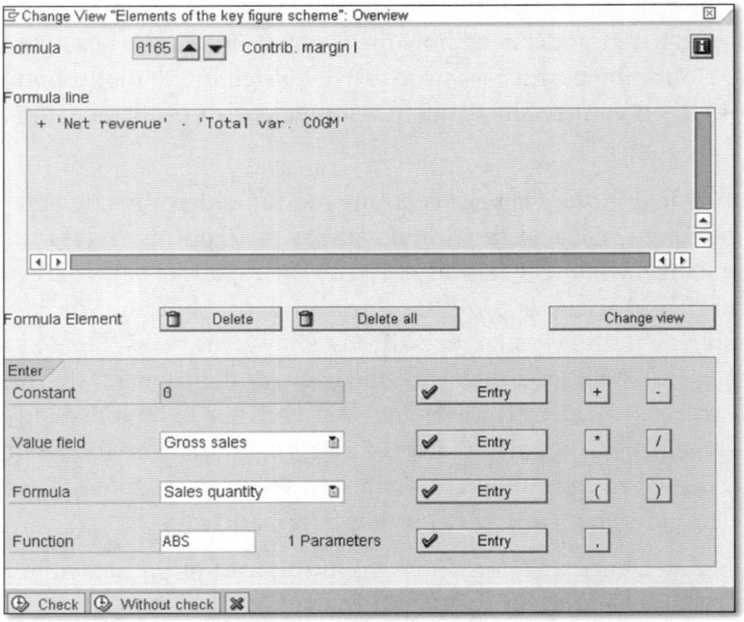

Figure 10.44 Reviewing the Formula Editor Environment

3. Also notice that there are different functionalities, as shown in full detail in Figure 10.44: the **Formula** element identifier (**0165**), the **Formula line** where the formula appears slightly differently from how it looked in the basic formula environment, the **Delete**, **Delete all,** and **Change view** buttons, as well as a variety of different operator buttons and icons.

To create a formula using the Formula Editor, follow these steps, referring to the information displayed in Figure 10.44 and 10.45:

1. First think about your formula and write it down on a piece of paper.

2. To add an operator to the formula (they are elements of the key figure scheme), in the **Formula line** area, type "+" (sum), "-" (subtraction), "*" (multiplication), "/" (division) , "(" and ")" (left and right parentheses), and "," (comma).

3. To add a constant, type the value (for example, "100") in the **Constant** field and click on the **Entry** button for **Constant**. This will add the constant to the formula, as long as an operator has already been added (an operator is required before a constant).

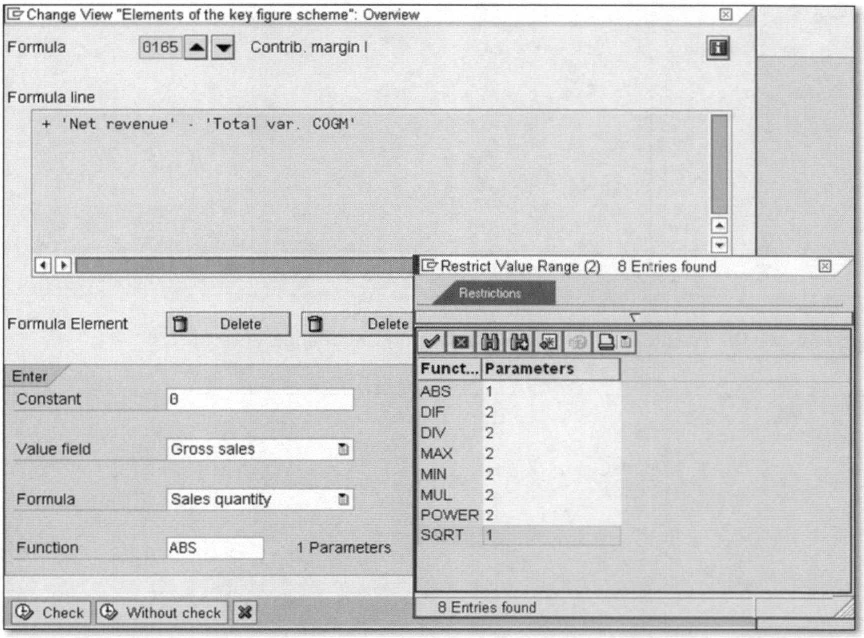

Figure 10.45 Analyzing a Formula in the Formula Editor Environment

4. To add a new value field, select a field from the **Value Field** dropdown list and click on the **Entry** button for **Value Field**.

5. To add a preconfigured formula, select a formula from the **Formula** dropdown list and click the **Entry** button for **Formula**.

6. As shown in Figure 10.45, there are also eight functions available that you can add, depending on the output for the calculated element and the number of parameters required in an equation. Examples include **ABS** for absolute value, **DIF** for difference, **SQRT** for square root, **MAX** for the maximum value, and so on. Explore these features on your own. They are simple mathematical terms that can be useful in more complex calculations.

   To add one of these functions to the formula, enter its name in the **Function** field, or select the function from the list in the **Restrict Value Range** window shown in Figure 10.45, and click on the **Entry** button for **Function**.

7. Finally, the **Change View** button, shown earlier in Figure 10.44, is useful if you would like to change the display of the formula from being based on its technical definitions, as shown in Figure 10.46, to showing a technical name description as illustrated in Figure 10.47.

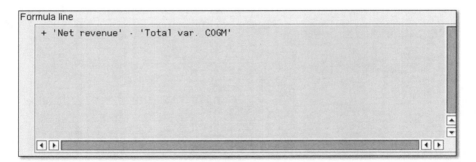

Figure 10.46 The Formula Editor Before Clicking on the Change View Button

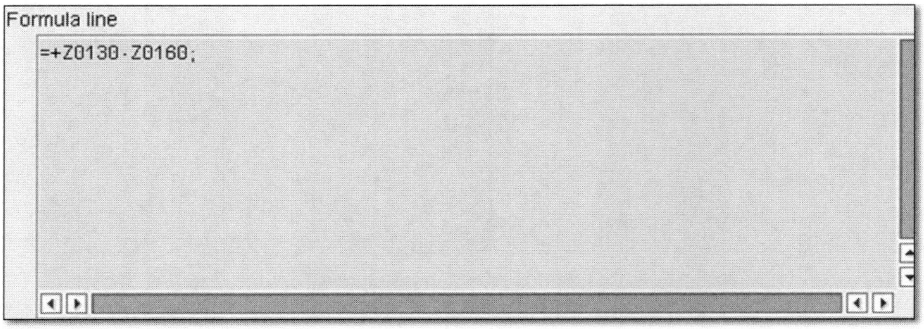

Figure 10.47 The Formula Editor After Clicking on the Change View Button

8. When you're finished, click on the **Check** button.

Using Key Figure Schemes and Elements

Now the question is, how do we use this? And where? The answer is simple: use key figure schemes and elements as if they were value fields (key figures) in reports and forms. You will be able to access this information along with your regular value field information:

1. Place the cursor into the **Key figure scheme** box and select **Detailed**, as shown in step 1 in the Figure 10.48.

2. Select the desired characteristics in the list of **Available Key figures**, in this case **Contrib. Margin I**, as shown in step 2 in Figure 10.48.

3. Move the characteristic to the left to make it a selected key figures (use the left arrow button), as shown in step 3 in Figure 10.48.

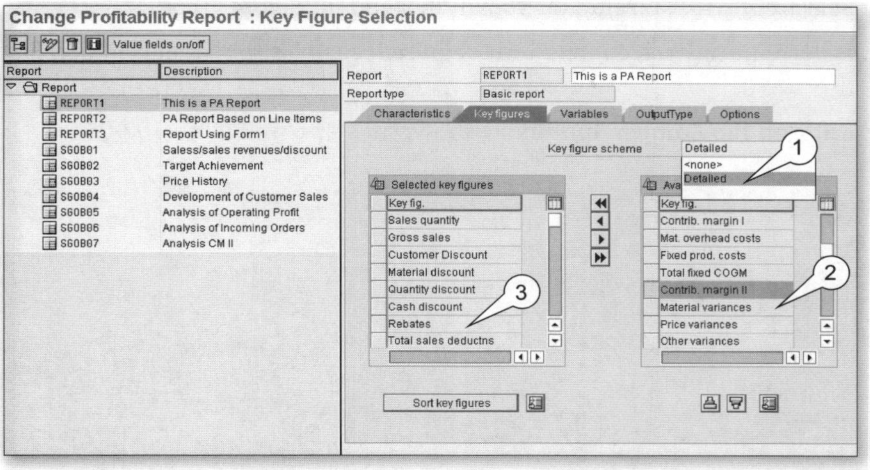

Figure 10.48 Accessing the Key Figure Scheme and Elements in the Report

Now, access the change report environment, and review **Form1** shown in Figure 10.49 and Figure 10.50:

1. Click to the right of the **Gross sales** column, as shown in step 1 in Figure 10.49.

2. When the window **Select element type** appears, select the second option: **Key Figure scheme element**, as shown in step 2 in the Figure 10.49.

3. Click on the checkmark icon, as shown in step 3 in the Figure 10.49.

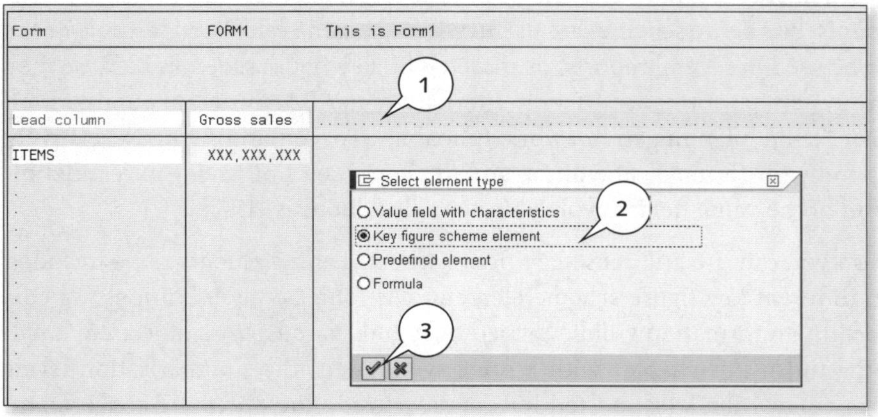

Figure 10.49 Adding a Key Figure Scheme Element to a Form Part I

4. Select **Sales quantity**, as shown in step 4 in Figure 10.50.

5. Select **Contrib. Margin I**, as shown in step 5 in Figure 10.50.

6. Determine any selection criteria required, again as shown in step 6 in Figure 10.50.

7. Click on the **Confirm** button, as shown in step 7 in Figure 10.50.

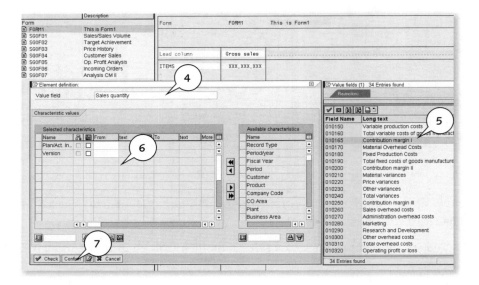

Figure 10.50 Adding a Key Figure Scheme Element to a Form

You have now seen how a key figure scheme can be used to optimize the calculation of complex values using the basic formula or formula editor environments. key figure schemes are useful when the same calculated formula needs to be used in several reports, or shared with key figure schemes because they are system performance-friendly alternatives to ABAP programs, and to even the CO-PA planning framework functions. The environment is relatively friendly for formula generation, and the importance of having a clear definition of the value fields involved in the calculations is critical.

Also you can use and reuse key figure schemes and elements to be included in different key figure scheme elements. As long as the definitions are correct, the information will be carried over and shared across objects. We will now finish this chapter with a brief overview of the summarization levels that control the latest posted information inside the operating concern and positively affect system performance.

10.3.3 Improving Performance in Reports and Forms Using Summarization Levels

This topic depends greatly on the concept of summarization levels discussed in detail in Chapter 12, but here's a quick definition. Summarization of data is a presummarized set of report data stored in the database. In CO-PA reporting, it can be used to display parts of information that reside in a particular segment level. This data can be read from the database and displayed immediately when you call up a report. Summarization is a technique for improving system performance when extraction is considerably slow. Normally, summarization data is created during background processing, as we previously discussed, to avoid overloading the system with multiple users running the same reports at the same time. The data controlled by summarization levels can also be updated with the created line items, and this data is valid for one combination of characteristic values (variables) for one report at a time.

At this point we will discuss how to work with the performance-related options available in CO-PA designed to improve report performance. You'll find these in the **Performance** area on the **Options** tab of a report, as shown in Figure 10.51:

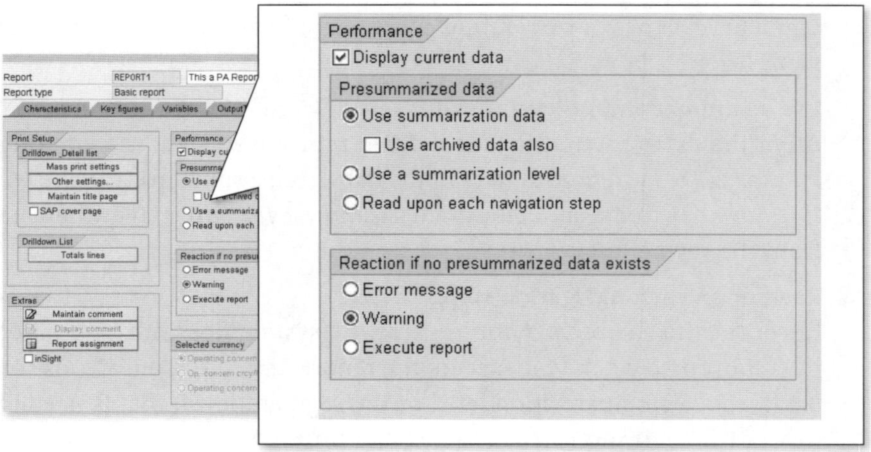

Figure 10.51 Reviewing the Options Tab in the Change/Report Environment

> **Note**
>
> **Performance** is a small area of the **Options** tab, feel free to explore the other items on this tab if desired.

► **Display current data**

Because presummarized data is updated on a periodic basis, it does not always contain the latest values of postings that have been made in Profitability Analysis since the information was last updated. Therefore, if you select this setting (it's the default setting), when you execute the report, the system will read the presummarized data plus the line items posted since that data was last updated. If you do not select this option, the system displays the data as it was when it was last updated.

► **Presummarized data**

There are a number of different methods for presummarizing data in CO-PA. Which method is better depends on which type of report you want to execute. The available options include:

  ► **Use summarization data**

  All of the data required for the defined report is loaded into working memory. First, the system tries to find summarization data for the report. If this does not exist, the system creates it by reading a summarization level or the segment level.

  ► **Use archived data also**

  The system reads the data that has been archived and deleted from the segment level of your operating concern as well as data from the segment level.

  ► **Use a summarization level** (default setting)

  All of the data required for the defined report is loaded into working memory. The system tries to read the data from a summarization level. If it does not find a suitable summarization level, it retrieves the data from the segment level.

  ► **Read upon each navigation step**

  In contrast to the other options, here the system does not load all of the report data when you execute the report. Instead, it only loads the data (from a summarization level or the segment level) that is needed upon each navigation step, and displays this on the screen. It does the same for each step you take when navigating through the report.

► **Reaction if no presummarized data exists**

Here you can tell the system how it should react if no presummarized data can be found for the report:

▶ **Error message**
The report cannot be executed. You first need to create the presummarized data in the background. You should select this option if executing the report without the presummarized data would lead to excessively long runtimes.

▶ **Warning** (default setting)
When you execute the report, you receive a warning message saying
that no suitable presummarized data could be found. You can then
decide whether you want to cancel or to execute the report anyway.

▶ **Execute report**
In this case, the system executes the report without displaying a message. The data is read from the segment level. You should select this
option only for reports that require a small amount of data.

10.4 Summary

In this chapter, we reviewed in more detail the different configuration elements related to CO-PA reporting to provide you with a view of its capabilities and functionalities from an advanced user or implementer point of view.
The information presented in this chapter, along with that presented previously in Chapter 9, should provide a project leader with enough background
information to consider if reporting outside R/3 or SAP ERP ECC 6.0 is
required, or if certain reports can be utilized within the CO-PA Report
Painter environment to make the required consolidation, and leave more
complex developments for the SAP BW/SAP NetWeaver BI platforms.
Remember, the SAP system is not about implementing the latest tools all of
the time, but about delivering requirements with tools that provide value to
your users, and improve the productivity of your implementation teams.

We have now covered the most important concepts and functionalities of
CO-PA with SAP. In Chapter 11, we briefly discuss how to perform the
switch from costing-based to account-based CO-PA. With account-based CO-
PA, it is possible to use cost elements to perform reconciliation with the FI-
GL module.

Working with costing-based CO-PA is not the only approach available. Account-based CO-PA allows reconciliation with Financials (FI) using cost elements by reusing the same previously configured components but changing specific elements within the operating concern to allow account-based transactions.

11 Working with Account-Based CO-PA

So far, we have dedicated our time and resources to reviewing applications using costing-based CO-PA, and studying other functionalities of the module, such as planning and reporting. Because the functionalities are relatively the same in comparison with account-based, we will only discuss the change in approach you'll need to take if you decide to be more specific and link your General Ledger (GL) information in FI and your cost elements in Controlling (CO) using account-based CO-PA. The switch to an account-based environment can be achieved with just some minor changes in your operating concern, but it affects how the information is displayed and reported. For example, value fields are exclusively applicable to costing-based CO-PA and do not exist in account-based environments.

11.1 Differences between Costing-based and Account-based CO-PA

Costing-based profitability is intended for short-term Profit and Loss (P&L) statements for sales management in evaluation of planned sales volumes or the sales volume transferred from billing or incoming sales orders using costing-based values, such as sales deductions and standard cost of goods manufactured, in real time. In comparison, account-based accounting using CO-PA allows users to access information reconciled with FI at the account level and post cost and revenue information in CO-PA and FI simultaneously.

It is important to remember that account-based and costing-based CO-PA can run parallel either using the same operating concern to extract the required information to switch back and forth between the two types of Profitability

Analysis, or with two operating concerns — one running account-based and another one running costing-based CO-PA. The latter is particular useful when working with SAP NetWeaver Business Intelligence (BI) extraction because the information for each type of accounting can be sent to different data targets, depending on the reporting needs. The account-based approach can be used as a "reconciliation bridge" between FI and costing-based CO-PA, and costing-based Profitability Analysis is mostly used for short-term data analysis.

In addition, in account-based CO-PA, the cost of goods sold (COGS) is updated at the time of delivery (goods issue); revenue, discounts, and freight are not updated in the system until the billing document is created. In comparison with costing-based CO-PA, the COGS is not updated at the time of delivery when the goods are issued, but at the same time when revenue, freight, discounts, and other related information is updated. This major difference when switching between costing-based and account-based CO-PA causes differences in the information report of time of delivery (goods issue) versus time of billing.

Because of these timing differences, a change of model from costing-based CO-PA to account-based CO-PA causes these two to be out of balance. This does not mean, however, that the information is incorrect, it is simply interpreted differently.

Now, let us begin our discussion of the elements and changes required to work with account-based CO-PA.

> **Note**
>
> In the next section we discuss comments related to SAP Note 69384, and complement this with information we consider meaningful to the reader. We will not, however, provide a complete discussion of the implications behind account-based CO-PA because this requires knowledge of FI and other areas of CO. However, at a minimum, the reader should have a clear understanding of account-based CO-PA to decide which CO-PA to use and under which circumstances.

11.1.1 Defining Cost Elements for CO-PA

Account-based CO-PA uses cost elements, which are the CO equivalents of GLs in the FI system. Cost elements are not created in CO-PA, and their creation is specific to the cost element accounting component of CO, shown in Figure 11.1. Use the path **Controlling • Cost Element Accounting • Create Cost Elements**, also shown in Figure 11.1, to access cost element accounting. The idea behind cost elements is that each transaction in the system has an account number that transfers and monitors the flows of money, materials, resources, and other components inside the system within the CO module.

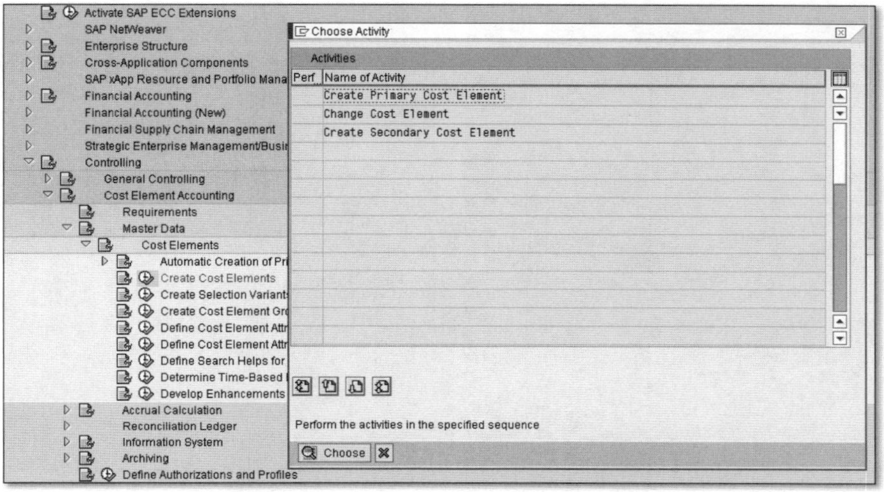

Figure 11.1 Accessing Cost Element Accounting

For example, you can monitor the materials consumed from a cost center by assigning cost element accounts that specifically control materials only inside the system, and that are defined as *secondary* cost elements (more on secondary cost elements in a moment). This lets you determine budget and actual costs based on the assignments and consumptions of this cost center. Further, you can generate reports based on these characteristics. Cost elements must previously exist inside your CO system to use account-based CO-PA, and its use is limited by the configuration options set up in the GL accounts and cost element accounting.

There are two types of cost elements: *primary* and *secondary*. Primary cost elements describe a one-to-one relationship between the GL transactions and cost elements inside the OLTP system associated with the FI module. Secondary cost elements are created inside the CO environment, and are related to internal transactions, such as cost center, profit center, and internal order postings that move and transfer costs or revenues among them.

As shown in Figure 11.2, cost elements such as **420000 Direct labor costs,** are part of a controlling area, **0001 SAP** in this case, and they have a validity period, **01/01/1995** to **12/31/2400,** in our example. In addition, a cost element has master data elements associated with it, as also shown in Figure 11.2 such as its **Name**, **Description**, **CElem category** (Cost Element Category, which describes its behavior within the system), **Indicators, Default Acct Assgnmt,** and others.

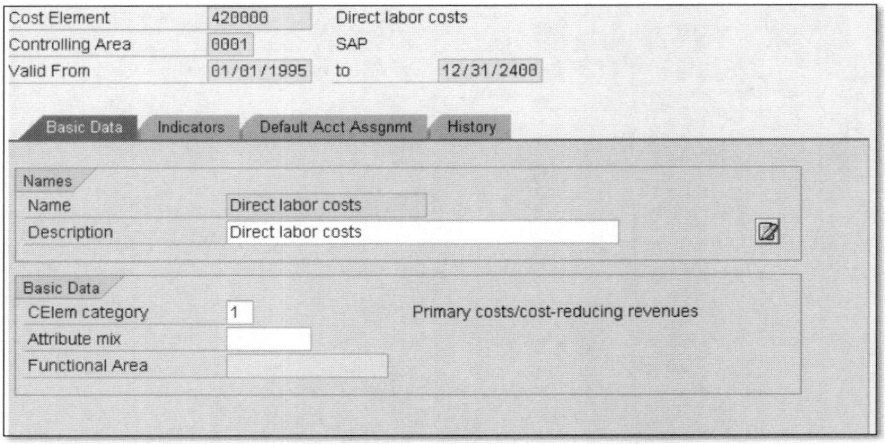

Figure 11.2 Reviewing the General Options of a Cost Element

As shown in Figure 11.2, in the cost element category (**CElem category**), we have defined the **420000** as a primary cost/cost-reducing revenue, by specifying a value of **1**. However, there are other classifications, such as the following:

▶ 3: Accrual/deferral per surcharge

▶ 4: Accrual/deferral per debit = actual

▶ 11: Revenues

▶ 12: External settlement

> **Note**
>
> Feel free to investigate the different types and classifications of cost elements, and how they impact your data display. As always, you can find help at *http://help.sap.com* or *http://sdn.sap.com*.

Next, let us review in more detail specific configuration settings required to switch to account-based CO-PA.

11.1.2 Changing the Operating Concern from Costing-Based to Account-Based CO-PA

As we previously reviewed in Chapters 3 and 4, several processes are required to configure an operating concern, the main component and object to perform profitability analysis. As shown in Figure 11.3, when setting up the operating concern **TEST,** the option you select in the area **Type of Profit. Analysis** changes the behavior of your operating concern object to either costing-based or account-based. Once you make a selection, your operating concern output will be immediately affected, so if you are using structures associated with a Data Source in R/3 or SAP ERP ECC 6.0 generated with Transaction KEB0, this change will directly impact the information coming out of your R/3 or SAP ERP ECC 6.0 system.

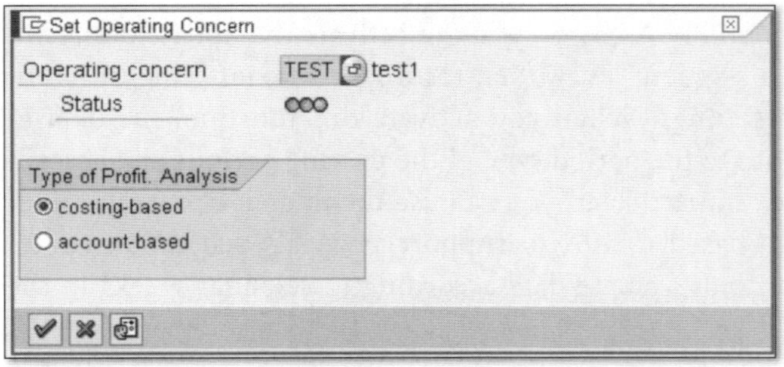

Figure 11.3 Switching From Costing-based to Account-based CO-PA

11.1.3 Controlling Areas and Account-Based CO-PA

As is the case in costing-based CO-PA, the controlling area is hierarchically subordinate to the operating concern in account-based CO-PA. Consequently, one or more controlling areas can be assigned to an operating concern. The operating concern determines the characteristics, and therefore the structuring, of the market segments for costing-based and account-based CO-PA. If you have configured both types of Profitability Analysis, you have the option to use one or the other, and with account-based CO-PA the data volume can be reduced considerably.

Further, controlling areas can have different currencies and different charts of accounts. However, as in costing-based CO-PA, the fiscal year variant of the operating concern and the fiscal year variants of all assigned controlling areas must correspond in account-based CO-PA as well. However, unlike costing-based CO-PA, in account-based CO-PA you cannot create cross-controlling area evaluations because the charts of accounts may differ. Cross-controlling area planning is not supported either.

11.1.4 Currencies and Account-Based CO-PA

With respect to currencies, costing-based Profitability Analysis requires an operating concern currency definition to maintain a common currency for all of the transactions. For account-based Profitability Analysis, the operating concern currency is irrelevant because the data is updated simultaneously using the information contained in the company code currency, transaction currency, and controlling area currency.

11.1.5 Data Structures and Data Retention

In costing-based Profitability Analysis, you can activate the update of data in calendar weeks at the segment level (total records) while entering different actual and plan data settings. When you activate this function, the data in CO-PA is managed both in the period type of the posting periods and according to calendar weeks. In particular, you can use the update of data in calendar weeks in account-based CO-PA to support a weekly schedule in sales planning and you can only valuate data according to calendar weeks in the line item reporting.

In terms of the data structures required to create an operating concern there are basically no differences in comparison for account-based CO-PA to what we discussed in Chapter 4 for costing-based CO-PA. However, value fields are only required in costing-based CO-PA. Therefore, if you configure your operating concern to use both types of CO-PA, value fields are only relevant when you are working with costing-based Profitability Analysis.

> **Tip**
>
> If you believe that both types of Profitability Analysis are required in your implementation, make a copy of your operating concern and have it switch independently of your options and required fields. This will help you avoid confusion during data reporting and provide more visibility.

11.1.6 Characteristic Derivation and Valuation

The same characteristic derivation-related functions and procedures shown previously in Chapter 5 using costing-based examples are applicable to account-based Profitability Analysis as well.

In account-based Profitability Analysis, posted values are always transferred from the primary document (goods issue posting, billing, direct postings from FI/MM, allocations within the CO system, settlements of orders). However, valuation does not take place in account-based CO-PA.

11.1.7 Actual Data Flow and Data Transfer

Costing-based and account-based Profitability Analysis is updated when actual postings relevant to profit are made. What is updated depends on which type of Profitability Analysis type is active.

The following is a general description of the main transfer components posted to CO-PA and their change when working in account-based CO-PA:

▶ **Sales order receipts**
The transfer of sales order receipts is not available when using account-based CO-PA.

▶ **Goods issued for the sales order**
When transfering billing data in account-based CO-PA when there is a stock change in FI, the goods are issued for the sales order simultaneously to CO-PA. Therefore, you must create a cost element in CO to monitor stock changes posted in FI.

▶ **Transfer of billing data**
When a billing document is released to FI, revenues, sales deductions, and imputed costs are transferred to CO-PA, whether they are FI-relevant or not. This way, the Cost of Goods Manufactured is transferred to account-based profitability when the goods are issued.

▶ **Cost center asssessments**
With account-based Profitability Analysis, the update is carried out using an assessment cost element under which the sending cost center is credited. When using both types of profitability analysis, you can specify if the distribution base is determined for costing- or account-based data.

▶ **Order and project settlement**
When you settle orders or projects in account-based CO-PA, you also must have settlement cost elements defined by the corresponding settlement structure.

▶ **Internal activity allocation**
If you allocate internal activities of cost centers to profitability segments you must also create allocation cost elements, which are assigned to a particular activity type.

11.1.8 Profitability Analysis Reports

When working with the CO-PA Information System menu, and the reporting components, there are a few considerations to keep in mind when working with the account-based profitability analysis:

▶ Forms, reports, and line item layouts apply to one type of Profitability Analysis only, and cannot be combined because they are directly dependent on the operating concern set current (active) and its type of Profitability Analysis to display information.

▶ You can use hierarchies for the cost element characteristic by entering a cost element group. There is no such structure in costing-based CO-PA because cost elements don't exist in that environment.

▶ Different currencies can be displayed in a report based on controlling area currency, company code currency, and transaction currency.

▶ For any form or basic report, a characteristic currency must be entered as a required entry for each currency needed in your report. If you want a report to be made in the company code currency, for example, the "company code" characteristic is compulsory; for a report in the transaction currency, the transaction currency (foreign currency) characteristic is required. However, in the form definition or report definition, you can use variables that are only supplied with a characteristic when they are executed. By the time you run the report at the latest, you must have specified a unique characteristic value for every cell of a report (intervals are not permitted).

▶ When working with line item reports both account-based and costing-based CO-PA can be used. You can define separate line item layouts for the account-based Profitability Analysis; if you do not specify a layout, the system uses the standard layout.

With account-based Profitability Analysis, you can only report on active characteristics, in comparison with the costing-based CO-PA that allows displaying non-active characteristics in a line-item report. In addition in the detail display of Account-based Profitability Analysis, the system goes to the general CO document display instead of the detail screens of the costing-based line item.

11.1.9 Assessment of Cost Center Costs

For costing-based Profitability Analysis, cost center costs are updated using a value field specified during the cycle maintenance. In account-based Profitability Analysis, the update is carried out by a cost element called assessment cost element. This special cost element credits the sending cost center and debits the receiving cost center. When using both types of profitability, the distribution base can be determined from the data of the costing-based Profitability Analysis or from the data of the account-based Profitability Analysis.

11.1.10 Order and Project Settlement

A *settlement* can be considered a process to assign costs from a sending object to one or more receiving objects, such as cost center, order, fixed asset, or account. When you settle orders or projects, the value fields for updating the costing-based Profitability Analysis are determined by the PA transfer structure that is assigned to the order. In account-based Profitability Analysis, the update of the settlement data is carried out under the settlement cost elements which are defined by the corresponding settlement structure. A PA transfer structure is not required for the settlement in Account-based Profitability Analysis.

11.1.11 Internal Activity Allocation

Allocations are useful when the breakdown of costs received to a cost object is not possible or not very clear. Some examples of allocations can be general and administrative costs. In the case of CO-PA, when you allocate internal activities of cost centers to profitability segments, the value field for updating costing-based Profitability Analysis is defined by the "CO" PA transfer structure. The update of the values from activity allocation in account-based Profitability Analysis is carried out under the allocation cost element which is assigned to the corresponding activity type. The "CO" PA transfer structure is not used for account-based Profitability Analysis.

11.2 Sales and Profit Planning

A main function of sales and profit planning for costing-based Profitability Analysis is the valuation of entered planning values, such as sales volume, with price lists of the Sales and Distribution (SD) system and imputed costs and sales deductions. In account-based Profitability Analysis, amounts and quantities can be entered by cost element for any market segments and user-selectable planning levels. However, no kind of valuation functions are available.

11.3   External Data Transfer

The only way you can transfer actual external or legacy data into account-based CO-PA is to post the corresponding data to FI. The long text of error message KE093 explains why this restriction applies. All FI document line items that have been assigned to a profitability segment automatically generate a line item in account-based Profitability Analysis as well.

11.4   Summary

In this chapter, we have briefly covered the general concepts and changes required to switch to the account-based model of CO-PA from the costing-based model. Costing-based CO-PA is derived from value fields. Account based CO-PA is often used for reconciliation of data between FI-GL accounting and CO cost element accounting. Costing-based CO-PA is more analytical but not as accurate as account-based CO-PA.

In addition, account-based CO-PA is updated during the delivery (goods issue) and the creation of billing documents. For this reason, the COGS is updated in CO-PA at the time of delivery (goods issue); revenue discounts and freight are not updated until the time billing documents are created. The update of COGS in account-based CO-PA might generate significant differences between revenue and billing. These differences make account-based CO-PA out of balance with costing-based CO-PA, and vice versa.

Next, Chapter 12 explores some tips and tricks relating to summarization levels, the Report-Report-Interface (RRI), and report splitting.

Tips and tricks are important techniques that can improve your reporting capabilities inside CO-PA. Some of the techniques explored in this chapter are designed to make your environment as user-friendly as possible without losing powerful reporting capabilities.

12 Tips and Tricks with CO-PA

We are close to coming to the end of our discussion of CO-PA with SAP, at least with the most general and basic components we addressed in this book.

In this chapter, we will cover some general and important tips and tricks to consider in your implementation. You do not need to apply them all; instead, select those that make sense based on your project requirements. Some of these tips come from the author's personal experience with different projects and clients, others from different literature and sources, such as *Financials Expert Magazine* and others. This chapter has been written for advanced users, so keep that in mind as you follow our discussion.

12.1 Integrate Planning Layouts with Microsoft Excel

This first tip might be important for users that do not feel comfortable working within the traditional SAP environment. For this reason, CO-PA includes a configuration checkbox that allows the layout to accept information after changing into a Microsoft Excel environment. Some consultants or advanced users may already know about this, but it is a tricky change, and it is not always clear if this capability is available.

In Figure 12.1 a screen shot from the CO-PA planning framework is displayed. Notice that in the **Integrated Excel** area at the bottom of the screen, the **Active** checkbox is selected. This changes the output of the CO-PA planning framework to display the information in a Microsoft Excel environment without leaving the SAP system.

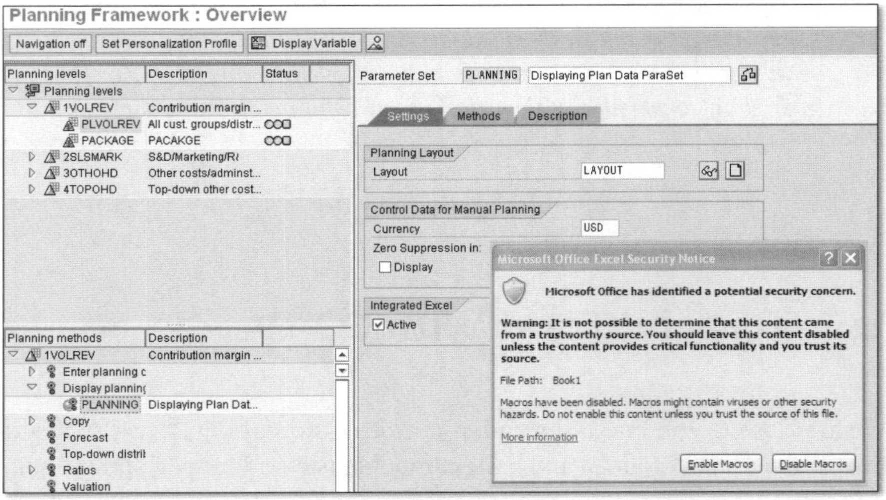

Figure 12.1 Changing a Planning Layout to Interact with Microsoft Excel

As also shown in Figure 12.1, once you execute the layout, you might receive a **Security Warning** message to notify you that the document you are opening contains macros. If this message displays, click on the **Enable Macros** button and then review the change in the environment, which will now look similar to that shown in Figure 12.2.

> **Caution**
>
> If you plan to use the Microsoft Excel environment inside CO-PA, verify with your system administrator that the Microsoft Excel integration with SAP has been correctly installed.

Note that you are only able to access Microsoft Excel with restrictions in place; that is, some of its functions will be either not available or not working.

As shown in Figure 12.2, on the right-hand side of the screen, the Microsoft Excel environment appears with the information controlled by the package **PLVOLREV**, selected on the left-hand side of the same figure. Just as with a regular layout, at the left bottom of the screen you can select any planning method, for example, **Enter planning data** or **Display planning data**. As shown in Figure 12.2, we are working in the **Enter planning data** planning method; therefore, we can modify the data available to users, save and go back to the SAP environment.

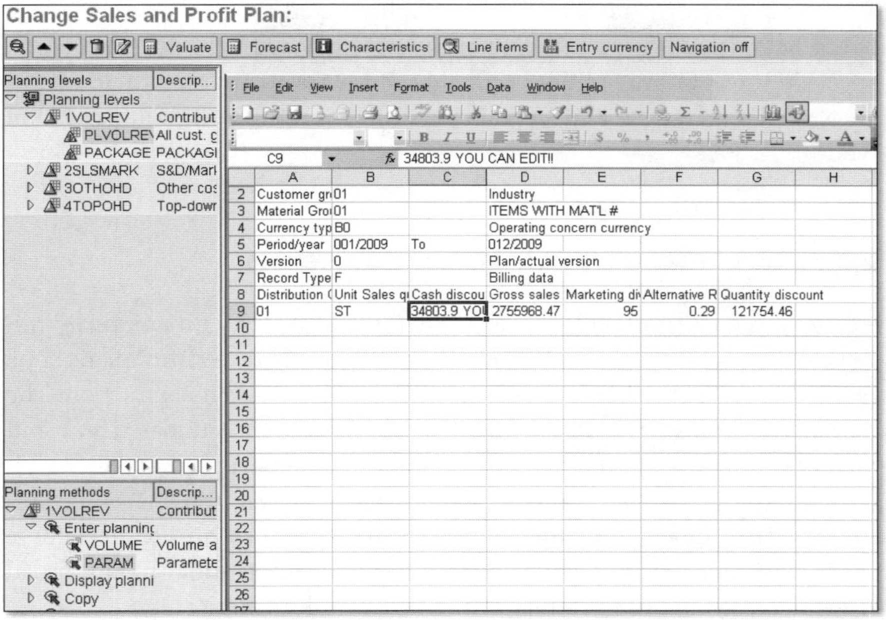

Figure 12.2 Working with a Planning Layout in Microsoft Excel

When you've made your changes, click on the back icon to return to the SAP GUI environment. For comparison purposes, review Figure 12.3 which shows the same layout but within the SAP GUI environment, after deselecting the **Active** option in the **Integrated Excel** area shown earlier in Figure 12.1.

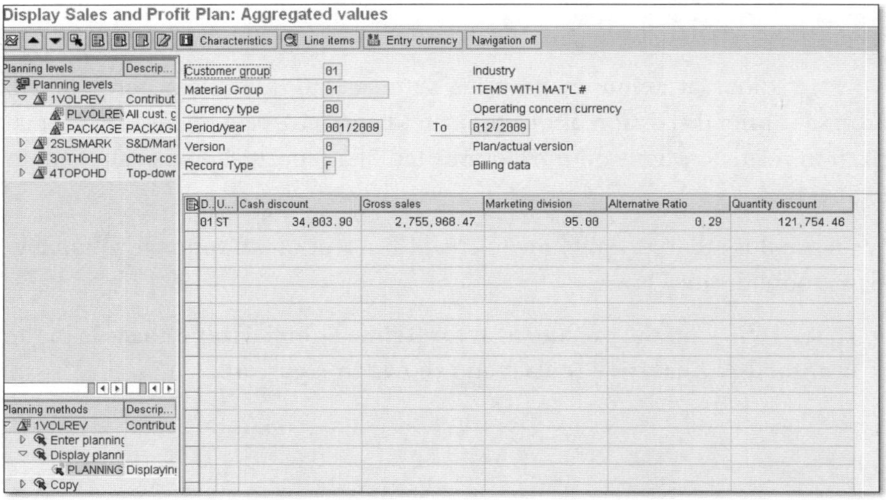

Figure 12.3 Planning Layout within the SAP Environment

Even though it might not be the most sophisticated tip or trick, this option should be quite useful to sell your planning applications to different users, especially those in finance who actively use Microsoft Excel in their reporting. Now, let us review a more important tip, working with summarization levels in CO-PA.

12.2 Working with Summarization Levels

In general, *summarization levels* can be defined as tables with an update frequency. They are presummarized data for selected characteristics that can be created to run as the first layer that the system uses for data extraction. The alternative, for the system to read the different transactional tables and extract the data every time that it is required by a report might take considerably more time. When summarization levels are used, the SAP OLTP system generates, loads, and updates tables when extracting the data for a report, thus maximizing your overall extraction performance. In broad terms, to create and use summarization levels, follow these steps:

1. Define summarization levels using Transaction KEDV (more on how to do this in a moment).

2. Tell R/3 or SAP ERP ECC 6.0 to load the level by executing a report with Transaction KEDU.

3. To update your levels, schedule the report to run periodically by creating a variant.

4. Schedule a batch job to run the variant.

Now, let's look at defining and using summarization levels in more detail. From our brief discussion of this topic in Chapter 10, remember the summarization-related options on the **Options** tab of a report, shown again here in Figure 12.4.

We'll use this tab to review how to create and work with summarization levels in more detail:

1. To start, click on the execute icon for **Define Summarization Levels** in the **Profitability Analysis • Tools** menu shown in Figure 12.5.

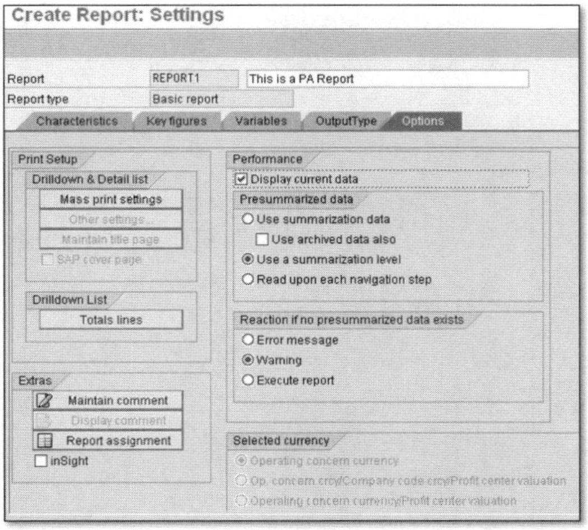

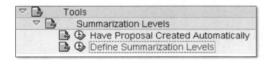

Figure 12.4 Reviewing the Options Tab of a Report

▽ 🗋	Tools	
	▽ 🗋	Summarization Levels
	🗋 ⊕	Have Proposal Created Automatically
	🗋 ⊕	Define Summarization Levels

Figure 12.5 Defining Summarization Levels

2. If this is the first time that you access the summarization option, click on the **Profitability Analysis • Tools • Have Proposal Created Automatically** object as shown in Figure 12.5 for the SAP system to generate proposed summarization levels based on the use of your different reports and data in general.

3. Review the screen shown in Figure 12.6, where the SAP system suggests possible summarization levels and the characteristics used in each of them. The information shown in Figure 12.6 also includes the percentage of records you can expect to simplify its extraction by using each of type of Summarization Level. For example, the proposal says that Summarization Level **80001** provides **42.86** % of savings, and it is the first one chosen by the system, including most of the characteristics included in your operating concern (identified with an asterisk (*) in the upper level of the report).

4. Accept the default summarization levels displayed in Figure 12.6, and identify the best choice: in this case summarization level 80001 provides the best savings in percentages.

5. Click on the **Create levels** button shown at the top of Figure 12.6 to generate your automatic summarization levels.

Create Automatic Suggestion for Summarization Levels

Create levels

Characteristics	800001	800002	800003	800004	800005
Product					
Industry	*				
Company Code	*	*	*	*	*
Sales district					
Fiscal Year	*	*	*	*	*
Business Area					
Customer group	*			*	*
Sales Office					
Sales employee					
Main material group	*	*	*	*	*
Customer					
CO Area	*	*	*	*	*
Material Group	*	*		*	*
Currency type	*	*	*	*	*
Period	*	*	*	*	*
Plan/Act. Indicator	*	*	*	*	*
Profit Center	*				
Division		*			
Version	*	*	*	*	*
Sales Group	*				
Sales Org.	*		*		
Record Type	*	*	*	*	*
Distr. Channel	*		*	*	
Plant					

Summarization Level	Estimated Number of	Saving in %
800001	3,019	42.86
800002	40	34.74
800003	379	13.40
800004	1,751	14.86
800005	745	6.92

Figure 12.6 Reviewing the Automatically Calculated Summarization Levels

The summarization levels we just created are empty tables that now need to be populated with data. To do so, we need to identify the default parameters based on the history of usage of the system, using the following steps:

1. Execute the **Tools • Summarization Levels • Define Summarization Levels** object, and the screen shown in Figure 12.7 appears. Notice that the automatically calculated summarization levels are **Active**, but **without data**.

2. Use Transaction KEDU to display the screen where you can populate the summarization levels (tables) with data, as shown in Figure 12.8. Here you must define the **Operating concern (S_GO)**, **Type of Profitability Analysis** (1=costing-based), **Summarization levels** (1= 80001), and make sure that the **Build new levels** option is checked.

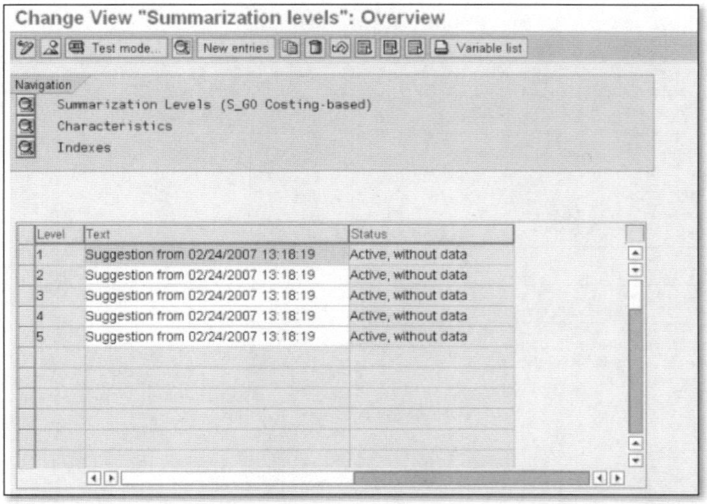

Figure 12.7 View the Summarization Levels

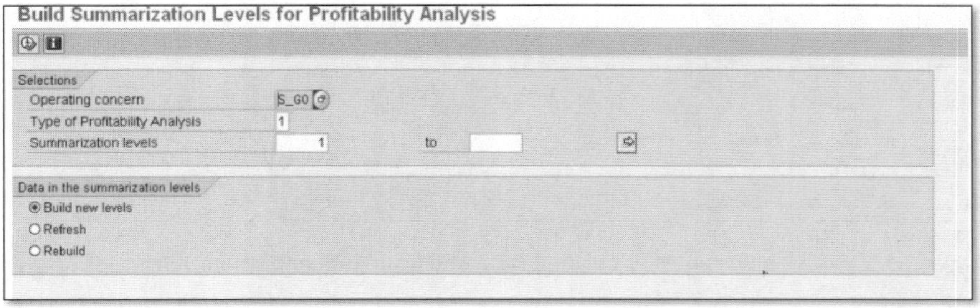

Figure 12.8 Loading Data into Your Summarization Levels

3. Click on the execute icon.

Tip

Summarization levels can be used for specific reports (and the fields used depend on each report) for manual and automatic planning, and cost center assessments, among others.

4. The screen shown in Figure 12.9 displays and notifies you that the summarization levels have been created without problems, based on the parameters established in the previous screen.

```
┌──────────────────────────────────────────────────────────────────────┐
│ Build Summarization Levels for Profitability Analysis                  │
├──────────────────────────────────────────────────────────────────────┤
│ ⌕ │🖨▽▼│⏏⟳▣⏱│ ⊞ │ ⓘ                                                   │
├──────────────────────────────────────────────────────────────────────┤
│ ┌──────────────────────────────────────────────────────────────────┐ │
│ │ Call parameter                                                   │ │
│ ├──────────────────────────────────────────────────────────────────┤ │
│ │ Operating concern: S_GO                                          │ │
│ │ Type: Costing-based                                              │ │
│ │ Summarization levels:                                            │ │
│ │ I BT 000001 000005                                               │ │
│ │ Data in summarization levels: Rebuild                            │ │
│ └──────────────────────────────────────────────────────────────────┘ │
│                                                                        │
│ ┌──────────────────────────────────────────────────────────────────┐ │
│ │ Statistics                                                       │ │
│ ├──────────────────────────────────────────────────────────────────┤ │
│ │ The data was read from the segment level. Data from the last 30 minutes │ │
│ │ was ignored for reasons of consistency.                          │ │
│ │                                                                  │ │
│ │                                                                  │ │
│ │                                                                  │ │
│ │                                                                  │ │
│ │ Runtime: 00:00:06                                                │ │
│ │ Of which for the update: 00:00:00                                │ │
│ │                                                                  │ │
│ │ No. of records read: 7,548                                       │ │
│ └──────────────────────────────────────────────────────────────────┘ │
│                                                                        │
│ ┌──────┬───────────┬──────────┐                                       │
│ │Level │Time (sec) │Comments  │                                       │
│ ├──────┼───────────┼──────────┤                                       │
│ │000001│     0.24  │OK        │                                       │
│ │000002│     0.19  │OK        │                                       │
│ │000003│     0.19  │OK        │                                       │
│ │000004│     0.28  │OK        │                                       │
│ │000005│     0.24  │OK        │                                       │
│ └──────┴───────────┴──────────┘                                       │
└──────────────────────────────────────────────────────────────────────┘
```

Figure 12.9 Revision Screen After Loading Data into Your Summarization Levels

---

Note

To update the levels periodically and automatically, you must define a variant; however, we will not go through this procedure. Also, you can run the screen displayed in Figure 12.8 and select either the **Rebuild** or **Refresh** option depending on the changes that might have happened in the data selection parameters of your system.

---

5. Return to the report, and select the **Options** tab previously displayed in Figure 12.4.

6. Select the **Use a summarization level** radio button. Your report performance should now be improved to make extraction faster because the system will first look in the data contained in the summarization levels to perform the extraction, which is more commonly used. If not available, the system will go directly to the different CO-PA tables to update the information.

We'll conclude our discussion of summarization levels with these tips:

▶ **Do not include constants**
Summarization levels are designed for characteristics or values that change, not for characteristics or values that are always the same. For example, customer group is more likely to change during the extraction than company code, when there is only one company code available in the system.

▶ **Avoid using redundant summarization levels**
If summarization level A contains characteristics X1 and X2, and summarization level B contains characteristics X1, X2, and X3, it does not make sense to use summarization level A because it is already part of summarization level B, and the difference at the segment level in number of records is not significant enough to use summarization level A instead of summarization level B.

▶ **Add dependent characteristics as part of your summarization levels**
A characteristic that depends on others will affect the performance during the extraction. Therefore, if, for example, you add the characteristic customer ID to your summarization level, and the characteristics customer group, customer region, and customer category are also part of your operating concern or your CO-PA data, it is much better if you include all of them in the summarization level to avoid delays during extraction because their information is highly dependant.

▶ **Avoid fixed characteristic values in your summarization levels**
Evaluate the data volume of each of your characteristics to avoid managing small data volumes in different summarization levels that are controlled with a fixed characteristic. In other words, avoid using fixed characteristics because they will perform similarly to constants.

▶ **Do not use more than six characteristics per summarization level**
Remember, summarization levels are about being selective. You do not need to use all of the characterstics available in your transaction data, only the ones that are used most often to simplify their extraction.

▶ **Do not create too many summarization levels**
Between eight and twenty summarization levels is more than enough! Summarization levels are not "free;" they also require resources, including memory and storage space.

▶ **Force all summarization levels to have the same timestamp**
In other words, build all of your summarization levels and update all of them at the same time so the data is consistent in your reports.

▶ **Delete older summarization levels**
Use Transaction KEDV and review the date-last-read status to avoid using summarization levels that are no longer used by any report or object.

▶ **Update your summarization levels daily**
Update your summarization levels each night by using a variant and a scheduled job.

▶ **Review your definitions periodically**
There are always changes during the lifetime of your implementation, and some characteristics will be used more often than others, but this might also change over time. Eventually you will know which characteristics you must include in your summarization levels and which ones you can remove. Perform this process periodically to achieve optimum performance.

12.3   Performing Report Splitting

Report Splitting (RS) means taking a report with a certain number of characteristics and generating two or more reports from it, to reduce the number of characteristics used to perform the data extraction. This improves system performance. Situations in which to use RS include:

▶ When you have reports that have many characteristics, and, for a specific level of users, only part of them are required.

▶ When reports use a lot of characteristics and values and take a long time to generate.

▶ When multiple users require the same drilldown with the same characteristics.

Tip

The reason for using RS and the Report-Report-Interface (RRI), discussed in detail in the next section, is to allow the breaking down of transactional data. As a general rule, R/3 or SAP ERP ECC 6.0 transactional data once posted in the respective value fields is indivisible, meaning you cannot go back to the original components that describe an account, unless each component was previously specified as an independent object. For example, if gross margin (GM) is calculated as the difference between total sales and cost of goods sold (COGS), the last two fields must be specified in addition to the GM before the values are posted; otherwise, it is not possible to go back and review the calculation performed. Using RS, you can have the GM value in one report and call the stored values of COGS and Sales in a different report, if required.

To create a split report follow these steps:

1. Using the regular SAP menu, access the following path, as shown in Figure 12.10: **Controlling · Profitability Analysis · Information System · KE3L – Split Report**. Alternatively, use Transaction KE3L.

> **Note**
>
> You cannot access the split report functionality by using the IMG Activity menu, (Transaction SPRO), that we have worked with throughout the rest of the book.

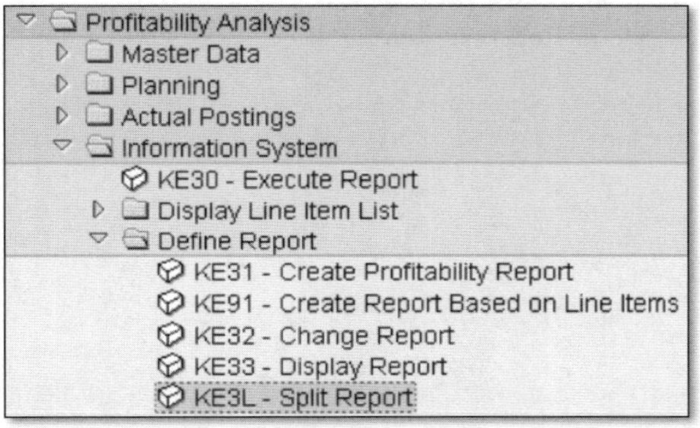

Figure 12.10 Accessing the Split Report Functionality

2. The **Split Report** screen appears, and requests the following parameters: **Operating concern**, **Type of Profitability Analysis**, and **Report name**. Enter "S_GO," "1," and "REPORT2" into the respective fields, as shown in Figure 12.11.

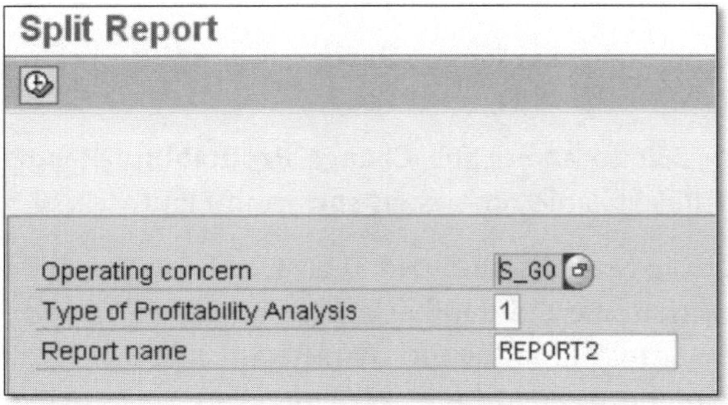

Figure 12.11 Reviewing the Split Report Screen

3. Click on the execute icon.

Tip

It may be obvious, but still: The minimum number of characteristics required in a report to perform RS is two. (Otherwise, why would you need to use this functionality?) In addition, if you select all of the characteristics available in your current report, why are you splitting the report in the first place? RS is meant to simplify the information being displayed, and to cut an original report into smaller pieces.

---

4. As shown in Figure 12.12, the **Split Report** screen requests you to select the characteristics to use in the new report and provide a name for the new report. For our example in Figure 12.12 select **Material Group** as the characteristic to use and specify **Receiver Report** as "ReportSplit1."

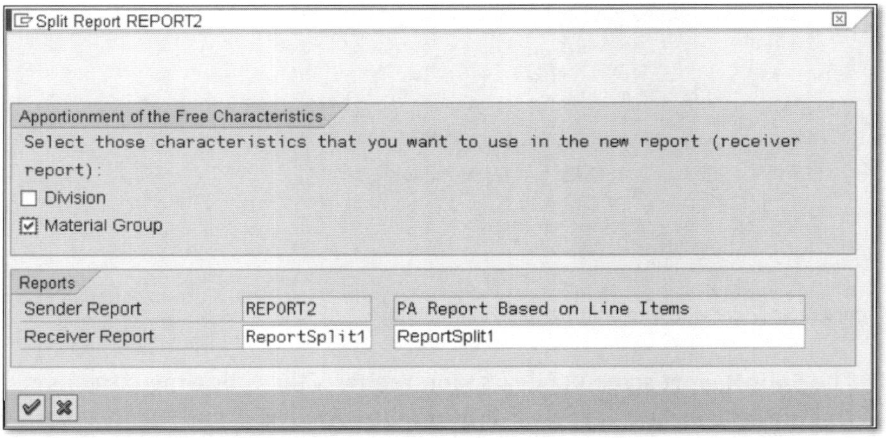

Figure 12.12 Creating the Split Report

5. Click on the checkmark icon.

6. You receive the information message **Report Report2 was split**. Click on the checkmark icon.

7. Now, use Transaction KE32 to access the **Change Profitability Report** object to see the list of the available reports, as shown in Figure 12.13.

Here you can see that you have generated **REPORTSPLIT1**, a reduced version of the original REPORT2 with a selected number of characteristics. In addition, you have reduced the search time for the characteristics because you narrowed down the size of the search! However, there are cases when another type of functionality might be useful, namely when you want to attach different reports with common characteristics and generate a drill-down. This is the function of the RRI discussed in the next section.

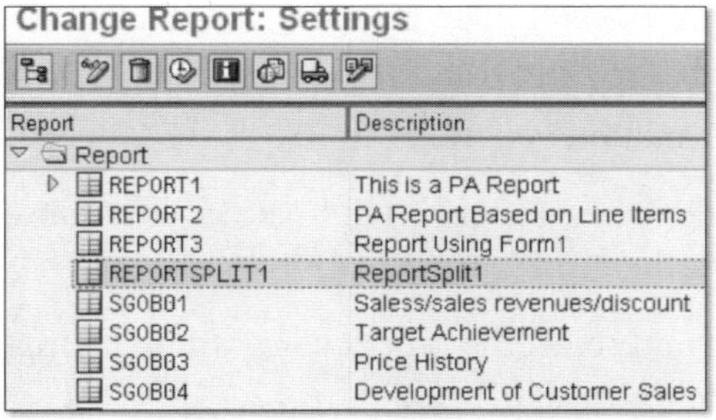

Figure 12.13 Reviewing the Creation of Your ReportSplit1 Report

12.4 Working with the Report-Report Interface (RRI)

What happens when you have multiple reports, and you have common characteristics between them? Can you integrate all of them to make them look like a single report without affecting performance? Can you configure a report list to manually navigate to the lower-level report using a menu path? The answer is yes to all of these questions, and the RRI has been created to address this issue.

In general, the RRI is a high-level analysis to improve interfacing with other elements besides simple reports, enabling you to connect a total of seven types of reports:

▶ Report portfolio

▶ SAP Business Warehouse (BW) query

▶ SAP query

▶ Drilldown reporting

▶ ABAP report program

▶ Report writer

▶ A basic transaction

The next issue is when to use RRI:

▶ When you want to link different types of reports, such as ABAP programs to Report Painter reports or SAP queries to drilldown reports.

▶ When users don't use a single drilldown approach so RS is not a viable option.

▶ When splitting a report, users are limited to specific drilldowns.

▶ When drilldown is the best way to present your data and based on a call-up chain that allows access to other SAP applications.

▶ When you want to combine information generated in RS.

Now, with a better idea of how and when to work with RRI, follow these steps to use the RRI process, as described in Figure 12.14:

1. Access the **Change Report** screen and select the report you want to configure, in this case, **REPORT1**, as shown in step 1 in Figure 12.14.

2. Select the **Options** tab as shown in step 2.

3. Click on the **Report Assignment** button as shown in step 3.

4. The **Assign Report** screen appears. Click on the plus sign icon, as shown in step 4.

5. The screen **Add Drilldown Report** appears, as shown in step 5.

6. Click on the **Other report type** button as shown in step 6

7. Now see the seven types of reports, as shown in step 7, and select the report of your choice.

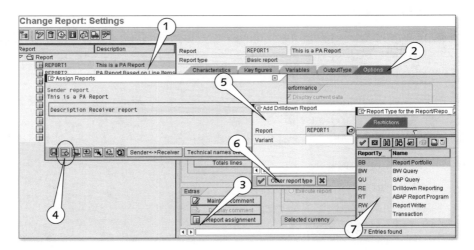

Figure 12.14 Working with the Report-Report Interface (RRI)

Now, let's say we want to perform drilldown and attach two reports to our basic report **REPORT1** following the steps described in Figure 12.14, but we want to create a drilldown structure attached to REPORT1, as shown in Figure 12.15, called **Price History** and **Analysis CM II**.

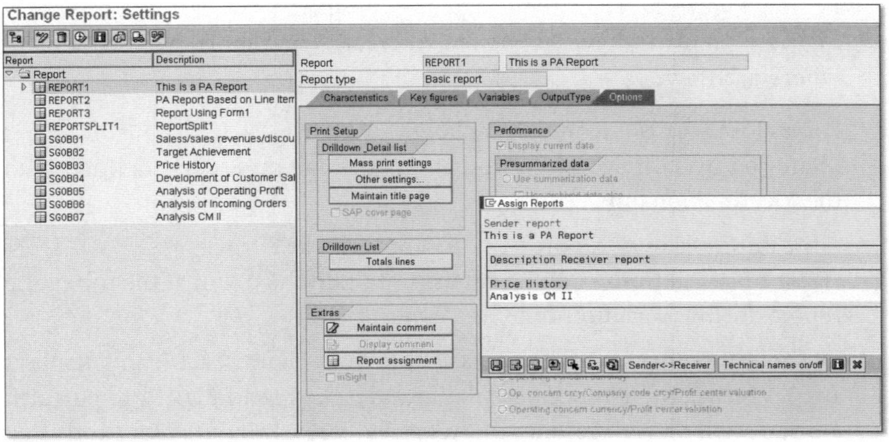

Figure 12.15 Attaching Two Reports to REPORT1 Using RRI

To create the drilldown structure based on RRI, follow these steps:

1. Using the **Report assignment** button, select the **Price History** and **Analysis CM II** reports, as shown in Figure 12.15.

2. Click on the save icon to attach the reports.

3. Save your changes to REPORT1 using the save icon in the upper portion of the screen.

4. Execute the report **REPORT1 This is a PA Report**, shown in Figure 12.15.

5. Fill out the report selection parameters like a traditional R/3 or SAP ERP ECC 6.0 report.

6. Select either **Current** or **Saved** (frozen) data, if available.

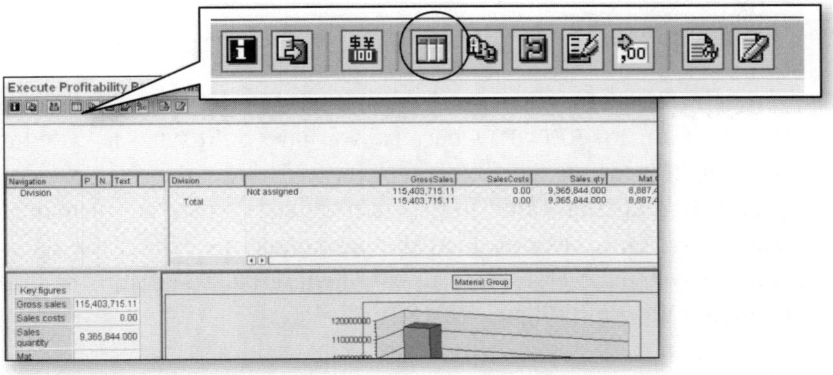

Figure 12.16 Results for REPORT1

7. Review Figure 12.16. It seems like the report ran successfully, but nothing new seems to have happened, correct? The reports we just added, where are they?

8. Look closely at the icon menu shown in Figure 12.16. The icon that is identified by a circle is how you access the call-up reports defined with the RRI functionality.

9. Click on the call-up-report icon, or enter the keystrokes $\boxed{\text{Ctrl}}$+$\boxed{\text{Shift}}$+ $\boxed{\text{F3}}$, or use the **Goto · Call up report** option in the menu at the top of the report during execution time.

10. The **Select Report** screen appears as shown in Figure 12.17, and displays any SAP executable objects available and linked to REPORT1 to perform a drilldown. Select the one you want, let's say **Price History**, and click on the checkmark icon.

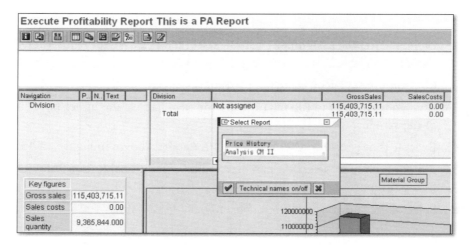

Figure 12.17 Accessing the Call-up Reports

11. The report **Price History** is executed, maintaining the report selection parameters input for **REPORT1** because we have built what is called a *call-up chain*. This means two object reports are sharing the same parameter definition at the same time, improving system performance because the system does not need the parameters to extract the data. Instead, the system accesses data already generated. The results of this drilldown are shown in Figure 12.18.

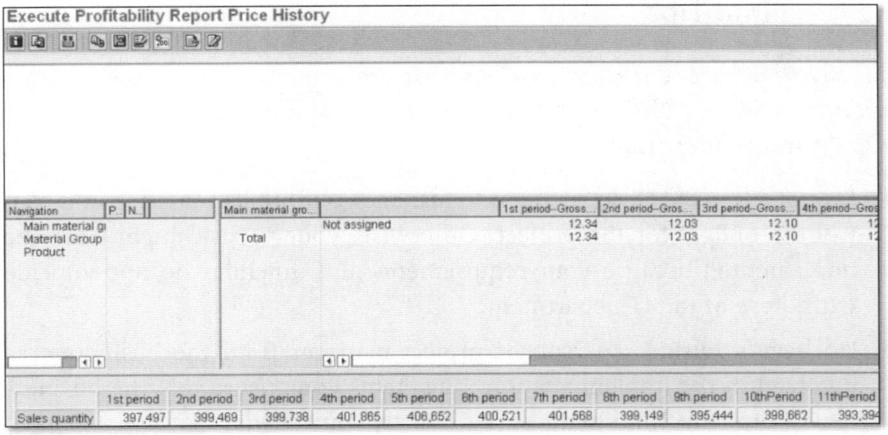

Figure 12.18 Accessing the RRI Report Price History

> **Tip**
>
> You can break the relationship created with the RRI at any time. Based on this information, experiment with the other types of objects, such as ABAP queries, Report writer reports, and so on, that can be linked to the call-up navigation functionality.

Now, let's think of a more complex scenario using the objects shown in step 7, displayed earlier in Figure 12.14. For example, you may have a report that depends on an ABAP program that must be generated, and once that is ready, you can access the information in another report. You can review your final SAP BW query that collects that information using scheduled variants that will run in the background after your ABAP program ran, and update your final information reports that are accessible in your SAP BW query.

Therefore, the functionalities and interactions that can be performed using the reports, SAP BW queries, SAP queries, drilldown reporting, ABAP report program, Report writer, and transaction objects make more sense of the power of the RRI functionality to improve navigation while improving the end-user interface. Regardless of the level of complexity you decide to use with your RRI reports, remember to maintain the best and easiest environment for your users. Try to keep things clear and simple.

12.5 Final Tips

Finally, here are a few suggestions that are important to consider when working with any type of SAP implementation, and that can also affect your CO-PA implementation:

▶ Do not allow the IT department to manage your implementation and control the budget for the project. Otherwise, your project might never be implemented because your requirements and timelines do not coincide with those of the IT department.

▶ Do have a business person or project manager from the business area involved in the implementation. This helps you ensure that the business needs, priorities, and budget are correctly controlled.

▶ Make sure to have an implementation plan that identifies times and activities required for your project. You do not have to be an SAP expert but having a clear idea of your goals written down in a document is a good idea to have for your implementation team.

▶ Have your requirements clearly defined in a formal document and communicated and reviewed with your IT department.

With these considerations in mind and a complete commitment to understanding your business processes and implementing that knowledge using the SAP functionalities of CO-PA, or any other module, you are on your way to a successful implementation.

CO-PA is a great tool to improve the consolidation, reporting, and planning capabilities of your R/3 or SAP ERP ECC 6.0 environment. However, remember to spend time reviewing your requirements and data volume to determine if CO-PA or SAP NetWeaver Business Intelligence (BI)/SAP BW is the best choice for your final goals, and for system performance.

12.6 Summary

In this chapter, we explored important and useful functionalities to improve the performance and interface of your reports generated in CO-PA. We reviewed key elements useful in most implementations, such as Microsoft Excel integration, RS, RRI, and summarization levels. All of them can make the life of your users better and improve the performance and look and feel of your application. Hopefully, these tips and tricks will be useful to you.

In Chapter 13, we will briefly summarize the contents of this book, providing you with a quick chapter-by-chapter review of what we've covered on CO-PA with SAP.

13 Concluding Remarks

In this book, we covered the key components and functionalities of the Controlling Profitability Analysis (CO-PA) module in SAP. Regardless of your role during an implementation, whether you are an end user, a manager, a team lead, or a consultant, we hope you have found something useful in this book to complement your current interest. In general, it is a great advantage to be able to obtain information in an environment that is similar to SAP Business Warehouse (BW)/SAP NetWeaver Business Intelligence (BI), Business Planning and Simulation (BPS), and Integrated Planning (IP), but without having to create complex structures to generate similar reports.

For users new to CO-PA, this book has been designed to be a reference guide. For advanced users, this book provides extensive configuration reviews and discussion of key functionalities to facilitate your data extraction, reporting, and planning within the SAP transactional system, in as simple a form as possible. Regardless of your knowledge level, however, using this module does require further study of the information contained in other SAP modules such as Materials Management (MM), Financials (FI), Sales and Distribution (SD), Controlling (CO), and others.

The book covered the following topics:

- Chapter 1 introduced the book and provided an overview of the information contained in it.

- Chapter 2 reviewed basic concepts and terminology quite common during any financial related projects. Terms such as EVA, revenues, direct and indirect costs and how an SAP system controls and generates such information must be completely clear during your implementation. Financial transactions are a delicate issue and how Profitability Analysis information is reported to external parties is sensitive, so make sure to include the people with more financial information of the organization when implementing CO-PA to make it truly successful.

- Chapter 3 provided a general overview and introduction to the functionalities of CO-PA, specifically the concepts of costing- and account-based accounting within the SAP system. Costing-based CO-PA is more complex to implement than account-based. Even though some minor changes in your operating concern are required to switch from one to the other, both approaches use the same functionalities, such as reporting and planning.

▶ Chapter 4 introduced the configuration steps toward the definition of the basic element for CO-PA: an operating concern. We have said several times throughout this book that you are not required to implement every single component of CO-PA, but it is highly recommended to at least use an operating concern object when possible to facilitate your data extraction and reporting from SAP ERP ECC 6.0 or R/3 into SAP NetWeaver BI/SAP BW or non-SAP systems. Remember, CO-PA interacts directly with the transactional system of SAP, and does not require exporting the data into third-party systems or SAP BW/SAP NetWeaver BI to execute similar tasks until a certain level. However, when the data volume is high, it might be a better idea to think of an OLAP environment.

▶ Chapter 5 explored additional functionalities in master data, such as characteristic values, valuation, derivation, and valuation strategies. Valuation, especially, is a functionality that is very difficult to replicate with alternative processes.

▶ Chapters 6 and 7 reviewed the concepts of the CO-PA planning framework, such as layouts, planning functions, planning packages, ratio schemes, and others. Using planning applications, you can create and modify data inside your transactional system that can also be shared later on during reporting.

▶ Chapter 8 explored flows of actual values to transfer data from other SAP modules into CO-PA. Because this is a function with quite an extensive number of menu options, only key components were reviewed, including incoming sales orders and the assignment of quantity and value fields.

▶ Chapters 9 and 10 provided an extensive analysis of the most important component for any SAP implementation: reporting. CO-PA reporting interfaces with the Report Painter functionality within R/3 or SAP ERP ECC 6.0, so it might be easy for users familiar with similar environments from other SAP applications.

▶ Chapter 11 provided a quick glance at the differences when working with account-based CO-PA, and how to switch to this environment. However, it is recommended to review SAP Note 74486 INFO: Overview of consulting notes for CO-PA for further details using your SAP Service Marketplace account.

▶ Chapter 12 provided an overview into advanced functionalities, such as RRI and RS that improve system performance. The best choice is to have reports that not only have precalculated data so the system does not need to spend time using parameters that are accessed frequently, but that also can be reduced with only required characteristics for each level of analysis.

It has been a pleasure to provide this comprehensive CO-PA review. Unfortunately, some topics had to be left out of this book due to their complexity, such as the integration of material ledger and CO-PA to access information related to material costs, prices, and movements. If you are looking for information on data extraction and retraction, which were also not covered in this book, you can go to the "how-to" procedures available in SDN at *http://sdn.sap.com*. Even though these procedures are not new, they can still be used as a good reference to create a data source in R/3 or SAP ERP ECC 6.0, or to save data back to the transactional system.

We hope that the information discussed in this book is useful for your SAP implementation efforts, and helps you provide the best service to your clients and users.

Appendix

A   About the Author

Dr. Marco Sisfontes-Monge is a consultant based in New York City and he has worked in the following industry sectors: automotive, logistics, software, gas and electric, discrete and process manufacturing, retail, and financial services in companies such as Matsushita, Schneider Electric, John Deere, Sara Lee, Conair, Pacific Gas & Electric, Peavy Electronics, New York Power Authority, Hyperion, PeopleSoft, Capgemini, MyITgroup, BTicino, and others.

His background combines different SAP ERP team lead positions, project management, profitability analysis, performance measurement, product- and activity-based costing, design optimization and robust design, discrete and process simulation, system dynamics, and structural equations modeling. Dr. Sisfontes-Monge is also the author of the book *CPM and Balanced Scorecard with SAP* by SAP PRESS. You can contact him at *msisfontes2001@yahoo.com.ar*.

B   Bibliography

Draeger, E. *Project Management with SAP R/3*. Addison-Wesley. London, England, 2000.

Franz, M. *Project Management with SAP Project System*. SAP PRESS. Bonn, Germany. 2007.

Greenspan, A. *The Age of Turbulence: Adventures in a New World*. The Penguin Press, New York, 2007.

Jacobsen, L. *Cost Accounting*. Second Edition, McGraw Hill, New York, 1988.

Kundalia, M. *"Ask the Financials Expert Should I Report in CO-PA or BW?" Financials Expert Magazine*. Volume 4, Issue 1.

Kundalia, M. *"Quick Tip: 7 Sets of Consulting Notes for CO-PA Analyst." Financials Expert Magazine*. Volume 6, Issue 7.

Quentin, H, et al. *Configuring SAP R/3 FI/CO*. SYBEX

Reilly, F, et al. *Investment Analysis Portfolio Management*. Thomson South-Western, USA, 2003.

Rogan, T. *"A Quick Look at How to Use Frozen Data, and Speed up your CO-PA Report Response speeds in the Process." Financials Expert Magazine*. Volume 6, Number 8.

Rogan, T. *"Pick the Right Reporting Tool for the Job: CO-PA or BW." Financials Expert Magazine*, Volume I, Issue 7.

Shizuo, S, et al. *Profitability Analysis for Managerial and Engineering Decisions*. Asian Productivity Organization (APO). Tokyo, Japan. 1980.

Sisfontes, M. *SAP CPM and Balanced Scorecard with SAP*. Bonn, Germany. SAP PRESS, 2007.

Thomas, K. *The Business of Investment Banking: A Comprehensive Overview*. Second Edition, John Wiley & Son, Inc. New York, 2006.

Williams, G. *Implementing SAP R/3 Sales & Distribution*. McGraw Hill. New York, 2000.

C   Glossary

ABAP   Advanced Business Application Programming language. Virtually the entire SAP system is written in ABAP.

Access Sequence   Determines the condition tables in which the system should search for valid condition records for a condition type.

Account-based CO-PA   Used to monitor cost elements and reconcile CO-PA data with Financial Accounting (FI) data. It is updated when goods are delivered.

BEx   SAP NetWeaver Business Intelligence (BI) tool that allows creating, setting up, and extracting specific information from SAP NetWeaver BI cubes.

Business Planning and Simulation (BPS)   SAP application that enables you to perform planning operations over data coming from SAP BW or R/3. It is quite similar to the SAP NetWeaver BI module Integrated Planning (IP).

Condition Types   Key used to define the attributes of a condition and identifies the condition in the system.

Costing Sheets   Contain the conditions that are used to calculate expected values. They also determine the order in which the conditions are processed and how the conditions are related to one another.

Characteristic   Describes the business event and creates relationships. Can be business characteristics (customer, cost centers, and company), units (currency and quantity), time characteristics (calendar day, calendar year, and fiscal year),

and technical characteristics (the number of a data-load procedure).

Characteristic Derivation   Rules used to generate new characteristic values based on inference rules.

Cost Center   Object used in Controlling (CO) to monitor internal cost assignments.

Cost Element   CO equivalent of a General Ledger (GL) that monitors both primary and secondary postings.

Costing-based CO-PA   CO-PA model that stores values and quantities in value fields. It is updated until the billing document is created.

Controlling (CO)   SAP R/3 or SAP ERP ECC component that controls and monitors internal transactions or reporting processes for non-external parties.

CO-PA Planning Framework   Environment used to generate planning applications within CO-PA. Similar to that of SAP SEM-BPS, SAP BW-BPS, and SAP NetWeaver BI-IP.

Condition Tables   Tables that store specific characteristic values and combinations to automatically control automatic procedures.

Derivation Rule   Automatic procedure used to generate or change values based on predefined criteria.

Discrete Manufacturing   Production environment where the end product is the result of operations using parts or components to assemble a product. Examples: automotive components.

Economic Value Added (EVA) Monetary value of an entity at the end of a time period minus the monetary value of that same entity at the beginning of that time period.

Extraction In CO-PA, setting up an operating concern using Transaction KEB0 to create a data source to transfer data from the transactional SAP system to SAP NetWeaver BI/SAP BW.

Forms CO-PA object used to create predefined templates that can be used as standard to maintain specific formats.

Financial Accounting (FI) SAP component that organizes and controls the financial accounting processes and transactions of an organization, and mostly oriented toward external parties.

Integrated Planning (IP) SAP NetWeaver BI planning application that uses J2EE technology using a similar environment to that of SAP BPS.

Key Figure Scheme Collection of any number of interrelated key figures, referred to as elements of the key figure scheme.

Material Management (MM) Component of the Logistics module designed to manage and control the material flow of information inside a company, such as requisitions, bills of material, inventory management, purchasing and supplier information, and others.

Operating Concern Basic CO-PA object that contains characteristics or value fields and is used to perform reporting, planning, and data extraction.

Order Settlements Internal orders used to close any open items used to post information from a cost sender to a cost receiver.

Planning Layout CO-PA planning object that accesses the data restrictions stored in a planning package. It is the object that displays any required planning information.

Process Manufacturing Production environment that uses production batches or jobs to create the final product. Example: beer production.

Profitability Segments Grouping of characteristics used to store selected groups of data. Think of profitability segments as data sets of an SAP NetWeaver BI InfoCube.

Project System (PS) Project management module of SAP systems that controls dates, activities, costs, networks, schedule, and interfaces with different modules to control how the information for a particular project is achieved.

Report-Report Interface (RRI) Reporting functionality that allows creating drilldown structures within a reporting environment to improve performance.

Report Splitting (RS) Reporting functionality that allows dividing a larger report with many characteristics into a smaller one with fewer characteristics.

Retraction Data transfer process from outside the OLTP into CO-PA using the operating concern as the connection.

SAP Abbreviation for SAP AG, Systeme, Anwendungen, Produkte in der Datenverarbeitung (Systems, Applications & Products in Data Processing).

Summarization Levels Performance optimization technique used to keep the most common extraction parameters in memory.

Valuation Automatic calculations based on costing-based CO-PA. Can be used for both planning data and actual data.

Value Fields R/3 or SAP ERP ECC equivalent of a key figure in SAP BW. They are objects that store quantity, amounts, dates, and counter-related information.

Index

Gain valuable insight into the workings of SAP NetWeaver BI Integrated Planning

Maximize your return on investment by learning to use this new, valuable tool

318 pp., 2007, 69,95 Euro / US$ 69,95
ISBN 978-1-59229-129-8

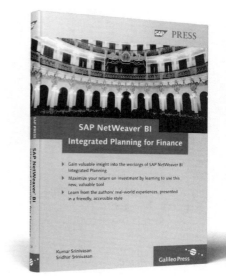

SAP NetWeaver BI
Integrated Planning for Finance

www.sap-press.com

Kumar Srinivasan, Sridhar Srinivasan

SAP NetWeaver BI Integrated Planning for Finance

If you are a functional analyst, consultant, business manager, or a developer this book helps you work on projects to build planning applications in support of business processes.

Readers learn how best to configure, develop, and manage planning applications in a simple and easy-to-follow manner. All the key features and most important aspects are covered in detail, providing you with everything you'll need in order to build a comprehensive planning application. The included examples provide you with a deep understanding of the various features.